The Great Transition

_ The Great Transition _

POLITICAL AND SOCIAL CHANGE
IN THE REPUBLIC OF CHINA

Hung-mao Tien

HOOVER INSTITUTION PRESS

Stanford University

Stanford, California

The Hoover Institution on War, Revolution and Peace, founded at Stanford University in 1919 by the late President Herbert Hoover, is an interdisciplinary research center for advanced study on domestic and international affairs in the twentieth century. The views expressed in its publications are entirely those of the authors and do not necessarily reflect the views of the staff, officers, or Board of Overseers of the Hoover Institution.

Hoover Press Publication 378

Copyright 1989 by the Board of Trustees of the
  Leland Stanford Junior University

First printing, 1989

95 94 93 92 91 90 89   9 8 7 6 5 4 3 2 1

Simultaneous first paperback printing, 1989

95 94 93   9 8 7 6 5 4 3

Manufactured in the United States of America
Printed on acid-free paper

Library of Congress Cataloging in Publication Data

Tien, Hung-mao, 1938–
    The great transition: political and social change in the Republic of China / Hung-mao Tien.
        p.   cm.
    Bibliography: p.
    Includes index.
    ISBN 0-8179-8781-9 (alk. paper)
    ISBN 0-8179-8782-7 (pbk.) (alk. paper)
    1. Taiwan—Politics and government—1975–   2. Taiwan—
Social conditions—1975–   I. Title.
JQ1522.T54 1989   88-39356
951'.24905—dc19   CIP

Design by P. Kelley Baker

For my wife, Amy

Contents

Preface

In 1945, at the end of World War II, the Kuomintang (KMT) regime on the Chinese mainland took control of Taiwan from the Japanese, who had ruled the island for fifty years. Four years laters, as China's civil war came to an end, the defeated KMT forces retreated to Taiwan. For about a quarter of a century since then, the KMT regime has exercised authoritarian rule over the island state. Significant political change began in the mid-1970s when Chiang Ching-kuo succeeded his father, Chiang Kai-shek; gradually native Taiwanese were recruited into the KMT's ruling circle. At the same time, the Republic of China (ROC) on Taiwan was suffering from diplomatic isolation, and the island's economy was rapidly growing. Political democratization proceeded in the next decade despite periodic setbacks.

Major breakthroughs in democratic reform and political liberalization occurred from 1986 to 1988, when opposition parties were finally formed and martial law was lifted. The KMT authorities also reformed outdated national representative institutions and liberalized the publication of newspapers. By the spring of 1988 Taiwan's political system had begun the transition toward representative democracy, and the one-party authoritarian dictatorship gave way to a dominant-party system with the establishment of about a dozen new political parties.

Political transformation on Taiwan is profoundly significant not only for the residents of Taiwan but also for the People's Republic of China, which has always pursued political unification with Taiwan. Moreover, the transition to democracy of the authoritarian KMT regime, based on a Leninist party structure, raises important theoretical questions for those who study politics in the Third World. Although the outcome of the current political transformation cannot be forecast precisely, Taiwan's experiences in liberalization and democratization are already significant enough to warrant a careful analysis of the island state's political dynamics.

The idea of writing a comprehensive book on Taiwan's politics was conveyed to me by Dr. Ramon Myers of the Hoover Institution, who began to plan a series of publications on East Asia in 1982. I am eternally grateful for Dr. Ramon Myer's initial suggestion to pursue this project. In the subsequent years, I benefited from two grants awarded to me by the Hoover Institution, which enabled me to spend two summers doing research there.

In preparing this study, I took several trips to Taiwan to observe the political changes in person and to interview and to hold conversations with a wide range of people, including government officials, journalists, opposition activists, scholars, and KMT cadres. These experiences helped me gain a deeper understanding of Taiwan's political dynamics. Throughout 1983–1986 I received valuable research assistance from Shih Shia-yin, then a graduate student of political science at the National Taiwan University. Other graduate students—Liang Shuang-lien, Huang Yueh-hua, and Yao Ch'ao-shen—also provided me with occasional help. All four of these graduate students were recommended to me by Professor Hu Fo of the National Taiwan University, to whom I feel deeply indebted.

I also greatly appreciate the contributions made by Professors David Buck, Michael Y. M. Kau, and Andrew Nathan. Professor Buck of the University of Wisconsin at Milwaukee made tremendous efforts to help improve the manuscript's final draft. Professor Nathan of Columbia University and Professor Kau of Brown University read the earlier draft and suggested valuable changes that improve the quality of the manuscript. Amy Klatzkin did a meticulous job of copyediting that helped correct many unintended errors. Her tireless efforts are fully appreciated.

I wish to acknowledge the support provided by the following institutions: the Hoover Institution, the China Times Cultural Foundation, the Committee for Scientific and Scholarly Cooperation with the United States of the ROC Academia Sinica, and the University of Wisconsin Centers administration.

Professor Cheng Tsai-fa of the University of Wisconsin at Madison offered valuable assistance in preparing the romanization. I also wish to thank Dr. Fu-mei Chen of the Hoover Institution for assistance during my research at the Hoover Library. Bonnie Siedlewski did a fine job of typing the final draft of the manuscript. Scott Swenberg helped with the graphics in the book.

Above all, I feel particularly indebted to my wife, Amy, and to my two children, Marvin and Wendy, for their encouragement and emotional support. Amy also spent endless hours helping me put the chaotic bibliography in order.

Needless to say, the views in this book are entirely mine and should not be ascribed to the persons and institutions acknowledged above.

— 1 —

The Nationalist Regime
in Perspective

INTRODUCTION

This book concerns government and politics in Taiwan under the rule of the Chinese Nationalist Party, or Kuomintang (KMT). The KMT forces were defeated in China's civil war of 1947–1949. Retreating to Taiwan in 1949, they formed a de facto state known as the Republic of China, representing the authority they salvaged from the mainland. For almost four decades they have claimed sovereign jurisdiction over the mainland, which has been under the legitimate control of the Chinese Communist Party. While maintaining an authoritarian dictatorship until 1986, the KMT regime successfully steered Taiwan toward prosperous capitalist economic development.

The KMT was reorganized in 1924 explicitly on the Leninist model of a single democratic-centralist, elite, disciplined, and revolutionary party exercising leadership throughout the political system (Chien 1950, 120; Tien 1972, 10–11; Jacobs 1978, 240–43). After arriving on Taiwan, the party was again reorganized during 1950–1952, although it continued to follow Leninist guidelines (Hsu 1984, 64). But the KMT differs from other Leninist parties. It has its own official ideology based on Sun Yat-sen's Three Principles of the People, which mix Chinese tradition with doctrines of European socialist democracy and modern nationalism. In keeping with Sun's ideas, the party is committed to progressive change from dictatorship to constitutional democracy. Moreover, as early as 1927, while still on the mainland, the KMT adopted an idealogy of anticommunism with procapitalist domestic and foreign policies (Chou and Nathan 1987, 278).

Thus there is a structural contradiction in Taiwan between a Leninist party-state and a capitalist socioeconomic system that promotes the values of liberal democracy in sociopolitical life. This contradiction has at times generated social strains and political conflicts, which have been brought under control by coercion and repression. Over the decades it has been tempered by the KMT's internal transformation and gradual adaptation to change. The ruling elite have advanced political reforms, particularly since the early 1970s, that have moved Taiwan from authoritarianism toward representative democracy. This transition has been accomplished in part through popular pressure for democratic reforms. On September 28, 1986, the Democratic Progressive Party (DPP), Taiwan's first true opposition party, formally came into existence. On October 15 the KMT decided to lift the 39-year-old martial law and to revise existing laws governing political associations. The changes made opposition parties legal for the first time and greatly liberalized political activities.

If the transition now under way succeeds, Taiwan will be hailed as a model not only of industrialization and economic growth but also of political development. The immediate prospects are difficult to gauge, for proponents and opponents of reform have entered a sensitive period of mutual accommodation. Behind the façade of authoritarian rule, the social, economic, and political transformation over the last three decades has affected both domestic forces and the elite's calculations. Social and economic conditions are maturing; social pluralism is gradually emerging; public mobilization and pressure from below have also contributed to change. In addition, pressure from the United States influenced the elite in favor of liberalization and democratic reforms. Thus internal and external conditions have pushed Taiwan toward democracy, and the elite now perceives such political change as a profitable option (Chou and Nathan 1987, 288–99).

In addition to the theoretical considerations of Taiwan's transition from authoritarianism to democracy, this book offers a comprehensive treatment of Taiwan's political dynamics for readers unfamiliar with the inner workings of the island nation's political process.

RETREAT TO TAIWAN

The People's Republic of China (PRC), with its capital in Peking, was officially established on October 1, 1949, thus ending the turbulent years of civil war on the mainland. Before that fateful day the Kuomintang had seen its military, economic, and political power steadily deteriorate along with its popular support ever since the end of World War II.

The KMT military resistance in North China had already collapsed by January 21, 1949, when Chiang Kai-shek was forced to withdraw from the presidency and vice-president Li Tsung-jen became acting president of the Republic of China (Riggs 1952, 32). Suffering from rampant inflation, black marketeering, and the collapse of the national currency, the economy continued to worsen. The KMT government had announced a series of emergency economic reforms in 1947 and 1948 to stabilize the deteriorating economy. On April 8, 1948, the U.S. Congress in a rescue effort passed the China Aid Act, which authorized U.S. $338 million in economic aid and U.S. $125 million in special grants for China's 1948–1949 fiscal crisis. In the end none of these efforts could reverse the trend (Pepper 1978, 74, 121–26). The KMT's alienation of China's intellectuals also undercut its political mandate. As C. Martin Wilbur concluded: "Battling in the cities, the Nationalists used their repressive mechanisms, secret police, censorship, and thought control...such repression in Nationalist China gradually alienated makers of public opinion—writers, teachers, and students" (Wilbur 1984, 46). In the last few months of the civil war defeatism prevailed, and many former KMT supporters defected to the communist side. From retirement in Chekiang, Chiang Kai-shek dispatched troops personally loyal to him to Taiwan for regrouping and, he hoped, the eventual military recovery of the mainland. By December 1949 the People's Liberation Army (PLA) had conquered the entire mainland.

Following the capture of Hainan island in the South China Sea, the communist forces under the command of General Su Yu mapped out a strategy for the conquest of Taiwan. Tension on the Taiwan Strait was on the rise. The U.S. government debated the desirability of military intervention. Many political and military leaders pressed for the protection of Taiwan against a communist onslaught. In December 1949 the U.S. Joint Chiefs of Staff, under the chairmanship of General Bradley, urged President Truman to defend Taiwan with U.S. troops (Chiu 1979, 149). But Truman apparently anticipated a final collapse of the KMT government in Taiwan. In fact on December 23 the Department of State issued a special guidance memorandum to its diplomatic and consular officers in the Far East instructing them that if Taiwan were lost, they should minimize its political and strategic significance to the United States in the Far East (Riggs 1952, 34; Chiu 1979, 149).

But the widely expected PLA invasion of Taiwan never happened. In June 1950 the Korean War broke out, forcing the Truman administration to alter its policy regarding the security and future of Taiwan. On June 27 President Truman ordered a fleet to patrol the Taiwan Strait to protect the island from any military action by the Chinese Communists from the mainland. This sudden change of U.S. policy not only saved Taiwan's inhabitants from the terror and destruction of a war but also prevented the annihilation of the KMT forces by the PLA. Since then Taiwan and mainland China have remained two separate political entities. Taiwan under the KMT regime has become a military stronghold and an economically prosperous nation.

THE KMT DEFEAT ON THE MAINLAND

The KMT's final defeat in 1949 ended an era of wars and conflicts set in motion about one hundred years earlier in the ancient land of the Middle Kingdom. The historical process and sociopolitical forces that eventually brought down the KMT—or, conversely, raised the Communists to victory—have been well documented in scholarly circles. Some view the success of the communist social revolution as inevitable, particularly given the long social, economic, cultural, and political disintegration of China since the nineteenth century combined with the KMT's failure to provide an acceptable program for national development. Many attribute the Communists' victory to their ability to mobilize the peasantry, especially their mobilization of peasant nationalism during the Sino–Japanese war, which provided the effective organization used against their KMT rivals (see, e.g., Schurmann 1968, prologue; Johnson 1962; Moore 1966, chap. 4; Kataoka 1974, chaps. 2, 4, 8; Meisner 1979, 3–54; Selden 1971, 79–176; Hofheinz 1969, 3–77). Historian Maurice Meisner stated another view: "The Japanese invasion undermined the foundations of the Kuomintang regime, for the Nationalists were driven from the major cities from which they derived their major sources of financial and political support. For the Kuomintang, the ravages of war resulted in incredible economic chaos and bureaucratic corruption—and, eventually, in almost total demoralization" (Meisner 1977, 37).

Whatever the explanation, the communist victory in China is an accomplished fact. Although intellectual debate on the causes and nature of the great revolution in China will continue, for the purposes of this book the KMT defeat in 1949 will serve simply as a point of departure. What follows is a discussion of the KMT's governance of Taiwan since 1949.

THE ROC POLITICAL SYSTEM

Since 1949 the Nationalist regime transplanted to Taiwan has operated according to the Constitution of the Republic of China, adopted on December 25, 1947, while the KMT was still on the mainland. Throughout the following decades the regime has maintained a system of government that claims to represent all of China. Thus the fundamentals of the regime's institutional framework and national power structure have remained intact for almost forty years. Over time incremental changes have been made periodically to accommodate the political demands of Taiwan's rapid socioeconomic modernization. Because the jurisdiction of the regime is confined to Taiwan and a few islands in the Taiwan Strait, the regime has been compelled to modify its political rules and institutional structures to account for the separation between the island and the mainland.

Given the institutional characteristics and conduct of the regime, how can we describe the ROC political system on Taiwan? One view suggests that Taiwan has the basic conditions for establishing a tutelary democracy (Liu 1985, 10). These conditions include the availability of a stable and internally coherent elite capable of modernizing the country, the minimum use of coercion to achieve consensus, a competent civil service to carry out development plans, and an effective security force to prevent subversion.

But the existence of these conditions alone has not yet produced a tutelary democracy in Taiwan. Edward Shils maintained that "the elite in a tutelary democracy must be attached to the idea of democracy and sincerely hope, in the course of time and ultimately, to see it flourish" (Shils 1966, 64). Gabriel Almond, in his classification of political systems, portrayed tutelary democracies as having, among other things, "freedom of party organization and competition," which Taiwan is only beginning to institute (Almond 1970, 176). We may infer from these conditions that the ROC, though not yet a tutelary democracy, is in the process of becoming one.

At the same time, if we use such variables as power distribution, civil liberties, political contestation, popular elections for public officials, and the autonomy of interest groups as criteria, the ROC political system is more authoritarian than democratic in the totalitarian-authoritarian-democratic continuum (Gastil 1987, 32–33, 44–45). An authoritarian system "emphasizes the centralization of power, the flow of decisions from the top down rather than of demands from the bottom up, deference to authority, limited pluralism, and the use of violent repression when other methods of co-optation and control fail" (Purcell and Kaufman 1980, 204). Even so, many writers acknowledge the possibility of limited political pluralism in authoritarian regimes (Linz 1975, 277–97). Political pluralism does not necessarily equal political democracy, but it represents an important step toward a genuinely democratic system (O'Donnell 1973, 7).

Many authoritarian regimes have been founded by military men, either in connection with national liberation movements or through military coups. The Nationalists fit the pattern. The current KMT regime inherited its authoritarian character from the pre–World War II revolutionary experience when it attempted to unite the nation and liberate the country from external subjugation. Still, what was an authoritarian regime can evolve into a democratic polity, as in West Germany, Italy, Japan, Greece, Portugal, Turkey, and perhaps Mexico (Dahl 1975, 181; Linz 1975, 274; O'Donnell, Schmitter, and Whitehead 1986, 3–186; Ward and Rustow 1964). One writer recently argued that Taiwan has started the transition from "hard authoritarianism" to "soft authoritarianism" by loosening political control to allow more political participation and by sharing political power with a broader segment of the native population (Winckler 1984, 482–99). With the recent establishment of an opposition party and the KMT decision to suspend martial law, a transition to representative democracy may be possible in the foreseeable future.

Juan Linz has argued that for an authoritarian regime to liberalize, there must be institutional channels for the political opposition to reach "the mass of the population" (Linz 1975, 273). This liberalization requires the regime to accept institutionalized political parties—a process that may take time to bear fruit. In summarizing the transition to democracy in southern Europe, Philippe C. Schmitter has argued that

> for an effective and enduring challenge to authoritarian rule to be mounted, and for political democracy to become and remain an alternative mode of political domination, a country must possess a civil society in which certain community and group identities exist independent of the state and in which certain types of self-constituted units are capable of acting autonomously in defense of their own interests and ideals. (Schmitter 1986, 6)

Since the 1950s many scholars have written on the social, economic, and cultural conditions that make democracy possible (Lipset 1959; Cutright 1963; Almond and Verba 1963; Lerner 1958; Neubauer 1967; Dahl 1971; Eckstein 1961, 1966). These theories describe the political environment, developmental outlook, and attitudes of democracies but fall short of analyzing the organic aspect of the transition to democracy (Rustow 1970, 342–54). Certain social and economic conditions—such as a high literacy rate, rising per capita income, exposure to mass media, and urbanization—may be conducive to the development of a democracy, but there is no definite causal relation. Guillermo A. O'Donnell's study of modernization in South American authoritarian regimes suggests that socioeconomic modernization may lead to more political pluralism, which cannot in itself be equated with the emergence of political democracy (O'Donnell 1973). On the contrary, socioeconomic modernization may enhance the authoritarian regimes' oppressive capacities or set the stage for a praetorian politics.

Thus even among nations with high rates of socioeconomic growth, the transition to democracy is not uniform. In fact, as Dankwart A. Rustow has concluded, during the preparatory phase after socioeconomic modernization, the dynamic process of democratization itself may set off a "prolonged and inconclusive political struggle" between protagonists of democracy and their entrenched opponents (Rustow 1970, 352–54). For the antagonism and struggle of the preparatory phase to end, political leaders must accept "diversity in unity" and undertake measures to "institutionalize some crucial aspects of democratic procedure" (Rustow 1970, 355). In short, the ruling elite's decision to pursue democracy is at least as important as the requisite socioeconomic and cultural conditions. Popular demands for political democratization may generate pressure toward democratic reform, but they do not necessarily lead to it.

Taiwan may have all the necessary conditions for democracy, but the transition from a soft authoritarianism or its present form of tutelary democracy to a truly representative democracy must await the ruling elite's support for further reform and the opposition leaders' willingness to compromise. Recent events in 1986–1988 suggest that the KMT leadership has undertaken reforms that should lead to a more democratic political system.

THE PARTY SYSTEM

Political parties have existed for only about one century. With the decline of the monarchy and aristocracy, political parties first emerged in the late nineteenth and early twentieth centuries in Anglo-American democracies and then spread throughout Europe. During the course of national independence movements, such parties assumed the leading role of organizing anticolonial struggles. The emergence of political parties is undoubtedly an important feature of modern political development.

But political parties reflect differences of political culture and historical experience in a wide variety of political systems at various stages of social, political, and economic development. Despite these differences, Joseph LaPalombara and Myron Weiner have argued that parties perform certain common functions in all political systems: the organization of public opinion, the communication of demands to the central government, the articulation to their followers of the concept and meaning of the broader community, and the recruitment of political leaders (LaPalombara and Weiner 1966, 3). In addition, political parties integrate otherwise segmented social forces, thus aggregating interests. In democracies where open and competitive elections are regularly held, the parties select candidates and often manage campaigns as well.

The party system refers to the aggregate of party activities in the political process. It describes the nature and pattern of interactions among party, state, and society. Where there is more than one party, the pattern of political interactions among parties also shapes the party system. In analyzing societies most scholars use the number of parties and party competitiveness as two major variables to classify party systems. Austin Ranney and Jerzy J. Wiatr have classified them into multiparty and two-party systems of democracy as well as one-party dictatorships, which include the three variants of monoparty, hegemonic party, and dominant-party systems (Ranney 1975, 208–28; Wiatr 1964, 281–90). Other writers include ideology in their classification schemes. Giovanni Sartori, for instance, has developed a typology of ten party systems as follows: (1) one-party totalitarian, (2) one-party authoritarian, (3) one-party pragmatic, (4) ideological hegemonic, (5) pragmatic hegemonic, (6) predominant, (7) two-partism, (8) moderate multipartism (three to five parties), (9) extreme multipartism (more than five parties), and (10) atomized partism (a great proliferation of parties) (Sartori 1964). Although this typology serves an analytical purpose, it is by no means easy to place the party system of any given state under one category or another. In the case of the Republic of China, no single category from the above list accounts for the characteristics of its party system.

Fred R. Von der Mehden has analyzed a wide variety of party systems in the developing nations. Von der Mehden used the number of parties and the degree of competitiveness to arrive at eighteen possible forms for party systems (Von der Mehden 1969, 49–59). As Table 1.1 indicates, of the 98 nations surveyed in the 1960s, 37 were noncompetitive state systems in which the political party did not play effective governing roles, 5 were one-party or multiparty proletarian states without political competition, and 24 had either two-party or multiparty democratic competitive systems. In between were 16 semicompetitive one-party-dominant systems, including those of India, Mexico, South Korea, and Malaysia (Von der Mehden 1969, 55–56). The ROC on Taiwan was classified as one of the 16 noncompetitive one-party states (Von der Mehden 1969, 52).

Von der Mehden argues that one-party systems share the following characteristics: (1) opposition parties are rarely permitted and have insuf-

_____ TABLE 1.1 _____
PARTY SYSTEMS IN THE THIRD WORLD

	Non-competitive	Semi-competitive	Competitive
Nongoverning-party states	37	—	—
One-party or multiparty proletarian states	5	—	—
One-party states	16	—	—
One-party-dominant states	—	16	—
Two-party democratic states	—	—	8
Multiparty democratic states	—	—	16

SOURCE: Von der Mehden (1969), 50–59.

ficient popular support; (2) the scope of the opposition parties' activities is restricted even though democracy is accepted in principle; (3) political opponents are forcibly co-opted by the ruling party or by legal and extralegal barriers to competition; and (4) there is minimal distinction between the party and the state (Von der Mehden 1969, 53). But he distinguishes one-party systems from both communist states and one-party-dominant systems. One-party-dominant systems have a higher incidence of legally and politically accepted competition, permitting opposition parties to survive, if not thrive, by holding seats in the national and regional legislatures. This conceptual distinction closely follows the classification schemes offered by Ranney and Wiatr, who define both monoparty and hegemonic one-party systems as ones in which organized opposition parties are either legally nonexistent or practically meaningless (Ranney 1975, 224–26; Wiatr 1964, 281–84).

Samuel P. Huntington, however, prefers not to distinguish between various types of one-party systems:

> In a one-party system the processes determining governmental policy and political leadership function almost exclusively through the framework of a single party. Minor parties may exist but they are so minor as not to exert any significant influence upon what goes on within the major party. In the mid-twentieth century one-party systems included the communist states, authoritarian regimes like Franco's Spain, and Nationalist China. (Huntington 1968, 419)

By referring to the ROC as a one-party system, Huntington makes no distinction between communist and noncommunist states.

But in a separate work Huntington and Clement H. Moore relate one-party systems to stages of modernization and differentiation of social forces (Huntington and Moore 1970, 11–12). They argue that "the great bulk of one-party systems . . . come into existence in societies in the early and early-to-middle phases of modernization . . . produced by social revolutions [that] come with the breakdown of traditional social structures and the mobilization of new groups into politics" (Huntington and Moore 1970, 12). They differentiate three forms: exclusionary one-party systems, which limit the scope of political participation; totalitarian revolutionary one-party systems that limit the scope of political participation; and totalitarian revolutionary one-party systems that liquidate subordinate social forces. Although they describe the KMT regime as an exclusionary one-party system, they acknowledge that "after its removal to Taiwan a somewhat looser exclusionary policy was followed with respect to the bifurcation between mainlanders and islanders" (Huntington and Moore 1970, 16).

The KMT's looser exclusionary policy is apparently a response to the socioeconomic changes brought about by Taiwan's modernization. Modernization has diversified the social and political elite, introduced disruptive forces within both the ruling party and society at large, and greatly complicated the dominant social division between mainlanders and ethnic Taiwanese. Thus a previously exclusionary authoritarian one-party system could, through socioeconomic modernization, eventually transform into a categorically different form.

The conceptual framework of Joseph LaPalombara and Myron Weiner goes one step further by separating three types of one-party systems according to elite structure, ideological orientation, and socioeconomic differentiation (LaPalombara and Weiner 1966, 37–40). In their view Marxist-Leninist and Nazi totalitarian party systems are fundamentally different from two other types, one-party authoritarian and one-party pluralistic systems. One-party authoritarian systems are dominated by a single, monolithic, ideologically oriented, but nontotalitarian party, such as Spain under Franco, Mali, Ghana, Guinea, and South Vietnam under Diem (LaPalombara and Weiner 1966, 38). In these systems opposition parties are regarded as traitors to revolutionary or nationalist causes and thus as threats to security. The ruling party personifies the development aspirations and mission of the nation. In contrast, one-party pluralistic systems are quasi-authoritarian systems dominated by a single party that is pluralistic in organization, pragmatic rather than rigidly ideological in outlook, and absorptive rather than ruthlessly destructive in its relations to other groups (LaPalombara and Weiner 1966, 38–39). A one-party pluralistic system tends to accommodate the conflicting interests within a society. Since parties are often the outgrowth of a development process, a one-party authoritarian system, in theory at least, could gradually transform into a one-party pluralistic system through socioeconomic modernization. We can argue that the ROC party system has followed this pattern. As democratization continues, a dominant-party system has emerged and may even stabilize.

In a dominant-party system only one party can govern, but two or more opposition parties contest openly in the electoral process. These opposition parties are strong enough to affect the operation of the political system. By virtue of their legal status and interaction with the ruling party, opposition parties can often influence the political process within the dominant party (Huntington 1968, 419). Furthermore, under such a system a plurality within the ruling party leads to flexibility and internal competition (Hardgrave 1980, 149). Maurice Duverger maintains that several Western democracies have in fact operated under a dominant-party system at either a national or a subnational level. Sweden and Norway under the socialists and the U.S. South under the Democratic Party are cases in point (Duverger 1963, 410–17). Moreover, Japan—where the Liberal Democratic Party has won every national election since the early 1950s—resembles a dominant-party system rather than a multiparty system with five contending parties.

Some dominant-party systems in the Third World also tolerate party competition, although the ruling party, which often emerged from a national liberation movement, regularly wins most of the national and regional/local elections. The ruling party monopolizes government power, and conflicts over public policy are generally fought out within the ruling party. To perpetuate its status, the dominant party absorbs groups and movements from outside the party, preventing other smaller parties from gaining strength (Hardgrave 1980, 149). India and Mexico are frequently cited as examples of this dominant-party system.

The Indian National Congress Party was founded in 1885. In the 1940s under the leadership of Mohandas K. Gandhi and Jawaharlal Nehru, the party led India to political independence from British colonial control. From 1947 to 1967 it dominated national elections by winning three-quarters of the seats in the national parliament. Its popularity subsequently declined; from 1967 to 1977 the National Congress Party at one time or another lost control of about half the state governments (Hardgrave 1980, 157). In the election of 1977 the Janata Front, an umbrella of four constituent parties, joined with the Congress for Democracy (CFD) party on a common slate of candidates and won 298 of the total 542 seats in the parliament, with 43 percent of the popular vote (Hardgrave 1980, 176). The National Congress Party gained only 154 seats, with 34.5 percent of the vote. Twenty-eight months later the Janata government fell as the party alliance was torn by factional conflict and defection. In the most recent parliamentary election in January 1985, the Congress Party regained its strength by winning over 50 percent of the popular vote and 400 of the 508 seats against 27 other political parties (Brelis 1985, 68).

In Mexico the politically dominant Institutional Revolutionary Party (PRI) is more entrenched than its Indian counterpart. The party was created in 1929 to carry out the social programs envisioned in the Mexican Revolution of 1910, which ended the dictatorship of Porfirio Díaz. The PRI has won all presidential contests by overwhelming margins, holding over 80 percent of the seats in the Chamber of Deputies (Ranney 1975, 228). From 1934 to 1982, according to available figures, PRI presidential candidates won at least 71 percent of the votes cast, sometimes garnering 90 percent or more (Cornelius and Craig 1988, 438). In fact none of the party's nominees for governor or senator has ever been defeated. In addition the party and government overlap because the top party officials usually also occupy government posts (Padgett 1976, 1). The government controls radio and television networks as well.

Although the PRI is a dominant political force in Mexico, it does not outlaw other political parties, which are legally free to contest elections (Rustow 1967, 214). The six opposition parties shared 25 percent of the seats in the Chamber of Deputies in 1985. In a presidential election held in 1982, opposition candidates received 26 percent of the popular vote (Wesson 1985, 273). Furthermore, the PRI itself has a pluralistic structure to accommodate specific groups, such as workers, peasants, and government employees. Each of these groups is assured of 15 representatives in the PRI National Council (Dix 1974, 297). That Mexican opposition parties cannot win a major office other than the lower house seats suggests the fragility of democratic competition in that country. During election campaigns, the mass media give little coverage of the opposition. Government control of the newsprint supply and electronic media also helps the PRI retain dominance. Compared with India, the Mexican dominant-party system is weak and sometimes looks more like a one-party system, but it is not a single-party system like that of the ROC before 1986.

POLITICAL DEVELOPMENT

According to the preceding analysis, the ROC polity is essentially a modernizing authoritarian regime with strong characteristics of a one-party pluralistic system in transition toward a dominant-party system. As Taiwan passes beyond the initial phase of industrialization and moves toward a higher level of socioeconomic modernization, both the general public and segments of the governing elite are increasingly demanding more rapid democratization. As Edwin A. Winckler has recently pointed out, "Taiwan's political leadership has proved remarkably good at adapting political institutions largely to absorb and selectively to repress" demands for broader participation (Winckler 1984, 483). The pattern and pace of adaptation evident in the past may not be sufficient to deter a possible crisis of participation should democratization stagnate. Clearly both the overall political system and the party system in particular are under pressure to move toward a new phase of development. In fact the process has already begun.

As recently as the 1970s Bruce Jacobs, a close observer of Taiwan's politics, portrayed the ROC as having a strong one-party system comparable with some of the Leninist one-party systems in Eastern Europe and elsewhere (Jacobs 1978, 240–42). Such a system has so far provided a level of political stability rarely seen in the Third World (Huntington 1968, 422–23). Although authoritarian and hierarchical, the KMT does offer the institutions and procedures for the assimilation of new groups into the system. Assimilation has been accomplished by competitive examination for civil servants, intraparty recruitment, and electoral contests. The party system has also fostered a political environment conducive to stable socioeconomic modernization.

Many problems emerging on Taiwan's political horizon should not be regarded as failures to modernize. On the contrary, they are products of that modernization and underscore Taiwan's rapid success. The institutional structures that have helped cement the KMT's authoritarian one-party system are gradually revised, albeit slowly, to accommodate public pressure for more intraparty pluralism and even a representative democracy at the systemic level. Such a transition has been regulated closely so as not to threaten the KMT's ruling position. Eventually these changes could lead to a stable dominant-party system unless the ruling elite abruptly reverses the course of political development.

During 1986–1987 two major political developments in Taiwan furthered the transition to a dominant-party system of representative democracy. At its May 12, 1986, meeting, a KMT Central Standing Committee task force decided that the ruling party would study the possibility of major political reforms. Subsequently, on October 15, the Central Standing Committee passed a resolution to draft a new National Security Law to replace martial law, later lifted on July 15, 1987. The existing emergency provisions restricting private associations were also revised in 1987 to legalize certain political activities, including the organization of opposition parties.

Another major political development was the formation of the new Democratic Progessive Party on September 28, 1986 (*SPCK*, no. 84 [October 4, 1986]: 7–9). Since the formation of this new party, the KMT authorities have taken no repressive actions. With the lifting of martial law and the legalization of political opposition, the ROC has clearly crossed the threshold to a competitive dominant–party system and, perhaps, a meaningful representative democracy.

The main purpose of this book is to study how the ruling KMT interacts with other major institutions of the state and society. It will show how a structurally Leninist party has adapted to govern a society with a large private economic sector and with emerging social pluralism. More important, it will investigate how the KMT accommodates demands for democratic political participation within a context of phenomenal socioeconomic modernization. Most common socioeconomic indicators suggest a pattern of growth highly conducive to democratization in Taiwan. Yet because of Taiwan's geopolitical situation, in particular the unresolved historical hostility between the KMT and the Chinese Communist Party (CCP) as well as the traditional elitist attitudes of the KMT power holders, the transition toward a more competitive and democratic political system has not been smooth. As Chapter 9 will show, the decline of Taiwan's international status together with threats from the PRC, both direct and implied, will continue to constrain the ROC's political system. Chapter 2 analyzes the pattern of development and current progress of Taiwan's socioeconomic modernization. Modernization expands economic opportunities and leads to social pluralism, urbanization, mass exposure to the media, rising expectations, popular demands for more civil liberties and political participation, organized political opposition, and growing differentiation of the elite structure. All of these changes conflict with institutional and policy constraints that deter development to a political democracy.

Chapter 3 will analyze the proliferating interest groups on Taiwan. As the society becomes more complex, organized groups are growing in number and diversity. Since the ruling KMT still plays a critical role in social control, Taiwan's interest groups have yet to achieve the autonomy commonly seen in Western pluralistic democracies. By and large the party still dominates the selection of group leaders. The Leninist practice of treating mass organizations as merely the transmission belts of the party-state continues to characterize the interaction between the KMT and major organized groups. The party thus remains an "overarching institution of interest aggregation," to quote John A. Armstrong, a noted authority on the Marxist-Leninist system in the Soviet Union (Armstrong 1978, 53).

Nevertheless, the impact of Taiwan's evolving social pluralism on the political process can be seen in the growing autonomy of certain socioeconomic groups, particularly since the 1986–1988 political reforms. Indeed a limited political pluralism has already arrived on Taiwan.

To put the KMT in perspective, Chapter 4 analyzes the party's development since its reforms in 1950–1952. Over the years the party has moved from a predominantly mainlander orientation to its present makeup, with a substantial number of Taiwanese in high posts and a Taiwanese majority in overall membership. The party's integrative function is reflected in the gradual convergence of elite interests among the major ethnic groups—the mainlanders, the Fukien-Taiwanese, and the Hakkas. As the KMT expanded its organizational network into the most remote corners of rural Taiwan, it fostered social control and provided social services, both of which have become essential to the party's continuing electoral success. Winning elections has gradually become an important measure of the regime's legitimacy. Chapter 4 will also outline the development of the political opposition and its relation to the ruling party.

Chapter 5 describes the institutional structure of the government at the national, provincial, and local levels. The executive branch of the national government constitutes the focus of our analysis. Special attention will be given to those elements of the executive branch that deal with economic development. Chapter 6 discusses the electoral process in Taiwan and the roles of the KMT and the opposition. As more public officials are subject to popular elections, the electoral process has gained importance in the overall political process. Chapter 7 will deal with the legislatures, particularly at the national and provincial levels. Although the legislatures remain relatively impotent in lawmaking and in the budgetary process, they have lately provided lawmakers with a crucial forum for policy debate and interrogation. In addition, Taiwan's interest groups have focused more of their attention on the legislators rather than just on the KMT and government officials. Their pressure is certainly felt in the Legislative Yuan, which until the 1970s had no meaningful connection with electoral politics or organized political pressure.

Along with interest groups and electoral politics, Chapter 8 will show a flourishing mass media fast becoming a salient feature of Taiwan's political dynamics. Until the 1970s the KMT authorities and individual KMT leaders practically monopolized the mass media. The press was anything but free. But with growing social pluralism and a market orientation, even the KMT media enterprises are locked in relentless competition. Consumer sovereignty is gaining ground. Moreover, as opposition political movements emerge, the media can no longer be treated as the transmission belt of the party-state. In January 1988 Taiwan's mass media entered a new era of free competition with substantially liberalized regulations.

This study has adopted familiar Western concepts and analytical theories to look at the dynamics of Taiwan's political evolution. I am not prepared to argue that a Western type of two-party or multiparty pluralistic democracy is superior in Taiwan's political context. The ROC political system has to operate within the context of its historical legacy, geopolitical constraints, distinct Chinese political culture, and level of socioeconomic development. For a polity governed by an essentially Leninist political party, the transformation toward a Western-style democratic system with more than one meaningful party is clearly a formidable challenge. By examining the interlocking relations between the party, the state, and society, I will show that although the party continues to play pivotal roles in many respects, its domination over the state and society is weakening. The political process in recent years has pointed Taiwan toward a dominant-party system of representative democracy.

— 2 —

Economic Development
and Social Change

Taiwan experienced outstanding economic development during the
period 1951–1987. The annual economic growth rate averaged 8.9 percent from 1951 to 1984 (*TCNC*, 1985, 62). With a mild recession in 1985
the growth rate slowed to about 5 percent. In 1986 the recovering economy showed an impressive growth rate of 10.87 percent; the rate rose
further to 11.2 percent in 1987 (*CYJP*, January 2, 1987, 1; January 4,
1988, 1). Per capita income increased from U.S. $3,748 in 1986 to U.S.
$4,991 in 1987 (*CYJP*, December 10, 1987, 1).[1] With an export volume
worth U.S. $53.5 billion in 1987, Taiwan became the eleventh largest ex-
porter in the world. By the end of 1986 the Central Bank's foreign reserves stood at U.S. $46 billion, surpassing Japan's and the United States'
as the second largest after West Germany's (*FCJ*, December 29, 1986, 1).
Total foreign reserves were approximately U.S. $76 billion by March
1988 (*CYJP*, March 15, 1988, 1).

These staggering figures mark the monumental achievements of this
island nation of 19.5 million people (in 1987) with scarce natural resources and heavy defense expenditures. If economic growth continues
at the projected 7.5 percent rate in 1988, with an exchange rate of U.S. $1
to N.T. $28, the nation's per capita income in 1988 would be U.S. $6,183,
reaching as high as U.S. $17,000 in the year 2000 (*CYJP*, December 10,
1987, 1). With such an economic performance, Taiwan would soon join
the family of economically developed nations. Moreover, compared with
other noncommunist nations, Taiwan has achieved this record of phenomenal growth since the 1950s with a relatively equitable distribution
of income.

There are reasons why Taiwan's economic development has been so successful. This chapter intends neither to offer a new interpretive theory nor to construct a possible model for other nations to follow, but rather to show the tremendous sociopolitical impact of almost four decades of continuous economic modernization on Taiwan's political development. Taiwan's authoritarian political system, as oppressive as it has been at times, has provided the economy with the long-term political stability it needed for development. Taiwan's technocratic elite and administrators have also been much more competent than those in most developing nations. But the relation between polity and economy does not end in these aspects alone. The significant sociopolitical changes in Taiwan raise a serious analytical question: How long can an authoritarian political system outlast its own economic success?

This chapter explores three interrelated issues: (1) the pattern and experiences of Taiwan's economic development, (2) their effect on the standard of living on the island, and (3) the sociopolitical change that results from economic development. These issues will help explain the current transformation in the political system, which has been moving toward Taiwanization, liberalization, and political democratization (Tien 1987a, 13–37).

ECONOMIC DEVELOPMENT

Economic Policy

During the Japanese occupation of 1895–1945, Taiwan acquired a sound economic foundation in its agricultural sector and in its economic infrastructure, with good roads, railways, and irrigation systems as well as local government administration (Ho 1978, 41–106; Lin Ching-yuan 1973, 13–22). Still Taiwan suffered severe damage during World War II when the United States conducted intense bombing in 1944–1945. The war curtailed industrial production and, together with the near cutoff of trade, caused severe shortages in all commodities. After the war, when Taiwan was brought under the control of the KMT regime in Nanking, inflation became rampant as prices increased 5-fold per annum from 1946 to 1948 and accelerated a phenomenal 30-fold in the first half of 1949 alone (Kuo 1983, 285). In 1949 the KMT government and armed forces retreated to Taiwan. Approximately two million mainlanders, mostly military servicemen, government and party officials, and their families, fled to Taiwan, creating additional economic pressure as Taiwan's economy, already depressed, faced the burdensome task of financing a vastly enlarged military establishment as well as an enlarged government bureaucracy.

Three major economic policies were pursued in the early 1950s: land reform, price stabilization, and import substitution behind a protectionist tariff policy. Land reform was a policy taken from Sun Yat-sen that the KMT had promised but never implemented on the mainland. Carrying out land reform in Taiwan gave substance to the KMT's claim that it was turning the island into a model province in accordance with Sun's Three Principles of the People. The land reform crippled the former economic base of the Taiwanese landlord-elite, who were not KMT allies at the time and might have challenged the KMT as carpetbaggers (Gold 1986, 65). By 1953 land reform, which involved both the redistribution of farmland and rent reduction, was largely complete. Monetary stabilization measures—including a thorough monetary reform, preferential interest rates on deposits, tight control of the money supply, and strict government budgets—were improved to slow the spiraling inflation (Kuznets 1979, 38; Kuo 1983, 286–90). To rehabilitate Taiwan's war-torn industries, an import substitution policy was designed to protect domestic light industry from foreign, particularly Japanese, competition. These import controls had the additional benefit of reducing the already sizable trade deficit. To promote import substitution the government relied on a combination of high tariffs, import quotas, and multiple exchange rates. According to Samuel P. S. Ho, the average tariff rate for all imports more than doubled, rising from 20 percent to nearly 45 percent between 1948 and 1955 (Ho 1978, 191). Items such as leather and leather manufactures, cement, chemical fertilizers, soap, paper, tin plate, sewing machines, bicycles, and motorcycles were placed under various degrees of import control (Lin Ching-yuan 1973, 49–50; Gregor and Chang 1983, 41). The importation of essential consumer goods, capital equipment, and raw materials was permissible within prescribed quotas. Luxury goods or dangerous items were totally prohibited. Partly because of these protectionist measures, Taiwan's industries—textiles, plastics, artificial fiber, glass, cement, fertilizer, and plywood—registered impressive growth. By 1956 inflation had been brought under control. These achievements were made possible mainly by U.S. assistance and the import-substituting industries instituted by the government (Haggard and Cheng 1987, 86–88; Gold 1986, 71–73). However, it soon became evident that the domestic market had been saturated. The import substitution strategy had to end, to be replaced by a strategy of export-led growth.

Between 1956 and 1958, with encouragement from the U.S. Agency for International Development (AID) mission in Taiwan, the government's economic planners decided to follow a forward-looking policy of export expansion. Over the next five years numerous reforms and programs promoted exports and stimulated industrialization. The government provided export insurance, direct subsidies to promising export industries, and export marketing research. In 1957 the state-owned Bank of Taiwan initiated low-cost loans as incentives for export industries. In April of the following year the government adopted a new economic package that simplified the multiple exchange rate system, reduced import restrictions, and rationalized the allocation of goods (Haggard and Cheng 1987, 115). The ROC augmented these economic reforms by a comprehensive nineteen-point Program of Financial and Economic Reform and the Statute for Encouragement of Investment introduced in 1960 to increase production, liberalize trade, and accelerate the export-induced industrial development during the Third Four-Year Plan of 1961–1964 (Kuo 1983, 300–301; Fei, Gustav, and Kuo 1979, 29; Haggard and Cheng 1987, 115).

The export promotion policy created a business climate that stimulated private local and foreign investment. The policy came at an opportune time because U.S. and Western European markets were growing and world trade was expanding rapidly with little protectionism curtailing growth. The termination of U.S. aid in 1965 had little impact on Taiwan's capital formation, which had already begun to depend on Taiwan's increasing net domestic savings derived from rising personal incomes.[2] In 1966 the KMT government established the first export-processing zone in the southern city of Kaohsiung; three years later two more zones were established in Nantze and Taichung.

The export-processing zones designated land for industrial use with tax advantages for foreign firms comparable to those found in free ports such as Hong Kong (Haggard and Cheng 1987, 91–92). The manufacturing firms in these zones were granted all the privileges and tax incentives given to other export producers in Taiwan, but without the red tape (Ho 1978, 197). By 1979 the three zones had attracted a combined investment of U.S. $280 million (Myers 1984, 518). The 250 factories in operation employed 78,000 workers. Their annual export value of U.S. $405 million was 9 percent of Taiwan's export total (Ho 1978, 90).

All these export-directed efforts contributed to the uninterrupted economic boom from 1962 to 1971. During that period industrial output rose at an annual rate of 17.3 percent, while the overall economic growth rate was just over 10 percent. As a result, from 1965 to 1972 per capita income more than doubled. But the significance of the export-processing zones declined, and by the early 1970s the government had to adjust the structure of the economy to retain export competitiveness. In fact as early as the mid-1960s the government tried to strengthen capital-

and technology-intensive sectors in the intermediate-goods industries to help fit the island's economy into the world trade system (Gregor and Chang 1983, 47).

In 1973 Taiwan's economic development policy entered a third phase with a growing emphasis on high-tech and capital-oriented industrial development. By then the economic environment at home and abroad had changed: the expanding world economy was slowing, energy prices were rising rapidly, the international finance system was in shambles, labor costs were no longer as cheap, and world technology was advancing quickly. Under the circumstances the government had no choice but to upgrade the technology and capital of Taiwan's industrial development.

Throughout the 1970s Taiwan's economy encountered difficulties. The effects of the oil shock and the general economic downturn in the industrialized West were severely felt in trade-dependent Taiwan because over half the nation's products were exported to the West. As Taiwan's economic outlook suddenly darkened, businessmen became cautious in capital investment and stagflation set in. Beginning in 1972, when Chiang Ching-kuo took over as premier, the government decided to invest public capital in ten major construction projects to sustain economic growth, provide additional employment, and improve Taiwan's industrial infrastructure. These ten projects developed a north–south freeway, railroad electrification, a railway in northeastern Taiwan, a new international airport in Taoyuan, a nuclear power plant, an integrated steel mill, a giant shipyard in Kaohsiung, petrochemical complexes, Taichung harbor, and Suao port.

By the end of 1978 these projects were nearly completed. During the following years the government continued to channel public investment into twelve new major construction projects (*China Yearbook*, 1978, 213). In addition a high-tech industrial park, modeled on Silicon Valley in northern California, was established in Hsinchu in 1980 to attract investment in technologically based industries (Gold 1986, 103; Wu Yuan-li 1985, 41–42). Since then the park has persuaded 73 research companies, three-quarters of them from the electronics industry, to set up shop there (Johnstone 1988, 70). In 1987 those companies generated sales of about U.S. $700 million, with nearly U.S. $500 million in exports (Johnstone 1988, 70). In 1985 the government initiated fourteen public-works projects, with a total capital budget of U.S. $23.5 billion over six to ten years (*FCJ*, April 14, 1986, 1). All these projects show the government's determination to strengthen the country's foundation for continued economic modernization. During 1986–1988 the government took measures to liberalize trade by relaxing import and foreign exchange restrictions. Such measures were clearly in response to U.S. pressure to reduce its trade deficit with Taiwan. Taiwan's economy is thus entering a new phase of challenges in trade as well as in structural and technological transition.

Land Reform

The Nationalist leaders have pursued economic development with balanced attention to the agricultural sector. During the 1950s land reform was a high priority. The reform was so successful that it brought the ROC on Taiwan its first international recognition in economic development. The reform program laid a solid foundation for agricultural growth throughout the 1950s. It also successfully resolved the issue of land tenure, which otherwise would have perpetuated socioeconomic conflict in rural areas. Thus Taiwan's developing economy did not experience the agrarian paralysis and rural unrest that have plagued many Third World nations.

Taiwan land reform rests on three policy measures implemented during 1949–1953. The first measure, rent reduction, was carried out in 1949. Before that time Taiwan's tenants, about half the farming population, paid, according to the quality of land, 40–60 percent of their agricultural output to landlords as rent (Ho 1978, 1600). The government's rent reduction decree set a compulsory rent ceiling of 37.5 percent of the annual standard yield of the chief crops, no matter what the actual harvest. Standard yield was appraised officially according to the grading of farmland, which was differentiated into 26 grades for both paddy and dry land (Ho 1978, 161). The fixed standard yield for each grade of land became the criterion for calculating annual rents. The government also specified provisions for the temporary relief of rent in the event of crop failure or natural calamity. According to Lee Teng-hui, Taiwan's leading agricultural economist and president of the republic, the average annual payment of rent per tenant was subsequently reduced by 1,116 kg of rice (Lee 1983, 3:1448). Tenant households as a whole gained an aggregate benefit of 134,922 metric tons of paddy rice, equivalent to 18 percent of the total 1948 rice output (Lee 1983, 3:1448).

The second measure was the sale of public farmland to tenant farmers. When World War II ended in 1945, land previously owned by Japanese citizens was confiscated by the Nationalist government. The total amounted to 170,000–176,000 hectares, or 20 to 25 percent of Taiwan's arable land (Fei, Gustav, and Kuo 1979, 46; Ho 1978, 161). During 1948–1958, 71,666 hectares were sold to nearly 140,000 tenant families (Lee 1983, 3:1446).

The third and most dramatic measure was the land-to-the-tiller program. According to a new law promulgated in 1953, each landlord family was compelled to sell to the government any land that it owned in excess of 2.9 hectares of medium-grade paddy field. The government purchased the land for 2.5 times the land's annual yield and then resold it to the tenant farmers. The landlords received payment not in cash but in commodity bonds issued by the government and in shares of stock for four public industrial enterprises previously owned by the Japanese colonial administration (Fei, Gustav, and Kuo 1979, 41). Under this program about 160,000 hectares, or another 22 percent of the total 681,150 hectares of private farmland, changed ownership (Lee 1983, 3:1446, 1449).

The program immediately increased the number of small owner-families, undermined the status and interests of the landlords, redistributed wealth and income in the rural community, and contributed to the rise of the farmers' political voice. From 1949 to 1957 the number of owner-families in the total farming population increased from 38 to 60 percent (Lee 1983, 3:1448-49). Before the land-to-the-tiller reform, 6 percent of the owner-families held 3 to 10 hectares of farmland and 1 percent (5,051 families) owned more than 10 hectares per family. By 1955 there was a substantial reduction in the number of families that owned over 34 hectares of land (Lee 1983, 3:1450). Conversely the proportion of tenant farmers dropped from 38 to 15 percent from 1950 to 1960 (Fei, Gustav, and Kuo 1979, 42).

The total value of redistributed land wealth was estimated at 13 percent of Taiwan's gross domestic product in 1952 (Fei, Gustav, and Kuo 1979, 43). The transfer of land wealth also equalized the income distribution between the agricultural sector and other sectors of the economy (Lee 1983, 3:1450-51).

The landlords, of course, suffered enormously. The commodity bonds they received from the government paid only 4 percent interest, substantially lower than the prevailing commercial interest rate. Furthermore many of them promptly resold their industrial stocks in state enterprises, which they had been compensated for, at prices well below their actual value (Fei, Gustav, and Kuo 1979, 43). Only a small number of them were later able to become industrialists, bankers, or businessmen (Gold 1986, 71). The effect on the rural political landscape was also noticeable. In field research conducted in the west-central coastal plain of Taiwan during 1956-1958, Bernard Gallin reported that "the loss of much of the leadership traditionally furnished by the wealthy, well-educated landlord class. . . [and] the exodus of the landlord families [to the city] has created a virtual leadership vacuum in some local villages" (Gallin 1964, 317). As the landlords lost economic interests, they lost interest in local politics. In a 1958 local election, for example, some villages in Changhua County did not have any candidates for the position of village headman, a status previously monopolized by landlords (Gallin 1963, 109–12). In another study Martin M. C. Yang disclosed that 70 percent of the 575 farmer-landlord households surveyed admitted that "they became either less interested or had felt no interest at all in the community's local politics since land reform" (Yang 1970, 483). In contrast, as beneficiaries of land reform the tenant farmers and owner-cultivators became more interested in politics and governmental affairs (Yang 1970, 482; Ho 1978, 174).

The KMT government achieved its intended economic and political goals. Land reform forestalled potential rural unrest. The economic base of Taiwan's landlord power was seriously weakened, if not eliminated, thus circumscribing local political opposition. The government carried out land reform not only "for what it might do for the economy and social justice but also for what it might do for its [the KMT's] own political survival" (Ho 1978, 162). In the end, a new rural leadership more attuned to the KMT's political requirements emerged and replaced the deposed landed gentry.

Industrialization and Structural Change

Taiwan's industrialization has gone through four phases (*TSDB*, 1984, 13–17). The initial phase, 1936–1952, was marked by postwar economic reconstruction and efforts to stabilize the price structure by controlling the skyrocketing inflation. The major targets for industrial development were fertilizer production, electric power generation, and textiles. The first two meshed with agricultural needs—raising production and increasing irrigation. During the second phase, 1953–1960, the government encouraged private investment in labor-intensive light industry. During this phase import substitution was pursued to protect domestic industry. Industrial products and consumer goods were manufactured mostly to meet domestic demand.

During the third phase, 1961–1972, the government adopted a series of financial reforms and incentive programs to increase industrial output for both exports and growing domestic demand. Labor-intensive light industry remained the primary focus. But the government also began to encourage large-scale industrial production and initiated the development of heavy and chemical industries. During the current fourth phase, the government has set forth measures to promote capital-intensive industries—such as electronics, communications, and machinery—and chemical industries to guide Taiwan from light to heavy industrial development. The government has made large capital investments to improve the economic infrastructure, as is evident in the adoption of major construction projects. More recently, since 1981 industrial development has been directed toward high-tech and energy-saving industries, with an emphasis on precision instruments, robotics, and communication technologies. Overall the electronic, petrochemical, and advanced machine tool industries have surged ahead during this latest phase of industrial development.

In the past 36 years industrial growth has been spectacular. Between 1953 and 1962 the average annual industrial growth rate was 11.7 percent, followed by growth rates of 18.5 percent from 1963 to 1972 and 9.8 percent from 1973 to 1987 (*TSDB*, 1988, 2). Taiwan's industrialization is also demonstrated by changes in the industry-agriculture-service component of net domestic product, exports, and employment. In 1952 agriculture accounted for 35.9 percent of Taiwan's total production, compared with 18.0 percent for industry and 46.1 percent for commerce, transportation, and services (*TSDB*, 1988, 41). By 1987 the relative positions of the three sectors had changed dramatically to 6.1 percent, 47.5 percent, and 46.4 percent respectively (*TSDB*, 1988, 41). Industrial output is expected to continue to exceed 50 percent of the nation's domestic product, thus qualifying the ROC as a highly industrialized nation.

Intrasectoral changes have been equally significant. In 1952 light industry constituted 75.2 percent of total industrial output, with heavy industry at 24.8 percent. By 1982 the ratio was 46.3 percent to 53.7 percent in favor of heavy industry (RDEC 1983, 112). The ratio between public and private enterprises was 56.6 percent to 43.4 percent in 1952. By 1987 the private sector had surged to 85.6 percent (*TSDB*, 1987, 88). Thus Taiwan's economy today is dominated by private enterprises with a broad heavy industrial base.

Exports have always been vital to the ROC's economy. The change in Taiwan's export component indicates the underlying structural transformation of the national economy. In 1952 industrial products constituted only 8.1 percent of total exports, compared with 91.9 percent for agricultural products and food. By 1986 industrial products accounted for 93.9 percent of total exports (*TSDB*, 1988, 213). Today Taiwan's exports are more characteristic of industrialized nations than of most developing nations, which export primarily agricultural products and raw materials.

Along with structural changes in production and exports, Taiwan's employment pattern has changed dramatically. In 1984 nearly 3.1 million people, or 42.3 percent of total employment, were in the industrial sector. The figures for agriculture and services were 1.3 million (17.6 percent) and 2.8 million (40.1 percent) respectively (*TCNC*, 1985, 38). Agricultural employment is expected to decline further, with increasing growth in the services industries predicted in the years ahead. C. E. Black, a leading scholar on modernization, once argued that "the most important indication of a society being transformed from traditional to modern is the transfer of more than one-half of the work force of a society from agriculture to manufacturing, transportation, commerce, and service" (Black 1967, 78). By this yardstick, and on the basis of figures cited above, Taiwan can be described as a modern industrial society.

Income and Living Standards

Aside from industrial growth, Taiwan's overall economic achievement is reflected in the high growth rates of both gross national product (GNP) and GNP per capita. As Table 2.1 indicates, during the early decade of 1953–1962 the average annual growth rate was 7.5 percent. Much of that growth was accomplished in light industry; land reform and U.S. aid were also major contributing factors. Because of the high population growth rate of 3.5 percent, GNP per capita grew only 4.0 percent per annum. In the next decade, 1963–1972, the GNP growth rate accelerated to 10.8 percent as Taiwan's light industry developed and trade expanded, particularly after 1968. Population growth declined to 2.9 percent. GNP per capita increased 8.1 percent annually for these years, twice the figure of the preceding decade. During 1973–1987 the GNP growth rate decreased to 8.0 percent, reflecting the effects of petroleum price rises and global economic recession. Meanwhile a continuing decline in population growth helped the GNP per capita retain a respectable 6.2 percent growth rate.

Indeed the high growth rate in GNP and the steady decrease in population growth have rapidly raised the income of Taiwan's population. In 1952 GNP per capita and per capita income stood at U.S. $50 and $48 respectively (TSDB, 1988, 29, 35).[3] By 1985 the figures had risen to U.S. $3,142 and U.S. $2,868 respectively (FCJ, January 27, 1986, 1). Per capita income increased further to U.S. $4,991 in 1987 (CYJP, December 10, 1987, 1). More important, these rises in income were achieved with more equal income distribution than in most countries. According to ROC official data for 1985, when disposable family incomes were divided into five equal groups in ascending order, the disposable family income of the highest income group was 4.5 times that of the lowest income group (QNET, August 1986, 57). Further, the income gap between the highest and lowest 20 percent in Taiwan is smaller than that in the United States, Japan, the United Kingdom, Thailand, Australia, South Korea, the Netherlands, Hong Kong, and West Germany (SI, 1983, 8).

_____ TABLE 2.1 _____
AVERAGE GROWTH RATES OF GNP, POPULATION,
AND GNP PER CAPITA IN TAIWAN, 1953–1987

	GNP[a]	Population	GNP per capita
1953–1962	7.5	3.5	4.0
1963–1972	10.8	2.9	8.1
1973–1987	8.4	1.7	6.5

SOURCE: *TSDB* (1988), 2.
[a]Adjusted for gain or loss due to changed terms of trade.

What do these figures indicate about Taiwan's standing in the world? Figures compiled by an independent source show that in 1984 Taiwan ranked 59th among 69 nations in the percentage of national income received by the richest 10 percent (Kurian 1984, 101). The higher the rank, the greater the disparity in income distribution. In fact only Australia, the United Kingdom, Norway, Sweden, and 6 Eastern European countries rated more favorably than Taiwan. Conversely Taiwan ranked 6th in the percentage of national income received by the poorest 40 percent of the population (Kurian 1984, 102). Sixty-one countries in the study fared worse than Taiwan; only Czechoslovakia, Bulgaria, East Germany, Hungary, and Poland, all socialist states, rated more favorably. The poorest 40 percent of Taiwan's populace apparently had a larger share of national income than counterparts in any noncommunist country in the world. Thus, according to available figures on income distribution, Taiwan society clearly has one of the most equitable distributions of wealth in the world.

High growth rates for income plus relative income parity have meant widespread improvements in the living standard for the island's twenty million residents. Comparative measures of living standards are difficult because there are many indices and their components vary from one political system to another. But modern societies tend to provide, among other things, the following common material goods: automobiles, motorcycles, telephones, televisions, radios, magazines and daily newspapers, air conditioners and/or heaters, refrigerators, and washing machines. Two questions are key: Are these goods available, and are the citizens able to purchase them? Only a developed economy can provide its consumers with abundant supplies of these goods, either domestic or imported. As disposable income increases beyond daily necessities (food, clothing, and shelter), the ability of a family to purchase consumer goods rises. A society with greater income parity will have more who can afford to acquire these modern goods. Therefore the possession of these goods signifies an overall higher standard of living.

Table 2.2 illustrates this point. The indices fall into two groups because of the way the data were gathered. The first three items are transportation and communication products; the second three are information media. In 1952 there were four telephones and one automobile per 1,000 persons and one motorcycle for every 5,000 persons. The ownership of these products per 1,000 persons has increased steadily over the years. By 1985 there were 70 automobiles, 342 motorcycles, 294 telephones, 230 televisions, 127 radios (1984), and 195 magazines and daily newspapers in circulation per 1,000 persons. If we use figures per 100 households as indicators, in 1985 there were 106 televisions (90 percent color), 12 privately owned automobiles, and 102 motorcycles (QNET, August 1986, 58). The record of escalating rates of ownership for these goods suggests rapid improvements in living standards for most residents. These figures compare favorably even with some Western European nations.

Access to modern living is also reflected in the possession of household goods such as air conditioners and heaters, refrigerators, and washing machines. As Table 2.3 indicates, in 1976 there were 4 heaters and air conditioners, 75 refrigerators, and 39 washing machines per 100 households. The figures have risen steadily since. By 1985 these figures had increased to 30, 99, and 79 respectively. If we calculate average household possessions, approximately 23 percent of Taiwan's families owned air conditioners and heaters, over 95 percent owned refrigerators, and 76 percent owned washing machines. By this measure, the household ownership of these goods is rapidly approaching the levels of advanced industrial societies. Today in Taiwan owning modern products such as televisions, refrigerators, motorcycles, washing machines, and telephones is commonplace even in rural communities.

SOCIAL STRATIFICATION AND SOCIAL CHANGE

Economic modernization has had a profound impact on Taiwan's social system. With rising living standards, better educational opportunities, and improved health care, the island's demographic composition has changed significantly. Infant mortality has declined while life expectancy has lengthened. Under Nationalist rule, annual population growth started at 3.3 percent in 1952, grew to 5 percent in 1969, and then slowed to 1.0 percent by 1986 (TSDB, 1988, 4). By 1995 the growth rate is ex-

——— TABLE 2.2 ———
SELECTED INDICES OF MODERN MATERIAL GOODS (1):
POSSESSION PER 1,000 PERSONS IN TAIWAN, 1952–1985

	Autos	Motorcycles	Telephones	Televisions	Radios	Magazines and daily newspapers
1952	1.0	0.2	3.9	—	—	—
1956	1.4	0.3	5.2	—	—	—
1961	1.9	3.9	9.9	—	—	—
1966	3.1	20.4	15.0	—	—	39
1971	7.5	55.7	33.2	101	—	61
1972	9.1	63.3	39.4	—	—	74
1973	11.3	76.0	48.1	—	—	76
1974	14.2	91.5	57.3	—	—	83
1975	16.6	106.6	69.9	—	—	89
1976	19.3	123.1	85.5	178	64	97
1977	22.6	143.7	101.2	194	67	120
1978	25.6	160.1	123.7	201	72	140
1979	32.4	192.7	148.3	207	86	141
1980	38.6	224.8	179.5	210	91	142
1981	44.7	225.5	212.6	215	103	161
1982	50.6	278.7	238.1	217	109	164
1983	56.6	198.7	258.7	220	121	169
1984	64.0	321.3	277.2	222	127	178
1985	69.8	342.1	293.5	230	130	195

SOURCES: *TCNC* (1984), 13; *RDEC* (1986), 227, 229.

pected to dip below 1 percent (Liao 1985, 8). The age structure of the population has also shifted, with the number of one- to fourteen-year-olds stabilizing while the number of citizens above 65 years of age steadily rises. In recent years the government has recognized this change by allocating a larger budget for social security expenditures. Furthermore, the high population growth rates of the 1950s and the early 1960s have produced an upsurge in Taiwan's working-age population, leading to employment pressures. Another important demographic trend is toward the formation of smaller family units. The traditional lineage system is breaking down so that fewer people live together in extended family networks, but nuclear family ties remain strong. The nuclear family now averages about 4.5 persons, down from 6.5 persons per family in the 1950s.

_____ TABLE 2.3 _____
SELECTED INDICES OF MODERN MATERIAL GOODS (2): POSSESSION PER 100 HOUSEHOLDS IN TAIWAN, 1976–1984

	Heaters and air conditioners	Refrigerators	Washing machines
1976	3.6	74.2	38.6
1977	5.3	81.2	47.2
1978	8.6	86.4	54.0
1979	11.7	89.6	60.1
1980	14.4	92.2	64.7
1981	16.4	94.0	68.9
1982	17.2	94.3	70.5
1983	19.7	95.4	73.6
1984	23.0	96.1	75.5
1985	30.3	98.8	78.5

SOURCES: *TCNC* (1984), 2; figures for 1983 from *QNET* (August 1986), 58.

Industrial development combined with an advanced transportation system has helped produce rapid urbanization. In 1950, 24 towns and cities in Taiwan had populations over 5,000. By the early 1980s such places numbered almost 70. Urbanization is caused by migration from rural areas as well as by the natural reproductive increase of urban residents and by the administrative expansion of cities. In 1981, 62.4 percent of the island's population lived in urban centers (Sun 1985, 117). But Taiwan's urbanization pattern differs from that of other countries, particularly the pattern in the Third World. The island is geographically compact, thus assuring even rural residents relatively easy access to a nearby urban center. Furthermore, many industries are located in smaller cities and towns, partly to absorb excess labor—part-time farmers and marginal agricultural workers. Hence Taiwan does not have a lopsided concentration of population in a few metropolitan centers.

The Impact of Modernization on Social Structure

When the Nationalists arrived on Taiwan in 1949, the island's social structure was simple. There was a small middle class. The upper class consisted mostly of landlords, a few industrialists, and physicians. Government employees and officials of Taiwanese origin were mostly clerks at the middle level or in local administration. With the arrival of the mainlanders, this social structure was profoundly disrupted. The subsequent land reform program further reduced the landlords' significance in society. As industrialization and urbanization picked up momentum, Taiwan's social structure became increasingly complex and differentiated. This transition has given rise to social pluralism, as in many industrialized societies (Yang Kuo-shu 1985, 73–81).

The impact of economic modernization on social differentiation is clearly reflected in the changing patterns of employment. As Table 2.4 indicates, employment in the industrial and commercial sectors has steadily increased, compared with a marked decline in the agricultural and forestry sectors. In 1953 the number and percentage of professionals and technicians, administrators and managers, and supervisors and clerks were insignificant; by 1983 these categories were growing rapidly, and their significance in the total employment figures had more than doubled. Both sales and service personnel also increased steadily. The most dramatic change took place in the categories of agriculture and forestry workers and production workers. In 1953 the former constituted more than half the total work force, but the numbers in this classification actually declined over the years so that by 1983 they represented only 18.3 percent. In contrast, the percentage of production workers doubled during the same period, from just over 20 percent in 1953 to over 40 percent in 1983.[4] That 30-year span has seen a net gain of almost 2.3 million production workers.

Changes in employment patterns have affected the island's social stratification. According to Hill Gates, Taiwan has five social classes (Gates 1981, 272–78). At the top are members of the upper class, divided into two elite strata. The first refers to high government officials and military leaders, who are both "wealthy and politically powerful" (Gates 1981, 272). The other consists of influential industrial and commercial entrepreneurs. An analysis of the 2,699 entrepreneurs listed in *Who's Who in Taiwan Business* (1979–1980) shows that, of the total, 806 (or about 30 percent) are mainlanders and 1,893 (or 70 percent) are Taiwanese (Alan P. L. Liu 1985, 19). At the bottom are the lower class and what Gates has described as the "lumpen proletariat"—the "deviant" and the unemployed. The lower class consists of mostly industrial workers, landless agricultural workers, salespeople, peddlers, and small-scale craftsmen. The lumpen proletariat refers to those in gambling, prostitution, and other illegal economic activities as well as those frequently unemployed or marginally employed. In between the two elite and two lower classes are the growing middle-class components of the social order. Gates also distinguishes the "new middle class" from the "traditional middle class" (Gates 1981, 277). The former refers to salaried employees of large bu-

TABLE 2.4
EMPLOYMENT PATTERNS IN TAIWAN, 1953–1983
(IN THOUSANDS OF PERSONS AND AS A PERCENTAGE
OF THE LABOR FORCE)

	1953		1963		1973		1983	
Professionals and technicians	79	(2.67%)	149	(4.15%)	266	(4.99%)	412	(5.83%)
Administrators and managers	8	(0.27%)	13	(0.36%)	33	(0.62%)	62	(0.88%)
Supervisors and clerks	176	(5.94%)	272	(7.57%)	561	(10.53%)	953	(13.48%)
Salespersons	295	(9.96%)	324	(9.02%)	647	(12.14%)	933	(13.19%)
Servicepersons	180	(6.08%)	232	(6.46%)	363	(6.81%)	557	(7.88%)
Agriculture and forestry workers	1,628	(54.96%)	1,755	(48.84%)	1,612	(30.24%)	1,295	(18.31%)
Production workers	596	(20.12%)	848	(23.60%)	1,848	(34.67%)	2,860	(40.44%)
Total	2,962	(100%)	3,593	(100%)	5,330	(100%)	7,072	(100%)

SOURCE: Wen Ch'ung-i (1985), 7.

reaucratic organizations—government institutions, schools, industries, and banks. The latter consists of those involved in owner-operated farms, commerce, and small industry. It is the emergence of this second middle class that has changed the island's political landscape. With its rising political and social consciousness, the new middle class acts as a reformist force in electoral politics and social movements (Tien 1987a).

But scholars cannot agree on the membership of this middle-class sector; estimates of its size vary from 25 to 40 percent of the total adult population (Hsiao 1985, 15; Lu 1984, 45–46; Kao 1985, 10–12). A detailed list of the socioeconomic groups in the middle class would probably include the following: (1) entrepreneurs who have emerged since the 1960s in small- to mid-size enterprises; (2) managers in public corporations and state banks; (3) managers in private corporations; (4) upper-middle-level government bureaucrats; (5) elected representatives in the Provincial Assembly and the national legislatures; (6) professionals such as college professors, lawyers, physicians, architects, accountants, and artists; (7) schoolteachers, especially in secondary schools; (8) foreign-trade businessmen; and (9) middle- and upper-middle-level KMT cadres.

But the middle class in Taiwan is not politically cohesive; indeed its diversity suggests to some a lack of class consciousness. Still the great majority of KMT electoral candidates and opposition activists come from this social stratum. Their voices and reformist demands are gaining the attention of the ruling authorities. Elements of the middle class have provided the impetus for democratic reform in recent years, so they are of great political importance even though they are not united.

Education

Compared with other developing nations, Taiwan has a high literacy rate. Even during the Japanese occupation Taiwanese children attended elementary school in large numbers. In 1943, for instance, 70 percent of all school-age children were enrolled in school (Mancall 1964, 2). But there were only four technical colleges and one university on the island then. Further, Japanese colonial authorities discouraged Taiwanese students from studying law or social sciences. Most college students of the colonial era majored in agriculture, engineering, and medicine. Japan's colonial policy sought to prevent college students from gaining knowledge and skills that could be used in anticolonial political activities.

Since 1949 the Nationalist government on Taiwan has popularized education through competitive examinations. From 1950 to 1985 the total number of schools at all levels has tripled. Student enrollment in schools also rose by 362 percent, nearly two and one-half times the 148 percent increase in the general population during the same period (Liao 1985, 3–4). In 1950 there were 1,231 primary schools with approximately 900,000 students, or 86 percent of the total student population.[5] In 1985, 2,474 primary schools enrolled almost 2.3 million students, or only 46.7 percent of the student population. During the same period the number of colleges and universities rose from 7 to 105. Enrollment in higher education jumped from 6,665 to 412,381. High school and middle school enrollment also grew from about 67,000 to over 1.7 million, a rise from 8.8 percent to 44.6 percent of the entire student population (*TCNC*, 1985, 309). By 1987 slightly more than 53 percent of the population over the age of six had had at least secondary education, and the illiteracy rate had decreased from 42 percent to 7.8 percent (*TSDB*, 1988, 7).

The rising enrollment reflects the government's egalitarian education policy as well as its parental attitudes. In Taiwan education is regarded as an important vehicle for socioeconomic mobility. The nation's examination system provides a fairly objective means of student recruitment. Over the years it has largely kept favoritism out of the admission process. Thus the examination system has provided a basis for upward mobility among people from lower socioeconomic strata.

Meanwhile industrialization demands a steady supply of progressively better educated workers. Between 1976 and 1985 employees with college degrees in Taiwan increased from 369,000 to 869,000 (Liao 1985, 11). But the supply of engineers with advanced degrees from Taiwan's graduate schools has fallen short of demand. Also, as Table 2.5 indicates, domestic graduate schools are not producing enough scientists and engineers with Ph.D. degrees. The gap is particularly severe for mechanical and electrical engineers and only somewhat better for civil and chemical engineers. An oversupply of master's degrees in the sciences, civil engineering, and chemical engineering contrasts with a gross shortage in mechanical and electrical engineering.

The continuing brain drain, particularly to the United States, accounts for some of these problems. This phenomenon produces a net outflow of needed talent; from an investment standpoint, it wastes public money in education. From 1952 to 1981 the Ministry of Education authorized 67,868 persons to pursue advanced studies abroad, but only 8,363 (12.3 percent) have returned to Taiwan (Wei 1983, 29). More recently, of the 41,823 persons who went abroad between 1973 and 1982, 6,587 (15.7 percent) returned—a modest improvement (Liao and T'ang 1984, 2). Especially troublesome are the 20 percent of college graduates with science and engineering degrees who have gone abroad, of whom only 10 percent have returned home (Liao and T'ang 1984, 2). Among the graduates of the nation's universities strong in the sciences and

⎯⎯ TABLE 2.5 ⎯⎯
DEMAND FOR AND SUPPLY OF ENGINEERS
WITH GRADUATE DEGREES, 1983–1984

	Master's degrees			Ph.D. degrees		
	Demand	Supply	Net difference	Demand	Supply	Net difference
Scientists	165	493	+328	102	17	–85
Mechanical engineers[a]	963	535	–428	241	6	–235
Electrical engineers[b]	958	673	–285	292	31	–261
Civil engineers	117	220	+103	67	12	–55
Chemical engineers	143	252	+109	60	11	–49

SOURCE: Wei (1983), 30.
[a]Includes engineering mechanics.
[b]Includes electronics, communications, and information sciences.

engineering—Taiwan University, Tsinghua University, Chaiotung University, and Chungyang University—53.7 percent of science graduates and 30.7 percent for engineering graduates go overseas (Chang Wang 1984, 65). Taiwan has lost 30,000 of its scientists and engineers to the United States, where they now work (Johnstone 1988, 70). The trend seems difficult to reverse. Government recruiting agencies are competing with the appeal of higher monetary rewards and a better work environment in the United States. In other fields of study the return rate is improving. For instance, 26 percent of business majors studying abroad had returned home by 1982, an improvement over the 8 percent figure of a decade earlier (Wei 1983, 29). Perhaps more are returning because it has become more difficult lately for foreign students with master's and Ph.D. degrees to find suitable employment in the United States. In addition, monetary rewards and career opportunities in Taiwan have become increasingly attractive. All these changes may work to relieve the brain drain in the years to come.

Ethnic Relations

Taiwan's population of twenty million comes from four ethnic groups. The largest group consists of Taiwan-born natives who speak a

Fukien dialect. Their ancestors migrated from Fukien province across the Taiwan Strait before 1895 and the Japanese occupation. Another Chinese group is the Hakkas from Kwangtung province, who speak a different dialect. The third group is the mainlanders who came to Taiwan after World War II, especially from 1948 to 1950 after the Chinese civil war. In nationality, all three groups are considered Han Chinese. The aborigines, the fourth group, are descendants of the earliest inhabitants of the island who are racially non-Chinese and live mostly in the mountainous regions. They number only about a quarter of a million (Thompson 1984, 554).

It is difficult to get an accurate count of mainlanders in Taiwan. Available figures range from 12 to 14.3 percent of the total population (Gates 1981, 255; P'eng 1983, 73; TCNC, 1985, 229). The discrepancy may stem from differences in counting intermarried couples and their children. The population census often records intermarried households headed by mainlander males under the mainlander category. At any rate, the latest government figures show that 14.3 percent, or 2,715,162 of the more than 19 million people in Taiwan in 1984, are mainlanders. But the proportion of Taiwan's population born on the mainland had declined from about 15 percent in 1950 to 5.7 percent by 1985 (Li Wen-lang 1987, 2). The majority of those classified as mainlanders are now Taiwan-born. Native Taiwanese who speak the Fukien dialect constitute almost three-quarters of Taiwan's population. They outnumber the Hakkas approximately 6 to 1.

Over the years ethnicity has been a salient factor in Taiwan's political, economic, and social life. Some argue that ethnic differences are almost solely the result of the political, social, and economic interaction of the Taiwanese and mainlanders since the war (Gates 1981, 252). Although some ethnic differences would exist with or without the mainlanders, political factors appear to have played a key role in generating ethnic consciousness.

When the war ended in 1945, the Taiwanese, who hated Japanese colonial control, welcomed the arrival of their Chinese compatriots from the mainland. But General Ch'en Yi, the newly appointed governor of Taiwan, brutally oppressed the islanders. On February 28, 1947, an incident involving the mistreatment of a Taiwanese woman by mainlander soldiers touched off an islandwide rebellion against Ch'en Yi's administration. Estimates of those killed by Ch'en Yi's forces range from several thousands to twenty thousand Taiwanese, mostly local elite and students (Kerr 1965, 310; Mendel 1970, 31–41; Myers 1987a, 10; P'eng Ming-min 1972, 59–73). Memories of the terror and brutality of the KMT soldiers under General Ch'en's command still linger. The February 28

Incident has become an important and unfortunate political legacy of KMT rule on Taiwan.

The rising tension between Taiwanese and mainlanders was further aggravated by the arrival from 1948 to 1950 of KMT supporters, who assumed a near monopoly over political power on the island. The asymmetry of political power between mainlanders and Taiwanese remains a source of ethnic antagonism. The land reform program that benefited tenant farmers stirred up new resentment among Taiwan's elite landlord families. During the course of economic development, many mainlanders with official or party connections have used governmental prerogatives for personal aggrandizement (Huntington and Moore 1970, 29). These abuses of power have alienated entrepreneurs—many of them Taiwanese—who lack such political access. Some KMT leaders have shown concern about the lack of ethnic harmony. President Chiang Ching-Kuo, when serving as premier in the 1970s, began to address the ethnic issue by appointing more Taiwanese to important party and government posts. His efforts began a process of Taiwanization, as political power is increasingly shared by both mainlander and Taiwanese elite. But the underlying ethnic distrust has yet to dissipate.

That ethnic differences remain salient in Taiwan is apparent in the continuation of disproportional representation in public office, de facto residential segregation, and language preferences that all favor mainlanders and in disparities in identity, expectations, and behavior patterns between Taiwanese and mainlanders. Disproportional representation in public office is evident in several respects. According to Table 2.6, in 1987 mainlanders held at least three-quarters of the key posts at KMT central party headquarters, in the cabinet, and in the Legislative Yuan. They still controlled 17 seats, or 55 percent of the total 31, in the ruling Central Standing Committee of the KMT. The composition of this party committee in 1988 (Table 4.1) represented another improvement as Taiwanese gained a majority 16 seats for the first time (see Chapter 4, Table 4.1); over a decade ago Taiwanese held only 4 of the total 22 seats (Tien 1987b, 4). But still the mainlander representation is disproportional, since over 70 percent of KMT party members are reportedly Taiwanese. At party headquarters 8 of the 11 leading cadres, or 73 percent, are mainlanders. In the Executive Yuan (or cabinet) in 1987, Taiwanese served as vice premier, ministers of interior, communication, and justice, and ministers without portfolios, holding a total of six posts. Ministerial posts—which carry more weight in such policy areas as defense, foreign affairs, finance, economic affairs, and education—remained exclusively in the hands of mainlanders. And despite changes in the KMT Central Standing Committee and the Executive Yuan in July 1988, which shifted the balance in favor of the majority Taiwanese for the first time, mainlanders still hold all top posts in the military and security apparatus except two, garrison commander and vice minister of defense.

Taiwanese are doing much better in elected posts and local government. As Table 2.6 shows, in 1987 Taiwanese accounted for all 21 mayors and county magistrates and held 97 percent of the 77 Provincial Assembly seats. As of 1981, of the 88,873 civil service functionaries in the provincial government, provincial enterprises, and public schools, 31,592—or 36 percent—were mainlanders, who make up less than 15 percent of the population (Gates 1981, 255). A study in 1969 showed that mainlanders occupied 31.5 percent of the positions in the military, police, and national security apparatus and 25.7 percent of positions in public administration and the professions (Wei 1976, 262). In the city government of Taipei, Taiwanese hold the greatest number of positions but only 6 of the 15 key administrative posts and 40 percent of the 100 civil service appointments (Yang Hao 1986, 6). Taiwanese fare better in low-level positions and local government administration, whereas mainlanders control the national levers of power in both the KMT and the government.

Economic power shows a more symmetrical distribution along ethnic lines than political power. Many more Taiwanese than mainlanders engage in small business, though the precise figure is unavailable. In big business mainlanders still hold a disproportionate edge, but in numbers Taiwanese have overtaken mainlanders in this area. Of the 2,699 leading entrepreneurs listed in the 1979–1980 edition of *Who's Who in Taiwan Business (Chung-hua min-kuo shih-yeh ming-jen-lu)*, 806, or 30 percent, are mainlanders, whereas 1,893, or 70 percent, are Taiwanese (Alan P. L. Liu 1985, 19). A 1978 survey of 100 business groups revealed that 78 percent of the chairmen of the board were Taiwanese (Greenhalgh 1984, 540). But in the large and economically important public corporations, the chairmen of the board and general managers are mainlanders—except in commercial banks, where the distribution of top positions is about even. Statistical data are not available.

Residential patterns for mainlanders and Taiwanese also show clear distinctions. About 70 percent of the mainlanders live in urban areas, including the major cities and their surrounding suburbs—Taipei, Taipei county, Kaohsiung, Kaohsiung county, Taichung, and Taoyuan county. Mainlanders compose 32 percent of all households in Taipei, 27 percent of the population in all urban cores, and 24 percent of residents in the urbanized areas surrounding these cores (Greenhalgh 1984, 537). Most mainlanders residing in rural and mountainous areas are military personnel, retired veterans, and their families. Within the cities, mainlanders

——— TABLE 2.6 ———
ETHNICITY OF TAIWAN'S POLITICAL ELITE, 1987

	Total number of positions	Percentage held by Taiwanese	Percentage held by mainlanders
KMT Central Standing Committee members	31	45	55
KMT central headquarters leaders[a]	11	27	73
Cabinet ministers[b]	30	20	80
Military generals[c]	—	16	84
Legislative Yuan members[d]	348	22	78
Control Yuan members[e]	78	44	56
Taiwan provincial assemblymen	77	97	3
Mayors and county magistrates	21	100	0

SOURCES: Wu Ying-ts'un (1987), 76. Percentages for the Legislative Yuan and the Control Yuan have been recalculated. Figures on military generals are from Chiang Liang-jen (1987), 9.
[a]Secretary-general, deputy secretary-generals, and heads of departments and commissions.
[b]Premiers, vice premiers, ministers, and deputy ministers of ministries and commissions.
[c]Percentages are for 1978–1987; the total number is not available.
[d]Of the 78 Taiwanese, 70 are subject to popular elections for three-year terms; 267 of the 270 mainlanders were elected in the mainland during 1947–1948 and serve for life.
[e]Of the 34 Taiwanese, 25 are elected by Taiwan provincial assemblymen and the councilmen of Taipei and Kaohsiung for six-year terms; 41 of the 44 mainlanders serve for life.

tend to reside in neighborhoods previously occupied by the Japanese before the war. Of the 17 administrative districts in Taipei, for instance, mainlanders concentrate in the Taan, Kut'ing, Mucha, Chingmei, Ch'engchung, Sungshan, and Neihu neighborhoods; mainlanders make up 37 to 58.7 percent of the total population in these areas (Gates 1981, 262). In recent years, as ownership of automobiles has become more commonplace, a growing number of affluent mainlanders are fleeing to the upper-middle-class suburbs of Shihlin, Peit'ou, and Nankang.

Residential segregation reinforces language barriers. Language is a crucial tool for social communication and sociopolitical integration. Taiwanese educated since the arrival of the Nationalist government on Taiwan can speak the official Mandarin dialect with varying degrees of proficiency. But many natives age 60 or older have difficulty mastering Mandarin, and uneducated or marginally educated Taiwanese still speak little Mandarin. By the same token, most adult mainlanders speak at best a smattering of the Taiwanese dialects. The younger generation from mainland families are learning to speak the local language through interaction with their peers in school, but those who live in the de facto segregated communities often do not need to speak any dialect other than Mandarin. Thus a linguistic gap yawns at various social levels, especially in communities outside the major cities. This gap constitutes a major hindrance to social integration.

Differences also persist in national identity, cultural affinity, future expectations, and behavior patterns. Compared with their native counterparts, mainlanders identify more strongly with "China" than with "Taiwan" (Chang and Hsiao 1987, 36–39). Many mainlanders look down on Taiwanese culture as "something beyond the pale of Chinese civilization" (Gold 1987a, 2). In contrast, Taiwanese attach much less of their political identity to the mainland; instead they identify with Taiwan and its local culture. Such differences in perception have profound political ramifications for the government's goal of political unification with the mainland. Mainlanders also show stronger support for the ruling KMT as well as for existing government institutions. According to a survey conducted in Taipei, mainlanders identify more positively with government authorities, stress stability in the existing political system, and perceive higher levels of social harmony and political order. They are also willing, if necessary, to restrict individual freedom (Hu and Yu 1983, 38). In contrast, Taiwanese voters value more highly the protection of civil liberties, freedom of speech, broader political participation, the sharing of political power, and the enhancement of Taiwanese status and influence in society and politics (Hu and Yu 1983, 38). Hu Fo and Yu Yinglung's survey of voting behavior in the Taan, Sungshan, and Neihu districts of Taipei in the 1983 parliamentary elections also showed that although KMT candidates drew about an even number of mainlander and Taiwanese votes, opposition candidates drew about 87.6 percent of Taiwanese votes but only 12.4 percent of mainlander votes (Hu and Yu 1983, 37–38). A separate survey of 704 college faculty members in eight leading universities in March 1986 indicated ethnicity as an important variable in the assessment of social and political developments. The questionnaires, administered by the ROC Association for Public Opinion Surveys, disclosed that mainlander faculty members expressed fears of the PRC military threat and the Taiwan independence movement three times more often than their Taiwanese colleagues (Chen Hao 1986a, 16). They also worried more about social disorder. And in the debate over parliamentary reforms, mainlanders were more inclined to favor a system that would guarantee a quota of political representation for them.

Patterns of social behavior further endorse these ethnic divisions. With the ROC government's cooperation, Wolfgang Grichting, a Swiss Protestant missionary, conducted a nationwide survey in 1970 of 1,882 households on interethnic social relations (Appleton 1976, 705–10). "Over 97 percent of the three best friends reported by Taiwanese respondents were also Taiwanese, while 87 percent of the three best friends reported by mainlanders were mainlanders" (Appleton 1976, 709). Social relations among those under 35 years old cut across ethnic lines more often. Even so, "93 percent of college-educated mainlanders said their best friend was from their own grouping" (Appleton 1976, 709). The situation since the 1970s has improved. Despite these statistics intermarriage between ethnic groups is on the rise as the Taiwan-born mainlanders grow up (Gold 1987a, 10). A survey that compiled registration data from 755 households in three Taipei districts in 1974–1975 endorsed this fact (Gates 1981, 265–66). More than 22 percent of the marriages were between mainlanders and Taiwanese. A 1987 survey of 1,261 students in 26 colleges and universities showed that 40 percent of their brothers and sisters had intermarried, a significant rise from about 17 percent for their parents' generation (Chang and Hsiao 1987, 40–42). The recent marriage of Chiang Hsiao-wu, the late President Chiang Ching-kuo's son, to a Taiwanese woman serves as an important reminder that intermarriage is becoming more common.

Time and modernization have brought about a social structure markedly different from that of the 1950s. Modernization has brought a much higher degree of social differentiation in all ethnic groups. As one U.S. researcher has observed: "Previously absolute ethnic advantages and disadvantages became relative as poor mainlanders and rich Taiwanese became part of the social landscape" (Gates 1981, 269). Social differences exist within each ethnic group, and the narrowing of social gaps between ethnic groups is gradually transforming a social system that was once heavily characterized by ethnic division. Today over 1.5 million, or 55 percent, of the mainlanders in Taiwan were born on the island (Chiu 1983, 158). In other words, about 93 percent of the total population is Taiwan-born. In recent years the continuing overwhelming concern about the PRC threat may also have fostered a common identity with Taiwan among the younger generations, diminishing ethnic differences (Greenhalgh 1984, 536). As a result, frequent travelers to Taiwan have noticed a gradual reduction of language barriers along with more inter-marriages and more frequent interethnic social ties.

CONCLUSION

Modernization is a continuing process involving the broad transformation of traditional and parochial values together with changes in institutions and behavior patterns. Change takes place simultaneously in the economic, political, social, and cultural sectors, even though the degree of change in each sector varies. The modernization of Europe and North America occurred over a period of two or more centuries. In Taiwan that time span has been compressed into a few decades, dating back to the late decades of Japanese colonial rule. In the advanced industrial nations the long process of modernization provided more time to make structural, attitudinal, and behavioral adjustments. Taiwan has had to adjust to many problems connected with modernization much more quickly. The tasks and challenges are simply enormous.

Taiwan's economic modernization has been accomplished with some pain, but its success is internationally acknowledged. Social transformation is an ongoing process, with many problems still to be resolved. Yet in less than four decades the social system has become highly differentiated, showing ample evidence of growing social pluralism. Its effects on ethnic relations are clearly visible. The indicators examined in this chapter point to rapid social mobilization with growing material comforts. All these developments have helped bring about a socioeconomic environment conducive to broader political participation. Over the years the emergence of an ever larger middle class has heightened social and political consciousness, increasing expectations for democratization. The middle class has pushed for KMT reforms, opposition political movements, and a variety of social movements concerned with ecology, consumer rights, civil rights, and trade unionism. Portions of the next two chapters will examine these movements and their impact on interest group activities and political parties.

— 3 —

Interest Groups

Over the past three decades of rapid economic development and social change on Taiwan, business and civic associations have proliferated. According to government statistics, in 1952 there were some 2,560 registered associations with over 1.3 million members. By 1987 there were nearly 11,306 with about 8.3 million members (*TSDB*, 1988, 303). Associations have flourished during the broadening political liberalization and social differentiation brought on by technological and structural changes in the Taiwanese economy. The social differentiation in Taiwan confirms what Robert H. Salisbury has observed elsewhere:

> Increasingly specialized sets of people...engage in a growing range of particular economic activities or special social roles, and from this specialized differentiation of role and function comes greater and greater diversity of interests or values as each newly differentiated set of people desires a somewhat different set of social goals. (Salisbury 1969, 3)

The proliferation of associations and enlarging group membership show that Taiwan is rapidly becoming a pluralistic society. The immediate questions of interest in this analysis are: How do these associations participate in the political process, and what are their relations with both the ruling party and the government? Social pluralism cannot be equated automatically with political pluralism, nor will it lead necessarily to a pluralistic polity. In Taiwan, as in other authoritarian systems, many associations are "officially created functional organizations serving as transmission belts and auxiliaries" for the ruling party (Linz 1970, 299).

Even those associations not formally affiliated with the party may still be dominated by groups with party connections that prevent real autonomy (Salisbury 1975, 178). Control or domination by the party may become increasingly difficult, however, as organized interest groups proliferate and channels for articulating their common interests grow more complex.

Politically Taiwan's interest groups are essentially corporatist with pluralistic characteristics. The ideal pluralistic polity comprises many roughly equal autonomous political groups affecting public policy through their political interests (Ligphart 1975, 3–5). These organized conflicting social forces contribute to "the dispersion of power and thereby check and balance governmental power" (Ligphart 1975, 7). If interest groups operate in close approximation to this model, the role of the state is reduced to mediating the groups' conflicting demands. In such a political system, as in the United States, interest groups with independently derived sources of power constantly pressure policymakers, legislators, and bureaucrats. Thus under extreme pluralism the government can be regarded as merely a policy instrument of the interest groups.

By contrast, corporatism explicitly acknowledges the state as the principal arbitrator that dictates or directs the configuration and behavior of interest group politics (Wilson 1983, 109). The term *corporatism* gained currency in the 1930s under the influence of Pope Pius XI's encyclical of 1931, *Qaudragesimo anno*, and through the politics of Fascist Italy (Harrison 1980, 184). According to Phillipe C. Schmitter,

> corporatism can be defined as a system of interest representation in which the constituent units are organized into a limited number of singular, compulsory, non-competitive, hierarchically ordered and functionally differentiated categories, recognized or licensed (if not created) by the state and granted a deliberate representational monopoly within their respective categories in exchange for observing certain controls on their selection of leaders and articulation of demands and supports. (Schmitter 1979, 13)

Despite its earlier association with Fascism, *corporatism* has since been applied to a variety of contemporary political systems in which the state assumes key economic and social functions. In the opinion of a leading writer, aspects of corporatism exist in Sweden, Switzerland, the Netherlands, Norway, Denmark, Austria, Spain, Portugal, Greece, Yugoslavia, and perhaps a majority of Latin American nations (Schmitter 1979, 16). As the structure of the state strengthens, even democratic societies may approximate the corporatist model (Harrison 1980, 185).

Both historically and structurally the configuration and behavior of interest groups in the Republic of China are essentially corporatist. This form reflects in part the impact of traditional Chinese views on government and politics. Lucian W. Pye, for instance, has argued that "in Chinese theory there was no need for either representation or the politics of interest groups... The moral righteousness of government provided an absolute answer to the problems of representation and interest articulation" (Pye 1968, 18–19). Certain types of informal associations were acceptable only if they acted as "protective associations assisting their individual members and made no generalized claims on government" (Pye 1968, 20).

The traditional Chinese view of politics was reinforced in Nationalist Chinese politics by the KMT's adoption of an essentially Leninist organization structure in the 1920s. This characteristic was transferred with the KMT to Taiwan, and so interest groups on the island, particularly those with a political orientation, have functioned much like Leninist transmission belts: they transmit messages, mobilize political support, and help implement policies for the ruling party and government. Furthermore, the political leadership seeks to control or eliminate all groups that might articulate independent interests to ensure that opposition forces, if they exist, do not coalesce around these groups (Jacobs 1978, 243). Consequently the Taiwan government has always controlled and supervised interest groups' activities, management personnel, budgets, and representation in the legislature.

The situation in Taiwan resembles what Juan J. Linz has described as "limited pluralism" (Linz 1974, 298). According to Linz, many new associations may be created spontaneously by categoric groups of people with common social and economic interests. Although they remain under the authorities' close scrutiny, their activities sometimes run counter to government and party policies. These associations start to acquire some autonomy in leadership selection and sources of funding. Those with substantial resources and a large mass base still fall under the ruling party's direct control; others, although regulated by state agencies, are able to operate with minimum intervention by the state and the ruling party. This limited autonomy has occurred in Taiwan as the growing private sector, social differentiation, and gradual political liberalization have affected the prevailing pattern of relations between organized groups and the authorities.

TYPES OF INTEREST GROUPS

Of the 11,306 civic organizations listed in 1987, 1,073 are considered national-level associations and 10,233 are provincial or local (*TSDB*,

1988, 303). They are further classified into two broad categories, trade associations and social associations. The former consist of almost 5,000 occupational groups, such as farmers' associations, labor unions, irrigation associations, commerce and industry associations, professional associations, and fishermen's associations. The latter consist of slightly over 5,000 associations in such areas as culture, academics, religion, athletics, and social service (Rotary International, Lions International, and so on). Most groups listed under the first category may be regarded as interest groups with activities that carry clear political significance. In the second category only certain groups, such as the Council of Presbyterian Churches, have played important political roles.

The following discussion will focus on those associations with large memberships and active political interests: farmers' associations, trade unions, irrigation associations, industrial associations, commercial associations, professional associations, and religious associations. Nearly all these associations are hierarchical, exclusive, and noncompetitive. All are registered with the government; once they are licensed, other competitive groups in the same trade are legally prohibited. Their relation to the government exhibits strong corporatist characteristics; some perform functions like the transmission belts in Leninist systems. Major groups such as the farmers, workers, and industrialists are given an official quota of representation in the Legislative Yuan and the National Assembly. By and large, membership in these associations for people in each occupation is noncompulsory.

Farmers' Associations

Farmers' associations were first established in 1900 under the Japanese colonial rule. They operated as an administrative arm of the government, providing farmers with a variety of agricultural extension services (Ho 1978, 63). Under Japanese administration, membership and fees were required of all farming households (Ho 1978, 63). By the late 1920s and early 1930s these associations, together with their associated agricultural cooperatives, already employed 40,000 people to provide services to farmers (Ho 1978, 64). Among those employees were 13,000 extension workers and 9,000 agricultural advisers, averaging 1 extension worker for every 32 farming households (Ho 1978, 64). The services provided by these associations contributed significantly to the success of Taiwan's prewar agricultural development.

In 1949 the agricultural cooperatives merged with the farmers' associations. A year later they were reorganized according to the recommendations of the Joint Commission for Rural Reconstruction (JCRR).[1]

Reform by the JCRR turned the farmers' associations into more popularly controlled institutions that provide better credit facilities for farmers to finance new technology (Jacoby 1966, 182). During land reform the associations' organizational networks did much to help the government implement the reform policies.

The associations are hierarchical, with the provincial farmers' association acting as the main managing unit. In Taiwan there are 34 associations at the municipality and county levels and another 268 lower down in the *hsiang* (village administration) and *chen* (town) levels (*SAI*, 1984, 200). The membership is drawn from owner–cultivators, tenants, hired farmers, agricultural extension workers, and employees of the state-run experimental farms. Membership is voluntary, and about 85 percent of farming households are regular members (Li Chan-t'ai 1982, 8). Those who do not qualify for regular membership may join as associate members. Total membership in 1984 was nearly 1.3 million (*SAI*, 1984, 192). About 80 percent were regular members and 20 percent associate members. As farmers' associations have expanded their credit activities, associate members, particularly small businessmen and small entrepreneurs, have steadily increased. In fact in urban and suburban areas associate members may account for between 40 and 50 percent of total membership (Wu Ch'ueh-yuan 1981, 21).

Members are organized into 4,364 agricultural teams headed by popularly elected team leaders. Periodically members also directly elect representatives to the *hsiang-* and *chen*-level farmers' associations. These representatives elect members of the board of directors (*li-shih-hui*) and the board of supervisors (*chien-shih-hui*) as well as county- and city-level representatives, who in turn elect the corresponding directors and supervisors as well as representatives to the provincial association. At each level of the organizational hierarchy, the board of directors selects one or two candidates for the position of general manager (*tsung-kan-shih*), whose official appointment comes from the Department of Agriculture and Forestry in the provincial government. The general manager is the chief executive in charge of the daily operations of the association. As credit activities increased, the general manager assumed an additional role comparable to the president of a cooperative bank. The position is regarded as the most lucrative of all public offices in rural Taiwan, drawing a salary comparable to that of a cabinet minister in the national government. Furthermore, since the position offers a unique opportunity to help friends get jobs or win export quotas for agricultural products, it provides a base that can lead to an exciting and lucrative political career (Stavis 1974, 101).

Because farmers' associations control enormous rural economic and financial resources, the key posts of general manager, directors, and supervisors have become highly political. Factionalism has permeated the elections for these offices (Li Chan-t'ai 1982, 49), as members of the rural elite compete furiously for the positions. Furthermore, the associations' extensive institutional networks are often used by political factions to mobilize votes for candidates running for government office (Stavis 1974, 61). Their political weight has made it all the more important for the KMT to control the associations through appointments of general managers by the KMT-controlled provincial government and government regulations. Consequently the associations at all levels operate more as quasi-governmental institutions, in part to implement the agricultural and credit policies of the government, than as bodies articulating the farmers' interests.

Irrigation Associations

Irrigation associations in Taiwan distribute water to the island's farmland. Adequate water supplies are particularly important for rice farming in paddies, which require a proper level of water throughout most of the growing season. Thus what the associations do clearly affects the rice farmers' interests. The associations also construct and repair dams, water-regulating devices, canals, and bridges (Stavis 1974, 107). In areas where water shortages periodically occur, the irrigation associations implement rotational irrigation programs.

There are fifteen irrigation associations in Taiwan, varying in size according to the farming areas served by the irrigation system. The four smallest cover one county each. The eleven larger ones cover from two to four counties and municipalities. The largest—Chianan Irrigation Association—supplies water for the municipality of Tainan and the county of Chiayi. These associations are not hierarchical but parallel bodies subject to the provincial government's close supervision. Each has several hundred staff members. In addition to an association headquarters, branch offices throughout the fifteen associations collect fees and monitor water uses. Membership is virtually mandatory for all farmers who own farmland within the authority of an irrigation association. Fees are collected according to the acreage and quality of the land as recorded in the county or municipal land offices (Stavis 1974, 106).

The fifteen associations are governed by a deliberative council and a president (hui-chang)—the executive officer—whom the council elects. There are 441 councilmen, with the number representing each association allotted according to its membership size. Electoral competition for the president and the councilmen is intense. The largest association operated an annual budget of almost U.S. $20 million in 1986 (Lin Chin-k'un 1986a, 73). Authority over construction and repair work as well as staff appointments often enables the president to extract a lucrative sideline income. The association president's salary, accrued business expenses, and benefits alone provide annual earnings comparable to a cabinet officer's.

Because of these material attractions, many politicians find the position of association president at least as rewarding as that of mayor, county magistrate, or member of the legislature. Hence local political factions are often drawn into the electoral competition to capture a majority of seats in a council and then to elect the president of their choice (Lin Chin-k'un 1986a, 69–73). Like the farmers' associations, these irrigation associations, with their rich institutional resources, provide victorious local factions with considerable political spoils. Candidates for president spend up to U.S. $1 million on their campaigns for office (Lin Chin-k'un 1986a, 70–71). Once elected, the president can use his position to recover the money he spent to get elected. Some individuals also view the post as a stepping-stone to further advancement in their political careers.

Trade Unions

The ROC has over 2,300 trade unions; most are organized functionally, but some have a territorial basis (*CHNC*, 1988, 337). Of these, 14 national unions and 171 unions in the export-processing zones are affiliated with the Chinese Federation of Labor (CFL) (Wang and Chang 1987, 85). The CFL moved to Taiwan from the mainland in 1950 and was restructured in 1975 (Galenson 1979, 425). The remaining unions are affiliates of the Taiwan Provincial Federation of Labor (TPFL), an organization that has been active since World War II (Galenson 1979, 425). Although the TPFL is a nominal affiliate of the CFL, it has in fact operated independently.

About 1.8 million of the 8.1 million workers in manufacturing, communications, construction, transportation, services, and mining are union members (*TSDB*, 1987, 15). Public employees are not allowed to unionize. According to labor law, 30 workers in an industrial enterprise may organize a union, but only one union is permitted for each plant. About 30 percent of industrial workers in the private sector in Taiwan are unionized. In occupations such as taxi and truck drivers, tailors, barbers, cooks, and waiters, as many as 70 percent are union members (Galenson 1979, 426). Membership rates are much lower among young workers and employees of small enterprises. By law annual membership dues must not be lower than the daily wage rate (*MCJP*, December 2, 1985, 2).

Trade unions, farmers' associations, and irrigation associations are heavily subsidized by government revenues. Their activities are also subject to strict regulation by law. The most controversial restriction concerns the deprivation of the workers' right to strike, which is guaranteed in the constitution but banned by the National Mobilization Law. Union members are not entirely free when electing their leaders, for the KMT carefully scrutinizes candidate selection. The resulting union leadership depends heavily on the authorities and thus is hardly equipped to fight for the workers against the wishes of the party or state. As a result, there is widespread apathy among union members. A 1984 survey indicated that 66 percent of the workers interviewed considered the unions useless in promoting their economic interests (Chang Ch'un-hua 1984, 27). Grass-roots union activists have reportedly suffered employers' reprisals, including demotion (Chang Chun-hua 1984, 28).

Despite these difficulties trade unionism is steadily gaining strength in Taiwan. Some unions, such as the National Chinese Seamen's Union and the Teamster's Union of Taipei, have helped secure concessions for better wages and working conditions (Galenson 1979, 428). Difficulties in collective bargaining have been mediated from time to time by the KMT or government agencies (Hung 1984, 9). In recent years the breakdown of collective bargaining has led to a drastic increase in worker-employer disputes. In 1963 there were only 20 such cases, involving 550 workers; by 1981 labor disputes numbered over 1,000 and involved about 7,000 workers (Hsu Ya-yuän 1983, 45). Between 1971 and 1982 a total of 6,398 labor-management disputes were reported, involving about 12,000 workers (Hung 1984, 7). The situation appears to have worsened since the passage of the Labor Standard Law in 1984 (Fang 1985, 14). Employers complain that the new law, which requires better labor insurance and retirement compensation, will substantially raise their costs, thus depriving Taiwan's industries of their competitive edge in the world market (Hung 1984, 13). The employers most affected are the small- and medium-size businesses or factories with a limited capacity to absorb the newly added costs.

Consequently many employers have increasingly resisted wage and labor demands. There have been reports of work stoppages, sit-ins, and even demonstrations by workers. The improvement of workers' benefits and working conditions may be overdue, but the new law has put many private firms in a financially precarious situation at a time when Taiwan's exports are encountering fierce foreign competition and growing protectionism. The result is a serious dilemma for the ROC authorities. If they enforce the new law, they will deter capital investment and undermine competitiveness in Taiwan's export-related businesses and industries. But if they ignore the workers' growing demands for better wages, benefits, and job security, they will risk labor unrest, an explosive political matter the KMT hopes to avoid. Over the years in Taiwan the party and state have walked a fine line, hoping to maintain a balance through careful arbitration and persuasion. But the KMT is losing labor support. In the December 1986 parliamentary election, both CFL and TPFL presidents who stood for the union seat in the National Assembly and the Legislative Yuan respectively were defeated for the first time by two non-KMT candidates. The outcome shocked the KMT leaders. Subsequently the government created a cabinet-level labor commission to address labor demands and grievances. By summer 1988, the provincial government had established worker service centers in each county and city to help resolve workers' problems (*CYJP*, January 4, 1988, 2). In addition, the CFL president is now elected directly by union members rather than indirectly by labor representatives.

The KMT is losing control over some unions. A grass-roots labor movement that began in spring 1987 has been gathering momentum since the suspension of martial law in July 1987. Independent unions have been organized in the industrial areas of Kaohsiung, Hsinchu, Taoyuan, and Miaoli. By early 1988 there were nine local unions formed under the common label of Brotherhood Association (*hsiung-ti-hui*) in northern Taiwan and a Union Cadres Solidarity Association (*kung-hui kan-pu lien-i-hui*) in Kaohsiung (*SPCK*, February 6, 1988, 48). Total members are not known; they appear to be mostly workers from the large manufacturing industries (*CKSP*, January 9, 1988, 2). Efforts were made in early 1988 to organize a national federation of independent unions to foster unity in the membership drive (*CKSP*, January 24, 1988, 3). This labor movement has so far had no direct ideological connections with Marxism. Its chief immediate goals are the promotion of autonomous trade unionism, workers' rights, and better working conditions (*CKSP*, January 24, 1988). The relation of these new unions to the newly created Labor Party and Democratic Progressive Party has yet to be defined (Chang Hsiao-ts'un 1988, 3; Wu Nai-te 1988, 3; Hoon 1988b, 18–19). Although it is premature to judge the outcome of this labor movement, it seems the KMT's corporatist relations with the trade unions will soon be substantially revised.

Commerce and Industry Associations

The ROC has 1,799 associations in commerce and industry (RDEC 1987, 153). There are 8 national federations; the remaining 1,791 form separate provincial federations or are organized at city and county levels.

These associations fall into three broad categories. First are industrial manufacturers and producers organized at the county, city, and provincial levels, including, for example, the Coal Mine Association, the Medicine Industry Association, the Paper Producers' Association, and the Cotton Weaving Industry Association. In addition an umbrella industrial council (*kung-yeh-hui*) represents the interests of all industrial federations. The Provincial Industrial Council, the first such council, was organized in 1948. By 1985 all twenty counties and major municipalities had organized their own branch councils. Across the island almost 1,300 manufacturers, or 3.8 percent of all firms, have joined the provincial councils. In Taipei 377 firms, or 10.6 percent of the total, have joined the Taipei Industrial Council (RDEC 1987, 54).

The second category encompasses commercial firms. Each commercial group has its own association, for example, the Tea Merchants' Association, the Rice Merchants' Association, the Hotel Association, the Movie Theater Association, and the Real Estate Brokers' Association. They are organized hierarchically into county or municipal bodies affiliated with a provincial or national federation. Chambers of commerce (*shang-hui*) also operate at the municipal, county, and provincial levels to represent the common interests of businessmen and their firms. The third category consists of export-import associations organized by trade. There is also a general import-export association to promote the common interests of the nearly 63,000 firms involved in international trade (Wu Keng, et al. 1985, 101). Since foreign trade accounts for about half of Taiwan's annual gross national product (GNP), activities in the third category have grown in importance.

Other Interest Groups

In Taiwan thousands of other groups are organized to represent their members' interests. Most have little interaction with the political process, although three types deserve some attention: professional associations, public interest groups, and religious associations.

Professional associations have proliferated with Taiwan's growing social pluralism. These groups organize their own associations at municipal and county levels. Many form a higher body at the provincial or national level, depending on the laws regulating their profession. The best known are the Association of Lawyers, the Association of Physicians, the Association of Doctors in Chinese Herbal Medicine, the Association of Architects, the Association of Newspaper Reporters, and the Association of Accountants. By and large these associations are well-heeled and operate with only rudimentary intervention from the KMT.

Public interest groups seeking the collective good without apparent economic self-interest have mushroomed since the 1970s as middle-class citizens have become concerned about consumers' rights, civil liberties, and the deteriorating environment (Berry 1984, 28–29). Among the more prominent are the Chinese Human Rights Association, the Taiwan Human Rights Association, the National Association of Consumers, and the Cultural and Educational Foundation for Consumers. Both human rights associations were organized in the late 1970s in response to international concerns over the human rights situation in Taiwan. The Chinese Human Rights Association is financed mainly by state revenue and has a strong official connection. The Taiwan Human Rights Association articulates the views and concerns of the political opposition and liberal academicians. The National Association of Consumers and the Cultural and Educational Foundation for Consumers were organized in the wake of acute consumer awareness growing out of the island's increasing commercialism. Both groups claim to speak for the broad interests of consumers. They appear to maintain cordial relations with the government.

Religion has taken on new life in Taiwan as the pace of social change quickens and the society grows affluent. Buddhist and Taoist temples are flourishing, and the number of religious believers has risen to 2.6 million (*CYJP*, May 25, 1985, 1). Religious associations have proliferated as a consequence; in 1985 there were about 80 such associations (RDEC 1987, 153). Of these the Council of Presbyterian Churches is the most active politically. Although there are only 170,000 Presbyterians, nearly all are native Taiwanese (Chu 1982, 46).

Over the years the Protestant churches, particularly in central and southern Taiwan, have battled the authorities on a number of sensitive issues. One concerns the language used in church services. Presbyterians have insisted on using the native Fukienese dialect in sermons as well as in reading the Bible. The authorities, however, have sought to restrict such practices on the grounds that the churches are perpetuating the native identity. The most serious confrontation came in August 1977 when the Presbyterian council issued "A Declaration on Human Rights," which came close to advocating independence for Taiwan (Jacobs 1981, 26; Chu 1982, 47–48). Since then relations between the council and the authorities have remained uneasy. Furthermore, many Presbyterian leaders are involved in political opposition movements and have often spoken out on democratization and civil rights. In March 1987 Presbyterians in Tainan staged a street demonstration to protest the government's confiscation of official church publications (Chang and Chi 1987, 64–65). The publications, which contained an article on the February 28, 1947, Incident, were subsequently returned. In October 1987 over 400 Presbyterians, including 120 ministers, staged a demonstration in Taipei to protest the arrest of two opposition activists for advocating independence for Taiwan (Chen Min-feng 1987, 19–21). Since the Presbyterians are the best organized of all religious denominations and have close international ties, the authorities have been reluctant to repress their activities outright.

POLITICAL ACTIVITIES

Interest group activities in Taiwan show both pluralistic and corporatist characteristics. Groups exert political influence through lobbying, participation in the electoral process, and public education. They engage in various political pressure activities at local, provincial, and national levels. Many also play what Philippe C. Schmitter has termed a "concertation" role, meaning that the groups work as recognized negotiators in concert with public authorities to incorporate their interests into the policy process. Schmitter believes such groups then "take on a characteristically semi-public or para-state quality" (Schmitter 1982, 263). In Taiwan the farmers' associations, the irrigation associations, most professional associations, the trade unions, and even numerous industry and commerce groups have usually operated in this manner. Yet some associations in all categories have adopted political pressure techniques from pluralistic systems in the West. Taiwan's interest group activities thus present a mixed character, reflecting the paradoxes in the ROC political system itself (Jacobs 1978, 243–44).

In 1959 Seymour Martin Lipset argued that interest groups promote many functions necessary for democracy:

> They are a source of countervailing power, inhibiting the state or any single major source of private power from dominating all political resources; they are a source of new opinions; they can be the means of communicating ideas, particularly opposition ideas, to a large section of the citizenry; they serve to train men in the skills of politics; and they help increase the level of interest and participation in politics. (Lipset 1959, 72)

But the ROC is not a full-fledged democracy. Interest groups on the island are not strong enough to countervail the power of the state. With rare exceptions, such as the Taiwan Human Rights Association and the Presbyterian council, they have not advanced the ideas of the political opposition. Nevertheless, they can articulate the interests of their members, and in the process they disseminate information and shape group opinion. More important, they provide an avenue for many future leaders to learn political skills, particularly in the farmers' associations, irrigation associations, trade unions, and some business and industrial associations. Many officers of these groups later run for public office. Interest groups, especially from the public interest and professional ranks, have helped broaden popular participation in the political process.

Aside from these general functions, Taiwan's interest groups engage in three major activities that require closer attention: lobbying, official concertation, and electoral participation.

Lobbying

Lobbying refers to activities designed to gain favorable governmental actions or to alter unfavorable ones. Unlike interest groups in Western democracies, where lobbyists often focus on the legislative process, interest groups in Taiwan disperse their attention among government administrators, legislators, and KMT party leaders. Taiwan's legislatures remain weak, so lobbyists must interact closely with both the ruling party and the government administration to influence policy and legislation. Furthermore, the implementation of policies and laws can be more important to the interests of associations or the general public than the formal content of policies and laws. Thus Taiwan resembles many developing nations where a large portion of individual and group demands usually reach the political system at the enforcement stage.

Until the 1970s lobbying activities at the national level were directed mostly at ministers and the upper echelon of the administrative bureaucracy in the Executive Yuan (or cabinet). In the 1980s, following the rise of popularly elected members to the Legislative Yuan, lobbying in the lawmaking body intensified. Bills on banking practices, defendants' rights in judicial procedures, the ban on arcade games, workers' benefits, election laws, the tax rate on unearned income, and environmental pollution, for instance, have generated intense lobbying from various organized groups (Ch'iu 1984b, 17–18; Huang Ssu-ch'i 1982, 19–20; Wu Ke-ch'ing 1985, 59; Wen 1987, 28–33). In the Taiwan Provincial Assembly and in the municipal councils of Taipei and Kaohsiung, lobbying has long been part of the legislative process (Lerman 1978, 221–35).

Lobbying methods are immensely complex (Ch'iu 1984b, 15; Lin Chia-ch'eng 1983, 19). Groups or individual members may submit petitions to the legislatures. They may hire retired military generals or former ranking party and government officials as legislative consultants and through them seek to influence the lawmakers. Some legislators are elected to represent various functional groups—agriculture, education, medicine, commerce, and labor—and are expected to represent the interests of their groups. Bribery and other extralegal forms of political exchange have also been noted at all levels of the ROC legislative bodies. Illegal solicitations, of course, are not confined to lawmakers. Powerful government administrators are frequent objects of corrupt lobbying activities as well.

In the national legislatures the most active groups represent commercial, agricultural, public interest, labor, manufacturing, and fishery interests, in that order (Lin Sheng-fen et al. 1983, 2). In the Provincial Assembly the farmers' associations have been the most active and the most influential (Lerman 1978, 225). Business and labor groups are also active in the legislature, usually engaging in cooperative log-rolling among the leading assemblymen recognized as interest group spokesmen. In the national legislature, however, lobbying activities are intended mostly to put pressure on the government officials who sponsor bills or the KMT leaders who mediate floor conflicts over legislation. Typically the affected legislators use question sessions to air their concerns. A strong objection from the floor can sometimes bury measures introduced from the Executive Yuan (Chiu 1984b, 17–18). At all legislative levels in Taiwan, lawmakers cannot initiate bills on behalf of interest groups or individual citizens. Hence interest groups must seek influence within the appropriate government agencies.

Official Concertation

From a corporatist point of view, the interaction between the ROC government and interest groups constitutes an organic relation, but the linkages are neither entirely instrumental nor adversarial. The government clearly does not perceive itself as a policy or administrative instrument of interest groups. Adversarial relations between voluntary groups and government authorities are more the exception than the rule. Typically the regime incorporates interest groups into its governing structure and assigns them functional roles in both the input and the output phases of the political process. As one writer put it, the "negotiation of policy between state agencies and interest organizations [arises] from the division of labour in society, where policy agreements are implemented through the collaboration of the interest organizations and their willingness and ability to secure the compliance of their members" (Grant 1985, 3–4).

By law all social organizations, including interest groups, must register with the government and are subject to regulatory and functional supervision by the government. The KMT oversees their political loyalty through its party branches and its influence over the appointment of key personnel.

Since the ROC maintains a unitary structure of government, regulatory agencies for voluntary organizations exist at all levels of the governmental structure: central, provincial, municipal, and county. But these agencies rarely articulate group interests or supervise voluntary associations in the policy implementation phase. Policy implementation falls under separate administrative agencies with jurisdiction over specific activities undertaken by the associations. For instance, the Agricultural Development Commission of the Executive Yuan directs the overall administration of the farmers' associations at all levels (Wu and Yeh 1984, 9). The Ministry of Finance and the Provincial Department of Finance supervise the credit activities of the farmers' associations. The Provincial Department of Agriculture and Forestry and its functional subordinates in the municipal and county governments oversee personnel and budgetary operations. To some extent the farmers' interests are articulated in the associations' functional interactions with those government agencies. In the case of agriculture, the Agricultural Development Commission frequently serves as a bureaucratic arm representing the farmers' interests in the central government's decisionmaking process. Other associations interact in a similar fashion with their functionally related government agencies.

In implementing state policy, government agencies rely on various interest groups for administrative assistance. The farmers' associations help carry out agricultural policies at the grass-roots level. Similarly all five bureaus of the Ministry of Economic Affairs delegate administrative responsibilities to business and industrial associations (Wu Keng et al. 1983, 18–21). These responsibilities include applications for export quotas, technical innovation, import-export negotiations, attendance at international nongovernmental conferences, standardized quality control for export goods, and the dissemination of technology (Wu Keng et al. 1983, 104–8). Many interest groups in Taiwan thus assume quasi-governmental roles. Also the appropriate government agencies solicit the associations' input in policy formation at all administrative levels. These agencies have come to depend on voluntary associations to execute policy decisions. As long as this relation serves the associations' interests well, they have little need to lobby outside the government administration.

Some legislative matters concern many interest groups. The ROC constitution dictates that both the Legislative Yuan and the National Assembly include representatives elected by various vocational groups. In the Legislative Yuan 16 of the current 78 members elected on Taiwan represent farmers, fishermen, workers, industrialists, businessmen, and teachers. This functional representation assures the major occupational groups a voice in shaping legislative bills and in reviewing the government's fiscal budget. Functionally elected legislators, in contrast to those popularly elected, play watchdog roles for the groups they represent. They become legitimate spokesmen for their specific interests during legislative question sessions.

Electoral Participation

Most voluntary associations in Taiwan involve their membership in intra-association politics. Economic growth has fostered a large group of successful entrepreneurs and professionals who seek social recognition and political influence by running for office within the associations. Competition for the top posts in associations, which command lucrative resources, is particularly intense. Rivalry for the control of farmers' associations, irrigation associations, chambers of commerce, trade unions, industrial associations, and even religious associations has become intense. At stake are not simply positions of social recognition and political influence but potential patronage in the form of personnel appointments and material rewards.

Voluntary associations also participate in the electoral process outside their own organizations at two levels. First, six vocational groups—farmers, fishermen, workers, industrialists, businessmen, and teachers—elect occupational representatives to the national and provincial legislatures (Li Chan-t'ai 1982, 39–40). Second, voluntary groups also actively attempt to influence the general popular elections of other public officials. Because the KMT dominates electoral politics, interest groups often back specific candidates for party nomination. For years voluntary associations kept unofficial spokesmen in the Provincial Assembly (Lerman 1978, 221–34; Chen Ch'ao-p'ing 1982, 23).

Voluntary groups also contribute campaign funds to candidates of their choice. Sometimes they follow the urging of local KMT offices soliciting for the party's candidates. Since associations also command a large membership, the KMT relies on them to mobilize votes for party candidates in accordance with schemes for vote distribution carefully mapped out at the local or provincial party headquarters. Registered interest groups rarely back nonparty candidates, although individual members and leaders of local disenchanted factions do. In such instances their support for the opposition candidate is discreet for fear of punitive actions by the KMT. Aside from vote mobilization, interest groups provide an organizational network for distributing campaign materials.

THE KMT AND INTEREST GROUPS

The KMT's organizational ties with many interest groups lends substance to the argument that corporatism remains a salient feature of the relation between the party, the state, and society in the ROC. Since the early 1920s the KMT, following Leninist patterns, has always attempted to penetrate voluntary associations and to subordinate them within the party ranks. The party's earliest efforts to create such transmission belts proved futile. By 1941 the KMT was able to establish organizational branches in less than 6 percent of the mainland's existing private secondary (interest group) associations (Ch'i Hsi-sheng 1982, 194). After the war with Japan, the KMT faced the monumental task of reestablishing central authority in Nanking. In southern China and the lower Yangtze River Valley in the immediate postwar years, the KMT had little energy to organize new associations or penetrate existing bodies. Only in a few big cities along the eastern seaboard did the party gain control over key personnel appointments in trade unions, industrial associations, and chambers of commerce.

On arrival in Taiwan the KMT immediately took measures to reestablish control over voluntary associations. Among the secondary associations, trade unions, farmers' associations, and chambers of commerce were singled out as the principal targets in the 1950–1952 reorganization period. Trade unions—particularly those in shipping, railroads, and highway transportation—received the most serious attention.

In 1951 the Central Reorganization Committee adopted a resolution entitled "A KMT Guide for the Current Labor Movement," which called for the strengthening of party efforts to organize industrial unions. Later the party's organizational branches actively recruited members and trained cadres, first among workers in public enterprises and then in private industry.

Party penetration soon spread to the farmers' associations and other voluntary groups. In July 1953 the provincial party headquarters instructed the party committees in municipalities and counties to work out a timetable for establishing party units in the farmers' associations (Taiwan Tang-wu 1953, 47–49). The KMT's Eighth Party Congress in 1957 adopted a more comprehensive plan to promote the organization and growth of secondary associations under party auspices. Since then the penetration of vocational and social organizations has remained an emphasis of party policy, subject to periodic review and re-evaluation.

According to the organization rules of the KMT Central Committee, its Department of Social Work directs all party activities within the secondary associations (*CHNC*, 1982, 86). Party units in these associations are brought under the direct control of the Provincial Party Committee, the Taipei Municipal Party Committee, or the Kaohsiung Party Committee, except those involved with the armed forces, the security apparatus, overseas Chinese communities, manufacturing industries, transportation and communication sectors, and college campuses. The party headquarters for manufacturing industries (*ch'an-yeh tang-pu*) was set up separately to take charge of party organization in all public and private industries. The party headquarters of employees (*chih-yeh tang-pu*) has jurisdiction over shipping, railroads, highways, the postal service, and communications (Yu 1977, 78). Both of these party headquarters receive direct organizational and functional supervision from the KMT's Department of Social Work.

In principle the KMT prefers the elected leaders of all secondary associations to be party members, but as social pluralism gains ground this goal is not always possible. Insisting on party membership as a prerequisite for association leadership can generate antagonism and thus be counterproductive. In some cases where interest groups do not command large human and material resources—such as Rotary International, Lions International, the Association for Comparative Law Studies, the Taiwan Human Rights Association, and the Council of Presbyterian Churches—the KMT has taken a progressively more liberal stand, permitting non-party figures to become officers. Conversely in all key occupational groups—workers, farmers, fishermen, industrialists, businessmen, and teachers—the KMT continues to insist on party membership for the key officeholders. The Yangming Institution on National Revolution and Development, the party's central cadre school, holds periodic study sessions for leaders of these groups (Yu 1977, 88; *SPCK*, 1988, 44).

Among secondary associations the KMT has devoted the most energy to two mass organizations, the trade unions and the farmers' associations. The party maintains cells in the various unions. Each union has its own cadre committee (*kan-shih hui*), consisting of the union's general manager (*tsung-kan-shih*), secretary, and members of the boards of directors and supervisors. All these officers, and indeed all union officials in county-level organizations and above, are KMT members (Yu 1977, 84).[2] Most union staff with administrative responsibility are also party members who periodically receive training from the KMT's central cadre school. Available information indicates that in 1973 over 12,000 union officials from various levels went to the KMT's Yangming Institution on National Revolution and Development, where they studied Sun Yat-sen's Three Principles of the People, KMT labor policy, union organizational matters, and workers' welfare programs (Yu 1977, 87–88). In recent years, as labor-employer conflicts have multiplied, the KMT has frequently intervened as a mediator to keep problems from getting out of hand (Hung 1984, 9). Maintaining social order and political harmony remains a top priority of KMT policy.

KMT ties with the farmers' associations are equally strong. Although party membership is rare among ordinary and associate members of the associations, it is extremely common among officers. Figures show that in 1965 only 5 percent of regular members and 5.9 percent of associate members held party membership. By 1969 these percentages had risen to 6.9 and 8.6 respectively (Li Chan-t'ai 1982, 46). As Table 3.1 shows, the rates of party membership among farmers' association leaders is far higher.

Three patterns can be seen in the data. First, the percentage of party membership correlates positively with the hierarchical ranking of the leadership posts. Thus in a local farmers' association the chairmen of the board of directors and the board of supervisors are almost always KMT members. In contrast, only 40 to 50 percent of representatives in the association assembly are party members. Second, for similar posts in the association, there are more party members at higher levels of the administrative hierarchy. For instance, in 1975, 56 percent of the assembly representatives at the local level were party members, but at the county/city level the figure was 82 percent and at the provincial level, 99 percent. A similar pattern is evident in all other leadership posts in the association. In the provincial farmers' association all high-level officers held party membership. Third, in practically all categories listed in the table, party membership figures for 1975 are higher than those in 1969. This pattern is consistent with the overall increase in KMT membership between 1965 and 1969 among association members, cited earlier. At the local level all general managers except one have been party members since the 1950s (Li Chan-tai 1982, 43). In the 1986 election all fifteen presidents of the irrigation associations were KMT members (Li Chin-k'un 1986a, 69–73).

CONCLUSION

The KMT has broadly penetrated all voluntary associations since the party was reorganized in the early 1950s. In some associations that control significant material and human resources, the party has resorted to direct intervention into management, especially by appointing key personnel. Thus the trade unions, the farmers' associations, and even industrial and commercial associations closely approximate the corporatist

— TABLE 3.1 —
Percentage of Party Members Among Elected Officers in the Farmers' Associations, 1969 and 1975

	Assembly representatives		Board of directors		Board of supervisors		Chairmen of the board		Chiefs of the board of supervisors[a]	
	1969	1975	1969	1975	1969	1975	1969	1975	1969	1975
Local farmers' associations	40	56	69	83	64	86	98	100	76	97
County/city farmers' associations	66	82	82	96	83	95	100	100	100	100
Provincial farmers' association	97	99	100	100	100	100	100	100	100	100

SOURCE: Li Chan-t'ai (1987), 45.
[a]*Ch'ang-su chien-shih*, literally standing member of board of supervisors.

model in their relations with both the KMT and the government. But KMT penetration is minimal in other associations, and this noninterference permits a growing autonomy. Although the party may continue to tighten its grip over resource-rich associations, it does not appear able to dominate the voluntary associations that flourish outside its network of control. The lifting of martial law and the revision of the emergency law governing civic organizations, expected to take effect in 1989, will contribute to the general trend toward group autonomy.

With regard to interest groups, Taiwan is clearly in a state of transition. The dynamics of social differentiation has produced many such groups and thereby enhanced social pluralism. But for the moment the growth of social pluralism has not been matched by a corresponding growth of political pluralism, and corporatist ties between society and the party and government remain strong. Yet there are elements of political pluralism in the emergence of relatively autonomous professional and public interest groups.

The essentially corporatist KMT regime will make it extremely difficult for a full-fledged political pluralism to emerge in Taiwan. The KMT has institutionalized an organic relation between the ruling party and the major socioeconomic groups. Without a substantial break in this pattern, group autonomy can never be complete. Given the ROC political system, the KMT is unlikely to loosen its grip on the major voluntary groups it controls so efficiently. If it does, the KMT's ruling position would be in serious jeopardy.

— *4* —

The Party System
The KMT and the Opposition

The ROC on Taiwan was essentially a one-party state before September 1986, when the opposition Democratic Progressive Party (DPP) came into existence (Tien 1987b, 140–41). Since then eleven smaller parties have formed (*CKSP*, January 18, 1988, 3). A newly revised Civic Organization Law, which regulates secondary groups and political parties, now legally permits the formation of opposition parties. As of 1988 Taiwan's party system appears to have begun a profound transition from a one-party dictatorship to a dominant-party system.

From 1949 to 1986 the ruling KMT had a virtual monopoly of power on the island. It dictated governmental policy, appointed government personnel, allocated public revenues, and could coerce through the military, police, and security forces under its complete control. Two smaller legal parties—the Democratic Socialist Party (DSP) and the Young China Party (YCP)—were essentially satellites, relying on the KMT's financial subsidy for survival. In any electoral contest their combined support was less than 1 percent of the total votes cast. Their status as legal parties dates from the mainland prior to 1949, when they attracted significant followings. Since their arrival on Taiwan, their leaders, almost all mainlanders, have been co-opted by the KMT. Hence the electoral participation of the DSP and the YCP had little impact on Taiwan's politics.

Although the number of new opposition parties may continue to proliferate, only the DPP and the Labor Party, founded in December 1987, are expected to attract significant followings. The remaining ten small parties in existence in early 1988 are likely to fade away or be inconsequential in electoral competition. They lack an organizational base, a well-articulated party platform, adequate financial resources, and a substantial group of committed activists (*CKSP*, January 18, 1988, 3). In contrast, the DPP has inherited the principal forces from the pre-1986 opposition movements and has considerable support from those who are against the ruling KMT, particularly among the native Taiwanese. The Labor Party, launched by a band of intellectuals and labor activists, has a potentially broad political base among the 7.7-million-strong industrial work force of Taiwan (Hoon 1988b, 18). In fact the party's manifesto proclaims its hope of becoming the political vehicle for the workers as well as the emerging independent trade unions. Thus the developing party system in Taiwan is likely to include the KMT, the DPP, and perhaps the Labor Party as the only three parties of political significance. The DSP and the YCP, if successfully invigorated, could affect future party politics, but such a prospect is unlikely. Conceptually these changes in party politics will add up to a new dominant-party system under which the ruling KMT continues to be the decisive factor in governing the nation.

This chapter analyzes the KMT and to a lesser extent the opposition parties, emphasizing the structure and process within the KMT and the roles it plays in Taiwan's political system. The party was substantially reorganized in 1950–1952 after the arrival of the ROC administration on Taiwan. Since then both the rank-and-file members and the leadership have increasingly diversified. The KMT has transformed itself from a mainlander-dominated, exclusive, elite party to one characterized by partnership between the mainlanders and the Taiwanese. Rather than emphasizing authoritarian control and mass mobilization, the KMT has devoted its energy, especially since the early 1970s, to electoral activities and the mediation of political conflicts. In the process the KMT has gradually adapted to the requirements of a democratic and pluralistic society. This self-proclaimed revolutionary party no longer looks toward a massive reshaping of society and politics. It announced in early 1988 that it will transform from a revolutionary party to a party of democracy. In discussing the opposition parties, this chapter will focus on the *tangwai* movement and the formation of the new DPP.

THE RULING KUOMINTANG

The KMT is the oldest political party in China. Its present name was adopted in 1924, when Sun Yat-sen led a fundamental reorganization of the political movement. Under Dr. Sun the movement had used various names since 1894, when it was called *Hsing-chung-hui* (Society for Regenerating China). The predecessors of the KMT engaged in revolutionary activities with the specific goal of overthrowing the imperial Ch'ing (Manchu) dynasty and then, after the Ch'ing fell in 1911, the goal of national unification based on Sun Yat-sen's teachings. In 1924 Sun Yat-sen directed a reorganization based on the Leninist principles of a cadre-led party and democratic centralism. From 1924 to 1949 the KMT was embroiled in a series of civil wars against regional warlords and the CCP. As the internationally recognized government of China after 1927, it provided national leadership during the Sino-Japanese war from 1937 to 1945.

This history has greatly influenced both the organizational structure and the operational style of the party on Taiwan. V. O. Key once argued that "a conception of the party system must take into account its dimension of time. It may even be more useful to think of the party system as a historical process than as patterned institutional behavior" (Key 1964, 243). Thus the pre-1949 experiences on the Chinese mainland created patterns that help explain both the ROC's political party system and the role played by the KMT. After arriving on Taiwan, the KMT has continued to reform and evolve, and these changes have modified its interaction with the newly emerging social and political forces.

The Reorganization (1950–1952)

The defeat of the Nationalists on the mainland shattered KMT morale and crippled the party organization. In the closing months of the civil war the party lost contact with most of its members. As many local and provincial party organizations ceased to function, even the identity of party members was uncertain. The loss of records, defections, and a pervasive sense of defeat affected the entire KMT apparatus. This state of disorganization provided the Communists with ready opportunities to infiltrate the ranks of the KMT as well as the government and the armed forces. Following the retreat to Taiwan, a fundamental reorganization of the party was imperative. Members had to be reregistered. Those considered disloyal, suspected of enemy connections, or found guilty of corruption were purged (Riggs 1952, 38). The party needed to lay a new foundation in Taiwan and began to recruit new members from the local Taiwanese population.

In May 1949 President Chiang Kai-shek appointed an ad hoc group of ten men personally loyal to him to study reorganization measures. The leaders of the CC clique—the brothers Chen Kuo-fu and Chen Li-fu—were kept out of the reorganization scheme because they were held responsible for the party's paralysis on the mainland. Other KMT leaders from the mainland who were frequently at odds with Chiang—T. V. Soong, H. H. Kung, and Sun Fo—were ousted from the KMT's Central Standing Committee. That committee then endorsed Chiang's call for reorganization and adopted six guidelines to reshape the party (Hsu Fu-ming 1984, 64):

1. The KMT would be a revolutionary democratic party.
2. Its membership would be substantially enlarged to cover farmers, workers, youths, and the intelligentsia.
3. Party structure would continue to follow democratic centralism.
4. Party cells would serve as fundamental organizational units.
5. The KMT would provide political leadership throughout society; all decisions would be made through the party's organizational procedures.
6. Members would be required to believe in Sun Yat-sen's Three Principles of the People, obey the party, and follow party policies.

In January 1950 a reorganization study group was formed to draft operational details, which were formally adopted in July. In August Chiang appointed a Central Reorganization Committee consisting of Ch'en Ch'eng, Chang Ch'i-yun, Chang Tao-fan, Ku Cheng-kang, Cheng Yen-fen, Chen Hsueh-p'ing, Hu Chien-chung, Yuan Shou-ch'ien, Tsui Shih-ch'in, Ku Feng-hsiang, Tseng Hsi-pai, Chiang Ching-kuo, Hsiao Chih-ch'eng, Shen Ch'ang-huan, Kuo Ch'eng, and Lien Chen-tung (Hsu Fu-ming 1984, 65). The only Taiwanese member was Lien Chen-tung, who had strong mainland ties since he resided on the mainland before 1949.

There are no reliable figures on party membership in 1949. Official sources indicate that by December 1950, eighteen months after the ad hoc reorganization group was formed, civilian party members totaled 80,043, or slightly over 1 percent of Taiwan's total population (*TWTW*, February 16, 1951, 24). At the end of the reorganization in October 1952, civilian members had increased to about 170,000 (Hsu Fu-ming 1984, 155). Over 49 percent of these were farmers, workers, and merchants (Chang Ch'i-yun 1952, 45). All members were organized into about 30,000 party cells—work cells and residential cells—with an average of about 6 members each (Hsu Fu-ming 1984, 155). According to the official in charge of the KMT reorganization, Chang Ch'i-yun, the ratio of party members to nonparty members in government agencies was 5 to 1 in the central government, 1 to 1 in the provincial government, and 8 to 13 in county and city governments (Chang Ch'i-yun 1952, 44). Party branches and cells were established throughout the island in rural villages, government offices, schools, enterprises, military units, and transportation operations. Party cadres used workshops and propaganda campaigns to teach new members party doctrine.

Party reorganization was also carried out in the armed forces, where Chiang Ching-kuo was instructed by his father, Chiang Kai-shek, to establish a system of political commissars. These political commissars were charged with forming and supervising party cells, conducting political indoctrination, and serving as the party's eyes and ears in the military. Membership drives in the armed forces intensified during 1952–1954; the goal was to recruit at least one member from every squad and to have a party cell in each platoon. During these two years 95,702 new members were recruited from military ranks; 18,087 were officers and 77,615 were soldiers. By 1954 about 210,000, or 35 percent, of the 600,000 members of the armed forces were party members (Chou 1957, 57). As a result, the armed forces were brought under strict KMT control through a network of party cells directed by the political commissars in all units.

Developments Since the Reorganization

The KMT Seventh Party Congress of October 10, 1952, formally terminated the reorganization campaigns. The congress elected 30 members to a revived Central Committee, which in effect replaced the reorganization group as the party's directing body. The Central Committee in turn elected 10 persons recommended by Chiang Kai-shek to serve in the powerful Central Standing Committee: Ch'en Ch'eng, Chiang Ching-kuo, Chang Tao-fan, Ku Cheng-kang, Wu Kuo-chen, Huang Shao-ku, Chen Hsueh-p'ing, Yen Shou-ch'ien, T'ao Hsi-sheng, and Ni Wen-ya. No Taiwanese was senior enough or powerful enough to be included. In June 1988, 36 years later, 4 of them—Ku, Huang, Yen, and Ni—were still members of the KMT's Central Standing Committee.

From 1952 to 1968 the party followed a steady policy of widening membership drives while maintaining the stability of the party leadership. During this period only a few Taiwanese rose to high party positions. Mainlanders continued to hold practically all key offices in the central and provincial party headquarters. Even at county and municipal levels mainlanders were almost always the party branch chairmen.

By the late 1960s Taiwanese who had been enrolled since 1949 began to rise in the party ranks. In an apparent effort to meet the popular demand for broader-based political participation, Chiang Ching-kuo had a subordinate, Lee Huan, begin a policy of co-opting Taiwanese through promotion (*SPCK*, May 23, 1987, 200). From 1968 to 1977 Lee, now secretary-general of the KMT Central Committee, occupied a series of key party posts and was instrumental in implementing Chiang Ching-kuo's order to recruit Taiwanese party members for various middle and upper-middle party positions. During these nine years Lee held such powerful positions as chairman of the Provincial Party Committee, director of the Organization Department at the central headquarters, director of the Chinese Youth Anti-Communist League, and director of the Yangming Institution on National Revolution and Development, the highest party school for KMT cadres (*China Yearbook*, 1978, 567). Although Secretary-General Chang Pao-shih was his immediate superior in party bureaucracy during that period, Lee Huan held more actual power in the party apparatus.

Party growth during this period reveals a number of significant features. One was the emphasis on improving party work at the local level to integrate the party administration into election-related activities (Chen Shun-chih 1984, 6). Throughout the 1960s urban and rural party leaders were criticized increasingly for their bureaucratic style. Most mainlander party branch chairmen and functionaries could not speak the native Taiwanese dialects, and this limitation contributed to the social gap between them and local residents. Both the Tenth Party Congress in March 1969 and the second plenum held a year later adopted resolutions to improve party work styles and to carry out political reforms (*China Yearbook*, 1984, 81). The objective of these resolutions was to upgrade the party's image through a congenial local leadership conducive to winning popular support in elections.

Beginning in 1969–1970, two important steps helped Taiwanese rise into the party's elite circle. The KMT initiated a rapid turnover of county- and municipal-level party executives, and Taiwanese in growing numbers were appointed to chair these local committees. By 1977 about one-third of the county and city chairmen were Taiwanese, a clear reversal of the previous mainlander dominance. Even at the upper party levels more Taiwanese party loyalists were rewarded with highly visible posts in the central party headquarters and even the Central Standing Committee. The party also made clear its attempt to recruit younger and better educated Taiwanese as well as mainlanders for future leadership.

In 1976, on the order of Chiang Ching-kuo, Lee Huan selected several dozen young party leaders for the highest-level cadre training program at the party school. Some sixty individuals, half of them Taiwanese, reportedly attended this special course. Among them were Chen Li-an (now a Central Standing Committee member and minister of economic affairs), Lien Chan (a Central Standing Committee member and minister of foreign affairs), Shih Ch'i-yang (a Central Standing Committee member and vice premier), Kao Yu-jen (a Central Standing Committee member and speaker of the Provincial Assembly), Soong Ch'u-yu (KMT deputy secretary-general), Wu Po-hsiung (a Central Standing Committee member and mayor of Taipei), Fredrick F. Ch'ien (a Central Standing Committee member and chairman of CEPD), and Kuan Chung (director of the KMT Organization Department). Lee Huan's reform initiative also produced a wholesale personnel change in the KMT's provincial headquarters, where 641 older functionaries, or 37 percent of the total staff, retired or left office between 1968 and 1971. In those three years 2,100 provincial party cadres went to the party school for refresher training (Chen Yang-te 1978, 145). Lee's weeding out of older and incompetent cadres created a fresh image for the party; in the process the KMT also stepped up its drive to co-opt Taiwanese into its leadership ranks.

But in 1977 Lee Huan relinquished all his party posts. Lee was demoted because he was held responsible for a major incidence of public rioting in the northern Taiwan town of Chungli, where discontented voters clashed with the police in November 1977 during a local election. Despite Lee's exit the KMT continued in the general direction of reform and co-optation under the leadership of Y. S. Tsiang, who served as KMT secretary-general from 1979 to 1984. To foster a reformist image for the party, Tsiang recruited additional members from intellectual circles. At the provincial and local levels Sung Shih-hsuan, then chairman of the Provincial Party Committee, brought a social service orientation to the KMT's grass-roots activities in an effort to win popular support. Sung's operational style was conciliatory and down-to-earth. Under him a large number of young Taiwanese with college degrees were appointed to head the party's local branches. Local KMT functionaries were instructed to foster social harmony through mediation, particularly in the wake of growing political activity by the nonparty opposition. By 1984, when Tsiang and Sung left office, about half the county and city party chairmen were young Taiwanese, a major change from the first two decades of KMT rule. Sung was subsequently promoted to take charge of the party's Organization Department at central party headquarters until he was forced to step down in 1987.

Kuan Chung, a second-generation mainlander with a Ph.D. from the United States, succeeded Sung as head of the Provincial Party Committee and later in 1987 as head of the Organization Department. He marked a clear departure from his predecessor, for his management style relied heavily on modern technology and organization theories of party work. He initiated (1) the publication of a periodical for internal communication and propaganda within the party ranks, (2) the use of computers to store and analyze party data, and (3) straw votes through opinion surveys of rank-and-file KMT members concerning the nomination of candidates for public office and other important party issues (Li Ya-ch'ing 1985, 61). With his combative organizational style, Kuan intends to upgrade administrative efficiency and the grass-roots mobilization of rank-and-file members. He is prepared to meet the opposition's mounting challenges in electoral politics with technological innovations and organizational techniques. Together with Sung Shih-hsuan, Kuan was removed from his provincial party post in 1987 after the December 1986 parliamentary election in which the newly formed Democratic Progress Party (DPP) scored surprising gains in both popular votes and legislative seats. But in late 1987 he was put in charge of the KMT's powerful Organization Department.

KMT Roles on Taiwan

As a ruling party the KMT plays several important roles, which can be conveniently discussed under six headings.

Governing. The party completely monopolizes power within the government, the armed forces, and the police force. In theory at least, the government carries out policies made by the party leaders. The vast majority of government officials and bureaucrats are party members. All key officers in the various branches of the government, the military, and the police force are party members. At times distinctions between the party and the government blur.

Political recruitment. The KMT recruits citizens for leadership positions in the government, the legislatures, and the party institutions from within party ranks. Individuals who serve in one institution often take on an additional post in a parallel institution. Recruitment for elected office is by party appointment or nomination. The vast majority of the KMT's nominees win in electoral contests. Thus the political elite on Taiwan rise steadily within the party hierarchy or through the party-sanctioned patronage network. Party membership and party loyalty become two critical criteria for upward political mobility.

Political socialization. The KMT serves as a propaganda instrument for the regime. It sanitizes publications and reading materials for schools. It organizes study sessions to propagate the ideologies of Sun Yat-sen and Chiang Kai-shek. It attempts to mold popular attitudes against com-

munism in general and against the Chinese communist regime in particular, thus inculcating a strong anticommunist belief system.

Political mobilization. The party manages various mass organizations
that mobilize political support for the regime. Schools and interest
groups such as trade unions, farmers' associations, and chambers of commerce are headed by party members. Through penetration and control
the party uses this extensive network of mass organizations for its political purposes.

Political integration. The party assumes an important role in mediating conflicts. As Taiwan modernizes, growing social pluralism creates
conflicts of interest and new political demands. Factionalism brought
about by electoral contests permeates Taiwan society. Potentially disruptive individuals may be induced to support the political system through
patronage and political spoils or through the mediation of the KMT. The
party emphasizes the political integration of ethnic and socioeconomic
groups on Taiwan to promote social harmony and political stability.

Social services and social control. Party cells and local party branches
permeate Taiwan society, monitoring the mood and social ties of local
residents village by village and ward by ward. The KMT gathers information to detect political suspects and provides a network of communications in all localities to facilitate harmonious relations among the
political and social elite. Since the party controls access to public resources, services can be provided to the needy or the potentially discontented to temper their resentment and to solicit their support. Such
services include arrangements for easy access to major hospitals, the establishment of a local library, free sewing and cooking classes, free legal
and other consultations, and material assistance to poor families.

In short, the KMT has grown beyond a single-minded Leninist
party. At the same time it performs far more functions than political parties in most democratic systems. Unlike Leninist parties in communist
countries, the KMT does not rely principally on coercion and control to
secure its dominant position. It has modified its control to fit more efficiently into a society where social and political diversity call for persuasion and conciliation. The KMT's methods of securing power ultimately
affect the political stability of the system; they also determine the character of Taiwan's party system.

THE KMT'S ORGANIZATIONAL STRUCTURE

The party organization forms a complex, interlocking hierarchy. Its vertical structure parallels the various levels of the government. Thus there are KMT units at the national, provincial, county/municipal, township, and urban district levels. As Table 4.1 shows, at each level the party organization is separated into three functionally related institutions: a representative body, an executive center, and an administrative apparatus. On the national level the representative body is the Party Congress, whose delegates usually meet once every four years to discuss and approve party policies and to elect members of the Central Committee. The Central Committee in turn elects its chairman and the Central Standing Committee members, who in the past were usually hand-picked by Chiang Kai-shek and later by Chiang Ching-kuo.

Routine party work is conducted by the executive center and the administrative apparatus. At the national level the executive center comprises the party chairman, the Central Standing Committee, and the Central Committee (see Figure 4.1). In theory they serve as the decisionmaking bodies for the party. Various functional departments and committees attend to the daily operations of the party under the coordinating leadership of the secretary-general. At the provincial, municipal, city, and county levels, the chairmen of party committees hold executive power and direct the daily work of the secretaries and other administrative functionaries. Subcounty organizations are progressively simpler. The KMT penetrates down to the grass roots, where party members are formed into work cells or residential cells, depending on type of employment or locality.

The Party Chairman

The post of KMT chairman is the most powerful in the party. From 1949 to 1988 only Chiang Kai-shek, Chiang Ching-kuo, and Lee Teng-hui have occupied the post. Chiang Kai-shek was referred to in party matters as director-general (*tsung-ts'ai*) until his death in 1975. Chiang Ching-kuo served, until his death in 1988, as top party leader with the less exalted title of chairman (*chu-hsi*). Lee Teng-hui succeeded Chiang Ching-kuo first as acting chairman and then as chairman following meetings of the Party Congress, the Central Committee, and the Central Standing Committee. He holds the final authority on all policy matters and major personnel appointments. As acting chairman he presided over the Thirteenth Party Congress in July 1988. The hierarchical structure of power enables the chairman to wield enormous power with few institutional constraints.

_____ TABLE 4.1 _____
KMT ORGANIZATIONAL STRUCTURE

Representative body	Executive center	Administrative apparatus
National Party Congress	Chairman Central Standing Committee Central Committee	Secretary-general Functional departments
Provincial and municipal party conferences	Party committee chairmen	Secretaries Functional divisions
County and city party conferences	Party committee chairmen	Secretaries
District (township and hsiang) party conferences	Party committees	Secretaries
Subdistrict members' conferences Cell members	Party committees	Party office directors

Other factors contribute to the chairman's power. One is the charisma of the two men who occupied the post from 1949 to 1988. Chiang Kai-shek had been a party leader for over two decades before the KMT shifted to Taiwan in 1949. Although he had rivals on the mainland, those KMT adherents following him to Taiwan were mostly his supporters. His earlier success in leading the Northern Expedition against the warlords in 1926–1927 and his role as national leader during the Sino-Japanese war elevated him to a position without equal in the party and in politics, at least in the eyes of his followers. After the party reorganization of 1950–1952, he began to prepare his son, Chiang Ching-kuo, for the succession. On Taiwan the younger Chiang filled various important assignments in the party, the military, the security apparatus, and the government. During these assignments Chiang Ching-kuo formed his own institutional bases of power and a personal following. When he succeeded his father in 1975, Chiang Ching-kuo had reached a position of unchallengeable power in the regime. His populist style and his serious attention to both economic modernization and political reform earned him wide personal support beyond his authority as his father's heir.

In Taiwan politics since 1949 the numerical minority, the mainlanders, have looked up to the Chiangs as the paternal protectors of their interests. The ROC's political institutions legitimize the power and positions held by the mainlander elite. But the character and membership of these institutions, which claim to represent all of China, are subject to question. Thus to ensure the regime's political stability, the ruling political elite, particularly the mainlanders, have relied heavily on the charisma of Chiang Kai-shek and then Chiang Ching-kuo to provide legitimacy. As Dankwart A. Rustow has observed in a different context: "The more the legitimacy of institutions is in question, the more is there a need to find legitimacy in persons" (Rustow 1970, 156). The Chiangs' character, Taiwan's peculiar political institutions, and the goal of maintaining the ROC have all shaped the qualifications required for the KMT chairman. The occupant of that powerful position has been glorified and even deified in the past. Lacking the enormous prestige of the Chiangs, Lee Teng-hui, the current chairman, may have to exercise the power of chairman within the context of a collective leadership.

But the party chairman does not conduct national affairs singlehandedly. He relies on the powerful institutionally based elite—in the party, the security and military apparatus, and the government—as well as technocrats and personal advisers to assist him in decisionmaking. As indicated earlier, the party leadership is particularly important in Taiwan because of its crucial role in the ROC's political system.

The Central Standing Committee

The KMT power structure still follows the Leninist pattern of centralization and collective decisionmaking. At the top of the party's organizational hierarchy is the Central Standing Committee. Its members are elected by the Central Committee according to the principles of democratic centralism to exercise party decisionmaking authority when the larger body is not in session. The number of Central Committee members has increased from 32 in 1952 to 150, with another 75 alternates, in the 1980s. The large size of the Central Committee, however, makes it unsuitable for policymaking; furthermore, it is in session only once a year at most, usually for about three days. Such plenary sessions are devoted to reports from the party, the government, and the military leaders. Under the Chiangs even the election of Central Standing Committee members had become a formality in which the Central Committee merely approved a slate of candidates designated by the party leader. Over the years membership in the Central Committee, as in the Party Congress, has carried more status than actual decisionmaking power.

The Central Standing Committee is a smaller body that meets every ednesday. In status and power it resembles the Politburo in the Leninist

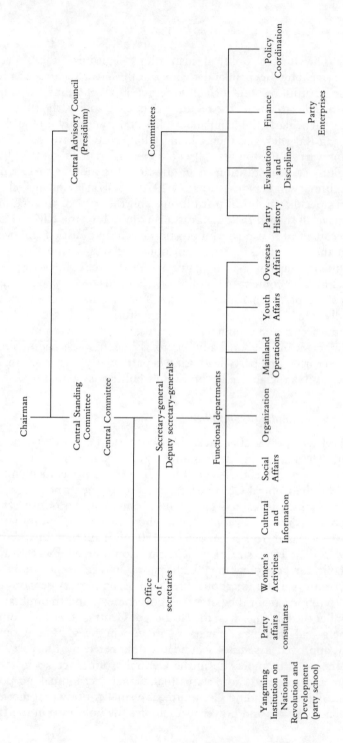

FIGURE 4.1

THE KMT CENTRAL ORGANIZATION

SOURCE: Ko (1980), 97–98.

parties of the Soviet Union and the People's Republic of China. It has 31 members, up from 10 in 1952, and members have the most prestigious positions in the KMT hierarchy. The party chairman or a senior member designated by him presides over the weekly meeting. The KMT's secretary-general, the directors of functional departments in the central headquarters, and party representatives in overseas diplomatic missions are all disqualified from membership, although those party leaders, along with the chairmen of the provincial and municipal party committees, may attend the weekly sessions as nonvoting participants.

According to Table 4.2, the average age of Central Standing Committee members in August 1988 was 63.7. As a result of the turnover in July 1988, only ten members were 70 years or older, compared with seventeen previously (*CKSP*, July 15, 1988, 2). Thirteen members were 60 years or younger, compared with only ten in the past. Moreover, over half (51.6 percent) were Taiwanese, although mainlanders had constituted a majority before the change in July 1988. The ethnic composition reflects the general trend of elevating more native Taiwanese to this symbolically important committee.

As recently as 1973 there were only 3 Taiwanese among the 21 Standing Committee members. In 1979 the figure increased to 9 of 27 (Nan 1986b, 43) and in 1984 to 12 of 31. The practice has been to create additional posts for younger Taiwanese, while the mainlander old guard continues to serve. As recently as 1986, 11 of the 13 members age 69 or younger were Taiwanese. Only 2 mainlanders—Hau Pei-tsun, chief of general staff of the armed forces, and Chen Li-an, director of the National Science Council—were younger than 70. The mainlander old guard was reluctant to step down. In fact about half a dozen of them had held their positions for over 35 years. But enlarging the Central Standing Committee increased Taiwanese representation at no direct risk to the old guard. As the senior members left office, they were partially replaced by second-generation mainlanders.

Central Standing Committee members on the whole have excellent educational credentials. Many hold degrees from elite universities in the United States, Japan, the United Kingdom, other European countries, the mainland, and Taiwan. As indicated in Table 4.1, 8 of the 31 members have doctorates and 4 have master's degrees. Their career backgrounds are highly diversified: 14 currently hold key government positions, 6 are leaders in the parliamentary bodies, and 3 are career military officers, with Chief of General Staff Hau Pei-tsun still on active military duty. Hsieh Tung-min and Li Kuo-ting are senior advisers to the president. Three are party bureaucrats, and only two are industrial or business leaders. Hsieh Shen-shan, a worker in his younger days and now president of

TABLE 4.2
MEMBERS OF THE KMT CENTRAL STANDING COMMITTEE, AUGUST 1988

Name (in order of rank)	Age	Birthplace	Position	Education
Hsieh Tung-min	82	Taiwan	Senior adviser to the president	Chung-san University
Li Kuo-ting	79	Kiangsu	Senior adviser to the president	Cambridge University, M.A.
Ni Wen-ya	84	Chekiang	President, Legislative Yuan	Columbia University, M.A.
Yu Kuo-hwa	75	Chekiang	Premier	Harvard University, London School of Economics
Lee Huan	71	Hupeh	KMT secretary-general	Columbia University, M.A.
Shen Chang-huan	75	Kiangsu	Secretary-general of the Office of the President	University of Michigan
Lin Yang-kang	62	Taiwan	President, Judicial Yuan	Taiwan University
Chiu Chuang-huan	63	Taiwan	Governor of Taiwan province	Cheng-chi University
Huang Tsun-chiu	65	Taiwan	President, Control Yuan	Central Police Academy
Hau Pei-tsun	69	Kiangsu	Chief of general staff	Military Academy, U.S. Army, Command and Staff College
Ho, Irwine W.	75	Fukien	Secretary-general, National Assembly	Chaoyang University
Soong, James C. Y.	47	Hunan	KMT deputy secretary-general	Georgetown University, Ph.D.
Wu Po-hsiung	50	Taiwan	Mayor of Taipei	Cheng-kung University
Chien, Fredrick F.	53	Chekiang	Chairman, Council for Economic Planning and Development	Yale University, Ph.D.

—— TABLE 4.2 (continued) ——

Name (in order of rank)	Age	Birthplace	Position	Education
Chen Li-an	52	Chekiang	Minister of economic affairs	New York University, Ph.D.
Lien Chan	52	Taiwan	Minister of foreign affairs	University of Chicago, Ph.D.
Shih Chi-yang	53	Taiwan	Vice premier	Heidelberg University, Ph.D.
Cheng Wei-yuan	75	Anhwei	Minister of defense	Military Academy, U.S. Army Command and Staff College
Mao Kao-wen	52	Chekiang	Minister of education	Carnegie-Mellon University, Ph.D.
Hsu Li-nung	68	Anhwei	Chairman, Vocational Assistance Commission for Retired Servicemen	War College, ROC
Koo Chen-fu	72	Taiwan	Chairman of the board, Taiwan Cement Company and China Trust Company	Tokyo University
Kao Yu-jen	54	Taiwan	Speaker, Taiwan Provincial Assembly	Taiwan University
Hsu Shui-teh	57	Taiwan	Minister of the interior	Cheng-chih University, M.A.
Chang Chien-pang	60	Taiwan	Speaker, Taipei Municipal Council	University of Illinois, Ph.D.
Chao Tzu-chi	74	Jehol	Member, Legislative Yuan	Nankai University, Military Academy
Tseng Kwang-shun	64	Kwangtung	Chairman, overseas Chinese affairs commission	Kwangtung College of Law and Business

———— TABLE 4.2 (continued) ————

Name (in order of rank)	Age	Birthplace	Position	Education
Kuo, Shirley W. Y.	59	Taiwan	Minister of finance	MIT, M. A.; Kobe University, Ph.D.
Su Nan-cheng	53	Taiwan	Mayor of Kaohsiung	Cheng-kung University
Chen Tien-mao	61	Taiwan	Speaker, Kaohsiung Municipal Council	Kimki University
Hsu Sheng-fa	64	Taiwan	President, National Association of Industries	Taiwan University
Hsieh Shen-shan	50	Taiwan	President, National Association of Trade Unions	Hua-lien Technical School

SOURCE: *CKSP* (July 15, 1988), 2.

the National Federation of Trade Unions, is the first and only member ever to represent the working class.

How the CSC conducts its weekly business is not public knowledge, but because of its size it probably cannot function effectively as a decisionmaking body. In recent years, as the number of members has increased, the party chairman has often appointed ad hoc committees from the membership to serve special functions. Thus every year since the early 1970s an ad hoc group has been named to approve a final slate of KMT candidates. In April 1986, after the Third Plenum of the Twelfth Central Committee, a twelve-member task force with a majority of old-guard mainlanders was formed to study measures for political reform. Reports by these ad hoc groups to the Central Standing Committee are only a formality.

The inability of the Central Standing Committee to function as an effective decisionmaking body can be seen in the creation of a "Liu Shao-k'ang Office" in 1979—the code name for an ad hoc leadership group consisting of General Wang Sheng, KMT Secretary-General

Tsiang Yen-si, Premier Sung Yun-hsuen, Secretary-General of the Presidential Office Ma Chi-chuang, and Defense Minister Kao Kuei-yuan (Tien 1984, 9; *KCJP*, March 16, 1988, 6). From 1981 to 1983, when Chiang Ching-kuo was suffering from serious complications of diabetes and underwent major eye surgery, this ad hoc group coordinated by General Wang became the de facto center of power. Alarmed by Wang's political ambition, Chiang Ching-kuo ordered the office disbanded in early May 1983. That same month General Wang's power in the armed forces was cut back with his removal from the post of director of the General Political Warfare Department.

In short, the Central Standing Committee has not exercised institutional authority efficiently or creatively. Rather, with its steadily increasing size and the periodic formation of informal power groups, it has become an archaic concertation body. Although it is a decisionmaking center under the party constitution, its importance should not be overemphasized (Bennett 1984, 11). In August 1987 Chiang Ching-kuo sought to rejuvenate this archaic power center by dividing its members into six functionally distinct ad hoc groups.[1] After Chiang Ching-kuo's death in January 1988, and in the absence of another charismatic leader, the Central Standing Committee could become quite important in party and government affairs.

Central Party Headquarters

In the KMT routine party affairs are initiated, coordinated, and executed by seven functional departments and four committees that are part of the central headquarters (see Figure 4.1). The leading post in the central administration is the secretary-general, who is considered equal in rank to the government's premier. He supervises daily party activities, coordinates party relations with the state and society, prepares the agenda for meetings of the Central Standing Committee, and reports directly to the party chairman on important party matters. Activities at the party center as well as vertical communication to party functional units are monitored through his office. The secretary-general usually plays a crucial role in the personnel selection process for significant party posts and for KMT candidates for publicly elected offices.

Since 1949 eight men have served as KMT secretary-general. Y. S. Tsiang, an agricultural specialist with a doctorate from the United States, brought a dynamic work style and high visibility to the position from 1979 to 1985. In January 1985 Ma Soo-lay, who has close personal ties with the Chiang family, succeeded Tsiang. Ma's strength is his experience in foreign affairs. From 1972 to 1984 he was the ROC's representative in Japan. Earlier he was involved in foreign affairs first as a journalist and later in KMT work (Sung and Ho 1986, 432). He appears to be fairly new to the KMT's domestic arena. In July 1987 Lee Huan succeeded Ma as secretary-general. Previously discharged as head of the Organization Department in 1977 after the Chungli Incident, Lee had been president of National Chungshan University and minister of education from 1978 to 1987. A lifetime protégé of Chiang Ching-kuo, he is widely regarded as the KMT's most able party bureaucrat. Chiang apparently entrusted him with the crucial task of steering the political reforms.

Among the seven central departments, the pivotal functions are organizational and cultural affairs. The Organization Department supervises nationwide party operations in matters of personnel, including cadre training, personnel evaluation, membership, and the recruitment of party leaders. Its director is often seen as almost the equal of the KMT secretary-general, since recommendations for appointments to party and government posts are initiated through him. The current head of the Organization Department is Kuan Chung, a Ph.D. from the United States who previously taught at a university and chaired the party committees of Taipei and Taiwan province. The Department of Cultural Affairs supervises the mass media and manages the party's propaganda activities and publication enterprises.

Interdepartmental matters are discussed at the weekly central work conference at KMT headquarters attended by all department directors and committee chairmen. Because of Chiang Ching-kuo's failing health, the conference was chaired for much of the 1980s by the secretary-general (Peng Huai-en 1983, 216). Potential conflicts between departments and committees are discussed and resolved there. More important, policy proposals regarding party affairs are drafted through the central work conference before they are forwarded to the party chairman or the Central Standing Committee for formal adoption. Thus the conference provides a useful forum for senior party cadres to articulate their interests and for the leadership to reach a consensus on party policy. The conference is not limited to discussions alone but can decide matters involving internal party operations.

The Policy Coordination Committee

The Policy Coordination Committee (PCC) is another important central party agency that has assumed an increasingly active role in liaison with other branches of the political system. This committee dates from 1955, when it was created as an ad hoc committee of the Central

Committee. Article 6 of the Central Committee Organization Rules specifies PCC functions as follows: (1) the study and review of matters concerning party policy, the legal system, and party-government relations at the national level; (2) research on the current political situation of the country; and (3) liaison with social notables and political figures who are not KMT members. To carry out its duties the PCC has about a dozen subcommittees to study various policy issues of concern to the party (Ko 1980, 100).

According to its bylaws, the PCC's membership consists of the following high-ranking officials: (1) the entire body of the Central Standing Committee; (2) the premier, the vice premier, and the presidents and vice presidents of the Legislative, Judicial, Control, and Examination yuans; (3) the secretary-general and deputy secretary-generals (one to three persons) of the PCC itself; (4) the directors of the Organization and Cultural Affairs departments, chairman of the Evaluation and Discipline Committee, and other appropriate department heads from central KMT headquarters; and (5) individuals designated by the ROC president. The large membership makes it difficult for the PCC to function efficiently, so full meetings are infrequent. Most of its affairs are conducted by the PCC secretary-general and his deputies. Although they must maintain communication with all members, their operational direction comes from the Central Standing Committee and the KMT secretary-general. Like his predecessors, the current PCC secretary-general, Liang Su-jung, is a member of the Legislative Yuan and was previously the KMT party leader there.

The PCC rarely deals with major policy issues, which are usually deliberated by the Central Standing Committee, the National Security Council, the central party work conference, or the Executive Yuan council. Two concerns preoccupy the PCC staff. First, the PCC coordinates three national representative bodies and mediates conflicts between party members in these bodies, especially in the Legislative Yuan. Maintaining party unity to ensure the swift passage of government bills and the annual government budget on the legislative floor is the PCC's top priority. Second, since the early 1970s the PCC secretary-general and his deputies have often made contact with the increasingly active and visible political opposition, with whom they discuss issues of mutual concern to correct misunderstandings and alleviate political tension. The PCC's role in mitigating political and policy conflicts is likely to enlarge since KMT Chairman Lee Teng-hui has instructed the PCC leaders to pursue a dialogue with their DPP counterparts on a regular basis (*CYJP*, February 11, 1988, 2).

Provincial and Local Party Organizations

The operational structure of the KMT includes both functional and territorial units. The former are an array of party branches organized in government bodies, the legislatures, and the military as well as in colleges, the transportation industry, the mass media, and government-run industries. The structure of these territorial organizations parallels the government administrative hierarchy. Below the national level is a provincial party committee with operational headquarters in Chunghsing New Town, the administrative center of the provincial government, near Taichung in central Taiwan. The municipalities of Taipei and Kaohsiung have separate party committees and headquarters with provincial status.

The organizational structure of these three territorial party units is essentially identical, but the provincial operation is much larger because it has jurisdiction over a large number of provincial territorial units. Each of the three provincial-level units has a party committee that serves as its executive arm. The chairman of the party committee supervises the personnel and party work throughout Taiwan except for Taipei and Kaohsiung. These three provincial-level party headquarters are divided by function into the following six offices (Ch'ü 1984, 128; Chen I-t'ien 1984, 31):

Division 1 supervises the membership organization, cadres, and party-government relation.

Division 2 acts as a liaison with interest groups and civic organizations.

Division 3 manages electoral campaigns and vote allocation for party candidates.

Division 4 promotes cultural and propaganda activities.

Division 5 supervises women's organizations and the activities of female party members.

Division 6 controls and monitors social activities, particularly among politically influential individuals.

In addition, an administrative office prepares the agenda for meetings and processes intraparty communications. An evaluation and discipline committee oversees the conduct of individual party members and recommends disciplinary action if necessary. And finally, a finance committee screens the expenditures of party agencies and disperses party funds according to the budget.

The local party organizations in cities and counties are much simpler. The party chairman assumes a variety of responsibilities, such as nominating local candidates for public office, winning local elections, mediating conflicts between local factions and socioeconomic groups, facilitating the progress of local development projects, and supervising political education (Winckler 1981, 54). He is responsible for the overall implementation of party policies. Since political stability and social harmony are among the KMT's primary concerns, the party chairman is vested with material and human resources to achieve those goals in his locality.

Below cities and counties are districts (*ch'u*), in which party offices are established. A full-time party secretary of rural townships or an urban district is appointed to run the unit known as the community service center (*min-chung fu-wu she*). Even at the village level there is a party committee headed by the village headman, who is usually a party member (Jacobs 1980, 26). These grass-roots committees supervise the activities of party cells, each composed of from 3 to 29 members (*CHNC* 1988, 150). For instance, in Kaohsiung county, a highly industrialized region in southern Taiwan, there are 4,000 party cells with an average of 15 party members per cell (P'an Fu-chien et al. 1987, 47). Cell leaders are instructed to hold monthly meetings with cell members. KMT units above the cells follow a similar practice to foster unity among party members in the face of growing competition from the opposition parties. The size of party cells varies according to locality and, in the case of functional party branches, according to the specific institution involved. Reportedly 70,000 cells fall under the direct jurisdiction of the Provincial Party Committee (*MCJP*, June 29, 1986, 5). That local government administrators and public school principals often serve on the standing committee illustrates the party's profound influence on local government.

Membership

In Taiwan KMT party members constitute about 12 percent of the total population and nearly 20 percent of the adult population; 70 percent of all KMT members are reported to be Taiwanese (Chiang Ping-lun 1985, 3). According to one official source, total membership in 1988 was about 2.4 million (*CYJP*, March 24, 1988, 1). Most leaders from all walks of life—politics, banking and finance, the armed forces, education, artistic circles, private and public enterprises, and the mass media—are KMT members. Party members represent a cross section of people from various vocational groups. According to Table 4.3, among the approximately 2.36 million members in 1986, 424,798, or just over 18 percent, were

_____ TABLE 4.3 _____
VOCATIONS OF KMT MEMBERS, 1986

	Number	Percentage
Peasants and fishermen	257,748	10.94
Workers	424,798	18.03
Businessmen and industrialists	276,004	11.71
Government and KMT employees	399,385	16.95
Students	207,228	8.80
Teachers	177,091	7.52
Others[a]	613,788	26.05
Total	2,356,042	100.00

SOURCE: Wen Man-ying (1988), 16.
[a]Includes professionals, housewives, veterans, active military servicemen, and so on.

workers, the largest vocational group. The second largest group of members were employees of the government or of the KMT apparatus, who accounted for almost 17 percent of the total. Many party members are also recruited from among businessmen and industrialists, peasants and fishermen, students, and teachers, in that order. But despite this large membership, many are inactive, failing to pay membership dues and rarely attending party meetings (Wen Man-Ying 1988, 16).

The KMT's finances depend on income derived from party-affiliated enterprises, membership dues, and government subsidies. The KMT operates at least thirteen enterprises, including the Chunghsing Electronics and Machinery Company, the Central Investment Corporation, the Central Glass and Synthetic Fiber Corporation, the Central News Agency, the Central Daily News, the Broadcasting Corporation of China, and the Central Motion Picture Corporation (*China Yearbook*, 1978, 76; Nan 1988, 22–23; Copper with Chen 1984, 52). Part of the income from these party enterprises is used to finance the central, provincial, and local party operations, which maintain "a cadre of at least 7,000 employees and 378 KMT community service centers throughout the island" (McGregor 1988, 19). Occasionally the party supplements its coffers by soliciting donations from party members who are successful businessmen and industrialists (Ko 1980, 69). Membership dues are set at 1 percent of a member's monthly income, although the actual amount contributed often falls short (Ko 1980, 68). A portion of the membership dues collected by the party cells is retained for their own operation; the rest is transmitted to higher levels of the party. The KMT receives a subsidy from the national government, but actual amounts have never been disclosed.

The Chinese Youth Anti-Communist League

In addition to its already elaborate network of organizations, the KMT maintains a special mass organization known as the Chinese Youth Anti-Communist League (CYACL), which bears a functional resemblance to the Soviet Union's Komsomol and the Communist Youth League in mainland China. Established in Taipei in 1952, the CYACL was not initially a party organization but answered to the General Political Department in the Ministry of Defense. In 1969 its administrative supervision was shifted to the Ministry of the Interior, and it was considered a civic organization devoted to social activism. In fact the CYACL's principal task is to mobilize youth, especially students, under party leadership. Its programs not only emphasize political socialization but also provide cultural and recreational activities for young people on Taiwan.

The CYACL has undergone three stages of organizational development and functional realignment (CYACL 1982, 61–63, 99–120). During the initial phase, 1952–1957, its primary responsibilities were administering reserve officer training programs on college campuses and in high schools and engaging student volunteers in combat drills during summer recess. These military activities were turned over to the Ministry of Education in 1960. During the second phase, 1957–1967, the CYACL abolished individual memberships and adopted a group membership system, with schools as the membership units. The CYACL's activities were reorganized to stress culture, sports, and recreation. A Young Lion Cultural Enterprise Company was founded to publish reading materials for these activities. Since 1967 the CYACL has expanded its highly structured organizational network beyond schools into factories, townships, and even administrative villages, taking on the character of a complex mass organization. To provide permanent facilities for its work, the CYACL built a number of elaborate youth activity centers throughout the island.

From 1952 to 1973 Chiang Ching-kuo assumed personal control of CYACL operations as its first general director. Since 1967 he has had six successors, including Lee Huan and Sung Shih-hsuan. Both have risen to high positions in the KMT, showing the importance of the CYACL in KMT political circles.[2]

Chiang Ching-kuo's personal commitment to the CYACL made it a politically important organization from its founding. Over the years it has expanded to involve a wide variety of young people and has developed a hierarchical structure parallel to the KMT territorial units. Beginning in 1972 the CYACL was charged with organizing the four hundred thousand young workers in the factories. To accomplish this task, it cast itself as a quasi–trade union, offering free services to young workers on matters of labor law and employment. In the rural areas and in Taiwan's eastern hilly regions, where the aborigines concentrate, the CYACL dispatches student teams to provide entertainment and simple health care. Political messages that boost the KMT's image are incorporated in all CYACL activities. Today the CYACL has a full-time staff of close to thirty thousand cadres (Lin Ch'ung-hsuan 1984, 18). Millions of people have participated in its activities at one time or another during their school years and youth.

The CYACL operates its own news wire service, a broadcasting station, several literary journals, nine youth activity centers in Taipei and at resort areas, and scores of commercialized retreat villas and cottages (CYACL 1982, 342–77). According to one estimate from the mid-1980s, these enterprises generated an annual income of close to U.S. $80 million (Li Chien-hsing 1984, 15). Each year the Ministries of Defense, Education, and the Interior as well as the Overseas Affairs Commission extend subsidies to the CYACL, ensuring its budgetary needs (Li Chien-hsing 1984, 13).

Although the youth organization operates under the scrutiny of the KMT, it has acquired an independent power base. The CYACL director is regarded as a powerful position in the KMT hierarchy. Many KMT leaders often hold positions in the CYACL during some phase of their careers. Over the years both Lee Huan and Sung Shih-hsuan have brought into the party apparatus their personal followers from the CYACL, many of whom now occupy important party posts, thus enhancing the power bases of these two men. Moreover, since the CYACL directs youth activities, it occupies a unique position to scrutinize and recruit young talent for the party's future. In short, the CYACL has been much more successful in its work than the PRC's Communist Youth League, which is plagued with overaged leaders and bureaucratism and serves primarily to control students rather than to channel their energies.

Party and Government

From the above discussion it is evident that the KMT plays crucial roles in the ROC's political process. There are interlocking relations among leaders of the party, the government, and the legislative institutions; personnel appointments often overlap and follow a path of interinstitutional circulation. In recent years KMT authorities have tried to reduce the level of party domination over administrative and legislative matters. Government administration is becoming more independent, but the KMT continues to dictate the legislative process through party branches in the legislative chambers. The party also tries to ensure that party policy is enforced in government operations and that interinstitutional conflicts at all levels are reduced to a minimum.

At the central government level, as discussed earlier, the Policy Coordination Committee is charged with resolving conflicts among and within the Legislative Yuan, the Control Yuan, and the National Assembly. It provides an institutional link between the Central Standing Committee and these three representative bodies, where party branches carry out directions from the party center. Party branches also exist within the Executive, Judicial, and Examination yuans. In each of these central government institutions there is a political cell (*cheng-chih hsiao-tsu*) consisting of party members who hold key administrative posts (Huang Yen-tung 1984, 80–81). For instance, in the Executive Yuan, cabinet members form a party political cell that reports directly to the party's Central Standing Committee.

First, at the provincial and local levels the party asserts its influence through three organizational devices in the government and the legislature. At the provincial level the governor and heads of departments and bureaus form a political cell. This pattern is replicated in county and city governments. The main purpose of these groups is to coordinate government administration with party directives. Second, at each level of these legislatures there is a party caucus (*tang-t'uan*) to which all KMT members belong. Each party caucus is headed by a party secretary who coordinates overall legislative action in conjunction with committee chairmen on the floor (Huang Yen-tung 1984, 82). The party secretary in the legislature, the speaker, the deputy speaker, and the legislative committee chairmen, all of whom are party members, form the party caucus's executive committee (*tang-t'uan kan-shih-hui*) (Lerman 1978, 67). The main responsibility of the executive committee is to seek party unity on votes in support of government bills. Third, a political coordination group (*cheng-chih tsung-ho hsiao-tsu*) serves as an interinstitutional link between party headquarters, government offices, and the legislature at each level of territorial administration (Lerman 1978, 83). The groups comprise (1) the party committee chairman and two members of the party committee designated by the chairman, (2) the governor (or mayor or county magistrate) plus two members of the political group appointed by him, and (3) the speaker of the provincial assembly (or local legislative council) plus two assemblymen who are party members.

The objective of these political coordination groups is to foster operational harmony between the party, the administration, and the legislature. As an interinstitutional instrument for conflict mediation, they make certain that disputes, when they occur, do not get out of control. Furthermore, legislative bills initiated by either the government or individual members of the legislature are subject to their review before entering the formal legislative proceedings of debate, amendment, and vote. This institutional device strongly suggests that governing power on Taiwan is not based on a notion of checks and balances but rather is a form of consensual politics emphasizing political harmony and stability. Even at the subcounty level the political coordination groups operate in this fashion. In the rural townships, police chiefs, school principals, general managers of local farmers' associations, and presidents of fishermen's associations are officials involved in ensuring a consensus (Lerman 1978, 83).

The KMT's close ties with the government administration and the legislatures show strong characteristics of a corporate state. But party leaders declared in early 1988 that an internal transformation was under way toward a party of democracy. In the future we can expect the KMT to revise its current operational procedures as well as its relations with the state and the society.

THE POLITICAL OPPOSITION

Despite the KMT's monopoly of power, opposition political groups are gaining strength in Taiwan, although their strength seems fragile at times. The emergence of opposition forces reflects both the legacy of the past and the impact of social change. In the 1950s leading opposition figures were either mainlander liberal intellectuals or those associated with minor political parties on the mainland before 1949. Taiwanese such as Li Wan-chi and Wu San-lien, who were involved in opposition movements, either had lived on the mainland before 1949 or were non-KMT politicians operating within the context of local politics. Some were drawn from the anti-KMT cause in reaction to the massacre of Taiwanese elite by General Ch'en Yi in the February 28, 1947, Incident. By the 1970s opposition movements had passed into the hands of the younger intelligentsia, mostly Taiwanese, who grew to maturity and were educated under KMT rule. Their demands for broader political participation derive from a more complex set of forces than the early movements. A major factor on the Taiwan scene today is the rising level of political expectations of most residents on the island. Taiwan's opposition movements have demonstrated a strong populist tendency, characterized by their antiestablishment political appeals and a pattern of leader-follower relations characteristic of mass society (Wu Nai-te 1988, 3).

In a one-party system the ruling political elite usually resist expanding political participation, particularly when they see it as a threat to their power (Huntington and Dominiquez 1978, 57–61). Studies suggest that a single-party government may respond to demands for greater political participation by repression, mobilization, or limited or full admission to the party system (LaPalombra and Weiner 1966, 401–3). These four responses need not be mutually exclusive.

Repression refers to the application of coercion such as forceful arrest, physical attack, imprisonment, execution, denial of freedom, and systematic surveillance. *Mobilization* means "controlled participation," that is, the government permits or even encourages participation, but only within prescribed limits (LaPalombra and Weiner 1966, 403). *Limited admission* signals a relaxation of rules against any and all organized opposition, allowing an opposition to operate in a quasi-party form. Only the category of *full admission* signals the transformation from a single-party system to a dominant or competitive party system in which repression either disappears or is reduced to unusual or accidental occurrences.

In Taiwan the KMT has preferred mobilization and limited admission in response to popular demands for greater political participation. Elections have been held regularly, with a gradual increase in the number and importance of contested offices. Since the early 1980s opposition groups have been allowed to assume a quasi-party form to nominate candidates and to campaign. In the fall of 1986 the opposition Democratic Progressive Party was formally organized without immediate official repression even though it was technically illegal. By 1988 Taiwan seemed to have crossed a threshold as it allowed the full admission of an organized opposition into the political system.

Nonetheless, the authorities periodically resort to repression when opposition activities exceed the limits of the KMT's tolerance. The arrest of Lei Chen and others in 1960 on the eve of the formation of the opposition China Democratic Party and the repression of *tangwai* (nonparty) leaders after the Kaohsiung Incident in December 1979 are well known.

Politically Taiwan's opposition falls into two categories. The first are two small but legal satellite parties—the Young China Party (YCP) and the Democratic Socialist Party (DSP)—both formed in China before 1949. These parties do not challenge KMT rule, however, and are regarded as the KMT's "party friends" (*tang you*). Their leaders are aging mainlanders; their activities are said to have diminished over the years

(Chang Ch'un-hua 1986, 44). The second category includes the newly formed opposition parties and, before 1986, the so-called *tangwai* movement that emerged in the 1970s. This movement specifically avoided the formation of a political party, but instead was composed of individuals and independent candidates whose chief bond was their lack of membership in the KMT. In 1986 most of these nonparty elements joined in organizing the Democratic Progressive Party, and in 1987 a few opposition activists formed the Labor Party.

The Satellites

Both the YCP and the DSP are small and relatively inactive. With few exceptions, their leaders were over 70 years old by the mid-1980s. Their combined popular vote in elections totals about 1 percent. Since their members sometimes encounter discrimination in public schools, administrative agencies, and banks, few are attracted to enroll (Jacobs 1981, 2). Both parties reportedly receive a monthly stipend of about N.T. $2 million, or U.S. $66,000, from the KMT government (K'ou 1983, 29; Chang Ch'un-hua 1986, 44). Most observers consider that the only political purpose of these two parties in the past was to validate the ROC's claim that it was not a one-party authoritarian state. On Taiwan they are described as "flower vase political parties" (*hua-p'ing cheng-tang*) because they are only for show. Some of their Taiwanese members, disenchanted with the ineptness of their leaders, joined forces with the *tangwai* movement.

Of the two, the YCP—founded in 1923 and with an estimated ten thousand members—is the more active (Chiang Ping-lun 1985, 5). As of 1987 their members held 7 nonelective seats in the Legislative Yuan and 45 in the National Assembly (Nan 1987a, 26). Since the 1950s its Taiwanese members have had a reputation for being involved in opposition movements. In 1960 Li Wan-chü and Kuo Yu-hsin—two YCP members—joined an abortive attempt to form a new China Democratic Party. To reactivate the party a YCP Democratic Reformation Committee was formed in 1980, but it quickly faltered before achieving concrete results (Chiang Ping-lun 1985, 5). Two years later a group of Taiwanese members failed in their attempt to challenge the YCP's aging mainlander leadership. Following the ROC's 1986–1987 political reforms, this party could regroup and enter the political arena with a fresh outlook. Whether the YCP could become a genuine opposition party depends on its ability to formulate an appealing platform, develop a social base, and produce new leaders with indigenous ties. The prospects appear gloomy.

The DSP, established in Shanghai in 1946, claims a membership of six thousand, most of whom have been inactive for over three decades

(Chiang Ping-lun 1985, 5). Its active membership may not exceed a thousand (*SPCK*, November 22, 1986, 44). Nevertheless, the DSP occupies 25 seats in the National Assembly, 4 in the Legislative Yuan, and 3 in the Control Yuan (Nan 1987a, 26). In ideology the party resembles European democratic socialism (Chang Ch'un-hua 1986, 43). Although six members have managed to win election as mayors, in recent years the party has not competed in Taiwan's electoral politics. In the national representative bodies DSP members, like their YCP counterparts, are rubber stamps for the KMT.

Frustrated by the aging leaders' procrastination on party renovation, young members of both parties have recently sought to revitalize themselves as a third force in Taiwan politics. In 1985 Hsieh Hsueh-hsien, a YCP parliamentarian, joined with Hsieh Cheng-i, a DSP leader in the Taipei party branch, and Li Ken-tao, a defector from the PRC, to form a new political group. In a statement published that year they argued that democratization in Taiwan would help stimulate democratic reform on the mainland and thus lay the ground for peaceful unification in the future (Chang Ch'un-hua 1986, 43). The generation gap in the satellite parties seems to presage the demise of the YCP and DSP, but only time will tell whether a new party with a substantial following will rise in their stead.

Opposition Movements Before 1977

Since the YCP and the DSP are mainlander-dominated parties, their grass-roots support on Taiwan has never been strong. They have contributed little to the growth of opposition political movements on the island nation. Historically opposition movements with a Taiwanese base have had two general stages of development, with 1977 as the turning point. Opposition movements before 1977 can be divided into mainlander and Taiwanese groups. The mainlanders concentrated their activities around the *Free China Journal*, which began publication in 1949 to promote political reform and a genuine constitutional democracy (Wei 1985, 344–46). Managed by a distinguished and forthright intellectual, Lei Chen, *Free China* attracted literary contributions from a group of liberal intellectuals such as Yin Hai-kuang, Mao Tzu-shui, and Chang Fu-ch'uan, who had established reputations on the mainland before coming to Taiwan. They idolized the philosopher-diplomat Hu Shih as their spiritual leader. Their reform program bore the strong imprint of Anglo-American liberalism, which Hu Shih had attempted to adapt and promote in China. The *Free China* group wanted the KMT authorities to replace the one-party dictatorship with a constitutional democracy (Lei

Chen 1952, 209–11). Articles in their magazine were often highly critical of the KMT, but *Free China* existed more as a literary forum than as a political journal of an organized opposition. None of the journal's editors was Taiwanese. Most contributors were not involved directly in electoral politics.

In contrast, a group of native politicians tried to win electoral contests against KMT candidates. These men—Wu San-lien, Li Wan-chü, Kao Yu-shih, Yang Chin-fu, Kuo Yu-hsin, and Kuo Kuo-chi—made individual electoral gains in their separate territorial bases in Taiwan's counties and municipalities, but overall they lacked the coherent party organization needed to challenge KMT power. In part this weakness reflected Taiwan's electoral policies in the 1950s, when all elections were at subnational and local levels, so no nationwide opposition could emerge.

In 1958 these local politicians organized the Association for the Study of China's Local Self-government to reform what they saw as corrupt electoral politics in Taiwan (*LHYK*, August 1983, 116; Yang Hsi-sheng 1983, 29). Their moderate effort fell short of organizing a party structure to challenge the KMT authorities. Nevertheless, the KMT refused to accept the association even as a civic organization. In 1960 these Taiwanese joined with Lei Chen and others in an attempt to form the China Democratic Party. As the formal announcement of the new party approached, political tension increased. Hu Shih retreated from his initial enthusiasm for the new party and expressed reluctance to back the new group at this critical juncture (Lei 1978, 328–29; Yang Hsi-sheng 1983, 40). Li Wan-chü, another key figure, became embroiled in serious financial trouble in connection with *Kung-lun pao* (Public Forum), a newspaper he published. The effort died when Lei Chen was arrested on September 4, 1960, on a highly questionable charge of associating with communist agents (Lei 1978, 278–90; Yang Hsi-sheng 1983, 43–44). The movement then quickly evaporated, and the KMT thus successfully blocked the first serious effort on Taiwan to create a real opposition party.

In retrospect the China Democratic Party affair was a watershed in the history of political opposition movements on Taiwan. Political opposition subsided on the island; even the intellectual ferment associated with liberalism was stifled for almost two decades. The only political episode of significance in the 1960s occurred in 1964, when Peng Ming-min—a Taiwan University professor—and his two students, Hsieh Ts'ung-min and Wei T'ing-ch'ao, were arrested for attempting to distribute anti-KMT materials (Peng Ming-min 1972, 125–74).[3] Political opposition activists were badly shaken by these two events and stopped trying to organize or lead political movements. The only surviving electoral challenges to KMT authority came from individuals who ran against KMT candidates in provincial and local elections. During the sobering years of the 1960s and the early 1970s, two periodicals—*Apollo (Wen-hsing)*, published from 1957 to 1965, and *The Intellectual (Ta-hsüeh tsa-chih)*, first published in 1968—kept the reformist flame alive, but their impact was slight (Jacobs, 1981, 37; Wei 1985, 357–69). Two major contributors to *Apollo*, Li Ao and Po Yang, were imprisoned for their opposition to KMT dominance. *The Intellectual* generated some popular excitement in the early 1970s when it pressed for political reform, but its liberal-minded editorial board was dominated by young KMT members. Also *The Intellectual* never attracted a mass following. Some of its leading figures were co-opted into the KMT power structure through patronage and left the journal. A few, like Chang Chun-hung and Hsu Hsin-liang, later switched loyalties to a political opposition group and embarked on careers in local electoral politics.

The Opposition Since 1977

Opposition politics in Taiwan has always involved the publication of political journals. Until the 1970s the writers and editors of intellectual magazines such as *Free China* and *Apollo* were usually mainlander intelligentsia. These people lacked a potential voter base, so they generally refrained from seeking elected office or from engaging in commonplace political activism. They were preoccupied with issues concerning all of China, not just Taiwan (Huang Kuang-kuo 1987, 6–9). Events in the mid-1970s changed all that. From then on, the Taiwanese have become the primary source of political activists and are newly important in both the literary activities and the electoral politics of the opposition movements. A growing number of second-generation mainlanders have also joined the opposition's ranks.

The first of the new-style political journals came out in 1975 when K'ang Ning-hsiang and his associates published the *Taiwan Political Review (Tai-wan Cheng-lun)*, with Chang Chun-hung as its chief editor. After only five issues, government censorship closed down the journal. K'ang and Chiang Ch'un-nan subsequently published another journal, *The Eighties (Pa-shih nien-tai)*, which expressed more moderate opposition views. The militant activists began a separate journal, *Formosa (Mei-li-tao)*, in August 1979 to criticize KMT authorities and to press for fundamental political reform. While K'ang's group proceeded cautiously in challenging KMT dominance, the *Formosa* group was more assertive. Leading members of the *Formosa* group included Yao Chia-wen, Chang Chun-hung, Huang Hsin-chieh, Hsu Hsin-liang, and Lin Yi-hsiung, all of whom belong to the generation of Taiwanese brought up and educated under KMT rule. Young (mostly in their thirties) and with a strong sense of their Taiwanese heritage, they were reluctant to identify with the Chinese mainland and a government structured to rule the mainland. This group has a character distinct from the mainlander intelligentsia of the 1950s and 1960s. In 1977 political candidates associated with the Taiwanese intelligentsia scored impressive victories as a new *tangwai* (nonparty) by winning 21 of the 77 seats in the Taiwan Provincial Assembly and 4 of the 20 magistrate and mayoral races (Jacobs 1981, 27). In the central Taiwan town of Chungli, a mass protest against alleged irregularities in vote counting touched off a serious clash between angry voters and the police (Lin and Chang 1978, 240–79). A district police station was burned, and a number of casualties were reported. The incident signaled a growing popular disenchantment with the KMT's domination in electoral politics. Since then the opposition movement has revived, led by the *tangwai* activists.

Following the Chungli Incident, Taiwan experienced the two turbulent political years of 1978 and 1979. In December 1978 the entire nation was stunned by the Carter administration's decision to normalize diplomatic relations with the PRC. Only a few days before the announcement, on December 5, the *tangwai* leadership had gathered in Taipei for a well-publicized political conference to create a sense of opposition unity (Yang Hsi-sheng 1983, 51). Encouraged by the results of the 1977 election, the *tangwai* leaders looked forward with optimism to broadening mass support through electoral campaigns. They hoped to make considerable gains in the 1978 elections for seats in the national parliament. But the elections were canceled after the U.S. decision to cut off diplomatic relations with the ROC government.

Beginning in the spring of 1979 the *tangwai* held a series of high-profile public rallies. Once *Formosa* began publication in August, the *tangwai* became bolder and increasingly extended opposition activism to street protests and mass assemblies. The journal became their rallying symbol and at its peak boasted a circulation of over one hundred thousand (Jacobs 1981, 38). Throughout the island "service offices" for the magazine quickly sprang up to serve as the local offices of *tangwai* activists. The establishment of these offices brought confrontations with the police and security forces. As the pace of political mass action quickened, KMT authorities grew seriously alarmed. On December 10 *Formosa's* office in Kaohsiung organized a rally to promote human rights. It was intended to be a prelude for an even larger public demonstration scheduled for December 16 in Taipei. The Kaohsiung rally culminated in a street confrontation between the participants and the police that quickly developed into an unexpected riot known as the Kaohsiung Incident. Scores of policemen and civilians were injured (Kaplan 1981, 16–20, 34–38).

Almost fifty hours later, leaders of the *Formosa* group—Huang Hsin-chieh, Yao Chia-wen, Chang Chun-hung, Lin Yi-hsiung, Lu Hsiu-lien, Chen Chu, and Lin Hung-hsuan—and dozens of other local activists throughout Taiwan were arrested. Shih Ming-te, the mastermind of the Kaohsiung rally, initially avoided arrest but was eventually captured. (His brief escape implicated Reverend Kao Chun-ming, head of the Presbyterian Church, who had offered Shih sanctuary in his home on humanitarian grounds.) These eight defendants—often referred to as the Kaohsiung Eight—were brought to trial in military court on March 18, 1980. After six days of semi-open hearings, during which each defendant testified in the absence of the others, the military tribunal sentenced the defendants to prison terms of from twelve years to life. Thirty-three minor defendants were tried in civilian court in April and received lighter sentences (Tien 1980, 61).

Evidence concerning the incident remains circumstantial. The government's charge that the defendants had instigated the riots seems dubious, although they had clearly organized the rally (Kaplan 1981, 39–42). The authorities argued that the incident was part of a plot to overthrow the government. Impartial analysts such as John Kaplan of the Stanford Law School believe otherwise, however, particularly because several of the eight key defendants did not arrive in Kaohsiung until the closing phase of the rioting (Kaplan 1981, 39–42).

The Kaohsiung Incident cannot be fully understood from the court proceedings, which cast it as an illegal challenge to public security. Rather, the Kaohsiung Incident was a political event in which the *tangwai* movement challenged the KMT monopoly of power both by holding a public demonstration and by revealing the autocratic nature of KMT rule in the trial itself. In most democracies disturbances such as the Kaohsiung Incident would not have led to such severe repression. The trial also disclosed that brutal methods might have been used to force the defendants to sign confessions prepared by the interrogators. The authorities' handling of the incident may have been especially severe because the Kaohsiung rally occurred when the shocking effects of Carter's diplomatic announcement preoccupied the KMT leaders' minds.

At any rate, the Kaohsiung Incident is a well-remembered event in the history of confrontations between the KMT and the *tangwai*. Neither the trial nor the sentences curtailed the opposition movement; they merely slowed the tempo of demands for political liberalization. In the two years after the incident, the *tangwai* recuperated and pressed ahead with its objectives to broaden electoral participation and distribute non-

party political journals. The relatives and defense lawyers for the Kaohsiung Incident defendants joined the ranks of the opposition movement,
carrying on the work of the *Formosa* group. K'ang Ning-hsiang (who was
also in Kaohsiung at the time of the incident but was never arrested) and
his moderate associates reemerged as champions of the democratization
movement but adopted a less confrontational, more conciliatory approach to KMT authority.

Toward an Organized Opposition

Since the Kaohsiung Incident, the *tangwai* movement has developed
unevenly. Fragmentation and internal conflict between militants and
moderates have sometimes brought the movement to the verge of anar-
chy; at other moments there seems to be hope for unity of action. This
zigzag pattern makes clear that the opposition requires a party organizational structure to unify its divergent ranks.

In the 1981 election, Legislative Yuan member and *tangwai* leader
K'ang Ning-hsiang initiated the practice of having the *tangwai* movement
endorse candidates for public office. In the following year K'ang and his
moderate associates—Chang Teh-ming and Huang Huang-hsiung—
were denounced publicly by the militant activists for their "conciliatory
stance" toward the KMT authorities in the Legislative Yuan. In 1982
K'ang invited *tangwai* activists and a number of reformist scholars to a
public rally at which a "common political demand" was adopted. One
year later a group of *tangwai* elected officials formed a campaign committee (*hou-yuan-hui*) to serve as an organizational arm in elections. A so-
called new generation of *tangwai*—younger and more militant—
organized a separate association for *tangwai* editors and writers in an apparent move of defiance (Ch'iu 1984d, 35). This splinter group reportedly had 150 members in 1985. Finally a third organization was formed
in Kaohsiung by several marginal *tangwai* politicians and supporters
(*TWMP*, August 24, 1985, 1). The divisiveness of this tripartite grouping
undermined the *tangwai*'s image in the eyes of the public and is believed
to have led to the defeat of K'ang and his incumbent associates in the
1983 parliamentary elections.

Out of the chaos and frustration the *tangwai* forces experienced in the
1983 election came a renewed push for unity. In February 1984 about
twenty elected *tangwai* legislators, provincial assemblymen, and Taipei
city councilmen formed the Association of Tangwai Elected Officials for
the Study of Public Policy. The association included several opposition
leaders, such as legislators Hsu Jung-shu (Mrs. Chang Chun-hung),
Chiang P'eng-chien, Fei Hsi-p'ing, Yu Ch'ing, Chou Ch'ing-yu (Mrs.

Yao Chia-wen), Fang Shih-min (Mrs. Lin Yi-hsiung), Chen Shui-pien, and Lin Cheng-chieh. Criticized for excluding nonelected officials, it was subsequently renamed the Association of Public Policy Studies (APPS) to encompass a broader membership base.

Several major developments in 1985–1987 had profound implications for the opposition movement. In the November 1985 elections—for city mayors, county magistrates, and provincial assemblymen—a Tangwai Election Campaign Committee was instituted to nominate candidates for public office. The new group openly used the label *tangwai* and was better organized so that it functioned much like a party. The government did not react with repressive measures to this *tangwai* political initiative.

Furthermore, beginning in March 1986, the Association of Public Policy Studies, under Yu Ch'ing's leadership, began to organize local branch associations (Chang and Lin 1986, 59–60). In April the KMT leadership called for a total crackdown on the unregistered APPS movement unless its activities were curtailed, but the KMT reversed its position on May 10 after a meeting with the *tangwai* leaders (*FCJ*, May 19, 1986, 1). The *tangwai* probably would have pressed ahead with the formation of branch offices even at the risk of confrontation with the authorities.

By the end of June 1986 the *tangwai* had instituted thirteen local chapters throughout the island, giving the APPS an appearance of a party rather than a loose coalition of opposition groups. Throughout the summer several *tangwai* leaders held secret meetings to plan the formation of an opposition party. A new party was finally born on September 28 at a convention in Taipei to nominate candidates for the forthcoming parliamentary elections. In the course of deliberations the 132 delegates at the convention unanimously approved a motion to form the new Democratic Progressive Party, even though such a party was still illegal in Taiwan (Lin Chin-k'un 1986b, 7–9).

On November 10 the DPP held its first party congress. The 165 delegates present, nearly all *tangwai* activists, adopted a party constitution and a party platform; they also elected 31 members to the Central Executive Committee (CEC) and 11 members to the Central Advisory Committee. At the CEC's first plenum, held the same day, Chiang P'eng-chien, a lawyer and member of the Legislative Yuan, was elected party chairman; 10 others were also elected to the CEC Standing Committee, the party's highest decisionmaking body (*SPCK*, November 15, 1986, 6–9). The chairman, who serves for one year, has little statutory power and is supposed to exercise collective leadership.

The party constitution gives the DPP an organizational structure similar to the KMT but stresses democratic processes within the party rather than the Leninist principle of democratic centralism. The party platform of 139 articles delineates the opposition's views on foreign policy, defense, civil liberties, political reform, and economic policy (*MCJP*, November 7, 1986, 2). The platform advocates a more flexible foreign policy, including an effort by Taiwan to reenter the United Nations. It calls for revamping Taiwan's defense structure and reducing the armed forces. Naturally it opposes the PRC's one-party dictatorship, but it also proclaims a strong opposition to any form of totalitarian dictatorship. The last element is an affirmation of anticommunism, a vital point if the DPP hopes to avoid suppression under the laws of the ROC. While denouncing violence, the new party emphasizes the necessity for sweeping political reforms, including retiring all members of the three national representative bodies not popularly elected on Taiwan. In its socioeconomic policies, the party endorses social services connected with the welfare state but favors free enterprise. The most controversial article is the party's call for self-determination for Taiwan's residents regarding their political future (*CP*, November 7, 1986, 1). The KMT authorities denounced this article for conflicting with the national policy of reunification with the mainland.

Reactions from the authorities on the "premature birth" of the DPP were mild. The KMT would have preferred the new party to emerge after the government had revised the laws on political organizations. Since the *tangwai* coalesced into the DPP before this revision was complete, the ruling party had either to suppress the DPP or to accept its extralegal existence (Mooney 1986, 19–20; Goldstein 1986a, 28–29). In the end the authorities chose the middle course of de facto acquiescence, a conciliatory gesture that was widely approved.

Whether the DPP can become a viable opposition party depends on its ability to foster internal unity, substantially enlarge its membership, and increase its share of parliamentary seats and the popular vote in the next election, scheduled for late 1989. Internal factions, which the party inherited from the *tangwai*, persist. The most divisive issue concerns whether or not to advocate Taiwan independence in the party platform. The militants, represented by National Assemblyman Hung Ch'i-ch'ang and DPP Deputy Secretary-General Ch'iu Yi-jen, favor independence. But a majority of the 31 members of the DPP Central Executive Committee are inclined to sidestep this issue for fear that a formal endorsement of independence would provoke KMT oppression and/or PRC military action. In the Second Party Congress held on November 9–10, 1987, the DPP failed to adopt a resolution that would have included "freedom of advocating Taiwan independence" in the party platform (Kuan 1987, 16–19; Yang Hsien-ts'un et al. 1987, 18–20; Goldstein 1987c, 40). However, the party has categorically rejected the PRC's claim to Taiwan.[4]

The issue of Taiwan independence, of course, will not easily be resolved. On the contrary, it will plague DPP leaders and activists alike. Part of the problem is that the pro-independence faction receives strong backing from the overseas Taiwan independence movement, centered in the United States. It also gains support from leaders of the Taiwan Presbyterian Church and released political prisoners. The KMT's decision to legalize visits to relatives on the mainland since the fall of 1987 has intensified concerns over an eventual KMT-CCP reconciliation. Discussing the issue of Taiwan independence has become all the more urgent lest political deals be made secretly between authorities in Beijing and Taipei without public knowledge. A majority of DPP leaders, such as party chairman Huang Hsin-chieh, remain convinced that a pro-independence platform would scare off many potential party members and voters, making the DPP strictly a party of Taiwan independence. They prefer a concentrated effort to push for further political liberalization and democratic reforms. The KMT authorities have threatened the advocates of Taiwan independence with harsh penalties. On January 16, 1988, the Taipei high court sentenced Ts'ai Yu-ch'uan and Hsu Ts'ao-teh to eleven and ten years respectively for promoting Taiwan independence (*MCJP*, January 17, 1988, 3). President Lee Teng-hui reiterated the official position that activities promoting Taiwan independence are illegal and will be punished.[5] Moreover, the PRC has said that Taiwan independence would constitute a major reason for Beijing to take military action against Taiwan.

The DPP faces a serious dilemma. The issue of Taiwan independence could eventually cause the new party to split apart. Even without an open split, the party is unlikely to avoid serious factionalism. With fewer than ten thousand party members in 1988, its growth potential could be severely hampered as elements of the DPP press for street actions to politicize the independence issue. Yao Chia-wen, DPP ex-chairman during 1987–1988, has pledged to reconcile internal differences, but the prospects remain uncertain. In the end the party has to decide whether it will develop into a responsible opposition party of democracy or continue to serve merely as a political instrument for Taiwan independence and other protest movements. In the latter case, the DPP would look increasingly like a mission-oriented revolutionary party with a goal of rearranging the current constitutional order. If that happens, the authorities would no longer tolerate it as an opposition party.

The Labor Party (Kungtang)

The Labor Party was established in December 1987. Its membership of about 500 in early 1988 and a limited core of activists make the party substantially smaller than the DPP. Nonetheless, this party, like the DPP, has an indigenous social base that could provide an important source of membership. The Labor Party's manifesto proclaims its hope of becoming the principal political vehicle for the 7.7-million-strong industrial work force of Taiwan (Hoon 1988c, 18). As Taiwan's employer-worker disputes intensify, an autonomous trade union movement has emerged to focus on workers' problems. The Labor Party could gradually provide leadership for this trade union movement or could simply ride on it. As in other industrialized democracies, the party could become structurally linked with certain organized unions if properly managed under able leadership.

The initial founders of the party were socialist intellectuals, concerned academics, and labor activists. Wang Yi-hsiung, the party chairman and a labor lawyer, is a member of the Legislative Yuan representing the industrial city of Kaohsiung. He was a DPP member until the summer of 1987. The party's vice chairman, Lou Mei-wen, is a veteran factory activist from the militant unions of Far Eastern Synthetic Fibers in Hsinchu.[6] Su Ch'ing-li, the party's secretary-general, has been an active member of the Summer Tide Association (*hsia-ch'ao lien-yi-hui*), a group of socialist intellectuals who favor eventual political unification with the mainland. This diverse leadership has made it difficult for the party to articulate a common platform. The left-wing intellectuals have had almost no experience in dealing with labor problems. Their political goal of unification with the mainland is directly at odds with the labor activists' concern for the material interests and collective bargaining rights of the workers on Taiwan.

Unlike similar parties in Europe and Japan, the Labor Party has not adopted a clear-cut ideology based on socialism, presumably to protect itself from charges of being soft on communism, which "would put it at loggerheads with the stridently anti-communist KMT" (Hoon 1988c, 18). In Taiwan's political environment the party has to tone down its ideological coloring by focusing on the more pragmatic issues of free unionism, wage and benefit disputes, and industrial health and hazards. In early 1988 the party was preoccupied with promoting independent trade unions and establishing party branches in southern Taiwan and a few industrial regions in the north (*CKSP*, January 4, 1988, 2). Grass-roots organizational work has been handicapped by a shortage of funds and a small activist core. Despite its intention, the Labor Party will not have a free hand in organizing labor support. Both the KMT and the DPP have strengthened their footholds in the industrial work force. The KMT has established party branches for industrial workers in Kaohsiung and in Taipei, Keelung, and Taoyuan counties, and a provincial party branch exclusively for recruiting workers may soon be established (Yang Tu 1987, 77). The DPP has declared its support for workers' democracy in state enterprises and has helped organize labor petitions (*CKSP*, October 26, 1987, 2). Competition from these two parties would limit the Labor Party's organization drive.

Still, the Labor Party is a natural ally of the workers. In employer-worker disputes it can take a firm stand for workers' interests. In contrast, the KMT has to protect the interests of both state enterprises and large private industries. Meanwhile the DPP has adopted a party platform closely linked to the interests of medium and small enterprises. Of the three, only the Labor Party has appealed chiefly for the workers' support. That focus alone could make it an important party to reckon with, particularly with the rise of independent trade unions.

CONCLUSION

By 1988 events had indicated the possibility of a transition from a one-party system to some kind of competitive party system on Taiwan. But in the foreseeable future there is little possibility for the DPP or the Labor Party to achieve equal status with the ruling KMT in either party membership or electoral strength. The KMT will continue to dominate all levels of institutional power, particularly in the armed forces, the police, and other security forces. Because the ROC's president, vice president, and premier and Taiwan's provincial governor are not subject to popular elections, the DPP cannot gain control over these powerful executive posts. Furthermore, the DPP—the emerging major opposition party—still faces the formidable challenge of holding together its own diverse factions. Divisions within the DPP follow ideological lines, reflect practical political differences on how to deal with the KMT or differences between mainland and Taiwan identities, or are based on personal experiences in the Kaohsiung Incident. A membership drive had enrolled only a few thousand regular members by early 1988, indicating much more modest support than most had predicted. A majority of the present DPP legislators are reluctant to endorse a party strategy that stresses confrontational politics through street rallies and protests, as advocated by the militant activists. Like Chinese politics in general, DPP politics is permeated with the drama of personal bonds and antagonism propelled by group divisions and locally based political interests.

The KMT's response to the growing challenge of the DPP also remains uncertain. KMT authorities have expressed their desire to see a smooth transition to a competitive party system, provided that the opposition leaders denounce independence for Taiwan and adopt a firm anticommunist policy. Such conditions have not been acceptable to opposition leaders. Meanwhile, there is a definite dissension within KMT ranks regarding the party's conciliatory attitude toward the DPP. Chiang Ching-kuo was the principal force behind the KMT reforms in the 1980s. After his death in January 1988, the KMT commitment to political conciliation was reaffirmed by Lee Teng-hui. Nonetheless, the political climate in the post–Chiang Ching-kuo era remains cloudy. If power falls into the hands of party conservatives, military and security leaders, and some economic technocrats, all of whom favor restrictive measures against the opposition, the political situation will heat up (Chou and Nathan 1987, 297). So far President Lee has been able to remain conciliatory toward the opposition despite dissension within KMT ranks.

Despite political uncertainty, there is little doubt that Taiwan politics has entered a new stage. Institutional changes will probably put an end to the one-party system. But given the KMT's predominant authority and command of resources, the emerging party system will probably not change the political balance between the ruling party and the opposition. Instead, more intraparty pluralism could appear within the KMT as it seeks to foster party unity between mainlanders and Taiwanese and between older and younger members. The future interaction between the KMT and the opposition party or parties may follow the pattern of dominant-party systems such as Mexico, where the ruling Institutional Revolutionary Party has won all national elections. Such a prospect may dampen optimism for a pluralistic democracy with full-fledged party competition. Yet the structural transformation of Taiwan's party system marks a dramatic step toward democratization.

— 5 —

The Government

The government on Taiwan is neither organized nor operated exactly as specified in the ROC constitution. So-called temporary provisions and emergency decrees—issued as a consequence of the hostility between the KMT and the Chinese Communists on the mainland—supplement or replace many key constitutional articles. Their combined effect on government operations is so important that the entire shape of the government departs from the constitution. As long as tense relations with the People's Republic of China continue and the KMT authorities maintain their claim of sovereign jurisdiction over the mainland, the Taipei regime will function more or less as an emergency regime and the constitutional order of government cannot be fully restored. In consequence, these temporary and emergency provisions retard Taiwan's political evolution into a constitutionally based representative democracy.

Furthermore, there is unnecessary duplication in administrative structure and in the division of authority between the national government and the provincial government of Taiwan, particularly in education, transportation, police, finance, and economic affairs. The resulting redundant staffing and functional confusion have been partially alleviated by a gradual rationalization of administrative jurisdictions, but the contradiction of having two governments—national and provincial—over essentially the same territory cannot totally be resolved unless the provincial government is eliminated as a separate entity and its structure absorbed into the national government. Such a prospect is unlikely in the near future because of the KMT's one-China policy, under which Taiwan is both a de facto national identity and a province of China.

CONSTITUTIONAL ORDER

The government structure of the Republic of China should follow the constitution promulgated in 1947. But the actual operation of the government on Taiwan has always been circumscribed by a series of emergency laws, administrative decrees, and interpretations by the grand justices of the Judicial Yuan, whose functions are like those of the U.S. Supreme Court. When the constitution was adopted, China was in the midst of civil war; then in 1949 the ROC government was forced from the mainland. Such extraordinary circumstances compelled the Nationalist authorities to modify the governing structure and procedure when they arrived on Taiwan. Consequently Taiwan's political system is subject to many extralegal constraints unforeseen in 1947. The authority of the ROC on Taiwan and the Taiwan government's structure derive from both the constitution and numerous extralegal constraints issued on the basis of Taiwan's state of emergency.

Article 1 of the 1947 constitution states that the ROC is founded on Sun Yat-sen's Three Principles of the People and thus is a democratic republic of the people, to be governed by the people and for the people. Although the drafters of this constitution disagreed over the authority and operating procedures of the national government's component parts, there was little doubt that Sun Yat-sen's teachings should provide the basis for the constitution. Thus the government's structure should fulfill Sun's belief in popular democracy and a system of checks and balances between the government's branches. The Chinese government Sun Yat-sen envisioned synthesized Chinese tradition and Western parliamentary democracy (Hu 1985, 4–5).

The ROC government organization is a cross between Western presidential and parliamentary systems and some institutional structures derived from imperial China. Governmental powers are divided among seven institutions: the president, the Executive Yuan, the Legislative Yuan, the Control Yuan, the Examination Yuan, the Judicial Yuan, and the National Assembly. The president is the head of state and also performs some of the functions of a chief executive.[1] He and the vice president are elected by the National Assembly to serve six-year terms. The National Assembly, the Legislative Yuan, and the Control Yuan are all representative bodies. Besides the authority to elect the president and vice president, the National Assembly's other principal authority is to

adopt constitutional amendments. The Legislative Yuan is given legislative powers commonly found in the parliaments of Western democracies,
including approval of the government's budget. The Control Yuan is a
peculiar Chinese institution from the days of dynastic government. It has
the powers of consent, impeachment, censure, and audit and is meant to
check malfeasance and corruption.

The Executive Yuan is equivalent to the cabinet in parliamentary democracies. Headed by the premier, it shares the executive powers of government with the president. The premier is nominated and, with the
consent of the Legislative Yuan, appointed by the president. The Executive Yuan administers ordinary government business through the administrative bureaucracy, composed largely of civil servants. It supervises the
government administrations at provincial, municipal, and county levels.
Personnel matters involving the civil service are under the jurisdiction of
the Examination Yuan, another institution derived from traditional Chinese practices. Its responsibilities include the recruitment of civil servants
through examination and matters involving salary scales, tenure, and
pensions. Finally, the Judicial Yuan is the highest judicial organ of the
state. It supervises the conduct of judges at all levels of the administrative
hierarchy. As in the French system, ROC judges are government employees recruited through competitive examination. The Judicial Yuan's
grand justices can also exercise the authority of judicial review over the
laws of the land, including the interpretation of the constitution.

The jurisdiction of each major government body is clearly delineated
in the constitution based on the principle of a division of powers. The
constitution also establishes a unitary form of government in that the
provincial and local governments are subject to the direct administrative
control and supervision of the central government. The limits of jurisdiction for the central, provincial, and local governments are spelled out
in the constitution (Articles 107–28). Although hierarchical, these levels
perform overlapping functions, with the central government holding
overall operational supervision. The central government may delegate
authority to lower-level governments, but there is no autonomy of
power at the provincial or local levels. On such critical matters as government personnel, budget, taxation, and policy formation, the provincial and local governments have only rudimentary authority. In short,
they do not have the kind of autonomy permitted in federal systems.

The constitution also lists the important civil liberties and individual
rights common to citizens in a democracy (Articles 9–24). Included are
freedoms of speech, assembly and association, writing and publication,
and religious belief as well as privacy of correspondence and the rights to
work, own property, receive citizens' education, and hold public office.

But although the ROC constitution resembles that of most democratic countries in the world in its regard for constitutional protection under a bill of rights, many of these freedoms and rights are circumscribed and limited by restrictions based on emergency provisions. Accordingly the democratic principles of the constitutional structure have succumbed to authoritarian governmental practice.

THE TEMPORARY PROVISIONS AND MARTIAL LAW

Until 1987 civil rights in the ROC were severely limited by at least sixteen laws, decrees, and judicial interpretations (Hu 1985, 6–23). Among them, the Provision Amendments for the Period of Mobilization of the Communist Rebellion and martial law had the most profound effects on the scope of governmental power and sociopolitical life on the island. The Provisional Amendments for the Period of Mobilization of the Suppression of Communist Rebellion, commonly known as the temporary provisions, were promulgated by the ROC on the mainland on May 10, 1948. Since then the provisions have been amended three times, in 1960, 1966, and 1972. The effect of these provisions and amendments was to broaden presidential power, giving the president an unlimited authority unintended by the framers of the constitution.

In 1948 the declaration of a state of emergency was justified by the ongoing civil war. The KMT leaders believed that extraordinary presidential power was necessary in the face of a national crisis. The provisions heightened the emergency power already given to the president in Articles 39 and 43 of the constitution (Li Hung-hsi 1983, 30). Still, the continuing application of these temporary provisions for several decades has raised controversy. Many people believe the military and political situation in Taiwan no longer justifies the president's emergency powers. The lessening of both military and political tensions across the Taiwan Strait supports this view.

The temporary provisions permit the president and vice president's tenure in office to exceed indefinitely the two-term restriction prescribed in the constitution. The president is empowered to make changes in the organization and personnel of the central government. He may also authorize additional members to be elected or appointed (in the case of overseas Chinese) to the three national representative bodies—the National Assembly, the Legislative Yuan, and the Control Yuan. The late President Chiang Ching-kuo used this authority to add the so-called supplementary representative members, elected by Taiwan voters, thus increasing Taiwan's representation above that constitutionally prescribed for the province. In that instance the temporary provisions were used to broaden the representation of the regime without restructuring the three outdated representative bodies.

More commonly, the temporary provisions give the president the power to "take emergency measures to avert an imminent danger to the security of the state or of the people—without being subject to the procedural restrictions prescribed in Article 39 or Article 43 of the constitution" (Article 1 of the temporary provisions). The president thus gains practically unlimited authority.

Perhaps the most important institutional outgrowth of the temporary provisions was the creation of the National Security Council (NSC) in 1967. The NSC was established at the order of the president to make policy decisions regarding "national mobilization and suppression of the communist rebellion (Article 4).[2] The president presides over NSC meetings. The other members are the vice president; the secretary-general of the Office of the President; the chief of the president's military staff (*ts'an-chun-chang*); the premier; the vice premier; the ministers of defense, foreign affairs, and finance and economic affairs; the chief of the general staff; the NSC's secretary-general; and the chairmen of the NSC's National Reconstruction Research Committee and the Committee for Science Development (*CHNC* 1988, 123–124). The president can also designate other members as he wishes.

Over the years the NSC has developed into one of the four major sites of institutional power in the ROC; the other three are the Office of the President, the KMT party headquarters, and the Executive Yuan. The NSC coordinates the nation's military strategy and security-related affairs, but its power also extends to initial approval of the ROC's annual budget, prepared by the Executive Yuan, before it is forwarded to the Legislative Yuan for passage (*FCJ*, March 10, 1986, 1). Under the temporary provisions and martial law, practically any major external policy and internal security matter may be declared a national security issue and thus may fall within the NSC's jurisdiction. In practice the president's personal decision determines if a matter is given to the NSC for disposition or if it is permitted to follow more regular channels.

The NSC played an important advisory role during the presidency of Chiang Kai-shek. Since 1978, when Chiang Ching-kuo became president, NSC meetings have been rare. Even so, the NSC has developed its own bureaucracy. Because the president did not attend to mundane matters, the NSC secretary-general became a powerful office in the functioning of the government. He coordinated NSC activities and provided access to the president. Since Chiang's death in January 1988, President Lee Teng-hui has gradually reduced the secretary-general's power.

The NSC's bureaucratic network has grown to include the National Security Bureau, the Committee for Science Development, and the National Reconstruction Research Committee. This last office comprises subordinate administrative sections—political affairs, military affairs, financial and economic affairs, and cultural affairs. The National Security Bureau is the ROC's highest intelligence organ, directing and coordinating all intelligence activities—including subversion, surveillance, espionage, and counterespionage—both internally and externally. The NSC headquarters, located in the presidential building in the center of Taipei, has developed close operational ties with the Office of the President through regular exchanges between the secretaries-general of the two offices. The NSC's power, however, does not derive from the 1947 constitution; rather it is based on extralegal power authorized to the president under the temporary provisions. The current NSC secretary-general is Chiang Wei-kuo (Wego), the younger brother of the late President Chiang and the last surviving member of the family to occupy an important office in the party or state apparatus.

The impact of martial law was as broad as that of the temporary provisions. Martial law was initially declared in the mainland in 1934 and remained in effect until July 1987. Its application was based on an administrative order issued in December 1949 by the Executive Yuan that designated Taiwan a combat area in China's civil war (Hu 1985, 16). In January 1950 President Chiang Kai-shek issued an emergency decree that activated martial law; the decree was subsequently ratified by the Legislative Yuan. Thereafter Taiwan was governed under martial law even though the island has never been a combat area.

Article 9 of the law stipulated: "During the enforcement of martial law the local administrative and judicial matters of the combat area shall be placed under the jurisdiction of the commander in chief in the said area, and the local administrative officials and judges shall be subject to the direction of the said commander in chief." A Taiwan Garrison Command headquarters was created in 1950 to take charge of all matters concerning the implementation of martial law. The Garrison Command is one of the active military commands under the Ministry of Defense. Its responsibilities include authorizing citizens to travel abroad, monitoring all entries into Taiwan, approving meetings and rallies, reviewing and sanctioning books and periodicals, and maintaining social order (Hu 1985, 17). In fact the Garrison Command headquarters never assumed control of local administrative and judicial matters as stipulated in Article

9 but rather confined itself to a supervisory role. Nonetheless, martial law authorized the extension of military authority into a broad segment of civilian life.

In addition, Article 8 specified ten categories of criminal offenses by civilians that were to be handled by military tribunals. This article greatly curtailed constitutional rights, since normal judicial procedure is not applicable in a military trial. An estimated ten thousand cases involving civilians were decided in military trials from 1950 to 1986 (Tien 1987b, 137). This practice violated Article 9 of the constitution, which prohibits the trial of civilians in military court. In 1970 the Defense Ministry issued a decree enlarging the Garrison Command's powers to include restrictions on civil rights such as the right to publish, privacy of correspondence, the right to practice religion, free speech, free assembly, and the right to petition and to give academic lectures (Hu 1985, 17–18).

Government officials justified these actions by stating that limitations on individual rights and freedoms were necessary because of the warlike state of relations across the Taiwan Strait. In practice the provisions of martial law were not implemented to the full. Nevertheless, the Garrison Command held tremendous extraconstitutional power over the political and social life of Taiwan's citizens. Moreover, the people of Taiwan were subject to restrictions and surveillance categorically forbidden by the constitution. Thus martial law was widely resented both on Taiwan and in the overseas Chinese communities, since it symbolized the political oppression that characterized the ROC's authoritarianism before its 1986–1988 political reforms.

For almost four decades, the temporary provisions and martial law have colored every aspect of Taiwan's political life. These laws created two powerful institutions—the NSC and the Garrison Command headquarters—outside the constitution and conferred virtually unlimited authority on the Office of the President. Such institutional developments have retarded the evolution of the constitutionally based parliamentary democracy that the ROC has yet to achieve. As long as these two extraconstitutional bodies exist, politics in Taiwan cannot keep pace with the ROC's economic affluence and social pluralism. Thus the operation and structure of the ROC government have been shaped by two conflicting standards—the constitution and extraconstitutional autocratic power—so that the decisionmaking process and lines of communication between power centers are exceedingly complex and often incomprehensible to those not privy to the ROC's inner workings.

In a bid to improve its international image and soften political opposition at home, the KMT Central Standing Committee announced on

October 15, 1986, its decision to lift the emergency decrees (*CYJP*, October 9, 1986, 1; *FCJ*, October 20, 1986, 1). The decision came as part of the party's reform initiatives. The late President Chiang Ching-kuo, the man behind the reform drive, insisted that "the party must accommodate itself to the changing times and environment" and added that only by adopting reform measures "will the party be able to keep pace with the changing times" (*FCJ*, October 20, 1986, 1). In July 1987 a new state security law formally replaced the martial law decree.

The end of martial law has had a profound impact on the ROC government and political life in the country. One immediate result was the legalization of new political parties previously restricted under the emergency decrees. Under the new conditions, all civilians will be tried in civilian courts; constitutional rights such as the rights of assembly and demonstration have been substantially restored, but only "if the organizers inform the proper authorities in advance" (*FCJ*, October 20, 1986, 1). Without martial law the power of the 25,000-strong Garrison Command still has to be substantially restricted—a thorny problem that has proved difficult to resolve. Article 3 of the new State Security Law strips the Garrison Command of the power to review applications for travel abroad and for visits to Taiwan, and Article 4 eliminates its authority over customs inspections (Shih 1987, 13). These provisions pave the way for less restrictive practices regarding travel to and from Taiwan.

The most controversial part of the ten-article State Security Law is Article 2, which regulates assembly and association among citizens. It clearly stipulates that such assembly and association, including political parties, are not allowed to violate the constitution by advocating communism or independence. These restrictions were later incorporated in Article 4 of the newly submitted Law on Assembly and Demonstration. The authorities believe that these provisions are necessary to maintain law and order in Taiwan (Shih 1987, 10–13). Their concerns are directed at both the PRC's peaceful unification campaign and the DPP's promotion of the Taiwan independence movement. The DPP, however, views these restrictions as a legal ploy to suppress its activities (*MCJP*, November 11, 1987, 3). As the opposition presses for the freedom to advocate Taiwan independence, this article could well be applied to sanction political actions or even public opinions that the authorities deem in violation of these three conditions. Thus the lifting of martial law has not really ended the kind of political conflicts associated with it in the past. However, the overall social and political atmosphere in Taiwan has substantially liberalized since the official end of martial law. On this evidence, Taiwan has indeed entered a new political era.

THE PRESIDENCY

The President

The ROC president holds the single most powerful office in the nation. According to both the constitution and the temporary provisions the president has the following powers:

1. He is the supreme commander of the nation's armed forces.

2. He appoints and dismisses all government and military officials at the provincial and municipal levels and above, except for popularly elected officials and civil servants. The appointments of the premier, the vice premier, cabinet members, and other high-ranking government officials require the consent of the Legislative Yuan or the Control Yuan. This consent has never been withheld from a presidential appointment.

3. He has the final power to conclude treaties, declare war, and make peace.

4. He may declare and terminate martial law.

5. He has the power to grant amnesties, pardons, remissions of sentences, and restitutions of civil rights.

6. He signs the legislative bills into law.

7. He may establish new offices during a national emergency.

8. He may adjust and change the organization of the national government.

9. He may increase the number of representatives in the national legislatures and appoint delegates from the overseas Chinese community to serve in the legislatures.

10. He may serve an indefinite number of terms.

This wide range of powers is rarely conferred on any other head of state in the world. But as with any leadership position, the effectiveness of the ROC president's power depends on the person who occupies the position. If the president serves concurrently as chairman of the ruling KMT, there is no party check on the president's power, as was the case with Presidents Chiang Kai-shek and Chiang Ching-kuo. The KMT chairman nominates candidates for the party Central Committee and the Central Standing Committee. He appoints the secretary-general of the Central Committee and all directors of functional departments at party headquarters. Approval by the Central Committee or the Party Congress of the chairman's appointments is usually a formality. When the president does not hold concurrent KMT chairmanship, the power of the presidency diminishes—as it did from 1975 to 1978 when Yen Chia-kan served as president and Chiang Ching-kuo as party chairman.

During the presidential terms of Chiang Kai-shek (1949–1975) and Chiang Ching-kuo (1978–1988), both men monopolized political power in the KMT regime. President Lee Teng-hui, who succeeded Chiang Ching-kuo in January 1988, is not likely to match the Chiangs in the exercise of presidential power. Although he was initially elected KMT acting chairman after Chiang's death by the party's Central Standing Committee, he has been the formal party chairman since the KMT Thirteenth Party Congress in July 1988. Lacking the enormous prestige of both Chiangs in the KMT and without a personalized power base in the governing institutions, President Lee will probably not become a supreme leader even though he heads both the party and the government. Most likely his power will be constrained by a collective leadership including KMT Secretary-General Lee Huan, Chief of General Staff Hau Pei-tsun, Premier Yu Kuo-hwa, President of the Judicial Yuan Lin Yang-kang, and NSC Secretary-General Chiang Wei-kuo, who is supported by the remaining influence of Madame Chiang Kai-shek. But Lee should still wield considerable influence.

As the first Taiwanese president of the ROC, Lee Teng-hui symbolizes the transition of power from the mainlander old guard to a younger generation of Taiwan-born leaders. Born into a family of rice farmers in northern Taiwan, Lee pursued an early career of academic rather than political achievement. His studies took him to Kyoto University, the National Taiwan University, Iowa State, and Cornell, where he received a Ph.D. in agricultural economics in 1968. After returning to Taiwan, Lee taught at the National Taiwan University and held several posts as agricultural specialist in the Taiwan provincial government and the U.S.-ROC Joint Commission on Rural Reconstruction. By the time he joined the KMT and began his real political career in 1972 as minister without portfolio in then Premier Chiang Ching-kuo's cabinet, he had won international renown among agricultural economists.

Under Chiang's stewardship, Lee rose quickly in the hierarchy of power. From 1978 to 1984 he was appointed mayor of Taipei and then governor of Taiwan and also became a member of the KMT Central Standing Committee. Lee's personal integrity, ability, broad knowledge of economic affairs, and unquestioned loyalty to Chiang Ching-kuo won his patron's confidence. Meanwhile, as Taiwan's opposition political movements intensified, Lee became an important liaison between the KMT and the opposition. As President Chiang moved toward the

Taiwanization of the regime, Lee's Presbyterian faith brought further advantages. Most Presbyterians on Taiwan are native Taiwanese, many of whose church leaders harbor anti-KMT sentiments. Lee was one of the few Taiwanese leaders in the KMT to enjoy the opposition's respect—a status that became Lee's biggest political asset.

In 1984, when Chiang Ching-kuo sought a second presidential term, he chose Lee as his vice president. As Chiang's health deteriorated from diabetes, Lee gained political stature as a potential successor to the president. Despite Lee's limited political experience (he has never run for elected office) and relatively short KMT membership, his expertise in agricultural economics, his image as an incorruptible public figure, and his diligence, personal integrity, and ethnicity have earned him widespread support and respect. His succession to Chiang's position marks a smooth transition of power rarely seen in developing nations.

The Office of the President

The crucial men who staff the president's office are Secretary-General Li Yuan-zu and Deputy Secretary-General Chiu Jin-yi (Cheyne). They control access to the president, coordinate staff work, and compile policy documents for his reference. Proximity to the president makes these two individuals powerful in their own right. They also serve as the eyes and ears of the president in personnel and policy matters. In the decisionmaking process their recommendations carry great weight. These two offices were particularly powerful during Chiang Ching-kuo's last years, when his failing health prevented him from much contact with the outside world.

The president also appoints a number of senior advisers (*tzu-cheng*) as consultants on major policies. Most advisers are of such advanced age that they are politically inactive. These appointments are regarded as political spoils, instituted to patronize officials retired from the ranks of premier, vice president, or the equivalent in the KMT hierarchy. At a slightly lower rank, retired party and government officials are appointed to the National Policy Advisory Committee; top military leaders are retired to the Military Strategy Advisory Committee. Both advisory committees are attached to the Office of the President but have few substantive responsibilities. A few committee members are sometimes given active responsibilities, in which case they remain influential, but the majority of positions are merely honorary.

Young staff members who begin their careers in the Office of the President often gain upward mobility from their boss—the president. Under Chiang Kai-shek and Chiang Ching-kuo, those who worked there or in the president's residence were known as the inner circle (*kung-t'ing p'ai*). Since personal association can be a paramount factor in politics on Taiwan, both Chiang Kai-shek and Chiang Ching-kuo made a practice of promoting their inner circle to high-level positions in the KMT, the government, and the military-security apparatus. Thus appointment to the Office of the President is an important step toward advancement from within the establishment power structure. Premier Yu Kuo-hwa, Chief of General Staff Hau Pei-tsun, and KMT Deputy Secretary-Generals James C. Y. Soong and Fredrick F. Chien, CEPD Minister, are but a few conspicuous examples. Their power derives ultimately from their association with the president; therefore they are not seen as politically accountable to either the voters in general or the party rank and file.

The Vice President

There have been four vice presidents on Taiwan. The first was General Chen Cheng, who served from 1954 to 1965. During the 1950s and the early 1960s General Chen was undoubtedly the second most powerful person in the ROC. A long-time loyalist to Chiang Kai-shek, Chen Cheng was instrumental in the consolidation of Nationalist power in Taiwan during the last days of the civil war. Before his appointment as vice president, when he was governor of Taiwan and premier, he played a crucial role in implementing land reform on Taiwan. Yen Chia-kan, Chen's successor, is a technocrat who played key roles in Taiwan's financial and economic policies during the 1950s and the early 1960s. His political loyalty, expertise in finance, U.S. connections, and lack of personal political ambition earned him the trust of Chiang Kai-shek. As vice president and later as interim president, Yen was never a political heavyweight.

In 1978 Chiang Ching-kuo appointed Hsueh Tung-min as the first Taiwanese to hold the post of vice president. Hsueh's appointment came as part of a new initiative to promote native Taiwanese into the upper echelons of power. Hsueh had a long working relationship with Chiang Ching-kuo. He was the first Taiwanese to be appointed governor of Taiwan after earlier service as vice speaker and speaker in the Provincial Assembly. His appointment as vice president was an important political gesture. Still Hsueh spent his youth on the mainland, and in local Taiwan slang that made him a "half-mountain"—half-Taiwanese, half-mainlander. Thus Hsueh's appointment was never seen as true power sharing between mainlanders and Taiwanese; its political importance was discounted.

In 1984 Chiang Ching-kuo elevated Lee Teng-hui from governor of Taiwan to vice president. In Taiwan and overseas many regarded Lee's selection as a wise move that helped alleviate political conflict in Taiwan from 1984 to 1987.

THE EXECUTIVE YUAN

The Executive Yuan is the administrative arm of the ROC government. Its organizational structure consists of a secretariat; eight ministries; seventeen commissions, councils, and bureaus; and the Central Bank.[3] As Figure 5.1 indicates, there are ministries of the Interior, Foreign Affairs, Defense, Finance, Education, Justice, Economic Affairs, and Communications. Of the seventeen commissions, councils, and bureaus, the most important are the Council for Economic Planning and Development (CEPD), the National Science Council, and the Government Information Office, which oversees the government's news releases and propaganda activities. The CEPD coordinates national economic planning and sets economic targets and priorities. The National Science Council plans and directs scientific research and development; it also provides funding for academic research. Technically only the premier, the vice premier, the ministers, some commissioners, and ministers without portfolio are members of the Executive Yuan's council with the status of a cabinet member.

These cabinet members and heads of administrative agencies are political appointees. The president makes these appointments at the recommendation of the premier, who is himself a presidential appointee with the consent of the Legislative Yuan. In the ROC the power to make high-level government appointments normally rests with the president. One exception was under President Yen Chia-kan (1975–1978), when Premier Chiang Ching-kuo dominated major appointments.

Each ministry has two deputy ministers; one is a political appointee, and the other represents the highest ranks of the civil service. Yet both deputies are appointed by the president, so distinctions in their career patterns are often blurred. A bureaucracy of civil servants carries out day-to-day administration under the order and supervision of these political appointees.

The Executive Yuan also supervises the administration of the municipalities of Taipei and Kaohsiung and the Taiwan provincial government, which in turn directs the administrative work of local governments. The Executive Yuan in effect sets the policy for all levels of government. Since ROC jurisdiction is limited to Taiwan and its offshore islands, the Execu-

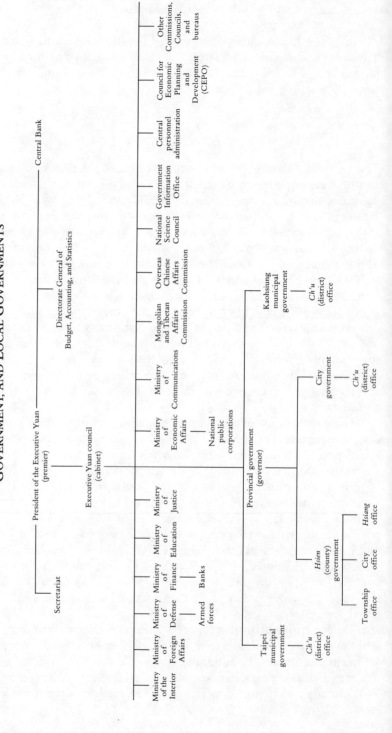

FIGURE 5.1

STRUCTURE OF THE EXECUTIVE YUAN, THE PROVINCIAL GOVERNMENT, AND LOCAL GOVERNMENTS

tive Yuan and the provincial government have overlapping functions, blurring the division of administrative authority.

The Premier and the Executive Yuan

In the formal structure of the ROC the premier is second in importance only to the president. As Table 5.1 shows, there have been six premiers since 1949: Chen Cheng (1950–1954; 1958–1963), Yu Hung-chun (1954–1958), Yen Chia-kan (1963–1972), Chiang Ching-kuo (1972–1978), Sun Yun-hsuen (1978–1984), and Yu Kuo-hwa (1984–present). Four premiers—Yen, Sun, and both Yus—are technocrats with wide experience in finance, economic affairs, and banking. This expertise suggests the importance of the premier in managing the ROC's finances and economic development. General Chen Cheng and Chiang Ching-kuo were the only two whose political power was the reason for, and not the consequence of, their position as premier. As Chiang Kai-shek's right-hand man in the military, General Chen was a stalwart supporter in the 1950s when the ROC faced a real military threat from the Communists across the Taiwan Strait. General Chen was a logical choice for managing the government in a time of national crisis. He later served a second term as premier in 1958–1963, when he was simultaneously vice president and deputy leader of the KMT. After the death of Chen Cheng, Chiang Ching-kuo emerged as the crucial second-echelon political figure behind President Chiang Kai-shek. His father arranged cabinet-level appointments that exposed him to a broad range of policy matters. In 1972 Chiang Ching-kuo became premier, a position that prepared him to succeed his ailing father.

The power of vice premier depends on the person in office. The position is usually an honorary post without specific duties. From 1950 to 1988 eleven persons have served as vice premier. With the exception of Chiang Ching-kuo (1969–1972), Huang Shao-ku (1954–1958; 1966–1969), and possibly Lin Yang-kang (1984–1987), vice premiers were not considered political heavyweights in their time. After 1972 Chiang Ching-kuo reserved that post for leading Taiwanese politicians as part of his effort to co-opt the Taiwanese. Prior to the appointment of Shih Chi-yang in 1988, four other Taiwanese—Hsu Ching-chung, Chiu Chuang-huan, Lin Yang-kang and Lien Chan—occupied the office; among them Lin, currently president of the Judicial Yuan, stood out in ability, popularity, and prestige.

Of the eight ministerial posts, those that deal with defense, finance, economic affairs, foreign affairs, and education are considered the most

TABLE 5.1
PREVIOUS POSTS HELD BY THE PREMIERS, 1950–1988

	Chen Cheng	*Yu Hung-chun*	*Yen Chia-kan*	*Chiang Ching-kuo*	*Sun Yun-hsuen*	*Yu Kuo-hwa*
Governor of Taiwan	•		•			
Finance minister	•	•	•			•
CEPD chairman						•
Economics minister			•		•	•
Central Bank president						•
Vice premier			•	•	•	
Defense minister				•		
Communications minister					•	•
Chief of general staff	•					
Minister without portfolio				•	•	•

SOURCE: Sun (1984), 104.

important. In the early years Taiwanese were kept out of ministerial appointments altogether. Under Chiang Ching-kuo Taiwanese were appointed as interior, communications, and more recently justice and cultural affairs ministers. Lee Teng-hui appointed Taiwanese to head finance and foreign affairs. As elderly cabinet members retire, second-generation mainlanders and Taiwanese succeed them. Of the current 24 cabinet members, 11 (or 45.8 percent) are Taiwanese (Wu Ching-feng 1988, 23). The percentage of Taiwanese holding these high offices has been steadily rising since 1972.

Unlike cabinets in Western parliamentary democracies, the Executive Yuan (see Table 5.2) is not a high policymaking organ. Most of the major policies are decided by the president and the KMT party chairman in conjunction with the National Security Council and the KMT Central Standing Committee. But the Executive Yuan is usually given a free hand in policy matters regarding finance, trade, and economic development, although on such matters the president often appoints an ad hoc group to coordinate policy planning. Thus the Executive Yuan is largely confined to developing policy proposals and implementing the policies already approved by the Office of the President and the KMT's Central Standing Committee.

The Administrative Bureaucracy

There are about 450,000 administrative functionaries in the ROC bureaucracy; 90 percent are employed at the provincial, municipal, and local levels. Approximately three-quarters of all government employees are classified as civil servants, who have passed examinations given by the Examination Yuan. The rest are unclassified personnel who hold their positions as a result of political appointment. From 1950 to 1984 the government held 35 general civil service examinations, which qualified about 53,600 candidates for future appointments (Sung and Ho 1986, 137). Political appointees at the upper levels of the bureaucracy must also pass special examinations to assume their bureaucratic rank. In recent years the ratio between Taiwanese and mainlanders who have passed the civil service examinations is roughly three to one in favor of the Taiwanese majority, though less than the seven-to-one ratio of Taiwanese to mainlanders in the total population.

In the Executive Yuan mainlanders hold the larger portion of administrative positions, but in local government the Taiwanese dominate. Many mainlanders were in government service before they arrived on Taiwan, so the situation in part reflects the ROC's history. In recent years the employment of Taiwanese has risen. As Figure 5.2 shows, among bu-

—— TABLE 5.2 ——
MEMBERS OF THE EXECUTIVE YUAN, AUGUST 1988

Name	Position	Age	Birthplace	Education	Experience
Yu Kuo-hwa	Premier	74	Chekiang	Harvard, London School of Economics	President, Central Bank, minister of finance
Shih Chi-yang	Vice premier	53	Taiwan	Heidelberg University, Ph.D.	Minister of justice
Hsu Shui-teh	Minister of the interior	57	Taiwan	Cheng-chi University, M.A.	Mayor of Taipei
Lien Chan	Minister of foreign affairs	52	Taiwan	University of Chicago, Ph.D.	Vice premier
Cheng Wei-yuan	Minister of defense	75	Anhwei	U.S. Army Command and Staff College	Chairman, VACRS[a]
Kuo, Shirley W. Y.	Minister of finance	58	Taiwan	MIT, M.A., Kobe University, Ph.D.	Vice president, Central Bank
Mao Kao-wen	Minister of education	52	Chekiang	Carnegie-Mellon, Ph.D.	President, Tsinghua University
Hsiao Tien-chan	Minister of justice	54	Taiwan	Taiwan University	Minister without portfolio
Chen Li-an	Minister of economic affairs	52	Chekiang	New York University, Ph.D.	Chairman, National Science Council
Kuo Nan-hung	Minister of communications	52	Taiwan	Northwestern University, Ph.D.	President, Chiaotung University
Wu Hua-peng	Chairman, MTAC[b]	63	Mongolia	Oregon State University, M.A.	MTAC representative in United States and Europe
Tseng Kwang-shun	Chairman, OCAC[c]	64	Kwangtung	Kwangtung College of Law and Business	KMT director of overseas affairs

TABLE 5.2 (continued)

Name	Position	Age	Birthplace	Education	Experience
Chien, Fredrick F.	Chairman, CEPD[d]	53	Chekiang	Yale University, Ph.D.	CCNAA[e] representative in the United States
Hsia Han-min	Chairman, National Science Council	56	Fukien	University of Oklahoma, Ph.D.	President, Cheng-kung University
Yu Yu-hsien	Chairman, Agricultural Commission	54	Taiwan	Purdue University, Ph.D.	Head, Department of Agriculture and Forestry, provincial government
Kuo Wei-fan	Chairman, CCPD[f]	51	Taiwan	University of Paris, Ph.D.	President, Taiwan Normal University
Ma Ying-jeou	Chairman, RDEC[g]	38	Hunan	Harvard University, S.J.D.	KMT deputy secretary-general
Chien, Robert Chun	Cabinet secretary-general	59	Chekiang	University of Minnesota, M.A.	Minister of finance
Kao, Henry Y. S.	Minister without portfolio	75	Taiwan	Waseda University	Minister of communications
Chang Feng-shu	Minister without portfolio	60	Taiwan	University of New Mexico, M.A.	Minister of the interior
Chow Hong-tao	Minister without portfolio	72	Chekiang	Wuhan University	Director of the general budget
Wang You-tsao	Minister without portfolio	63	Fukien	University of Iowa, Ph.D.	Chairman, agricultural commission
Huang Kun-huei	Minister without portfolio	52	Taiwan	University of North Dakota, Ph.D.	KMT director of youth affairs

──── TABLE 5.2 (continued) ────

Name	Position	Age	Birthplace	Education	Experience
Shen Chün-shan	Minister without portfolio	56	Chekiang	University of Maryland, Ph.D.	Dean, Tsinghua University

SOURCES: Wu Ching-feng (1988), 23; *CHNC* (1988), 427–94.
[a]Vocational Assistance Commission for Retired Servicemen.
[b]Mongolian and Tibetan Affairs Commission.
[c]Overseas Chinese Affairs Commission.
[d]Council for Economic Planning and Development.
[e]Coordination Council for North American Affairs.
[f]Council for Cultural Planning and Development.
[g]Research, Development, and Evaluation Commission.

reaucrats at the upper levels of the Executive Yuan in 1980, 26 percent were ages 55–59, 29.75 percent were 60–64, and 18.27 percent were over 65, for a combined total of nearly 75 percent aged 55 and older. From 1980 to 1982 the proportion of high-level bureaucrats over age 65 drastically declined to a mere 2.72 percent. This trend toward a younger age structure should bring more native Taiwanese into the bureaucracy.

A comparison of these data shows that in less than three years the age 35–49 cohort increased from 11.5 percent in 1980 to 27.6 percent in 1982. At the same time the proportion of officials aged 50 and older declined from 88.8 percent in 1980 to 71.6 percent in 1982.

The changing distribution among age groups has a political impact as more Taiwan-born and younger personnel replace the aging mainlanders. A 1983 random survey of 504 section chiefs and lower-level administrative functionaries in the Executive Yuan indicated that about 61 percent of those 49 and younger were Taiwanese, whereas mainlanders constituted 87.7 percent in the age groups over 50 (Liang 1984, 185, 337). Nevertheless the vast majority of civil servants appear to be KMT members regardless of their origins. The same survey revealed that 404, or 80.2 percent of the 504 persons in the study, were KMT members (Liang 1984, 218–219). So although the central administrative bureaucracy is clearly entering a period of transition in both age structure and provincial origin, appointment is still closely connected to KMT membership.

Economic Planning and Technocracy

Technocrats in finance and economic affairs have been critical to Taiwan's economic success, particularly from 1950 to 1970, when crucial decisions about economic development were made. The technocrats in the ROC include most ranking officials of the Council for Economic Planning and Development, the Finance Ministry, the Ministry of Eco-

_____ FIGURE 5.2 _____

AGES OF BUREAUCRATS IN THE UPPER RANKS OF THE EXECUTIVE YUAN, 1980–1982

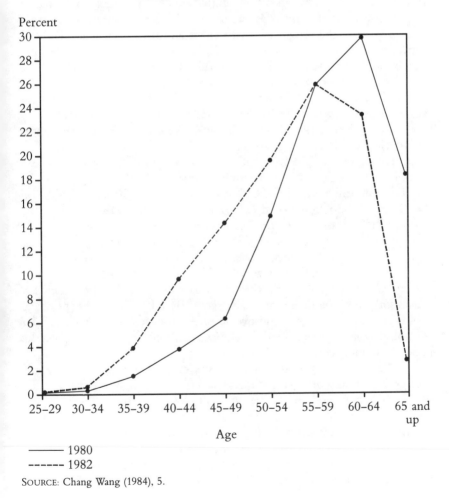

Percent

SOURCE: Chang Wang (1984), 5.

nomic Affairs, and the Central Bank. Of these the CEPD and its predecessors were responsible for formulating economic plans, especially during the years 1958–1984. Although the ROC economy is based on free enterprise, public enterprises are numerous and important. Government planning, which affects both private and public industries, has been a major part of the ROC's development strategy (Gold 1986, 68–69, 76–78; Haggard and Cheng 1987, 114–15; 123–27). Today the CEPD is less active in economic policy formulation, but it still conducts economic research and supervises major construction projects.

All major government construction projects require CEPD review before implementation. Table 5.3 shows the projects the CEPD reviewed from 1980 to 1985. About 52 percent of the 772 projects originated in central government ministries or agencies, whereas about 48 percent were projects of the provincial government and the two municipalities of Taipei and Kaohsiung. On average the CEPD screens 98 to 185 projects per year, so it needs a large staff and specialized civil service personnel. The CEPD reviews these projects in relation to overall economic direction and priorities. When Yu Kuo-hwa was chairman of the CEPD (1977–1984), it was extremely powerful, for its operations were free from intervention by the premier. Since Yu's promotion in 1984, the CEPD's power and status have declined.

Changes in the CEPD's structure over the years illustrate Taiwan's economic development. As Figure 5.3 indicates, CEPD's origin can be traced to both the Council for U.S. Aid (CUSA), established in 1948, and the Taiwan Production Board (TPB), established in 1949. CUSA, consisting of the premier and some cabinet members, was in charge of implementing U.S. aid programs (Gold 1986, 69). In contrast, the TPB was set up by the Taiwan provincial government, then under the governorship of General Chen Cheng, to stabilize the inflation-ridden economy and to help manage and develop all productive enterprises in Taiwan. In 1953 the TPB was absorbed by the Economic Stabilization Board (ESB), whose principal goal was to bring currency and overall financial-economic volatility under control; it was also to plan and develop Taiwan's industries and to promote basic economic reconstruction projects.

In 1958 the restructured CUSA was chaired by Chen Cheng, although its actual work was handled by Yen Chia-kan, Yin Chung-yung (K. Y. Yin), and a group of internationally known economists including Chiang Sho-chieh, Liu Ta-chung, and Wang Tso-jung (Wen Hsien-shen 1984, 22). They drafted reform programs on taxes, finance, investment, and exchange rates that were implemented from 1958 on. The political weight of Premier Chen Cheng contributed to the smooth functioning of the reorganized CUSA. As U.S. aid was drawing to an end, a new

───── TABLE 5.3 ─────

CONSTRUCTION PROJECTS REVIEWED BY THE CEPD, 1980–1985

Origin of projects	1980	1981	1982	1983	1984	1985	Totals
Ministry of Economic Affairs	38	36	61	31	15	20	201
Ministry of Communications	9	27	24	21	28	17	126
Ministry of Finance	6	7	6	5	5	5	34
Central Bank	1	1	0	0	0	0	2
Other ministries and agencies	2	6	11	6	7	9	41
Taiwan provincial government	33	42	63	36	46	55	275
Taipei and Kaohsiung governments	9	6	20	11	21	26	93
Total	98	125	185	110	122	132	772

SOURCE: Wen Hsien-shen (1984), 1.

Council for International Economic Cooperation and Development (CIECD) was created in 1963 to obtain foreign investment and long-term loans for infrastructure projects and to construct an export-processing zone in Kaohsiung. The CIECD was further reorganized under Chiang Ching-kuo in 1969, with some of its powers and functions dispersed to various ministries in the Executive Yuan. A special group to coordinate finance, economic affairs, and currency matters was formed within the Executive Yuan under then Vice Premier Chiang Ching-kuo. The group assumed much of CIECD's authority from 1969 to 1971. Once Chiang Ching-kuo became premier, the CIECD was replaced by the smaller Economic Planning Council (EPC), chaired by a technocrat, Chang Chi-cheng. Major authority in financial and economic planning and evaluation thus shifted to an ad hoc group headed personally by Chiang Ching-kuo.

The current CEPD was formed in 1977 to replace the EPC. With Yu Kuo-hwa—a lifelong confidant of the Chiang family—as chairman,

CEPD's authority and activities were considerable. When Yu became premier in 1985, Chao Yao-tung, a technocrat with few connections, succeeded him as chairman of CEPD. The CEPD's authority under Chairman Chao seems to have been substantially reduced. However, President Lee's July 1988 appointment of Chien Fu (Fredrick F. Chien), previously the ROC's representative in Washington, D.C., signals a step

——— FIGURE 5.3 ———
EVOLUTION OF ECONOMIC RECONSTRUCTION AND DEVELOPMENT AGENCIES, 1949–1988

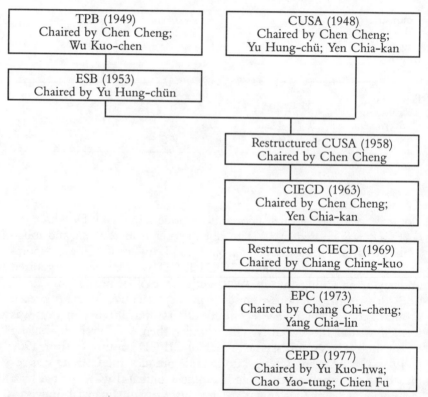

SOURCE: Wen Hsien-shen (1984), 16.

NOTE: CEPD = Council for Economic Planning and Development; CIECD = Council for International Economic Cooperation and Development; CUSA = Council for U.S. Aid; EPC = Economic Planning Council; ESB = Economic Stabilization Board; TPB = Taiwan Production Board.

toward reviving the CEPD's rule in economic development in a changing international trade environment.

Despite the complex pattern of institutional development and functional change, the CEPD and its predecessors have been instrumental in promoting Taiwan's economic modernization. Technocrats in these agencies generally are well educated and professionally competent. Compared with their counterparts in some of the high-growth countries of the Third World, such as South Korea or Brazil, ROC technocrats are cautious planners. They favor a project-by-project approach to development to achieve stability. This approach can probably be attributed to their educational background. A study of 44 key technocrats in Taiwan indicates that 97.7 percent of them have had a university education—about half with degrees in engineering and one-third in the social sciences (Alan Liu 1985, 14). Over 60 percent of them received graduate education in the United States and Western Europe. Their educational background appears to have contributed three important elements to their work style: a commitment to the market economy, a receptivity to modern management, and a style of planning that emphasizes steady growth, reflecting in part their engineering and science backgrounds.

PROVINCIAL AND LOCAL GOVERNMENTS

For administrative purposes the geographical entity of Taiwan is divided into two municipalities and a province. The province has five cities and fifteen counties, which are subdivided into 358 smaller cities, townships, and rural administrative villages (*hsiang*). The municipality of Taipei has a population of about 2.5 million and Kaohsiung about 1.4 million. In the ROC administrative hierarchy these municipalities are considered equivalent to a province. Thus the Taipei and Kaohsiung municipal governments fall under the direct administrative supervision of the Executive Yuan. The other cities and counties are administered by the Taiwan provincial government, located near the city of Taichung.

The Provincial Government

The governor is both the chief executive of the provincial government and the chairman of its executive council, which comprises department heads and 23 council members without portfolio in the provincial administration. The president of the ROC appoints the governor, so the office wields great power. From 1949 to 1988 there were eleven governors, four of them military men of mainlander origins. After 1972

Chiang Ching-kuo appointed four Taiwanese as governors. The governor is also a member of the KMT's Central Standing Committee.

As one of the most sought-after posts in Taiwan, the governorship is seen as a stepping-stone to higher positions in the central government. Two of the three Taiwanese former governors—Hsueh Tung-min and Lee Teng-hui—later became vice president. Lin Yang-kang, the other Taiwanese former governor, became vice premier and is now president of the Judicial Yuan. Chiu Chuang-huan, the governor since 1984, was previously minister of the interior and vice premier in the national government. In short, the four most prominent Taiwanese officials in the ROC in the late 1980s have at one time or another served as governor. The governor controls some provincial expenditures and personnel appointments, so the office has many favors to bestow. That the governorship is not determined by popular election has become a matter of growing controversy in Taiwan.

Unlike the national government, the provincial government has no authority over defense, foreign affairs, the judiciary, and intelligence. All other administrative functions are roughly divided between the Executive Yuan and the provincial government, obscuring the boundaries of responsibility. The provincial government has seventeen departments or equivalents that supervise administrative work at the county and city levels and monitor some public corporations and banks.

Local Governments

There are sixteen county and five city governments under the jurisdiction of the provincial government. Unlike the governors, the chief executives of the counties, known as magistrates, and the mayors are popularly elected. The vast majority of these local chief executives are KMT members. Competition for these positions is keen, for the office is considered the leading official position in each locality. Like the governor, these magistrates and mayors have at their disposal public revenues and personnel appointments that can go to their supporters. Some candidates spend millions of U.S. dollars as a political investment to win the KMT nomination and election. Once they are in office, local reconstruction projects and the zoning of land for urban or industrial development usually become sources of patronage, since these projects involve public monies as well as appreciation in land values. Further, citizens seeking official appointments or public school teachers anxious to be transferred to a more desirable location may buy their opportunities through the county or city chief executives. Local governments penetrate the most remote sections of the island. At the township or rural administrative district level a popularly elected executive heads another layer of administrative offices. At the village level administrative functionaries (*ts'un-kan-shih*) are appointed to provide links between local citizens and the government. The extensive administrative penetration of Taiwan is in part the legacy of efficient Japanese colonial control and also reflects the impact of extensive communication and transportation networks. Through these networks the authority of the ROC is felt on a daily basis even at the grass roots. The majority of government personnel at the county levels and below are subject to civil service classification.

Problems of Local Administration

Even though the administrative bureaucracy penetrates society at the county and local levels, serious problems remain in local government. One is the growing inability of local administrations to provide the services needed for a rapidly modernizing society. As Taiwan industrializes, the volume of needed services also increases. Recently the demand for services, especially those related to urbanization, has accelerated. The construction and repair of roads, building of additional public schools, and provision of adequate health services, drinking water, and industrial waste disposal are but a few of the issues that local governments must address. Yet the staffing of local administrations has not kept pace with population increases. For example, in 1953 San-ch'ung and Yung-ho, both suburbs of Taipei, had 69 and 31 local officials for their 46,000 and 16,300 residents respectively. By 1973 the population of San-ch'ung increased almost sixfold to 264,000 and Yung-ho almost tenfold to 115,400. Yet the number of administrative personnel in San-ch'ung barely increased to 74 and remained constant at 31 in Yung-ho (Tung 1974, 35). At Feng-yuan, a central Taiwan city, the population in 1974 was 110,000; Hsin-tien, in the north, had a slightly larger population of 113,000 residents. Nonetheless, Feng-yuan had 53 city government employees, whereas the more populous Hsin-tien had only 35 (Tung 1974, 31).

These examples reflect serious disparities in the provision of local administrative services during the 1970s. Since then the situation has not improved much. Although the ROC as a whole has made enormous progress in modernizing, its public services have not improved at the grassroots level, particularly in towns and rural communities. Because of the neglect of local government, county and subcounty administrations have had difficulty attracting and retaining well-trained personnel. In 1973 of the 14,735 regular administrative functionaries at township and rural district offices, only 147 had college degrees (Tung 1974, 31).

The problems of local government are compounded by inadequate sources of revenue. The current taxation system deprives local administrations of sufficient funding. Income taxes together with customs duties, commodity taxes, and other major sources of revenue go to the central government. The provincial government derives its revenue from such sources as the monopolistic sale of tobacco and alcoholic beverages, sales taxes, and business license fees. Municipalities and major cities collect revenue from land taxes, property taxes, capital gains from land appreciation, mortgage taxes, and the major portion of recreation taxes. But the county and subcounty administrative offices draw their revenues mostly from miscellaneous taxes or subsidies from the provincial government. The revenues of subcounty administrations barely cover the salaries of public employees, leaving almost nothing to provide services for local citizens.

As Table 5.4 indicates, in 1984 the central government received 57.8 percent of the total tax revenue collected, whereas county and city governments and subcounty governments received only 9.8 and 2.9 percent respectively. The revenue of the Taipei and Kaohsiung municipalities alone almost equaled the combined revenues of all county, city, and subcounty governments. On the expenditure side, the county and city governments and subcounty administration offices spent 13 percent and 3.5 percent respectively of total national expenditures in that year. Their deficit spending was compensated by subsidies from the provincial government, which in turn received funds from the national government. But there are no detailed guidelines for the allocation of these subsidies; the amount received by local governments depends as much on politics and favoritism as on merit and need. Revenue allocation thus becomes a means for political and administrative control of the local governments; it makes the magistrates, mayors, and subcounty executives responsive to wishes of the national and provincial governments.

In 1973, 219 townships and rural administrative districts, or about two-thirds of the total, failed to generate enough revenue for their annual budgets. Available figures suggest that in 1980, 52.3 percent of local budgets were funded by subsidies (Chiang Chia 1984, 29). Revenue allocation among cities also shows significant disparities. Despite rapidly growing populations, suburban cities are typically underfunded. In Pan-ch'iao and Chung-ho, two Taipei suburbs with populations approaching half a million each, per capita expenditures are only about one-eighth to one-third as large as those of other cities of comparable size (*LHYK*, 1984, 74). After paying the salaries of public employees, some cities and counties had almost no funds for public services (*CYJP*, January 3, 1988, 5). This disparity suggests that only politically loyal mayors may receive

_____ TABLE 5.4 _____
PERCENTAGE DISTRIBUTION OF REVENUES AND EXPENDITURES
BY LEVEL OF GOVERNMENT, 1984

	Central government	Province	Taipei and Kaohsiung	County and city	Subcounty
Revenues	57.8	17.4	12.1	9.8	2.9
Expenditures	56.3	16.0	11.2	13.0	3.5

SOURCE: *TCNC* (1982), 138–40.

subsidies. The KMT office's recommendations on these matters greatly influence local administrations, even where a nonparty person holds local executive power.

The Central Government's Budget

In general the ROC leaders are fiscal conservatives. In the 1950s the government was compelled to practice deficit spending out of the need to support large armed forces and a substantial national government bureaucracy on a modest economic base. U.S. aid eased the deficit but did not entirely eradicate it. Later, as Taiwan's economy improved, there was an accompanying increase in government revenues. As Table 5.5 indicates, over the 23 years from 1964 to 1987, the government achieved a budget surplus each year; this surplus had reached almost N.T. $1 billion by 1973. An aberration in this favorable situation appeared in 1982–1983 as a world recession affected Taiwan's exports. The fiscal 1982–1983 budget registered a deficit for the first time in years of about U.S. $75 million (Myers 1984, 526). Since then budget surpluses have continued.

The ROC's unitary administrative structure clearly favors the central government as far as revenue extraction is concerned. Central government revenues derive mainly from various taxes as well as profits from public corporations and such monopolies as liquor, cigarettes, and salt; some of these sources also provide revenue to the provincial government. Based on 1987 figures, public corporations and monopoly incomes constituted 21 percent of total revenues, and tax revenues amounted to 56.1 percent (*TSDB*, 1988, 170). Major tax bases include income taxes, customs, duties, commodity taxes, business taxes, and taxes from stock transactions. The income tax rate in Taiwan is lower than in all industrialized nations, where social spending tends to be high, but is higher than in other Asian nations such as Japan, South Korea, and Thailand (RDEC

_____ TABLE 5.5 _____
ROC NET REVENUES AND EXPENDITURES, 1964–1986
(IN MILLIONS OF N.T. DOLLARS)

	Revenues	Expenditures	Balance
1964	19,054	18,486	+568
1968	35,235	33,002	+2,233
1973	89,637	79,856	+9,781
1978	233,644	226,900	+6,744
1983	501,155	498,159	+2,996
1987	707,843	662,135	+45,708

SOURCE: *TSDB* (1987), 169, 171.

1983, 199). From 1976 to 1988 Taiwan's income tax rate stayed within 20–22 percent.

Four major categories account for the bulk of central government expenditures: (1) defense and foreign affairs, (2) social welfare, (3) economic construction and transportation, and (4) education, science, and culture. The defense and foreign affairs category includes all expenses related to national security. From 1954 to 1968 such spending comprised 51 percent to almost 64 percent of the annual budget (*TSDB*, 1988, 172). Although defense spending has continued to grow in recent years, it has declined as a percentage of the total central government budget since 1969. The budget for fiscal 1987 showed a decrease in this category to 33.4 percent of total spending (*TSDB*, 1988, 172). The decline can be attributed to a manpower reduction in the armed forces owing to a shift in defense posture to stress modern weapon systems and to place more emphasis on air and sea defenses and less on a large land army. But as long as the PRC military threatens Taiwan, the manufacture of sophisticated weapons or their acquisition from abroad will continue to be a top priority in national spending. Thus the current defense spending rate may not decline further in the years ahead.

Conversely expenditures for social, economic, and educational purposes have been on the rise, reflecting Taiwan's socioeconomic modernization. Plans for more structural change in the economy toward further technological applications will require an even higher level of funding for scientific research, technical education, and improvements of the infrastructure. In fiscal year 1987 spending for economic and transportation projects amounted to 17.3 percent, with education, science, and culture at 20.3 percent (*TSDB*, 1988, 172). The social welfare budget, which increased from 10 percent in 1975 to 15.5 percent in 1987, will continue to rise (*TSDB*, 1988, 172). As the population begins to age, spending on social welfare for the elderly will probably increase. In the ROC changing budget allocations are usually not a function of lobbying and politicking; rather they reflect the national leaders' perception of changing social and economic circumstances.

Public Enterprises

To influence the economy the ROC government licenses firms, regulates foreign exchange, and controls a cumbersome tariff structure (Silm 1976, 18). More important, the government owns, operates, and invests in many enterprises, mostly in basic industry and banking. In addition the KMT and the Vocational Assistance Commission for Retired Soldiers, which is heavily subsidized by the government, run some forty firms, including many of the island's largest so-called private enterprises (Silm 1976, 21). These public enterprises fall under the sponsorship of either the national or the provincial government, with the former in charge of basic industries.

Of the 27 national corporations, the largest 12 operate under the supervision of the Ministry of Economic Affairs. Some, such as China Steel, China Shipbuilding, China Petroleum, and Tai-power, rank among the largest in the nation. In 1985 these public enterprises employed more than a hundred thousand people. A majority of the past and present board chairmen and general managers are former officials of the government, retired senior military officers, or former KMT county and city executives (Hsi 1985, 77). Another 13 enterprises are run by other ministries and agencies. In 1984 these national corporations, with total assets of U.S. $70 billion, generated over U.S. $3 billion in profits (*SY*, 1985, 149).

The provincial government also supervises or owns 33 enterprises in addition to the Taiwan Wine and Tobacco Monopoly Bureau, which it operates. Among them are 11 major commercial banks, insurance companies, and trust banks, including the Bank of Taiwan, Taiwan Land Bank, First Commercial Bank, and Taiwan Life Insurance Company. These banks in 1984 provided a total of over U.S. $22.8 billion in loans, or about four-fifths of the value of all bank loans for the country in that year (Tai-wan sheng-cheng-fu 1985, 487–88).

The assets of these provincial government enterprises were valued at U.S. $54 billion in 1983 (Tai-wan sheng-cheng-fu 1985, 490). In 1984 these 33 enterprises generated a combined profit of about U.S. $325 million, of which U.S. $120 million was turned over to the provincial government treasury (Tai-wan sheng-cheng-fu 1985, 501). Beyond that the Wine and Tobacco Monopoly Bureau alone earned over U.S. $4 billion in profits, of which one-third went into provincial government coffers (Tai-wan sheng-cheng-fu 1985, 513).

Despite the earnings generated by government-owned enterprises, critics have argued that their profit margins are too low. In fact many of the national corporations lost money for years; only a special few, such as the China Petroleum Corporation and Tai-power, are making huge profits—partly because they are monopolies. Some government enterprises are overstaffed and poorly managed, often by retired generals, old bureaucrats, or semiretired politicians with little knowledge of modern management. For example, 130 retired generals serve as consultants to provincial banks and rarely work (*PSNT*, December 28, 1985, 13). As in many socialist countries, the majority of Taiwan's public corporations are wasteful and inefficient. Overstaffing in conjunction with a political spoils system is the heart of the problem.

CONCLUSION

Government on Taiwan as defined by the constitution could become a democracy that mixes presidential and parliamentary systems. Under such an arrangement there would be sufficient checks and balances between the executive branch and other branches of government. Unfortunately the actual government strays from the constitutional prescriptions. Both governmental structure and real authority are circumscribed by the temporary provisions and various emergency decrees. These extraconstitutional provisions have limited liberalization and slowed democratic evolution.

The current practice of government endows the president with virtually unlimited authority. He is accountable neither to the populace nor to any parliamentary body. Under him, the premier and his cabinet officers may be stripped of their real policymaking powers and may conduct government business essentially as the president's administrative subordinates. Like other major officials in the national government and the provincial governor, they serve at the president's pleasure. The president's extraconstitutional power derives from the temporary provisions and emergency decrees and from his chairmanship of the KMT. If the ROC is to become democratic in the future, the president's power must be curtailed and dispersed broadly through the government as specified in the constitution. That development would require abrogating the current extraconstitutional legal apparatus that makes such a concentration of power possible. The separation of party and government power is also needed.

The Executive Yuan does not have enough authority to meet the challenges of mounting social and economic change. It has been timid in initiating new policy measures and even administrative reform, perhaps because of the pervasive sense of powerlessness among cabinet officers. In earlier years the Executive Yuan adopted forward-looking economic measures. Taiwan's economic success can be attributed partially to the efforts of officials and technocrats in finance and economic affairs, particularly those connected with the Council on Economic Planning and Development and its predecessors. Most of that first generation have aged; their younger successors seem neither as able nor as forward-looking, in part because many of the most capable young people have chosen to work either in the United States or in Taiwan's prosperous private sector. New challenges inherent in the structural transformation of Taiwan's economy toward a high-technology base will prove difficult if the planning apparatus remains less competent than it was in the 1960s and 1970s.

New problems associated with economic development have yet to be tackled seriously. Four issues in particular have captured the most attention: ecology, trade, potential labor unrest, and energy. The national government does not have an administrative agency with enough power and resources to handle the ecology issue. Environmental problems are indeed serious and have been increasingly publicized. Foreign trade is the lifeblood of Taiwan's flourishing economy; yet it is administered by a mere bureau within the Ministry of Economic Affairs—an office with limited authority, budget, and staff. Labor unrest is becoming more serious, as is evident from the growing number of employer-worker disputes (Tien 1987a, 31). The number grew from twenty cases in 1960 to over a thousand in 1981 and is believed to have gone even higher since then. At issue are workers' rights to collective bargaining, job security, and compensation, social insurance, working conditions, and retirement benefits. Only in 1987 did the authorities finally decide to elevate the administrative agency dealing with labor rights from a bureau to a commission. The ROC also has no ministry-level administrative unit concerned with energy matters, despite Taiwan's steadily growing energy consumption and heavy dependence on Middle Eastern oil. The governmental structure has not adapted to a changing economy and society.

Restrictions on local government's tax base and limitations in staffing further compound the problems associated with social and economic modernization at the grass roots. Local governments at county and subcounty levels are financially starved. Thus Taiwan's economic affluence has not properly benefited small cities, towns, and rural communities. Rural roads are generally in poor condition; learning and recreational facilities are seldom available outside large cities. Modern public toilets are seldom available. Sewage is largely untreated in most small cities and rural communities. Although Taipei has rapidly become a modern metropolis, a large portion of Taiwan remains underdeveloped. The national government does not deal directly with these problems; the provincial government leaves them to local governments, which lack the financial and human resources to manage them effectively. In the prevailing system of political patronage, local government executives are rewarded with needed funding on the basis of political loyalty and personal ties. When local executives are either opposition activists or independent-minded KMT members, the funds for their projects are even harder to obtain. In short, Taiwan's unitary form of government together with a system of public finance based on political loyalty hampers modernization in small cities and rural communities and restricts the ability of opposition politicians to compete in local politics.

— 6 —

Representative Institutions

The major responsibilities of a legislature are to make laws, to scrutinize the conduct of government officials, and to approve the government's budget. But the specific functions performed by a legislature may vary considerably from one political system to another. Legislatures in representative democracies are usually more independent and powerful than their counterparts in authoritarian or totalitarian systems. In most developing nations, however, legislative institutions are often controlled by the executive branch, the ruling party elite, or military oligarchies. Even parliamentary democracies have seen growing executive domination over the legislature by the leaders of majority parties who control the government. Only in presidential democracies such as the United States does the Congress, the legislative arm, continue to hold fully independent legislative and budgetary authority. In one-party states, particularly Leninist ones, the legislative bodies are reduced to rubber stamps.

The roles and functions of legislatures are still evolving throughout the Third World. In these nations the legislatures generally play three major roles in the political system—the legitimation of the government; the recruitment, socialization, and training of the political elite; and decisionmaking—though to varying degrees (Packenham 1970, 528–35). Simply by giving a stamp of approval on initiatives begun elsewhere, the legislature widens and deepens the sense of the government's moral right to rule. In addition, the legislature also recruits, socializes, and trains politicians for other posts that may wield more power in the political system. The decisionmaking role, though real in some instances, is usually limited. Even though the power of the legislature is restricted, it often provides a public forum for policy debate, interest articulation, conflict resolution, and administrative oversight. In the Republic of China the functions performed by the legislatures are circumscribed by two important conditions. The first is the KMT's control over the legislative and budgetary processes. In a single-party system such as the ROC from 1949 to 1986, the regime's structure denies the opposition effective use of the legislature to propose alternative strategies to those presented by the government (Foltz 1974, 163).

Meaningful discussions on legislative bills in ROC legislatures often take place in a private caucus organized under KMT auspices where party leaders can crack the whip. At most, dissenting legislators—a few opposition and maverick KMT members—can attempt to affect policy and the passage of bills through legislative foot-dragging or outlandish behavior on the floor. In the KMT's self-legitimizing version of Chinese history, the party has appropriated the right to determine the ground rules under which the legislatures at all levels must operate (Lerman 1978, 23).

The second important condition is the domination of the national legislature by representatives elected on the mainland back in 1947–1948. Because of their old age these legislators are inactive in the three chambers of the National Assembly, the Legislative Yuan, and the Control Yuan but cannot be held accountable to Taiwan's voters. By 1988 the average age of these permanent representatives—those elected in 1947–1948 but not subject to reelection since—was 82 in the Legislative Yuan and 78 in the National Assembly (see Table 6.1). Numerically they constitute at least three-quarters of the total membership in each chamber. The majority rarely attend deliberative sessions; meanwhile of those physically present only a few participate in floor and committee activities. With some exceptions they decline to confer with citizens and organized groups. In short, they have no real electoral constituency and are free of pressure from the public. The presence of these aging and unrepresentative members hampers the normal operation of the three parliamentary bodies.

The hierarchy of representative institutions in the ROC corresponds to the administrative structure. At the national level each of the three bodies—the National Assembly, the Legislative Yuan, and the Control Yuan—performs distinct functions not exactly like legislatures in other nations. But in 1957 the Council of Grand Justices in the Judicial Yuan, which exercises the authority of constitutional review, ruled that the three bodies together would serve as the "functional equivalents to parliament in a democratic country" (Lin Chin-k'un 1986c, 38). At the subnational level are the Taiwan Provincial Assembly and the municipal councils of Taipei and Kaohsiung. Further down the administrative hierarchy are city and county councils. The subcounty levels of township and rural administrative districts have assemblies of local delegates.

THE LEGISLATIVE YUAN

Of the three national parliamentary bodies, only the Legislative Yuan actually functions like the parliament in a representative democracy. It has a number of parliamentary powers. According to the constitution, the consent of the Legislative Yuan is required for the presidential appointment of the premier. The Executive Yuan must present to the Legislative Yuan an annual state-of-the-nation report and an annual budget three months before the fiscal year begins. Members of the Legislative Yuan may question the premier and any cabinet ministers on policy matters and administration. Moreover, the Legislative Yuan holds deliberative authority over a broad range of government bills. In the event that it disagrees with the Executive Yuan on important policies or bills related to statutory law or to the budget and treaties, a two-thirds vote of opposition can force the Executive Yuan either to comply with the legislative resolution or to have the premier resign.

In practice, however, the Legislative Yuan has seldom disagreed with the Executive Yuan on proposed budgets and government bills. Although there have been rare instances of disagreement, the differences were ironed out through KMT mediation or by patronage given to key legislators by cabinet officials (Huang Su-chi 1983, 20). At times legislators use interpellation sessions to criticize the government or individual cabinet officials. But interpellation does not pose a political threat to the premier or to his cabinet members. It merely provides an avenue for discontented legislators to air their views or to seek clarification on the specifics of a government action.

When Chiang Ching-kuo was premier, he personally responded to all questions raised by legislators during the interpellation sessions. In subsequent years Premier Sun Yun-hsuen replied only to questions related to finance and economic affairs while he relied on his cabinet ministers to respond to questions relating to their jurisdictions. Thus for six years, from 1978 to 1984, the interpellation sessions established regular channels of communication between legislators and cabinet officials. There was some media coverage of interpellation sessions during that time, so the public became aware of some government policies that had been confidential or not widely publicized. Under Premier Yu Kuo-hwa (1984 to the present), executive-legislative relations have occasionally been strained. The source of the difficulty may be the premier's personality, for he does not have Chiang Ching-kuo's charisma and power or Sun's reformist image and popularity. Yu's lesser political stature adversely affects his cabinet's ability to exercise legislative leadership, and the responsibility for coordinating activities on the legislative floor devolves on the KMT organization in the Legislative Yuan.

Floor Organization

The Legislative Yuan consists of the following five categories of legislators:

1. Members elected on the mainland in 1947, who are not subject to reelection (216 members)

2. Members elected in Taiwan for permanent tenure in the 1969 supplementary election (7 members)

3. Members appointed by the president from the overseas Chinese communities for three-year terms (22 members)

4. Members popularly elected in Taiwan and Quemoy for three-year terms (55 members)

5. Members elected by certain organized groups representing workers, farmers, businessmen, industrialists, fishermen, and teachers for three-year terms (19 members)

Of these legislators, only the 74 elected in Taiwan (categories 4 and 5 above) can truly claim to represent their constituents. They compose slightly less than one-quarter of the 312 Legislative Yuan members in early 1988.

Members meet in two regular sessions during the year. The first session lasts from February to May, the second from September to December. Each member receives a total monthly income (salary plus other compensation) of N.T. $75,000, or about U.S. $2,700.[1] Additional compensation is provided when a legislative session extends beyond the normal four months, something that occurs regularly. Furthermore, legislators from the 1947–1948 group are given free housing in the affluent suburbs of Taipei. The material benefits to Legislative Yuan members compare favorably with those to cabinet ministers and when appraised quantitatively are more than double the wages and benefits of college professors on Taiwan.

Since the legislators of the 1947–1948 group no longer serve a real constituency, their jobs are less demanding. But legislators elected on Taiwan can be extremely busy. They are bombarded with such social duties as attending weddings and funerals; both types of events require sub-stantial monetary contributions. The Legislators must run endless services for their constituents on such matters as getting an illegal gambler released from police custody, finding jobs for the relatives of supporters, and ex-tending other personal favors. These chores form an important part of constituency service in Taiwan, and they are important to winning votes in an election. One survey estimates that Taiwanese legislators receive an average of 3.5 such requests a day, and over half have 30 or more wed-dings and funerals to attend each month (*CKSP*, June 30, 1982, 2). Most maintain an office in their home districts at their own expense. Because of these obligations, about 70 percent of Taiwanese Legislative Yuan members need to seek additional funding to cover their living and oper-ating expenses (*CKSP*, July 2, 1982, 2). Typically they enter business joint ventures, hold paid advisory posts in corporations, or draw com-missions for providing social brokerage functions.

Ironically, as demanding as these obligations are, the ability of a leg-islator to meet constituent needs does not seem to have much bearing on the individual legislator's mobility within the chamber's power structure or on committee assignments. There are twelve standing committees: in-ternal affairs, foreign affairs, national defense, economic affairs, finance, budget, education, communications, frontier affairs, overseas Chinese af-fairs, judicial affairs, and legal institutions. Four special committees deal with the Legislative Yuan's own affairs: credentials, rules, accounts, and the maintenance of order. Each legislative member may serve on only one committee. A committee chairman (*chao-chi-jen*) may be quite influ-ential, particularly as chair of one of the big four committees: defense, fi-nance, economic affairs, or budget.[2] Almost all chairs are controlled by KMT officials and faction leaders within the chamber. One or two are set aside as plums for popularly elected members from either the KMT or the DPP. Usually KMT faction leaders hand-picked by party stalwarts monopolize the chairs. Such practices have recently been challenged by the popularly elected KMT members, who threatened either to form their own faction or to make an alliance with the DPP members (Chen Cheng-nung 1987a, 48–50; Kuo Ch'ung-lun 1987, 50–54).

Legislative committees in the ROC are not nearly as powerful as their counterparts in the U.S. Congress. Much of the legislative work is done in the Executive Yuan before the bills are submitted to the Legisla-tive Yuan. After the bills leave the Executive Yuan the committees rarely make substantive changes. In fact the committee on which a legislator serves does not really make much difference, since committee actions and those of the Legislative Yuan as a whole are tightly controlled by the ranking KMT members.

The Legislative Yuan has a president (*yuan-chang*) and a vice president, both elected by the members at large. In practice, this election has little meaning since the candidates are ordinarily designated by the KMT chairman. And on Taiwan legislative authority is subservient to party power. Since 1950 there have been only four presidents and three vice presidents. There were no restrictions on length of tenure until 1981, when a three-year term was instituted; election to unlimited consecutive terms is still allowed. Ni Wen-ya, the current president and a member of the KMT's old guard, has held the office since May 1972 and is expected to step down soon. The vice president is Liu K'uo-ts'ai, a Hakka Taiwanese who rose to that position through party loyalty and a successful career in electoral politics. Liu is not regarded as a key member in the inner power circles of the Legislative Yuan.

The president, chairmen of the key committees, and party leaders on the floor are important figures in the legislative process. All these individuals operate in concert with the KMT organizations in the Legislative Yuan, which dictate committee assignments and coordinate floor and committee activities. Intraparty rivalry and disputes between the KMT and the opposition DPP are mediated through the party leaders. Since opposition members were not allowed to form any partylike organization until 1987, they have had to rely on ad hoc caucuses to shape positions during legislative battles. And since they number only thirteen, opposition has held little leverage in the legislative process. The best tactics they have found are disruption of floor procedure and "united interpellation," joining together on an issue to question the premier and other cabinet members.

The KMT organization on the legislative floor reports directly to the party Central Committee and the Central Standing Committee through the party secretary-general (*mi-shu-chang*) of the Policy Coordination Committee, who is in practice also a member of the Legislative Yuan. Although the Policy Coordinating Committee is attached to the KMT's central headquarters rather than the Legislative Yuan, its principal activities are liaison work with the Legislative Yuan and other parliamentary bodies. It is not surprising then that the positions of secretary-general and his deputies are considered among the most desirable for KMT legislators.

Within the Legislative Yuan the KMT branch is headed by a general secretary (*shi-chi-chang*) who takes charge of legislative floor work. This post is usually offered to the leader of the largest KMT faction in the legislature, and the three deputy posts are earmarked for leaders of minor factions and legislators elected from Taiwan. A KMT standing committee serves as the party's executive arm in the Legislative Yuan; a majority of its seats were held by the 1947–1948 group until August 1988, when 5 of its 9 seats were given to the Taiwan-elected legislators (*CYJP*, August 18, 1988, 1). Another KMT party committee has 25 places for members of the Legislative Yuan. Of these, 17 are reserved for members of the old guard and only 8 for those elected in Taiwan (K'ou Ssu-lei 1982, 19). All 12 functional committee chairmen in the Legislative Yuan are included automatically in this party committee. The remaining 13 slots are filled by appointments made at KMT central headquarters in consultation with key KMT legislators. In short, the general secretary, his three deputies, and members of the standing committee form the KMT leadership core in charge of all mediation and coordination activities in the Legislative Yuan. The general secretary works closely with leaders of the Policy Co-ordinating Committee to establish functional links between the legislature's party units and the party center.

Background of the Legislators

According to the 1947 constitution the Legislative Yuan should have 773 members. But logistical problems and the civil war made elections on the mainland impossible in some localities that year; consequently only 760 persons were elected to the legislature in 1947. Two years later only 470 of them retreated with the ROC government to Taiwan. The balance either decided to stay on the mainland or emigrated elsewhere overseas. Table 6.1 shows that in February 1988 only 216 of these permanent legislators were still alive.

With the steady reduction in the original membership and the greater demand for broader political participation in Taiwan, ROC authorities have taken three steps to add new members. According to one analysis, each time the ROC suffers a major diplomatic setback it takes an additional step to liberalize the pattern of representative government to quiet critics and enhance political harmony on Taiwan (Chiu 1986a, 9–10). In 1965 for the first time a United Nations resolution to expel the ROC delegation received a 47-to-47 tie vote, threatening the ROC's status as the government representing China. On Taiwan demands for internal political reform intensified. In the following year the National Assembly amended the temporary provisions and empowered the ROC president to add legislative members from Taiwan by popular election. Subsequently 11 new members were elected in 1969 to serve indefinite terms. At the same time 15 seats were added to the National Assembly and 2 to the Control Yuan.

In October 1971 the ROC was finally unseated from the United Nations. That diplomatic crisis touched off another wave of demands for political reform. The result was another amendment to the temporary

_____ TABLE 6.1 _____
COMPOSITION OF THE NATIONAL LEGISLATURES OF THE ROC, FEBRUARY 1988

	National Assembly	Legislative Yuan	Control Yuan
Constitutionally required members	3,045	773	223
Members elected in 1947–1948	2,961	760	180
Members who came to Taiwan in 1949	1,576	470	104
Total members in 1988	922	312	67
1947–1948 group	838	216	36
Members elected in Taiwan	91	74	24
Appointed overseas Chinese	0	27	7
Nonattending members[a]	179	10	0
Average age	75	72	71
1947–1948 group	78	82	83
Members elected in Taiwan	49	51	57

SOURCES: *CKSP* (February 4, 1988), 2; *CYJP,* international ed. (February 4, 1988), 1.
[a]Because of illness or permanent residence overseas.

provisions that created an additional 51 seats for the Legislative Yuan, 53 for the National Assembly, and 15 for the Control Yuan. Among the new seats in the Legislative Yuan, 15 were filled by appointment from overseas Chinese communities.

In December 1978, when the United States ended formal diplomatic relations with the ROC, pressure again mounted for further parliamentary reform. A supplementary election was held in 1980 to address this problem; in it the number of new legislators was increased to 97, of whom 27 were appointed from overseas Chinese communities. In addition to 70 new posts in the Legislative Yuan, the National Assembly opened 76 seats to popular election and the Control Yuan opened 32.

Still the addition of new members through supplementary elections has not solved the basic issues of parliamentary legitimacy and balanced representation. Since the average age of the 1947–1948 group is already over 80, only a few of these 1,190 members will survive through the 1990s. The ROC authorities are concerned that once these three bodies have only Taiwan-elected members and overseas appointees, the government can no longer claim to represent all of China, a development that could further erode the foundations of the regime on Taiwan.

A more fundamental reform in the parliamentary institutions has become urgent. In April 1986, after the Third Plenum of the KMT Twelfth Central Committee, Chiang Ching-kuo appointed 12 members of the Central Standing Committee to a task force to study and make proposals on political reforms, including major modifications of the parliamentary system. At issue were the attrition of the 1947–1948 group and an appropriate formula to strengthen the representative character of the government. Most likely the KMT authorities will substantially increase the number of representatives in the three parliamentary institutions in the election scheduled for November 1989 and will institute a program to induce the 1947–1948 group to retire voluntarily (*TLWP*, August 17, 1988, 1).

In December 1986, 74 members were chosen in parliamentary elections, constituting about 24 percent of the Legislative Yuan. An additional 27 members were appointed by President Chiang as delegates from overseas Chinese communities. Since the overseas representatives reside abroad, their involvement in legislative activities is limited. With the passage of time, therefore, those elected from Taiwan are certain to carry more weight in the legislative process. In fact the injection of the so-called supplementary members by election since 1969 has been the chief source of the legislature's modest vitality.

One important indicator of legislative vitality is the number of interpellations. Interpellations can be either oral or written. Since 1973, when 36 elected members were added, the total number of interpellations in the Legislative Yuan increased markedly. As Figure 6.1 indicates, from 1972 to 1973 the number of interpellations more than doubled. The number declined somewhat in subsequent years, partly because the KMT tightened party discipline, but it remained much higher than before 1973. The dramatic increase in 1978 can be attributed to a large number of questions about the change in diplomatic relations between the United States and Taiwan. And after the 1980 election, when Taiwan's elected members rose to 70, there was another sharp increase in interpellations to almost 2,000 in the 1981 legislative sessions. Although figures are not available, members elected in Taiwan have remained active since 1981. In contrast, during 1981–1987, 158 of the 216 members in the 1947–1948 group failed to make any oral interpellation (Su 1987, 51). Thus the addition of legislators elected in Taiwan has revived the legislative process in the ROC, and future elections should continue this trend.

Factionalism in the Legislative Yuan

Legislative politics on Taiwan have been characterized by factional realignments within the KMT and the emergence of DPP members as

——— FIGURE 6.1 ———
NUMBER OF INTERPELLATIONS, 1971–1981

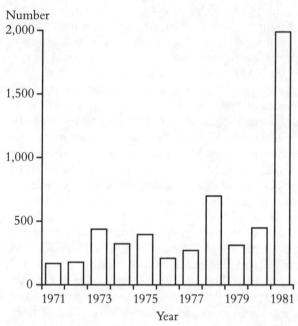

SOURCE: Engstrom and Chu (1984), 457.

important actors in both floor and committee activities. Factionalism has plagued the KMT since its early years in pre-1949 China. After arriving on Taiwan, Chiang Kai-shek was determined to eradicate intraparty factional conflicts, which he believed had contributed to the KMT's downfall on the mainland. For the 39 years the two Chiangs controlled Taiwan, they maintained extra caution to prevent factionalism from returning to the KMT. Because of their relentless efforts, factional politics have been brought under control, though not completely eradicated.

The Legislative Yuan still has five factional groups.

    1. The United Caucus clique (*lien-ho tso-t'an-hui p'ai*) is a coalition of the following pre-1949 groups:
        a. Graduates of the Whampoa Military Academy
        b. Members of the Three People's Principles (*san-min-chu* I) Youth Corps, founded in 1938 on the mainland with General Chen Cheng as its first leader

    c. Members of the Renaissance Society (*fu-hsing-she*), an extreme right-wing group connected mainly with security and intelligence activities previously under Tai Li's leadership

    d. Followers of Chu Chia-hua, who succeeded Chen Cheng as head of the Three People's Principles Youth Corps and later headed the KMT Organization Department on the mainland (Chen Cheng-nung 1987b, 34–40; Chen Hao 1984, 27–30; Han 1984, 11–13)

These four groups formed a united faction in the 1950s in support of then Premier Chen Cheng. Since his death in 1965, they have consistently supported government policies. With 146 members in 1988, the United Caucus is the largest and most important faction in the Legislative Yuan. Major figures include Ni Wen-ya (president of the Legislative Yuan), Chao Tzu-ch'i (former Policy Coordinating Committee secretary-general), Lin Tung (the KMT general secretary in the Legislative Yuan), Chen Ts'ang-cheng, and Chou Mu-wen. In addition, the faction is given three seats in the KMT's 7-man standing committee in the Legislative Yuan. It is not surprising then that the majority of elected KMT members in Taiwan belong to this faction.

    2. The CC clique were followers of the Chen brothers—Chen Li-fu and Chen Kuo-fu—in pre-1949 China, where the two men dominated the KMT Organization Department from 1927 to 1949. In the 1950s on Taiwan they formed what was initially the largest faction, reflecting CC strength in 1949. Throughout the first two decades of Nationalist rule on Taiwan, the CC clique gradually lost political strength. In the 1960s Chow Hung-t'ao, under instructions from Chiang Ching-kuo, persuaded the CC clique's younger members to form separate groups, thus splitting the faction into three elements (Ch'en Cheng-nung 1987b, 36). There are now about 60 members remaining; leaders include Liang Su-jung (the current Policy Coordinating Committee secretary-general), Chang Tzu-yang, and Wu Yen-huan (Han 1984, 11).

    3. The New Center clique (*hsin chung-yang*) consists of 35 members who split away from the CC clique to form their own group in the 1960s. They are considered an ally of the large United Caucus clique in legislative politics.

    4. The Central Society clique (*chung-she*) is a coalition of several former CC members plus a handful of Young China Party and Democratic Socialist Party members. The group has about 25 members.

5. The One-Four Caucus clique (*i-szu tso-t'an-hui*)[3] consists of a handful of legislators whose earlier careers were closely linked with the Kwangsi clique headed by Li Tsung-jen and Pai Ch'ung-hsi. This faction, although still in existence, has not played a significant role in legislative politics (Chen Hao 1984, 27).

Each of these factions is bound internally by personal ties, the demands of political expediency, and the members' career experiences. None possesses a formal organizational structure, but each has nominal leaders recognized by both its members and the KMT. Except for the partial breakup of the CC clique in the 1960s, there have been no other important factional realignments. Once a person becomes identified with a particular faction, that identity holds.

Legislators elected in Taiwan have not been able to form their own factions. The KMT leadership has been firmly against such a faction for fear that it would pit Taiwanese against mainlanders within the KMT and thus cause difficulties in party discipline. In 1981 KMT authorities ordered a newly formed mutual assistance club (*hu-chu-hui*) to be dissolved when it became apparent that it was a group of Taiwan-elected KMT members who might emerge as a power bloc in the legislature. Three years later Ts'ai Ch'en-chou, then Taipei's financial tycoon, formed the Thirteen Brothers group, consisting of thirteen legislators elected in Taiwan (Wu Ke-ch'ing 1985, 59). The group also had connections with a financial-business conglomerate headed by Ts'ai. In March 1985 a major scandal involving Ts'ai's Tenth Credit Cooperative in Taipei led to his arrest, bringing an end to this venture by ambitious Taiwanese KMT members to form a new clique (Lin Chien-hsing 1985, 14–16; Goldstein 1985b, 93).

After the December 1986 election, legislators elected from Taiwan have become more assertive in the Legislative Yuan. In early 1987 several abortive attempts were made to form factionlike associations; some were even based on cooperation between the KMT and the DPP (Kuo Ch'ung-lun 1987, 50–53). Finally in 1988, 28 KMT legislators elected in Taiwan successfully formed a "common views club" (*chi-szu-hui*), and another 12 countered with a "construction club" (*chien-she-hui*) (*Tzu-li Morning Post*, November 2, 1988, 2). There seems to be a consensus among Taiwan-elected members, KMT and DPP alike, that they must gradually take over legislative power from the old guard. Such feelings stem from the belief that they, rather than the old guard, truly represent the people. The emergence of this new consciousness comes at a time when the legislative activities of the old guard are clearly in decline. Moreover the nationwide debate on parliamentary reforms has put the old guard on the defensive. Although the newly elected KMT members may not succeed in creating alternative bases of factional power in the Legislative Yuan in the near future, a new kind of factional politics may be developing in the ROC after 40 years.

Opposition legislators have also shown interest in initiating new legislative tactics. Before the birth of the DPP, the nonparty opposition in the Legislative Yuan was small and ineffective. But the situation changed in the 1987–1989 legislative session. The thirteen DPP members formed a party group and have elected two spokespersons each year. So far the DPP members have acted as a unified new force in legislative politics.

The DPP members have been exceptionally active in both floor and committee work. Some, notably German-educated Chu Kao-cheng from southern Taiwan, have resorted to verbal abuse and outlandish behavior against the old guard and the legislative establishment. Chu's purpose is to discredit those legislators not subject to periodic popular election. Other DPP members, such as K'ang Ning-hsiang, have joined important committees as a result of careful floor maneuvers. The KMT even agreed to cut its proposed 1988 budget for the first time because of objections from the opposition. It appears at this juncture that the DPP members are revitalizing the Legislative Yuan. In time the old factions may be replaced by new groups formed by Taiwan-elected members from either the KMT or the DPP. New rules for legislative floor procedures and committee deliberations may be adopted even before the anticipated reform of parliamentary membership.

THE CONTROL YUAN AND THE NATIONAL ASSEMBLY

The Control Yuan

The Control Yuan is a peculiar Chinese institution. Its members are elected indirectly by members of the provincial assembly and municipal councils of Taipei and Kaohsiung. It has the investigating power of a modern legislature and performs what were the inspection functions of the censorate in imperial China. Its powers include approval of the appointments of the grand justices as well as the presidents and vice presidents of the Judicial Yuan and the Examination Yuan; impeachment and censure of government officials; supervision of examinations conducted by the Examination Yuan and other government agencies; and field investigations of government conduct at all levels (*China Yearbook*, 1978, 120).

The impeachment of the president or the vice president of the republic requires the initiative of at least one-fourth of the Control Yuan plus a majority vote. Once a motion for impeachment was adopted, it would be forwarded to the National Assembly for action. Impeachment of the president or vice president has never occurred in the ROC. Impeachments of lesser public officials, once finalized, are referred to a committee on the discipline of public officials within the Judicial Yuan for a hearing and sentencing. Censure of government officials usually involves an initial investigation of the charges and then requires the concurrence of at least three members of the Control Yuan before the case goes to trial. When there is evidence of a violation of law, a civil or military tribunal will try the case, depending on the offense. According to the Law for the Discipline of Public Functionaries, once a censure case is adopted by the Control Yuan, the offender's superior is obligated to take punitive measures against civil servants who have committed misdemeanors. The tribunal or the offender's superior decides on the appropriate punishment; the Control Yuan can only make recommendations to the Executive Yuan for action. In short, the Control Yuan exercises important investigative functions in the ROC political system.

Whether or not such functions are carried out may indicate the vitality of the Control Yuan as an institution. Figure 6.2 shows a steady decline in the total cases of impeachment, censure, and corrective measures between 1950 and 1984. Since 1971, the year Chiang Ching-kuo took over the premiership, the Control Yuan's activities have shown a modest, sporadic revival. The total cases went up to 27 in 1976 before declining again in 1981. The year 1984 shows a mild upsurge with 21 cases, but the figure remains considerably lower than any year prior to 1971.

Impeachment cases are most likely to target high officials. A close look at the number of impeachment cases from 1950 to 1984 shows further evidence of the institutional decay of the Control Yuan. In 1949 there were 33 impeachment cases (Liu Jen-yüan 1983, 9). Throughout the 1950s and the 1960s the annual average number of impeachment cases was 13 (Li Chieh 1984, 12). As Figure 6.3 indicates, there were only 2 to 3 cases each year in 1971, 1976, and 1981. The increase in impeachment cases to 7 in 1984 coincides with the mild upsurge in total cases that year. Whether this reversal signals the beginning of institutional revitalization is not yet clear. Furthermore, during the earlier years cases of impeachment were initiated against such high-level officials as Premier Yu Hung-chun in 1957, Taipei Mayor Huang Ch'i-jui in 1964, and Economics Minister Li Kuo-ting and Finance Minister Chen Ch'ing-Yu in 1966 (Li Chien 1984, 13; Liu Jen-yüan, 5–9). Since the 1970s, however, impeachment cases have involved only middle- or lower-level functionaries. In early 1988 several members of the Control Yuan initiated impeachment cases against Kaohsiung Mayor Su Nan-cheng (*CKSP,* March

10, 1988, 2). In a separate case, attempts to impeach Economics Minister Li Ta-hai and his two deputy ministers were also widely publicized (*CKSP,* March 12, 1988, 3). But neither impeachment case had been formally adopted by April 1988. Recent actions by the Control Yuan suggest a serious attempt to revive its constitutional functions.

Why did the Control Yuan become inactive and increasingly ineffective until 1984–1988? One reason may be the aging of the old guard in the Control Yuan. The 36 members initially elected in 1947–1948 now average 83 years of age. The KMT's growing intervention has also reduced the number of impeachment cases, since such cases are considered

——— FIGURE 6.2 ———
CONTROL YUAN TOTAL CASES, 1950–1984

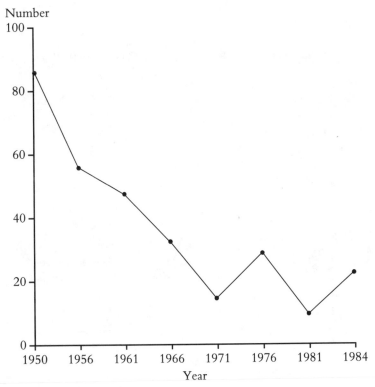

SOURCE: *TCNC* (1985), 1010.
NOTE: Figures include cases of impeachment, censure, and corrective measures.

damaging to political harmony on the island. As the party stepped up its mediation efforts, potential cases rarely surfaced. Moreover the 22 new members added since the 1970s to represent Taiwan have been cautious, fearing that investigations might antagonize powerful individuals in the party. After all, their bid for reelection depends heavily on party patronage. Most Taiwan-elected members therefore look to party authorities for instruction on potential cases. Since the KMT is bent on maintaining a façade of political harmony in the face of growing challenges from the opposition, most KMT members of the Control Yuan have learned to follow the well-known saying, "To do less is to make fewer mistakes." Finally, there is a shortage of qualified staff in the Control Yuan for investigative work. The total staff numbers less than a hundred, and only a portion has investigative responsibility. Even in lesser cases involving censure and corrective discipline, investigation may be either put off or left incomplete because of understaffing. When the Control Yuan inves-

_____ FIGURE 6.3 _____
CONTROL YUAN IMPEACHMENT CASES, 1950–1984

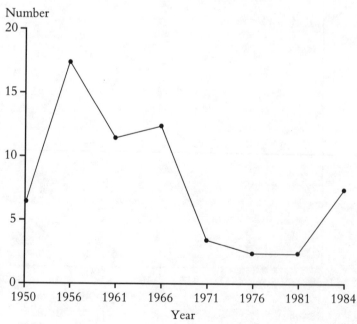

SOURCE: *TCNC* (1985), 1010.

tigated the illegal financial activities of the Taipei Tenth Credit Cooperative and its affiliated Cathay Trust in 1985, its recommendations of punitive actions against major government officials were ignored even by the higher authorities (*SPCK*, 1985, 14–15; Goldstein 1985b, 94).

In short, for two decades since the mid-1960s the Control Yuan has been a status institution. Rather than performing investigative functions, it is a quasi-governmental institution with membership awarded to KMT politicians in a scheme of political spoils. The ruling party uses it to patronize elected politicians who are seeking upward political mobility and who are not expected to rock the boat once in office. Since the KMT has initiated a broad range of political reforms in recent years, the Control Yuan could rejuvenate itself by becoming more active. But its efficiency as an investigative institution will be compromised as long as the KMT continues to intervene in the Control Yuan's internal affairs.

The National Assembly

The National Assembly's duties are scant and insignificant. According to the constitution it elects and recalls, if necessary, the president and the vice president of the republic. It may also amend the constitution by referendum. In reality, however, the election of the president and the vice president has been reduced to a ceremony. In the current political structure, the KMT party or its leader selects the candidates for these offices. After coming to Taiwan, national assemblymen routinely rubber-stamped the selections made once every six years by Chiang Kai-shek and Chiang Ching-kuo.

Although the National Assembly has not altered the constitution, it has on several occasions amended the temporary provisions enacted in 1948 to circumvent many of the constitution's important articles. These amendments have provided the president with a broad range of emergency powers not contained in the constitution (see Chapter 5). The underlying aim has been to strengthen the legal foundations of the emergency regime without appearing to suspend constitutional provisions. The National Assembly has carried out these maneuvers under the direction of the KMT's highest authorities.

When the National Assembly was first instituted in 1947, its exercise of power with regard to the constitution was meant to be periodic; its members were not full-time legislators. Since coming to Taiwan, however, the ROC has transformed it into a permanent assembly. Members receive payments and benefits equal to those of the two other national representative institutions. To justify such treatment the authorities have created two operational committees to which each National Assembly member belongs. The Committee for the Study of the Constitution meets from time to time to study various aspects of the constitution or the temporary provisions, presumably to make alterations. The other functional committee is charged with studying future ROC development on the mainland in the event that the KMT realizes its goal of unification.

As a representative institution the National Assembly is clearly superfluous. Most of its rudimentary functions cater to the interests of the ruling elite. From the regime's perspective, it performs the important tasks of legitimizing the presidential authority and constitutional alterations desired by the KMT authorities. Its existence also symbolizes the continuity of the ROC's constitutional order from the mainland to Taiwan. For Taiwan's elected politicians, a seat in the National Assembly is a political status symbol rather than a post with real power. Many elected national assemblymen from Taiwan also see the position as a stepping-stone to a more important elected position.

THE TAIWAN PROVINCIAL ASSEMBLY

Compared with the Legislative Yuan and the National Assembly, the Taiwan Provincial Assembly is more of a functioning representative body. Members are elected, engage in active legislative work, and provide many services for their constituents. The Provincial Assembly was established in August 1959 according to the provisions of the Organic Law of the Taiwan Provincial Assembly promulgated by the Executive Yuan. Its predecessors were the Provincial People's Political Council (1946–1951) and the Taiwan Provisional Provincial Assembly (1951–1959). Members of these earlier bodies were elected indirectly by city and county councilmen until 1954, when popular elections were instituted. Before 1972, when a substantial number of supplementary seats were created for the three national parliamentary bodies, provincial assemblymen were the highest level of elected representatives in Taiwan.

The jurisdiction of the assembly is limited to provincial affairs as specified in the constitution. The affairs of the municipalities of Taipei and Kaohsiung are excluded from its jurisdiction. The Provincial Assembly has the power

1. To pass regulations concerning the rights and obligations of the people

2. To approve the administrative budget and screen the provincial accounts

3. To decide on the disposal of provincial property

4. To review the proposals of the provincial government
5. To listen to reports from the provincial administration and to make interpellations
6. To submit proposals for administrative reforms
7. To consider petitions from the people
8. To approve the bylaws of provincial public enterprises

These powers enable the Provincial Assembly to play a major role in governing the island (*CHNC,* 1978, 140; Mu 1979, 9).

During the 1950s and 1960s assembly seats were the most rewarding elected offices available to Taiwanese. The island's social notables and local elite—wealthy merchants, physicians, lawyers, and industrialists—competed furiously for the KMT nominations (Chen Yang-te 1978, 65–107). On the assembly floor assemblymen jockeyed intensely for factional alignment, important committee assignments, and the prize posts of speaker or deputy speaker (Lerman 1978, 173–179). The rivalry between Speaker Huang Ch'ao-ch'in and Vice Speaker Lin Ting-li, as well as the factional strife between Hsu Chin-te and Li Chien-hsing, dramatized the intensity of assembly politics in the early years. Famous nonparty assemblymen, such as Kuo Yu-hsin, Wu San-lien, Kuo Kuo-chi, Li Wan-chu, and Li Yuan-chien, used the assembly as a forum to air their criticism of the government's policies. Debate and political maneuvering in the assembly captured popular interest throughout the island.

The KMT has always controlled a large majority of the seats in the assembly (Ho, 1985b, 26). In 1977 the opposition scored an unprecedented victory when non-KMT candidates captured 21 (17 percent) of the 77 seats in the provincial legislature. Furthermore, several of this "class of '77"—such as Chang Chun-hung, Hsu Hsin-liang, and Lin Yi-hsiung—belonged to a new breed of nonparty activists who were well-educated, articulate, well-versed in democratic ideas, and raised in Taiwan under KMT rule. For two years, until some of them were arrested after the 1979 Kaohsiung Incident, they used the assembly to debate controversial political issues, creating headaches for the KMT leadership. Although unable to stop the passage of government bills, they used floor speeches to ridicule government officials even on matters unrelated to the bills (Chen Li-ching 1980, 93). In response, the KMT frequently resorted to parliamentary maneuvers on the floor to limit the opportunities of nonparty assemblymen to give political speeches.

The speaker who presides over the assembly has the task of maintaining order on the floor. Since the 1950s there have been only four speakers: Huang Ch'ao-ch'in (1946–1965), Hsueh Tung-min (1963–

1970), Ts'ai Hung-wen (1970–1981), and Kao Yu-jen (1981 to the present). The speaker enjoyed more prestige before 1972, when few powerful posts were open to Taiwanese in either the party or the government. As more Taiwanese have been appointed to high positions at the national level, the speaker's prestige and relative importance have declined. But the position is still powerful, and the speaker is also a member of the KMT Central Standing Committee. Appointment as speaker is viewed as a stepping-stone to higher appointive office, such as governor or cabinet minister. A deputy speaker assists the speaker and has minor formal powers (Lerman 1978, 174).

Bills are reviewed in the Provincial Assembly by six standing committees: agriculture and forestry, civil affairs, education, finance, reconstruction, and transportation. The last three are the most significant because they deal with large amounts of public money. For example, commercial bank affairs are supervised by both the provincial government and the Provincial Assembly. Thus members of the assembly's finance committee, particularly the chairman, are often able to expedite loans as favors. Since most banks in Taiwan offer commercial loans on stringent collateral requirements, a seat on the finance committee can bring a valuable exemption from these requirements. The reconstruction committee supervises public works projects. A skillful committeeman can use his position to solicit benefits from the contracting firms. Finally, the transportation committee oversees the affairs of railways and buses, including the determination of bus routes. Over the years this committee has been dominated by assemblymen who own or have personal connections with bus companies.

Unlike the Legislative Yuan, the Provincial Assembly has a reputation for dealing in political favors. Assembly members have a relatively high degree of autonomy in bargaining for reciprocal favors. Without an old guard of mainlanders serving life tenure in the assembly, the assemblymen operate with fewer constraints and in a setting of relative equality. The matters that come up for consideration are not tied to fundamental national policies but rather affect people's daily lives on matters such as the price of public transportation, agricultural subsidies, road construction, and commercial regulation. Even the authorities are less alarmed when bills are substantially revised by bargaining in the assembly. Because of its propensity for wheeling and dealing, the Provincial Assembly was usually livelier than the Legislative Yuan until 1987, when some DPP members initiated dramatic acts and debates in the Legislative Yuan for the first time.

But the legislative maneuvers of the provincial assemblymen are not without constraints. KMT assembly members must follow party directives in voting and in interpellation sessions. A KMT party secretary and three deputy secretaries are responsible for coordinating party activities on the floor and in the committees. Across the street from the assembly hall at the special complex of provincial government offices in Chunghsing New Village is a KMT branch office that provides a convenient location for the party's caucuses. The responsibility of that KMT branch is primarily to keep KMT assemblymen in line to offer strong support for government bills and secondarily to dampen any criticism aired by party members. A KMT member who takes on a more independent stance in the assembly runs the risk of losing the party's backing in the next election. Most KMT assemblymen look to the party for assistance in upward political mobility, and compliance with party discipline is a proven route to future rewards. But despite party efforts to maintain discipline, it cannot restrain activity over matters that are not of major political importance. For example, the KMT permits the assemblymen to serve their constituents' requests in a wide range of matters since the party understands that responding to these needs is necessary for reelection. As Taiwan's socioeconomic system differentiates, however, conflicts have occurred between assemblymen who are KMT members but who represent different interests. In such cases KMT officials must mediate to avoid severe conflicts.

Provincial assemblymen have many social obligations to fulfill. Even more than members of the Legislative Yuan, they must run countless errands for individuals from their constituency seeking favors. Obtaining a bank loan, having a road paved, gaining public employment, and getting someone released from police custody are all activities provincial assemblymen perform daily. There are also countless weddings, banquets, and funerals to attend. People feel offended if their invitations are not honored, particularly by elected representatives. Attention to social functions can play as important a role as party loyalty in shaping an assemblyman's political career. Social obligations initiated by factional leaders in the assembly or an influential social notable also require an assemblyman's time and energy.

The nonparty members are free from the constraints of party discipline. The DPP is not yet organized well enough to apply party discipline over its ten assemblymen. The opposition caucus, formed in May 1987, consists of fifteen members, five of whom are not formal members of the DPP (Wang Po-jen 1987, 77). Thus the caucus coordinates its legislative actions without any disciplinary authority over the five non-DPP assemblymen. The opposition's role is often frustrating because members have little control over floor actions. A non-KMT vote rarely affects the outcome of an issue, but the assemblyman can use the legislative sessions to raise issues, to criticize party or government conduct, and to pressure government officials through verbal attacks on the floor. Such verbal threats can also provide a skillful nonparty figure with leverage against party and government officials. He can use that advantage to seek favors on behalf of his constituents. Moderate nonparty assemblymen who cooperate with the KMT are likely to be rewarded. Still, even in an assembly dominated by one party there is room for assemblymen, KMT or otherwise, to influence the legislative process. Although mainly concerned with issues of little political sensitivity, the Provincial Assembly has been lively since 1959, and the KMT lacks both the intention and the ability to turn it into a rubber stamp.

CONCLUSION

Taiwan's three national representative institutions are important sources of both regime legitimacy and political change. The old guard of these institutions, elected on the mainland during 1947–1948, symbolize the regime's continuity; they also help perpetuate the myth of Nationalist representation of the whole of China. But with the passage of time this rationalization is fading. Besides, the aging and death of the mainland-elected members have severely undermined the integrity of these institutions. The addition of popularly elected members from Taiwan since the 1970s has helped somewhat to revitalize these institutions but cannot fully restore their eroded foundations. Ironically, these new members have made one point clear to Taiwan's voters: legislators provide a legitimate base of representation only if they are subject to periodic reelection. The most serious dilemma in parliamentary matters that the ruling authorities face is how to strengthen the representative character of the institutions on Taiwan while continuing to preserve the regime's mainland connections.

At this juncture a sweeping reform that could undermine the KMT officials' own positions seems unlikely. But a reform scheme may try to preserve elements of continuity while broadening the popular basis of these representative bodies. The logic of political evolution would require such a compromise. Then a revitalized legislature could accommodate the growing demands for political democratization and make more room for ambitious Taiwanese seeking elected office.

Nevertheless the DPP will not be satisfied with this type of limited reform. Without elections for all National Assembly members, the mainlander-controlled KMT will be able to choose the ROC's president, who is elected by the assembly. Thus the DPP would never stand a chance of capturing this powerful post. Besides, the National Assembly has the authority to revise the ROC constitution. The DPP also wants reform measures to include the possibility that the National Assembly may some day be controlled by a Taiwanese majority that could revise the constitution and tailor it to Taiwan's local identity. Since neither change is likely, the best the DPP can hope for is a compromise in which the National Assembly preserves a mainland quota but the Legislative Yuan and the Control Yuan are popularly elected. This compromise would give the DPP leverage in the Legislative Yuan over the selection of the premier and the cabinet members, who are appointed by the president with the consent of the legislators. Under this arrangement if the DPP ever won a majority of seats in the Legislative Yuan it could force the ROC's president to appoint a premier satisfactory to the DPP, or even a DPP premier.

The future of parliamentary reform seems uncertain at this writing. A realistic forecast would predict that Taiwan's representative institutions, particularly the Legislative Yuan, will acquire much more power in the system as the political reforms set in motion by Chiang Chung-kuo are carried through.

— 7 —

Electoral Politics

Instituted by the ROC government in 1950, the concept and practice of popular elections are fairly new on Taiwan. During the latter part of Japanese colonial rule elections were held for representatives to advisory councils in townships but with only limited franchise (Crissman 1981, 101). Under the ROC elections were first initiated at the township, county, and city levels; later, in 1954, a popular election of provincial assemblymen was held for the first time. In 1969 the first popular election at the national level took place on Taiwan for a limited number of members to the Legislative Yuan. Since the 1970s the number of national parliamentarians subject to periodic election has steadily risen.

The record of elections on Taiwan shows two important characteristics. First, by the time local elections were instituted by the ROC, the principle of universal suffrage had already been implemented, thus eliminating a potential source of political conflict over franchise issues. Such franchise questions figure prominently in the histories of American and European electoral politics, but not on Taiwan. Second, whereas the right to vote has never been an issue, the question of which public officials are to be elected has been a matter of public debate and at times a source of deep political differences. Although the ROC has gradually opened more official posts to popular election, key government officials—the provincial governor, the mayors of Taipei and Kaohsiung municipalities, and the vast majority of representatives in the National Assembly, the Legislative Yuan, and the Control Yuan—are still not elected. The president and vice president of the republic are indirectly elected by members of the National Assembly, according to the constitution.

Despite these limitations, why have popular elections become an important component in the ROC's political process? Experts have delineated seven functions for elections in the overall political system on Taiwan (Copper and Chen 1984, 18; Wu Nai-te 1982, 14–15).

1. Elections mirror the progress, or the lack thereof, toward democracy and effective mass participation in the political system. Thus elections help legitimize the political structure and organization of the ROC government. The work and decisions of elected officials depend on the mandate of the people, which legitimizes their authority.

2. Elections give political voice to a number of underprivileged socioeconomic groups, most notably the ethnic Taiwanese, women, farmers, factory workers, and low-level mainlander soldiers.

3. Elections provide channels for political interaction between public officials at various levels of the territorial administration. They also create and mobilize local supporters of the regime.

4. Elections facilitate the role of the national government as broker and mediator in local political conflicts. The KMT central party headquarters often performs these functions.

5. Elections articulate and bring to the fore the differences between Taiwanese and mainlanders in outlook and purpose.

6. Through elections the ruling elite share political power and material benefits with local elite in exchange for their allegiance to the regime.

7. Elections symbolize the KMT's sincerity in implementing the democratic principles and concept of local self-government in Sun Yat-sen's Three Principles of the People, the party's official ideology.

Elections are not likely to be terminated in the future; on the contrary, the scope of elections should broaden gradually to include such public officials as the mayors of Taipei and Kaohsiung and additional members of the national representative institutions. As an important avenue for political participation, Taiwan's electoral politics has followed several significant trends over the years:

1. Candidates for elections are no longer confined to a narrow social strata of landlords, merchants, and social notables. There has been a participation explosion, characterized by widespread interest in seeking elected office at all levels.

2. Competition for office has intensified as more people with diverse backgrounds compete for KMT nomination and as opposition political forces become stronger and better organized.

3. Since the ruling KMT has come to look on election results as a test of its popular mandate, it has engaged in tenacious efforts to win elections.

Despite the growth of opposition forces, the KMT has performed strongly in all kinds of elections. This continuing success may be explained by the party's control over public resources, its meticulous election strategies, its effective media and campaign mechanisms, and the lack of organized opposition efforts. To continue winning, the KMT has increasingly relied on Taiwanese members to help manage electoral campaigns. Their participation has spurred the Taiwanization of the KMT as more Taiwanese are promoted within the party in concert with their increasing responsibilities in mobilizing votes. Even though Taiwanization cannot be equated with democratization, the two are intertwined and mutually reinforcing.

FACTIONALISM AND ELECTORAL POLITICS

Elections on Taiwan are not simply a contest in which voters exercise rational choices for representation from among competing candidates with different policy views. Factionalism often intervenes in the electoral process; it plays an important role at the nomination stage, in campaign activities, and in vote getting. Since most ambitious politicians join the KMT, factions are generally, although not exclusively, intraparty political groupings competing for political patronage delivered by the party.

Characteristics of Factions

Factions can be defined as dyadic noncorporate groups based on patron-client relations (Landé 1977, xiii). Such relations allow the established elite to mobilize lower-status individuals in traditional societies (Huntington and Dominiquez 1978, 44). The dyadic ties within factions are cemented on the basis of supportive exchange between patron and client. In the political arena the patron is a superior figure who commands or has access to resources (public revenue, employment, power, and official connections) that can be dispensed to the client in exchange for his support (vote, delivery of votes, and campaign contributions). The institution of competitive elections gives the client an important resource—the vote—to exchange with his patron for other benefits (Huntington and Dominiquez 1978, 44; Lerman 1978, 136). Thus in a true electoral competition a faction comes to resemble a political machine—a "mass political organization which buys electoral support with particularistic rewards distributed through a leader-follower network of clientelist ties" (Nathan 1978, 390).

Factionalism is a common characteristic of politics in many Third World nations (Schmidt et al. 1977, 75–82; Huntington 1968, 44). Even in a highly developed democracy like Japan, factionalism continues to play a central role in the Liberal Democratic Party (LDP), which has governed Japan for over thirty years (Ike 1957, 19; Masumi 1964, 431–32; Fukui 1978, 45–49). According to Nobutaka Ike, Japanese democracy follows a patron-client pattern whereby "individuals. . . relate to the political system through their patrons, who typically are local notables, political bosses, union leaders, local politicians, and leaders of local organizations" (Ike 1957, 19). In patron-client relations, voters trade their votes for particular benefits—jobs and favors or schools, roads, hospitals, and other public works projects for the community. In the LDP a faction that controls a local party apparatus can nominate loyal followers as candidates without concern for the party's overall interest (Masumi 1964, 431). Factional leaders and their networks thus become preoccupied with protecting their own political turf, leading to fierce intraparty competition for high party posts. In the case of Japan this competition even involves the LDP president, who usually becomes the premier.

Although factionalism in Taiwan's electoral politics is similar to that in Japan, it is confined mainly to local administrative units at the municipal, county, township, and village levels for two reasons. First, before the 1970s elections for public officials at city and county levels were organized by geographic units that also served as electoral districts for provincial assemblymen. When electoral districts for some of the new national representatives began to depart from county boundaries, factions were already well entrenched in various localities. Second, there are no general elections for major national government posts, which are filled either by appointment or by indirect election by the National Assembly. Not surprisingly, then, strong competing factions are found mainly in county, city, and township politics. These factions in turn establish a network of alliances with individuals and other factions in the lower levels of the local administrative hierarchy.

The Social Base of Factionalism

Taiwan's dyadic factions often share certain distinguishing character-istics. Factionalism tends to be fostered by the strong affective social ties among Chinese referred to as relationship ties (*kuan-hsi*), mutual affection (*kan-ch'ing*), or reciprocity (*jen-ch'ing*). Relationship ties can be described as "personalistic, particularistic, non-ideological ties between persons—based on a commonality of shared identification" (Jacobs 1976a, 81). The shared identification may derive from a shared native place or sur-name, a family relationship, marriage, educational institutions (class-mates), or places of employment. The influence of relationship ties depends on the affective content of mutual sentiment in dyadic relations. In Taiwan mutual obligation requires reciprocal favoritism and thus pro-vides an important attitudinal basis for the patron–client exchange in politics (Lerman 1978, 108–9). Bernard Gallin observes that local fac-tions recruited supporters on the basis of personal relationships such as friendship, sworn brotherhood, and marriage. Factions have also enlisted some supporters by calling for the "repayment of obligations acquired by villagers for past favors rendered by powerful and influential faction leaders" (Gallin 1968, 391).

Although social relations on Taiwan are conducive to political clien-telism, they are not the only explanation for the pervasiveness of factions in Taiwan's politics. Additional factors such as a need for security, affec-tive familism, an elitist community structure, and corporate institutions may also account for the strength of clientelism. The Chinese tend to es-tablish personal dependency relationships to safeguard their self-interest. This need for security may be related to the socialization pattern of Chi-nese children, which stresses the threat of insecurity and dangers within human relations and hence "the need for protection against these dan-gers" (Lerman 1978, 195).

Others have pointed out that the Chinese propensity for achieve-ment is motivated by a desire to satisfy the expectations of family mem-bers (Huang Kuang-kuo 1984, 3–8). According to this argument, familism dictates that able family members work to satisfy the material demands of other family members. It helps explain why many factions are traditionally family derived. The reluctance of the Chinese to rely on contractual relations built around impersonal institutions may be rooted deep in the cultural and behavioral characteristics of the Chinese tradi-tion. But factionalism may also be explained as a function of a develop-mental stage in Chinese society. A close observer of Taiwan's factional politics believes that urbanization and the concomitant social change have cast a pall over the continuation of factional groups (Wu Nai-te

1982, 22). Dyadic factions appear to be weaker in urban settings than in rural communities. According to this argument, as Taiwan modernizes factionalism may progressively diminish in importance.

Still factionalism will remain an important factor in Taiwan politics for the foreseeable future partly because of the KMT's relations to local factions. Over the years the party has not taken decisive action to suppress local factionalism. On the contrary, it has manipulated factional rivalries for its own benefit (Lerman 1978, 48–51). As long as local factional leaders support the regime, they serve as a powerful barrier against the expansion of opposition forces in a given locality. Since local factional leaders are almost all KMT members, local factions provide additional means for mobilizing votes in behalf of party candidates. Under the circumstances factionalism and the KMT's electoral interests are closely interrelated.

County- and City-Level Factions

Local factions in Taiwan are often related to electoral contests. Their geographic boundaries are usually the administrative territories of a county or municipality, which have served traditionally as the election districts for mayors, magistrates, and provincial assemblymen. Of the 21 counties and municipalities in Taiwan today, 16 have strong factional networks (Hu and Lin 1981, 20; Chao Yung-mao 1978, 50–54). Taipei, Nantou, Yunlin, and Penghu do not have districtwide networks of factional clientelism, but numerous factions exist in their subordinate townships and rural districts. Only Taipei appears not to permit stable factionalism within the KMT; electoral contests are divided sharply along party lines—the KMT against the nonparty group or, since 1986, the DPP.

Nearly all of the county- and city-level factions originated in 1951 when popular elections for mayors, magistrates, and provincial assemblymen were first instituted (Huang Wei-hsiang 1986, 30). As Table 7.1 shows, all the cities and counties have at least two factions; some (Kaohsiung and Tainan) have four or five. Most factions take the surnames of their founding leaders as faction labels. For instance, Miaoli county has a Liu faction and a Huang faction, but in more urban Kaohsiung county the factions have adopted colors (red, white, and black) as their labels. In Changhua county faction labels have both surnames and colors. In Tainan and Ilan counties labels represent geographic areas. In two counties—Taoyuan and Hualien—where ethnic rivalry between the Fukienese and the Hakkas is politically significant, faction labels either use ethnic identity or mask ethnic identity slightly by using the geo-

TABLE 7.1
FACTIONS IN TAIWAN'S CITIES AND COUNTIES, 1981

	Faction labels	Founding leaders	Current leaders
Keelung	Su faction	Su Te-ling	Su Te-ling
	Hsieh faction	Hsueh Kuan-i	Hsueh Hsiu-ping
	Main current faction	Chen Cheng-hsiung	Chen Cheng-hsiung
Taoyuan county	*Hakka*		
	Yeh faction	Yen Han-ching et al.	Yeh Han-ching et al.
	Wu faction	Wu Hung-lin et al.	Wu Po-hsiung et al.
	Fukienese	Hsu Hung-te et al.	Hsu Hung-te et al.
	Old faction	Hsu Hsin-chih	Hsu Hsin-chih
	New faction		
Hsinchu county	West faction	Hsu Chin-te	Hsu Chin-te
	East faction	Hsu Chen-kan	——
Miaoli county	Liu faction	Liu K'uo-ch'ai	Liu K'uo-ch'ai et al.
	Huang faction	Huang Yun-chin	Chin Wen-kuang et al.
Taichung	Chang faction	Chang Chi-chung	Chung Chi-chung
	Lai faction	Lai Jung-mu et al.	——
Taichung county	Chen faction	Chen Shiu-tan	Li Ching-yun et al.
	Lin faction	Li Ho-nien	Chai Hung-wen
	Third force	Hung Chen-tsung	Hung Chen-tsung
Changhua county	Lin-white faction	Lin: Lin Tu	Su Chen-hui
	Chen-red faction	White: Su Chen-hui	Lu Shih-ming
		Chen: Chen Chien-chang	Chen Ta-fu
		Red: Lu Shih-ming	Hung Tiao

County	Faction		
Chiayi county	Huang faction	Huang Jao-ta	Chai Chang-ming
	Lin faction	Lin Chen-jung	Lin Chien-chih
Tainan county	Pei-men (north gate) or sea faction	Wu San-lien	Wu San-lien
	Hu or mountain faction	Hu Lung-pao	Chang Wen-hsien
Tainan	Wang faction	Wang I-chi	Wang I-chi
	Hsin faction	Hsin Wen-ping	Hsin Wen-ping
	Lin faction	Lin Chuan-hsing	Lin Chuan-hsing
	Shang-lin faction	Chang Kun-San	Chang Kun-San
	Su faction	Su Nan-cheng	
Kaohsiung municipality	Chai-ti (local-born) faction	Wang Yu-yun	Wang Yu-yun
	Tainan faction	Wu Chung-ling	Wu Chung-ling
	Peng-hu faction	Hsueh Cheng-chiang	
	Mainlanders faction		
Kaohsiung county	Red faction	Hung Jung-hua	Wu Shang-ch'ing
	White faction	Chen Hsin-an	Chen Hsin-an
	Black faction	Yu Teng-fa	Yu Teng-fa
Pingtung county	Chang faction	Chang San-chung	Chung Feng-hsu
	Lin faction	Lin Shih-cheng	Tung Chien-shih
Taitung county	Huang faction	Huang To-jung	Huang To-jung
	Wu faction	Wu Chin-yu	Wu Chin-yu
	Shao-chung or youth faction	Cheng Lieh	Cheng Lieh
Hualien county	Fukienese faction	Yang Chung-ching	Ko Ting-hsuen et al.
	Hakka faction	Lin Meo-sheng	Wu Shui-yun et al.
Ilan county	Chen faction	Chen Chin-tung	Chen Chin-fu
	Hsu faction	Hsu Wen-cheng	Hsu Wen-cheng

SOURCE: Hu and Lin (1981), 21–23.

graphic name of an ethnic stronghold. In short, faction labels are not uniform in Taiwan, but some patterns are clear.

In most regions the founding leaders of factions are still alive and active in politics. Leadership of the faction is hereditary whenever a capable successor—son, son-in-law, or daughter-in-law—is available within the family. Most factional leaders are either wealthy individuals or social notables (Chao 1978, 63; Wu Nai-te 1982, 21). At any rate they usually command economic resources that can be used to support electoral activities. County-level factions tend to form a network of allies among smaller factions at the subcounty levels. When succession by a family member is not feasible, the factional leadership passes to a major ally or a protégé of the founder. No matter what, factions have proved durable once they have formed.

Each faction consists of a leader, his key lieutenants, grass-roots supporters, and reliable voters in given geographic areas or local bodies, such as farmers' associations, fishermen's associations, irrigation associations, teachers, local government, and civil servants. The concentration of reliable votes in a locale or group is referred to as the faction's domain (*ti-p'an*). Factional leaders and their key lieutenants may be mayors, magistrates, provincial assemblymen, or national parliamentarians; some may not now hold these elected offices but have previously served. Leaders and lieutenants perpetuate factional strength by offering material benefits, favoritism, and channels of upward social mobility for faction cadres, local allies, and regular election supporters. Thus even though factions lack an organizational structure, their informal networks of affiliation can be broadly extended.

Kaohsiung county has perhaps the most widely publicized competition among factions in Taiwan. There are three countywide factions: the red faction, headed by Wu Shang-ch'ing; the white faction, headed by Chen Hsin-an; and the black faction, headed by Yu Teng-fa. The red and white factions are affiliates of the KMT, whereas the black faction has always been nonpartisan. All three are considered roughly even in voter strength and monetary resources. For example, in the November 1985 election Ts'ai Ming-yao, an incumbent KMT member of the white faction, lost the magistrate's race to Yu Chen Yueh-ying, daughter-in-law of Yu Teng-fa, the leader of the black faction.

Over the years the rival factions have alternated in winning the magistrate's post, the most coveted office. As Table 7.2 indicates, in the February 1986 election each faction won a significant share of the seats in the county council and subcounty district executive races. Only 9 of the 53 county councilmen and 3 of the 27 heads were not affiliated with any faction and were under direct KMT control. In the light of these factional

_____ TABLE 7.2 _____
FACTIONS IN KAOHSIUNG COUNTY, 1986

	White faction	Red faction	Black faction[a]	Direct KMT control	Total
County councilmen	21	10	13	9	53
Heads of townships and rural districts	9	11	4	3	27

SOURCE: Chen Wen-tse (1986), 71.
[a]Also known as the Yu family faction.

alignments, the KMT is compelled to agree to nominate candidates from the white and red factions for major elected offices in each election.

Throughout the island there are also small factions at the subcounty level competing for positions in the local farmers' association and administrative offices. The most sought-after posts are the association's general director, members of its board of directors, and the head of the township's administration. In most communities with factional competition, the rival factions usually control either the farmers' association or the administration, providing a factional symmetry of power. These subcounty factions frequently ally with the countywide factions at election time. Since the vast majority of the factional leaders are KMT members, they help mobilize votes for party candidates for these subcounty posts.

THE SELECTION OF CANDIDATES

The ROC employs two basic types of electoral systems: a single-vote, single-member plurality system for the election of mayors and magistrates and a single-vote, multimember system for the election of national parliamentarians, provincial assemblymen, and city and county councilmen. In a single-member district each voter casts one vote for a preferred candidate; whoever wins the largest number of votes, even with less than a majority of votes when the contest involves several candidates, is elected. In a multimember district each voter casts only one vote for any of the contestants, but if the district elects several representatives then the top vote-getters win the contest.

The single-member system clearly favors the ruling KMT candidate in a two-way contest. The multimember system has an adverse effect on minor-party or nonparty candidates only when their numbers are proportionally higher than the percentage of votes they are likely to receive. Thus, for example, in a multimember district the ideal number of non-KMT candidates is one because that will not split the non-KMT vote and should give the candidate a chance to win one of the seats. To maximize the possibility of winning at least three of the four seats in these contests, the KMT has to allocate votes so that none of the party candidates receives a substantially higher vote than is required for victory and thereby causes the defeat of fellow party candidates.

The elections for mayor, magistrate, provincial assemblyman, and member of the National Assembly are held by county and municipal voting districts. But to elect members of the Legislative Yuan, Taiwan's 21 cities and counties are regrouped into six electoral districts. In addition, Taipei, Kaohsiung, and Quemoy each serve as separate districts. Because of these variations each election presents a different challenge to the KMT and the DPP. The KMT chooses its electoral strategies to fit the special circumstances in each district. The selection of candidates, a critical aspect of KMT efforts to win the maximum number of seats, is subject to cumbersome intraparty competition and procedural scrutiny. The nonparty elements, or the DPP since the December 1986 elections, have so far proved unable to exercise organizational discipline in their nomination process.

KMT Candidates

In the selection of candidates for various offices, the KMT follows different sets of procedures. Local party committees and their chairmen have the power to nominate candidates—to decide whether the nomination is necessary and who should be nominated—for city or county council and subcounty executive elections. In such elections the party may remain neutral or simply endorse candidates without formal nomination (Crissman 1981, 106). But since KMT members monopolize elected offices at these levels, the party cares little who may be elected. The election of delegates to the local associations and irrigation associations is usually handled with little KMT intervention. The party steps in to mediate only when electoral disputes threaten to get out of hand.

But the KMT scrutinizes potential candidates for the more important offices: mayors of major cities, magistrates, provincial assemblymen, and national parliamentarians. Party members seeking formal nomination register with the KMT's county or city office. Once the registration period is over, the chairman prepares a list of potential nominees subject to initial review by local party cadres, who then express their preferences by ranking the individuals during a party caucus. Three types of cadres are involved in this initial selection process: (1) political cadres (*cheng-chih kan-pu*), consisting of party members who hold important administrative and legislative positions in the local government and subcounty administration; (2) social cadres (*she-hui kan-pu*), who are leaders in functional organizations like trade unions, chambers of commerce, and farmers' associations in the locality; and (3) party functionaries (*tang-wu kan-pu*), such as party committee members who are full-time party officials (Ch'u 1984, 52–53). A caucus of party cadres may involve elaborate mobilization efforts. In 1983, for instance, the KMT Taipei branch office mobilized 3,600 cadres in five separate caucuses to assess KMT hopefuls for nomination as candidates for the Legislative Yuan (Cheng Nan-jung 1983, 15). In 1985 nearly four-fifths of the party cadres throughout the island reportedly attended such caucuses (Chiang Ping-lun 1985, 7).

In recent years such candidate review sessions—almost like U.S. primaries—may include all party members within an election district. Party members participate in forums where the aspirants for party nomination present their views. Party members at the meetings express their preferences for the candidates by casting straw votes. This practice provides a strong measure of intraparty democracy by allowing ordinary members a voice in the selection of nominees. Statistics from review sessions in 1985 show that over half the KMT membership attended 1 or more of 500 such forums (Chiang Ping-lun 1985, 7). In 1983 in Taipei alone 60 percent of some 200,000 KMT members participated in 1 or more of 16 such forums (Cheng Nan-jung 1983 , 15). The choices party members make are not necessarily binding on the party committee when a slate of candidates is finalized for review and approval by higher authorities. Although the results of the cadre review sessions and the straw votes are never released, they provide additional information that the party can take into account in its decisionmaking.

Once the cadre reviews and closed caucuses are finished, the city or county KMT committee assembles a slate of candidates, who usually number more than the seats to be contested. Candidate slates from the cities and counties other than Taipei and Kaohsiung municipalities are forwarded to the Taiwan Provincial Party Committee for scrutiny; at this stage the order of potential candidates may be altered from the first round of review. These higher-level KMT committees then present their approved slates to the central party headquarters for final approval. At the headquarters a small ad hoc committee chaired by the KMT's secretary-general and comprising the director of the Organization Department and other key party officials assesses the proposed candidates.

Additional names may be added to the slates at this point (Wu Ke-ch'ing 1983a, 21). The final stage in the nomination process transpires in the Central Standing Committee, where a task force of five to seven members appointed by the KMT's chairman decides on the final slate. For the national parliamentary election in December 1986, a seven-man committee consisting of former President Yen Chia-kan, former Vice President (and now President) Lee Teng-hui, Premier Yu Kuo-hwa, Secretary-General of the Presidential Office Shen Chang-huan, President of the Legislative Yuan Ni Wen-ya, Governor Chiu Chuang-huan, and Interior Minister Wu Po-hsiung provided the final approval of candidates (*CYJP,* August 21, 1986, 1).

Historically the KMT has used different processes to select candidates. In the 1950s, when the KMT organization was being rebuilt, it usually endorsed only a few candidates but allowed other party members to run on their own. Local party committees also had more power in the selection process. But since the 1970s the nomination process has become more centralized and the procedure more cumbersome. Party members without formal nomination can still run, but at a higher risk to their party career. The practice is either tolerated to prevent the disenchanted party members from joining the opposition or used to diffuse potential antiparty votes. In the face of the growing outcry for intraparty democracy, the party has lately sponsored more frequent forums of rank-and-file members to satisfy those sentiments.

The nomination within the KMT is influenced by a complicated set of factors. It must take into account party loyalty as well as the results of the cadre reviews and the closed caucuses. The age, sex, education, and financial resources of potential candidates are also carefully assessed. Further considerations are given to factional rivalry, the social base of the candidate, his social image, the odds of winning, and matters of vote distribution among KMT hopefuls (Ch'u 1984, 62–88). Overall the party's nominees fall into four basic categories: (1) KMT members who are drafted by the party or are long-term activists in party affairs; (2) co-opted candidates—famous athletes, scholars, and social notables—whose achievements, visibility, and social standing increase the luster of the KMT ticket; (3) career politicians who are invited to run for public office and who use the elections as a means of upward political mobility; and (4) entrepreneurs who see the instrumental value of public office to promote their industrial or business interests (Kim, Green, and Patterson 1976, 83; *SPTC,* October 27, 1985, 7). Many of those in the last two categories are factional leaders or their lieutenants.

The Tangwai *and the* DPP

Unlike the KMT, the nonparty (*tangwai*) group did not have a party organization system to select candidates. Even though the nonparty movement formed the Democratic Progressive Party in the fall of 1986, the new party did not come into existence in time to go through the process of party nominations. Fragmentation within the *tangwai*—personality clashes, generation gaps, factional interests, ideological and policy differences, and conflicting personal ambitions—made the coordination of a slate of candidates impossible. Quarrelsome and largely inexperienced, these non-KMT groups have not been able to consolidate their efforts in elections; they often wind up competing with one another for the limited votes available to them.

Despite these difficulties, the opposition has begun to foster electoral unity. Beginning in 1981 several opposition leaders decided to use a unified mechanism to endorse (*t'ui-chien*) candidates and assist their campaigns. The nonparty Campaign Assistance Committee (*hou-yuan-hui*) operated in the 1981, 1983, 1985, and 1986 elections.

The Campaign Assistance Committee's endorsements have been plagued with internal conflicts as the committee, lacking formal institutional authority, has attempted to reconcile the need to support the best possible candidate with the need to satisfy group interests within their forces. The performance of their candidates has been uneven. As Table 7.3 indicates, their success in contests for Taipei council seats was impressive in 1981 and in 1985. In contrast, their achievements in Kaohsiung were more modest in those elections. The Campaign Assistance Committee's candidates did well in the elections for provincial assemblymen, as 11 of their 21 candidates (52 percent) were elected in 1981 and an equal number of their candidates won in 1985. In the mayoral and magistrate races their victorious candidates dropped from 43 percent in 1981 to 17 percent in 1985. But the sharp reduction may not be as politically significant as the percentages seem to indicate, because in 1985 4 of their candidates lost only by a small margin. With only six posts in question, one or two victories would have changed these percentages dramatically. Furthermore, non-KMT candidates won the mayoral and magistrate races in Changhua, Ilan, and Chiayi, although they were not connected with the Campaign Assistance Committee. Overall, more than 50 percent of these candidates were elected in 1981 and almost two-thirds in 1985.

As the opposition leaders have become better organized, they have encountered major obstacles. One is internal dissent, which can be resolved only if the DPP establishes some disciplinary authority. Moreover

_____ TABLE 7.3 _____
CANDIDATES ENDORSED BY THE *TANGWAI* CAMPAIGN
ASSISTANCE COMMITTEE, 1981 AND 1985

	1981 ELECTION			1985 ELECTION		
	Endorsed	*Elected*	*Percentage of vote*	*Endorsed*	*Elected*	*Percentage of vote*
Taiwan provincial assemblymen	21	11 (52%)	13	18	11 (61%)	16
Magistrates and mayors	7	3 (43%)	20	6	1 (17%)	15
Taipei councilmen	9	8 (89%)	16	11	11 (100%)	21
Kaohsiung councilmen	2	0 (0%)	2	6	3 (50%)	8
Total	39	22 (56%)		41	26 (63%)	

SOURCE: *TLWP* (December 2, 1985), 2.

many popular non–KMT political figures refused to identify with the Campaign Assistance Committee in earlier elections and may dissociate themselves from the DPP in the future. Finally there simply have not been enough strong non–KMT candidates to run for elected office at the county and subcounty levels. Even the races for city councilmen failed to attract enough serious candidates to the *tangwai* ticket. These problems, typical of minor parties throughout the world, will be resolved only when the DPP strengthens its institutional base. It would then be able to attract more qualified candidates and improve its nomination process.

Still the Campaign Assistance Committee's performance in past election years represents concrete steps toward the formal organization of an opposition party. Before 1986 there were clear signs that a new party was gaining strength. Table 7.3 shows that more *tangwai*-endorsed candidates were elected in 1985 than in 1981. A similar pattern can be seen in the national parliamentary elections. In 1983 about a quarter of the candidates backed by the Campaign Assistance Committee were elected to the Legislative Yuan (*LHP,* November 21, 1985, 2). Three years later, in 1986, nearly two-thirds won seats. In the National Assembly race 41 percent of the Campaign Assistance Committee's candidates were elected (*MCJP,* December 7, 1986, 1). At the subcounty level, the forerunner of the DPP did not recommend any candidates until 1986. In the February 1986 election the committee recommended 10 candidates for the 309 township administrator positions and 82 candidates for the 837 city and county council seats; a total of 35 were elected (Liu Feng-sung 1986, 69). This represented only an initial step toward serious subcounty electoral contests, especially since the KMT nearly monopolizes elected local offices.

ELECTION CAMPAIGNS

Legal Regulations

Taiwan's election campaigns are subject to stringent legal requirements. In May 1980 the government promulgated the Public Officials Election and Recall Law, which was subsequently revised in July 1983. Its 113 articles set forth in great detail the conditions governing national elections. The rights and responsibilities of candidates are spelled out. The law is notable in part because it provides the *tangwai* with a formal legal foundation to participate in electoral politics (Gregor and Chang 1983, 73).

This 1980 election law also contained several important provisions to prevent acts of violence during elections, to eliminate vote buying and bribery, and to prohibit illegal campaign activities (Copper with Chen 1984, 93). It also revised the method for indirectly electing new members of the Control Yuan from the single- to the multiple-vote system. Previously each member of the Taiwan Provincial Assembly and the municipal councils of Taipei and Kaohsiung cast only one vote for a candidate, enabling the *tangwai* to concentrate their votes and elect at least one member of the Control Yuan. The new regulations allow each councilman or assemblyman to cast multiple votes, making it difficult for the *tangwai* to win any seats. Accordingly KMT members in these legislative bodies can each cast votes for as many as half the open seats of the Control Yuan (Articles 3 and 61).

The new law limits legal campaign activities to five categories and provides detailed restrictions in each. According to Article 46 these activities are (1) establishing a campaign headquarters and employing campaign assistants, (2) holding open meetings to present political statements, (3) printing and disseminating name cards and handbills, (4) operating campaign vehicles and loudspeakers, and (5) canvasing and visiting the voters in the candidate's constituency. No individual is allowed to act as a campaign assistant for more than one candidate (Article 47). Campaign meetings are divided into two types: candidate-sponsored meetings and meetings sponsored by the election commission before the day of voting. Candidates may hold a maximum of six meetings each day, and a meeting is restricted to two hours' duration (Article 49). Name cards and handbills can be posted only at places provided or assigned by the election commission, and the sizes of name cards are officially specified (Article 51). A candidate may employ no more than five campaign vehicles; local elections involving small constituencies are allowed only two or three vehicles, depending on the level of public office being contested (Article 52). Loudspeakers can be installed only in campaign vehicles, at the sites of candidate-sponsored meetings, and at campaign headquarters. There are also specific provisions outlining what is forbidden for the candidate and his assistants. These include setting off firecrackers, assembling a crowd for a parade, and engaging in campaign activities outside the candidate's constituency.

Some provisions impose harsh restrictions; others are in direct contradiction to prevailing custom, such as the rule against setting off firecrackers. The opposition particularly objects to two provisions. One is the requirement that handbills and other printed materials contain a stamp bearing the printer's name and address (Copper with Chen 1984, 64). The opposition believes that this rule might prevent a printer from taking work from non-KMT candidates for fear of future reprisals by the KMT authorities. Another provision earmarks the last few days before the election for the campaign meetings sponsored by the election commission. The opposition feels that the provision will restrict the non-KMT candidates' ability to select places and times during the most crucial days of the campaign. Article 45 of the law limits the duration of campaign activities to fifteen days for those seeking positions as national representatives, ten days for provincial assemblymen, mayors, and magistrates, and three to five days for subcounty positions. Lacking the extensive organizational structure and financial backing of the KMT, opposition candidates are clearly at a disadvantage in a short campaign (Parris H. Chang 1984, 11).

Limitations on campaign finances are also unrealistic. Spending is limited by the size of the electoral district, the number of elected offices to be filled, and the consumer price index (Articles 45–51). For the 1983 parliamentary election the range was from N.T. $2.5 million (U.S. $62,500) in the smallest district to N.T. $5.4 million (U.S. $135,000) in the largest (Copper with Chen 1984, 95).[1] Yet in practice the average candidate spent an estimated U.S. $500,000 during the 1983 campaign (Copper with Chen 1984, 64). In the 1985 election one major newspaper estimated that many candidates for the Provincial Assembly spent at least U.S. $1–2 million and that the expenses of some mayors and magistrates were even higher (*LHP,* November 20, 1985, 2). In most cases, however, only KMT candidates spent these sums, since most opposition candidates are short of campaign funds and exercise great caution in campaign expenditures lest they be charged with violating the 1980 law.

In addition to excessive campaign spending, numerous other violations of the campaign law are common. One leading newspaper discovered 236 violations during the first ten days of the two-week campaign in November 1985 (*CKSP*, November 18, 1985, 3). The election commission and the courts do not stringently enforce the campaign rules. Enforcement, if it occurs, is highly selective.

The KMT's Election Campaign

Unlike the opposition, the KMT commands enormous human and material resources for waging election campaigns. The party has a smooth-running organization, a well-established media network, and a substantial number of safe votes to be allocated among party candidates. It is little wonder then that KMT campaign efforts are often described in Taiwan as organizational warfare (*tsu-chih-chan*). Although the results of any one election would not threaten the party's dominant position, the party believes that a poor performance could undermine its mandate to govern effectively. Hence the KMT makes a determined effort in each election and each constituency.

The KMT's entire organizational machine is set in motion when elections approach. At each level of the organizational hierarchy KMT officials establish a campaign coordinating council (*p'u-hsuen hui-pao*) to direct its electoral activities. The coordinating council at the national party headquarters, chaired by the secretary-general, usually includes his deputies, the director and deputy director of the Organization Department, directors of other major functional departments, and the chairman of the Provincial Party Committee (Ch'u 1984, 122; Wu Ke-ch'ing 1983a, 21). The coordinating council reviews field reports, plots election strategy, issues instructions, and supervises the KMT's nationwide campaign. The provincial, municipal, and county party organizations also form campaign coordinating councils to direct activities within their jurisdictions. The members consist of major local party officials and functionaries. Thus the headquarters coordinating council forms a national command post to provide maximum political support through a complex organizational network to KMT candidates during the elections.

The KMT also establishes a meticulous timetable for the elections (*SGK*, 1983, 8–11). About five months before election day the KMT offices begin collecting and reviewing previous election data; in the process they gradually create a data bank with a profile of the voters in their district. In each district the party establishes a campaign control center to implement party instructions and to coordinate daily campaign activities. Meanwhile the campaign budget has been laid out in detail. One month before balloting the party prepares a comprehensive estimate of the vote distribution and sets in motion a network for mobilizing votes that extends down to the level of small neighborhoods. A well-coordinated media campaign is prepared. By this time the party candidates will also have visited various public institutions and all socioeconomic groups in the district to drum up support. As election day draws near, local KMT offices usher the candidates on door-to-door visits to those voters likely to cast ballots for a KMT candidate according to information on voting behavior provided by party analysts. In recent years the KMT has used the latest techniques, such as computer analysis and vote simulation, to improve their already well coordinated campaigns.

Two of the principal tasks for the campaign coordinating committees and various party offices are (1) to mobilize reliable votes and allocate them to the proper KMT candidate to gain winning margins for as many party candidates as possible and (2) to stage efficient media campaigns that polish the KMT candidates' image and counter opposition efforts. The KMT assigns each of its nominated candidates a discrete territorial or functional constituency and informs its loyal voters of those assignments (Winckler 1984, 497). Within each territorial constituency, which coincides with a voting district, the KMT delineates work responsibility areas (*kung-tso tse-jen ch'u*) and assigns a district KMT functionary to maximize the mobilization of votes. The creation of discrete territorial constituencies for KMT candidates presumably avoids competing head-on with each other within a district. Potential votes for each candidate in a multiseat race are carefully estimated so that all nominated candidates will receive just enough votes for victory. Similar calculations are made in functional constituencies, where each candidate is assigned a particular group of veterans' organizations, trade unions, farmers' associations, schools, and government agencies that are expected to provide him votes. All these activities supplement campaigns conducted by the individual candidates.

Campaign activities pursued by the KMT office and the candidate's own headquarters are supposedly coordinated. Any rivalry between KMT candidates is mediated by the party. KMT members who are public officials are supposed to use their institutional bases to support the party ticket (Ch'ing 1985, 7–8). Their performance—measured by votes delivered for the party ticket—constitutes one criterion for future advancement. Thus ROC government officials and public functionaries find it difficult to remain neutral in the election process; they and the votes they can harness are part of what the KMT needs to win.

The 1980 election and recall law prohibits the candidates from using the regular mass media—daily newspapers, television, radio, and periodicals—for campaign promotion. But the KMT can conduct campaign publicity through the party-owned media (Ch'u 1984, 203). In addition, candidates are allowed to use the following forms of media in campaigns (Ch'u 1984, 206–7):

1. Printed materials such as name cards and promotional pamphlets

2. Campaign vehicles with installed loudspeakers

3. Electronic materials such as videotapes

4. Public forums sponsored by the election commission and private forums organized by individual candidates according to the time sequence specified in the election law

5. Billboards and handboards posted in campaign headquarters and on campaign vehicles

6. Gifts such as calendars and bus and train schedules imprinted with the candidates' names

7. Face-to-face meetings with voters during which campaign messages, criticism of the opposition, and even unfounded rumors may be circulated

Since most of Taiwan's major mass media are owned by either the party or party members, it is difficult to expect fair media coverage for opposition candidates. In the past, two relatively independent daily newspapers—the *People's Daily (Min-chung jih-pao)* in Kaohsiung and the *Independence Evening Post (Tzu-li wan-pao)* in Taipei—did provide more balanced coverage of the candidates and their positions.

Taiwan's voters rely on many sources for information on the candidates and their campaigns. According to a survey conducted in Chiayi in 1972, one-third of the 320 voters interviewed said that the mass media were the principle source of information (see Table 7.4). Almost one-quarter used the handbills distributed by the government, while 18 percent learned about the candidates from attending campaign forums. Another 14 percent acquired information directly from friends and relatives. In short, approximately 90 percent of those interviewed indicated that the mass media, government handbills, campaign forums, and per-

_____ TABLE 7.4 _____
SOURCES OF CAMPAIGN INFORMATION IN CHIAYI, 1972

	Number of voters surveyed	Percentage
Mass media	107	33
Election handbills from the government	77	24
Friends and relatives	45	14
Campaign rallies	57	18
Other	34	11
Total	320	100

SOURCE: Wang Tuan-chen (1972), 153.

sonal contacts with friends and relatives were the major sources of their information about elections and candidates. The unspecified category of other may include direct contact with the candidates in door-to-door visits or postcards and handouts distributed by the candidates' headquarters. Overall the mass media remained the single most important source of voter information.

The Opposition Campaign

Unlike the KMT, the opposition does not have an organizational machine to coordinate nationwide campaign activities. The opposition's Campaign Assistance Committee is both financially starved and short of full-time staff. To overcome these problems, the opposition began to organize seminars in 1985 to train campaign workers (Ch'ing 1985, 8). The seminars featured opposition leaders and sympathetic academicians as guest speakers; participants were mostly young activists. The seminars stressed methods of publicizing campaigns, but since there were only a few dozen participants in all, they had little impact on the 1985 election campaign. The importance of these efforts may become more evident in the future as training and preparation become institutionalized under DPP auspices.

So far the opposition's campaigns have relied mainly on direct appeals to the voters through officially sanctioned public forums or by means of campaign vehicles, a variety of posters, and printed materials distributed during the official campaign period. At the national level the Campaign Assistance Committee published an opposition platform to publicize its candidates' common program. In the past opposition plat-form statements have included self-determination by Taiwan residents of Taiwan's political future, the legalization of opposition parties, the aboli-tion of martial law, a reform of the national representative system, in-creased civil liberties, and freedom of the press (Copper with Chen 1984, 66; Goldstein 1985a, 21–22; *TWMP,* August 24, 1985, 1). These high-interest political demands have attracted support in urban areas, where the intelligentsia and middle class are concentrated. In the small towns and rural areas interest in the opposition's platforms is limited, particu-larly among farmers, workers, and lower-middle-class people, who are typically more interested in issues that affect their daily lives.

Without a nationwide organizational machine most opposition can-didates rely on strong local campaigning. Each candidate assembles a campaign staff of relatives, friends, and a handful of like-minded activists in an election district. Their chief tactic is to stir up anti-KMT and anti-government sentiment. Many witnesses, including this writer, can report extraordinarily heavy turnouts at many *tangwai* forums. It is not unusual to have over twenty thousand people attend each meeting, compared with the several hundred that show up at rallies for KMT candidates. During these forums opposition candidates criticize the authorities and put the KMT candidates on the defensive. These large rallies have pro-vided the principal means by which opposition candidates wage cam-paign warfare against their KMT counterparts.

VOTING BEHAVIOR AND ELECTION RESULTS

Popular elections for public officials in Taiwan fall into three categories. The first category involves the supplementary election of members for the Legislative Yuan and the National Assembly. The former serve a three-year term, the latter a six-year term. Elections for these posts are held at the same time once every six years; every three years an election is held for members of the Legislative Yuan. In the second category are elections for mayors of the larger cities and for magistrates and members of the Taiwan Provincial Assembly and the municipal councils of Taipei and Kaohsiung, which are held concurrently every four years. In the third category are races for mayors of the smaller cities, township and subcounty executives, and councilmen of cities and counties, which are also held concurrently every four years. Elections for these three levels of public positions are held on different dates.

National Supplementary Elections

Since members of the Legislative Yuan are more actively involved in the legislative process, their elections have received more attention than those for the National Assembly. The Legislative Yuan also attracts better-known candidates and generates more competitive electoral contests. In 1969, when the first supplementary election was held, 11 members were elected to the Legislative Yuan for life tenure as representatives from the Taiwan area; 3 of those elected were nonparty candidates who have since lost their seats because of death or conviction for wrongdoing. From 1972 through 1986 five separate elections were held for new members, who serve three-year terms. In the last contest 55 popularly elected seats were at stake, an increase from 28 seats in 1972. The change results from a new allocation formula for seats and population growth on Taiwan.

As Table 7.5 indicates, KMT candidates have received from 67 to 79 percent of the popular vote over the years. Elections since 1975 have seen a gradual reduction of the KMT share of the vote, while the opposition's percentage has increased. From 1975 to 1986 support for the nonparty opposition grew from 17 percent to 32 percent of the vote. Nonparty elected seats increased from 4 in 1972 to 14 in 1986. Among the nonparty opposition, those connected with the *tangwai* or the DPP in 1986 held 12 of the 14 non-KMT seats. The importance of the two minor parties—the Young China Party and the Democratic Socialist Party—has dwindled both in numbers of seats and as a percentage of the vote. In the last three elections their combined popular vote dropped below 1 percent, and the two parties failed to win any seats. The success of the DPP in the 1986 election demonstrates its impact as a new party that managed to unify major groups of otherwise fragmented opposition movements.

Elections for Provincial Assemblymen and County-Level Executives

The total number of seats in the Taiwan Provincial Assembly increased from 57 in 1954 to 77 in 1985. The first popular election for provincial assemblymen took place in 1954; before then assemblymen were indirectly elected by county and city councilmen. As Table 7.6 shows, popular votes for KMT candidates from 1954 to 1958 ranged from a low of 65 percent in 1960 to a high of 76 percent in 1968. At the same time, the percentage of total seats won by the KMT was consistently higher than its share of the popular vote. This discrepancy reveals the advantages of the KMT organizational machine, especially in managing the nomination process and allotting votes to its candidates. But the percent-

Table 7.5

Number of Members Elected to the Legislative Yuan (with Percentage of Votes), 1972–1986

	KMT[a]	Non-KMT[a]				Total[a]
		Nonparty[b]	CYP[c]	DSP[d]	Subtotal	
1972	22 (74%)[e]	4 (20%)[e]	2 (6%)	0 (0%)	6 (26%)	28
1975	23 (79%)	5 (17%)	1 (4%)	0 (0%)	6 (21%)	29
1980	41 (73%)	11 (26%)	0 (0.7%)	0 (0.1%)	11 (27%)	52
1983	44 (71%)	9 (29%)	0 (0.4%)	0 (0%)	9 (29%)	53
1986	41 (67%)	14 (33%)[f]	0 (0.8%)	0 (0.2%)	14 (33%)	35

SOURCES: Wu Ke-ching (1983b), 16. Figures for 1986 from *Hua-ch'iao jih-pao*, New York (December 9, 1986), 12; *CKSP* (February 2, 1988), 3.

[a]Excludes representatives of the overseas Chinese communities and vocational groups in Taiwan.

[b]Consists of the *tangwai* and other independent candidates.

[c]China Youth Party.

[d]Democratic Socialist Party.

[e]Percentage of the popular vote won by all candidates in that group.

[f]Includes twelve members of the new Democratic Progressive Party and two independent candidates; the DPP candidates received 22.17 percent of the popular vote.

—— TABLE 7.6 ——
PROVINCIAL ASSEMBLY ELECTIONS, 1954–1985

		KMT		NON-KMT	
	Total seats	Seats	Percentage of popular vote	Seats	Percentage of popular vote
1954	57	48 (84%)	69	9 (16%)	31
1957	66	53 (80%)	68	13 (20%)	32
1960	73	58 (79%)	65	15 (21%)	35
1963	74	61 (82%)	68	13 (18%)	32
1968	71	60 (85%)	75	11 (15%)	24
1972	73	58 (79%)	69	15 (21%)	31
1977	77	56 (73%)	66	21 (27%)	34
1981	77	59 (77%)	72	18 (23%)[a]	28[a]
1986	77	59 (77%)	69	18 (23%)[b]	31[b]

SOURCES: *TLWP* (November 17, 1986), 2; Ho (1985b), 26.
[a]In 1981 the candidates of the Campaign Assistance Committee, the forerunner of the DPP, won 8 seats and 16 percent of the popular vote.
[b]In 1986 the Campaign Assistance Committee candidates won 11 seats and 22 percent of the popular vote.

age of seats occupied by the KMT decreased modestly in the last two elections. In all provincial assembly elections, non-KMT candidates received more than 30 percent of the popular vote except in 1968 and 1981. Yet the non-KMT's share of total seats has never matched its share of the popular vote. The opposition's best showing was in 1977, when opposition candidates captured 21 seats and 34 percent of the popular vote. After the 1979 Kaohsiung Incident and the subsequent arrest of many *tangwai* leaders, the opposition lost ground in elections during the 1980s. In the 1985 election nonparty candidates won 18 seats and again garnered more than 30 percent of the vote, but candidates endorsed by the Campaign Assistance Committee won only 11 seats and 22 percent of the popular vote.

Elections for mayors and county magistrates differ from the multi-member constituency system used in provincial assembly races. Mayors and magistrates are single-member contests typically involving only two candidates in a district in a winner-take-all rivalry. KMT candidates are generally favored to win, but opposition candidates have attracted large numbers of votes.

As Table 7.7 shows, the KMT has won at least 80 percent of all contested positions in the mayoral and magistrate elections since 1950. The KMT popular vote reached a height of 79 percent in 1972 and has declined gradually ever since. Meanwhile non-KMT candidates have gained ground both in the number of offices won and in the percentage of the vote. In the last three elections nonparty candidates won four contests each time, or approximately one-fifth of the available posts. These results compare favorably with the 1968 elections, when opposition candidates won only three posts, and with the 1972 elections, when the KMT swept all 21 offices. In popular votes the gap between the KMT and the opposition has narrowed. In the 1981 and 1985 elections the KMT received about 60 percent of the vote, compared with almost 80 percent in 1972. The trend in voting patterns indicates an increasing popular support for the opposition in mayoral and magistrate contests, but the strength of this trend is unclear.

Since the mayor of Taipei is an appointed post, elections for municipal councilmen have become especially important. Taipei, the capital city and home of the national government bureaucracy, is the most urban

——— TABLE 7.7 ———

ELECTIONS OF MAYORS AND MAGISTRATES IN TAIWAN, 1950–1986

		KMT		NON-KMT	
	Total posts	Posts	Percentage of popular vote	Posts	Percentage of popular vote
1950	21	17 (81%)	—	4 (19%)	—
1954	21	19 (90%)	72	2 (10%)	18
1957	21	20 (95%)	65	1 (5%)	35
1960	21	19 (90%)	72	2 (10%)	28
1964	21	17 (81%)	73	4 (19%)	27
1968	20	17 (85%)	72	3 (15%)	28
1972	20	20 (100%)	79	0	21
1977	20	16 (80%)	70	4 (20%)	30
1981	19	15 (79%)	59	4 (21%)[a]	41[a]
1986	21	17 (81%)	62	4 (19%)[b]	38[b]

SOURCES: *TLWP* (November 17, 1986), 2; Ho (1985a), 17.
[a]In 1981 the candidates of the Campaign Assistance Committee, the forerunner of the DPP, won 3 seats and 16 percent of the popular vote.
[b]In 1986 the Campaign Assistance Committee candidates won 1 seat and 4.8 percent of the popular vote.

area on the island. The city's residents include a substantial middle class, a large concentration of the island's professionals, and over four hundred thousand mainlander voters. The KMT is always anxious to do well in Taipei city elections, but the socioeconomic composition favors neither the KMT nor the opposition. A large number of mainlanders, party members, public employees, and professionals are loyal KMT voters; yet the opposition has natural allies and supporters in working-class neighborhoods and among intellectuals, small businessmen, and the socially dislocated lower-middle-class voters.

According to Table 7.8 the KMT controlled the great majority of council seats from 1968 to 1985. Nonetheless, their dominance has been eroding. In 1974 the KMT at its peak held 45 of the 49 seats. By 1985 its share had dropped to 38, or 75 percent of the council seats. The decline in the portion of the popular vote going to the KMT is even more obvious. In 1968 KMT candidates won 85 percent of the popular vote, but they won only 62 percent in the 1985 election. In contrast, non-KMT candidates have steadily gained ground. The increase of non-KMT influence is dramatically demonstrated by the rapid growth of the opposition's percentage of the popular vote. In the five elections from 1968 to 1985, popular votes for opposition candidates grew from 15 to 38 percent. The candidates backed by the Campaign Assistance Committee also did well. In 1981 they won 8 seats; four years later all 11 of their candidates were elected.

Subcounty Elections

Local elections below the county level have been dominated by the KMT; most non-KMT candidates at this level do not even have political ties with the opposition movement. As Table 7.9 indicates, of the 309 subcounty executive posts, the KMT won 94 percent in the February 1986 election. There were only 19 non-KMT winners; the opposition won only 5 contests. Although the KMT's domination of the city and county councils was not nearly as overwhelming, it still captured 79 percent of the contested seats. Among the 172 non-KMT councilmen, only 30 were endorsed by the opposition's Campaign Assistance Committee. If these subcounty executive and local council elections are combined, the KMT held 83 percent of the 1,146 posts, while the non-KMT share was only 17 percent. Those associated with the forerunners of the DPP were able to win only 3 percent of the elections. Thus at the subcounty level the KMT's control over elected offices shows little sign of erosion.

_____ TABLE 7.8 _____

ELECTIONS OF TAIPEI MUNICIPAL COUNCILMEN, 1968–1985

		KMT		NON-KMT	
	Total seats	Seats	Percentage of popular vote	Seats	Percentage of popular vote
1968	48	42 (88%)	85	6 (12%)	15
1974	49	45 (92%)	84	4 (8%)	16
1977	51	43 (84%)	76	8 (16%)	24
1981	51	38 (75%)	69	13 (25%)[a]	31[a]
1985	51	38 (75%)	62	13 (25%)[b]	38[b]

SOURCE: *TLWP* (November 17, 1986), 2.
[a]In 1981 the Campaign Assistance Committee, the forerunner of the DPP, endorsed 9 candidates, 8 of whom were elected with 16 percent of the popular vote.
[b]In 1985 all 11 Campaign Assistance Committee candidates were elected with 22 percent of the popular vote.

_____ TABLE 7.9 _____

PARTISAN DISTRIBUTION IN SUBCOUNTY ELECTIONS, 1986

			NON-KMT	
	Total seats[a]	KMT	Subtotal	CAC[b]
Subcounty executives[c]	309	290 (94%)	19 (6%)	5 (1.6%)
City and county councilmen	837	665 (79%)	172 (21%)	30 (3.6%)
Total	1,146	955 (83%)	191 (17%)	35 (3.0%)

SOURCES: *SCJP* (February 3, 1986), 1; *CP* (February 4, 1986), 7.
[a]Excluding the large cities of Taipei, Kaohsiung, Taichung, Tainan, Keelung, Chiayi, Hsinchu, and Changhua.
[b]Campaign Assistance Committee candidates.
[c]Mayors of small cities and chief executives of *hsiangs* and *chens*.

Voting Behavior

Taiwan has 19.8 million people and 12 million eligible voters, of whom 52.4 percent are males and 47.6 percent females. Approximately one-third are age 30 or younger, while 8.4 percent are senior citizens age 65 or older (Ch'ai 1983, 10). There are 3 million blue-collar workers and nearly 1.3 million people in the agriculture and fishery industries. About 850,000 people work for government and public enterprises. The armed forces have 450,000 enlisted men and women. The balance of the voters are mainly businessmen, industrialists, managers, professionals, and those engaged in trade and service work.

About 1.7 million of these voters are mainlanders and their descendants, accounting for 16 percent of the voting population (Ch'ai 1983, 16). One-quarter of them reside in the metropolitan area of Taipei and another 7 percent in Kaohsiung. The rest are distributed around the island, mostly in urban centers. In Taipei mainlanders constitute 30 percent of the city's voters. Among the native Taiwanese the minority Hakkas are heavily concentrated in Miaoli and certain sections of Kaohsiung county, Hsinchu, Ilan, and Taipei. Three million of Taiwan's voters (one-sixth of the total) declare an affiliation with a religion; 1.2 million are Taoists, 820,000 Buddhists, and 650,000 Protestants and Catholics. But religious faith is not a clear determinant of voting behavior, although many Presbyterian leaders among the Protestant Christians have supported the opposition candidates.

There are two fundamentally different interpretations of voting behavior in Taiwan. One argues for rational choice by the voters; the other stresses particularistic voting behavior. A study of Taipei voters conducted by Hu Fo, a leading political scientist in Taiwan, identified 24 factors affecting voting patterns in the city (Hu and Yu 1983, 233–45). The six most important are (1) the issues, (2) the candidate's record of achievement, (3) the candidate's personal character, (4) the candidate's education, (5) the candidate's perceived knowledge, and (6) party affiliation. Implicit in Hu's findings is a growing rationality in the voters' choice of candidates. In contrast, Bruce Jacobs believes that Taiwan voters cast their ballots on the basis of particularistic ties founded on personal relations (*kuan-hsi*). According to Jacobs "political leaders support the candidate with whom they have the closest guanxi [kuan-hsi], and voters cast their ballots either for the candidate with whom they have the closest guanxi or for the candidate supported by the local leader with whom they have the closest guanxi" (Jacobs 1981, 34).

These two perspectives are clearly at odds, but they need not be regarded as mutually exclusive. As the pace of socioeconomic change accelerates, the political ethos and behavior patterns of the urban residents on Taiwan differ markedly from those of voters from towns and villages. Since Hu's study was confined to Taipei voters, his conclusions probably indicate urban middle-class behavior. Jacobs's conclusions, however, are strongly influenced by his field research in a rural community in southern Taiwan.

Voting behavior on Taiwan, as elsewhere, is shaped by a matrix of socioeconomic factors, in this case the issues, KMT identification, and character of the candidates. Given the changes in electoral contests on Taiwan, perhaps the most important focus of study should be the partisan orientation of the voters. In another study Hu Fo conducted on Taipei voters in the 1980 supplementary election, he found significant differences between those who vote for KMT candidates and those who vote for the opposition. (Hu and Yu 1983, 31–53). According to this study, Taipei voters' partisan orientation had a significant correlation with their birth origins, educational levels, ages, and vocations. KMT candidates drew heavy support from the military, police, KMT functionaries, college professors, college students, civil servants, elected representatives, professionals (lawyers, physicians, engineers, and accountants), journalists, writers, those engaged in other media work, and mainlanders (Hu and Yu 1983, 31–53). Over half the KMT votes in Taipei were cast by mainlanders. Nonparty candidates received substantial support from youths other than college students, native Taiwanese, farmers, fishermen, workers, small entrepreneurs, business clerks and managers, and housewives (Hu and Yu 1983, 31–32). Among the non-KMT voters, 87.6 percent were Taiwanese and only 12.4 percent were mainlanders.

Furthermore, voters with different provincial origins have significantly different issue orientations, which further reinforce partisan divisions. The mainlanders tend to identify more strongly with government authorities and favor political stability, social order, social harmony among ethnic groups, and restrictions on freedom of speech. These attitudes coincide with the basic political views of KMT voters. But Taiwanese voters stress the importance of freedom of speech, better protection for human rights, broader political participation, the plurality of political forces, and higher status and more influence for Taiwanese in the political system (Hu and Yu 1983, 38). These views reflect the political orientation of opposition voters.

Urban-rural differences also help account for partisan voting patterns in Taiwan. Huntington has argued that opposition support is stronger in the urban areas of developing nations. Opposition leaders in the Philippines, Turkey, Pakistan, Morocco, El Salvador, and the Dominican Republic draw most of their votes from the cities, receiving less support in the countryside (Huntington 1968, 436–37). In Taiwan small cities and rural communities have consistently given KMT candidates greater support, whereas the opposition has scored better in urban than in rural areas. These urban-rural contrasts show up in the races for mayors and county magistrates. Among the 42 urban mayoral contests from 1950 to 1981, non-KMT candidates won 38 percent of the elections, but they won only 8 percent of the races in the 144 contests for rural magistrates (Huntington 1968, 436–37).

Vote buying by candidates may also influence voting behavior. On Taiwan candidates are not reluctant to buy votes because the successful candidate can use his post to acquire wealth. Close observers of Taiwan's electoral politics have reported that the illegal practice of vote buying is widespread (Copper with Chen 1984, 82; Lerman 1978, 112–13; Crissman 1981, 110). In recent years the price per vote has escalated to about five hundred New Taiwan dollars, or about U.S. $20. Even in a local election for irrigation association representatives, N.T. $300 (U.S. $12) per vote was a common price in 1986 (MCJP, May 5, 1986, 1). Although there is no systematic documentation of vote buying, charges of the practice have damaged the reputation of the KMT. So far government efforts to crack down on vote buying have been ineffective.

Such behavior reflects both the political culture of Taiwan and the character of Taiwan's democratic experiments. Although electoral corruption by vote buying has been an issue of great concern to many on the island, it needs to be put in perspective. The purchase of votes is a form of corrupt behavior partially bred by modernization, which creates new sources of power and wealth (Huntington 1968, 59–61). The election behavior found in advanced democracies has yet to take root among many of Taiwan's voters. As in many other Third World nations, voters on Taiwan are still learning about the true meaning of voting in the process of creating a representative democracy.

CONCLUSION

Taiwan has had only 38 years' experience with elections, and the electoral system is still maturing. Over the decades the authorities have gradually broadened the scope of electoral contests. Under the current reform initiatives many more parliamentary seats are likely to be subject to popular election. Even with the present limitations elections have become important channels for political recruitment and debate over public policy. Opposition candidates have used the election process to air their grievances and even to press their views on fundamental reforms, including respect for civil rights and the nation's political future. In a generally restrictive political atmosphere, elections on Taiwan have provided "holidays for democracy" (min-chu chia-ch'i), since the ROC authorities have permitted more freedom of speech during campaigns.

So far the KMT has achieved overwhelming success in elections. Several factors weigh heavily in favor of their candidates (Jacobs 1974, 28):

1. KMT candidates are able to campaign more openly than their opposition counterparts before the brief official campaign period.

2. Limitations on the number of sanctioned campaign forums are advantageous for KMT candidates, who can depend on the KMT organization and existing factional network to mobilize votes.

3. Professional functionaries provide additional manpower to KMT candidates, since there are legal limits to the number of campaign staff a candidate may hire.

4. The campaign platforms and speeches of opposition candidates are subject to greater official scrutiny and restrictions than those of KMT candidates.

5. Press coverage favors KMT candidates, particularly since many of the media are directly owned and managed by the KMT and government agencies.

6. The inability of all candidates to appoint poll watchers at every poll offers KMT candidates a potential advantage.

7. KMT candidates feel fewer constraints on illegal practices such as vote buying.

Election politics on Taiwan could change over time. Already the opposition has gained ground by winning both a larger number of popular votes and more contested seats in the 1985 and 1986 elections. Now the DPP is practically a legal opposition party (pending the imminent passage of a law governing political organizations) and can expand its membership and party organization. It publishes an official magazine, *Min-chin pao* (DPP News) and has a committed and growing number of supporters. In future elections the DPP should be able to nominate candidates, run better-coordinated campaigns for its candidates, and win non-KMT votes that previously went to independent candidates. Furthermore, DPP candidates are now subject to fewer legal and political restrictions with the suspension of martial law and the possible revision of election laws. The more open and competitive elections expected on Taiwan should benefit the DPP.

Under the circumstances the KMT may lose both popular votes and seats. Still the ROC authorities are not likely to reverse the trend toward more electoral contests and more even-handed election procedures. So much is at stake for the ROC's reputation, its commitment to political democratization, and even its dependence on popular elections as a source of legitimacy that the liberalization of the electoral process has a strong momentum. There are reasons to believe that the KMT will continue to hold onto a respectable majority of the popular vote. The KMT now has over two million members, a well-oiled party machine, deep-rooted alliances with powerful local factions, strong support from the stability-conscious industrialists and businessmen, and perhaps even a dominant position among the middle class. The mass media and the nation's security apparatus will continue to be on the KMT's side. Winning the majority of popular votes and holding the majority of elected offices at all levels should not be difficult unless, of course, the nation's economy slackens so drastically that voters defect en masse to the opposition—an unlikely prospect.

In Taiwan's transition to a representative democracy, elections will become an even more important part of the nation's political life. Thus improved election results for the DPP and some erosion of KMT electoral strength may benefit overall democratic political development if not the particularistic interests of the KMT. At this point no one expects a drastic reversal of electoral fortune for the KMT in favor of the DPP or any other new party.

— 8 —

The Mass Media

The influence of the mass media in Taiwan has increased as a result of rising affluence. As Chapter 2 indicates, the mass media have greatly widened their audience during the past decade. In 1976 for every 1,000 persons on the island there were 178 televisions, 64 radios, and 97 magazines and daily newspapers (see Table 2.2). By 1985 the rates had increased to 230, 130, and 195 respectively. Thus in less than ten years about twice as many people owned or had access to a radio, newspapers, and magazines, and 25 percent more owned a television. In 1987 an estimated nine out of ten families on Taiwan owned a television, there was almost one radio per person, and two out of three families subscribed to a newspaper or magazine.

The broadening exposure to mass communication raises new questions about relations between the authorities and the media on the one hand and the media and the citizenry on the other. In most pluralistic democracies the mass media are usually privately owned, although governments may hold a substantial ownership share in the electronic media (as in Canada, the United Kingdom, and most Western European countries). But in these cases the mass media are still highly commercialized and have only limited state regulation. Electronic broadcasting can be an important means of public information, presenting diverse viewpoints and even permitting the articulation of alternative policy positions. In contrast, highly ideological and authoritarian systems use the mass media as socializing agents for the ruling party. In these cases political sanitization transforms the media into a channel for enunciating state policy. Most nations, especially in the Third World, combine some qualities of commercial mass media with a degree of state-controlled political sanitization (Alan Liu 1982, 43). The Republic of China is a case in point. It has highly commercialized radio and television broadcast systems as well as newspapers and periodicals, and it also has substantial official sanitization. Consequently the balance between KMT control and independence in the media varies across a narrow range and periodically tilts toward one side or the other.

TYPES OF MAJOR MEDIA

Like many nations, Taiwan has both electronic and printed media. The electronic media are owned and operated largely by the government or the KMT. Both the government and the party also own a significant number of newspapers and periodicals; many privately owned newspapers are in the hands of loyal KMT backers. Among the 31 daily newspapers in 1987, only 2—the *Independence Evening Post (Tzu-li wan-pao)* in Taipei and the *People's Daily (Min-chung jih-pao)* in Kaohsiung—are owned and operated by native Taiwanese without close KMT connections. Most magazines are not owned or controlled directly by either the KMT or the government.

The Electronic Media

Radio broadcasting on Taiwan started under Japanese colonial rule. In 1945, 5 broadcasting stations were already operating in Taipei, Taichung, Tainan, Hualien, and Chiayi, and there were around 97,000 radio receivers throughout the island (Tai-wan sheng-cheng-fu 1985, 121). In 1950 the KMT established the Broadcasting Corporation of China (BCC) with 9 additional transmitting stations in Taipei and other major cities (Tai-wan sheng-cheng-fu 1985, 98). By 1985 there were 33 broadcasting networks and 177 stations owned either privately or by the government, the KMT, or the armed forces (*ROC Economy Yearbook,* 1985, 636). The BCC remains the most influential of all radio broadcasting networks; its powerful transmissions reach practically every corner of Taiwan from transmitters in all major cities. With over 17 million radios and a population of almost 20 million, radio broadcasting on Taiwan reaches virtually every household.

The first television transmission began in 1962. From the start television has forged an alliance of the KMT and government with private commercial interests. In the 1980s Taiwan has three television stations: the Taiwan Television Corporation (TTV), the China Television Corporation (CTV), and Chinese Television Services (CTS). The party-state has major ownership in each of the corporations that own these stations. TTV is the oldest and has a close connection to the provincial government. CTV is controlled by the KMT central office. CTS has minority investments from both the Ministry of Defense and the Ministry of Education, but with a majority private interest.

TTV was founded in 1962 as a joint venture of the provincial government, some Japanese corporations, and Taiwan commercial interests (Jao et al. 1982, 261; Li Chan 1973, 34). The provincial government, through its affiliated commercial banks, contributed approximately 49 percent of the start-up capital for TTV. The investment share of Japanese corporations has varied over the years; in 1987 the Japanese still held a 20 percent interest (Li Chan 1979, 35; *Yuan Chien,* April 1987, 46). The remaining shares are owned by private investors, KMT-affiliated enterprises, and semipublic corporations (Li Chan 1979, 35). Chairmen of TTV's board have always been prominent KMT officials of Taiwanese origin (Jao et al. 1982, 289).

In 1969 a second commercial network, CTV, was established following a directive issued by Chiang Kai-shek. After prolonged negotiations the KMT-controlled BCC emerged as the senior partner in CTV with 50 percent of the shares, while private radio stations owned 28 percent and other commercial interests 22 percent (Li Chan 1979, 36). Since 1979 KMT shares have increased to around 60 percent. For all practical purposes CTV operates as a KMT enterprise; its posts on the board of directors are plums of political patronage dispensed by the KMT.

CTS, the third television network, was established in 1970. It developed from a small public education station founded by the Ministry of Education in 1962. CTS was initially co-owned by the Ministry of Education (49 percent) and the Ministry of National Defense (51 percent). Over the years it gradually accepted private investment, though in 1987 the two ministries retained a combined interest of nearly 41 percent (Yuan Chien, April 1987, 46). The CTS network has maintained strong ties to both ministries through personnel and programs.

Newspapers

In 1987 Taiwan had 31 daily newspapers with an estimated circulation of 3.5 million copies (Sung and Ho 1988, 323). Since the publishers treat the exact circulation figures as private information, the figures are estimated from the consumption of newsprint rolls.

Of these 31 newspapers, 20 are privately owned while 4 are owned by the KMT, 2 by the government, and 5 by the military (Sung and Ho

1988, 323). Table 8.1 shows that the *China Times (Chung-kuo shih-pao)* and the *United Daily News (Lien-ho pao)*, both privately owned, had the largest circulations, with more than a million each. The *Industrial and Commercial Times*, which claims a circulation of 100,000, is owned by Yu Chi-chung, who also publishes the *China Times*. Wang Tih-wu, the owner of the *United Daily News*, also owns the *Economic Daily News* and *Min-sheng News*.

Both Yu and Wang are members of the KMT Central Standing Committee. Together the five newspapers they own claim a circulation of more than 70 percent of the total daily papers sold. Consequently Yu and Wang are regarded as the two most influential men in Taiwan's media circles. Their two press syndicates in 1985 collected about 60 percent of all newspaper advertising revenue (Goldstein 1986e, 27). Competition between the two press lords is intense. Yu's newspapers and magazines are more reformist in their treatment of internal politics and on informal contacts between Taiwan and the mainland. Wang's publications are more conservative on internal politics and take a hard line against communism on the mainland. Yet both press syndicates support the KMT and ROC government on major policy issues. Yu's publications definitely articulate views representing the KMT's reformist wing. Wang's express policy preferences generally held by the military and security service leadership.

The other privately owned papers are the *Independence Evening Post*, the *People's Daily*, and the *Taiwan Times*. The first two are considered relatively independent on many politically sensitive issues. Wu San-lien, publisher of the *Independence Evening Post*, is a well-regarded non-KMT political figure. Wu served as Taipei's mayor in the 1950s and was involved in an unsuccessful effort in 1960 to form an opposition party. His personal ties with Chiang Kai-shek and friendly relations with Chiang Ching-Kuo reportedly account for the newspaper's relative freedom from KMT interference (Goldstein 1986e, 28). *People's Daily*, published in Kaohsiung by Li Jui-piao and his son, Li Che-lang, has been under more KMT pressure because of its efforts to maintain an independent journalistic position. The newspaper was required to stop publication for one week in 1985 and since then has been pressed to downplay its coverage of opposition activities.

As indicated in Table 8.1, the *Independence Evening Post*, the most widely read evening paper in Taiwan, has a daily circulation of only around 100,000 copies; the circulation of the morning *People's Daily* was near the 200,000 mark in 1985 and may be approaching 300,000 after a major leap in circulation during 1988. Public institutions and official agencies are rarely permitted to subscribe to either of these newspapers. Sales of the *Taiwan Times*, another Kaohsiung daily, have slipped since the

——— TABLE 8.1 ———
MAJOR NEWSPAPERS IN TAIWAN, 1985

	Ownership	Location	Daily circulation
China Times (Chung-kuo shih-pao)	Private	Taipei	1–1.2 million
United Daily News (Lien-ho pao)	Private	Taipei	1–1.2 million
Economic Daily News	Private	Taipei	200,000 claimed
Industrial and Commercial Times	Private	Taipei	100,000 claimed
Independence Evening Post	Private	Taipei	80,000–100,000
Min-sheng News	Private	Taipei	Unknown
People's Daily	Private	Kaohsiung	160,000–200,000[a]
Taiwan Times	Private	Kaohsiung	Unknown
Central Daily News	KMT	Taipei	550,000 claimed
Chung-hua Daily News	KMT	Taipei and Tainan	650,000 claimed
Taiwan Hsin-sheng News	KMT	Taipei	450,000 claimed
Taiwan Hsin-wen Journal	Government	Kaohsiung	Unknown
Youth Daily News	Defense Ministry	Taipei	200,000 claimed
Taiwan Daily News	Defense Ministry	Taichung	250,000 claimed
China Post (English)	Private	Taipei	50,000
China News (English)	KMT	Taipei	20,000 claimed
Free China Journal (English)	Government	Taipei	Unknown

SOURCES: Goldstein (1986e), 27; Yang Su-min (1984), 21.
[a]Information provided by the publisher to this author.

change of management from Wu Chi-fu, a respected physician, to Wang Yu-fa, a Kaohsiung tycoon with broad KMT connections.

Eight major newspapers are affiliated officially with the KMT or the ROC government. Three of them—the *Central Daily News,* the *Chung-hua (Chinese) Daily News,* and the *China News* (published in English)—are directly owned by the party. The *Central Daily News* is the official publication of the KMT Central Standing Committee. Its editorial line and treatment of controversial issues enunciate the current views of the party's policymakers and set the direction for the other newspapers (Lai 1979, 23). As Table 8.1 shows, the *Central Daily News* claims a daily circulation of 550,000 copies but the actual figure is probably about 250,000 as of mid-1988 (Liao 1988, 77). All public official agencies are obligated to subscribe to it. The *Chung-hua Daily News* is a primarily KMT-controlled paper with Tainan and, until 1987, Taipei editions. Its claim of a 650,000 daily circulation, however, may be grossly inflated. Unlike the *Central Daily News,* the *Chung-hua Daily News* emphasizes local news and shows more flexibility in its interpretation of policy matters even though it echoes the KMT party line. The English-language *China News* caters mainly to foreigners residing in or visiting Taiwan. It is published by the Cultural Affairs Department of the KMT Central Committee.

Various government agencies own or control five other daily papers. The Hsin-sheng (New Life) Press Company, an affiliate of the Taiwan Provincial Government, issues two dailies: the *Taiwan Hsin-sheng News* in Taipei and the *Taiwan Hsin-wen Journal* in Kaohsiung. The circulation figures for the latter are unavailable; its circulation is limited to southern Taiwan.

Two newspapers connected with the General Political Department in the Ministry of Defense—The *Youth Daily News* (previously known as the *Young Soldiers News)* and *Taiwan Daily News*—have substantial circulations. The former circulates mainly among active military personnel and students and maintains a strongly conservative editorial tone. Despite efforts to become a partially commercialized press, the *Youth Daily News* has achieved only limited acceptance among the general public, so its influence is restricted chiefly to military ranks and some ultraconservative readers. *Taiwan Daily News* was owned privately until 1978, when the Taiwan Press Company took control. On the surface it still appears to be a private business venture headed by the industrialist Ch'en Mao-pang; actually it has close connections with the Ministry of Defense, and the ministry is believed to have a large financial stake in the newspaper. Both newspapers claim a circulation figure in the range of 150,000 to 200,000.

Most of the newspapers backed by the KMT, the government, and the military also have commercial investors, typically with ties to the KMT and the ROC government. Although the newspapers are obligated to support the official policies, the competition for readership and market share gives grounds for some to adopt a more independent journalistic approach to gain popular acceptance. Privately owned newspapers, including the *China Times* and the *United Daily News,* are more likely to publish editorials critical of government policies or decrying the conduct of public officials (Wu Feng-shan 1972, 233–34). Newspapers published by the authorities and leading KMT figures have a circulation advantage, since public institutions, agencies, and offices ranging from national government bodies to local police stations must subscribe to these newspapers. Government enterprises such as railways, bus stations, gas stations, and even some tourist hotels often offer only these so-called public dailies for sale. This practice restricts the market share of the independent newspapers.

In January 1988 the ROC government lifted its previous restriction on the publication of new daily newspapers. In three months several new dailies went into publication. Both the *China Times* and the *United Daily News* now issue separate evening newspapers, and the *Independence Evening Post* publishes a morning edition. All newspapers are permitted to add pages. A privately owned tiny *Liberty Times (Tzu-you shih-pao)* has been substantially expanded. Many local newspapers have since come into existence. The lifting of restrictions inevitably leads to intense competition over market share and a growing liberalization in reporting and press commentary. To survive, most newspapers are compelled to commercialize even further to gain readers' acceptance. Under the circumstances an official sanitization policy becomes more difficult to implement. Newspapers catering to official lines are reportedly doing poorly in circulation as readers expect the emergence of a free press. The privately held *People's Daily, Independence Morning Post,* and *Liberty Times* have gained market share since January 1988. The circulation of the *Central Daily News* and the two major newspapers—*China Times* and the *United Daily News*—reportedly have declined significantly. Financially shaky and smaller newspapers may eventually lose out in a market of fierce competition. After a period of consolidation only the financially strong major newspapers hold enough circulation to continue publishing.

Magazines

Magazines are also an important media forum, although they are not nearly as influential as the daily press. Magazines are popular in Taiwan because they publish views critical of the government much more than the newspapers do. The authorities have been less restrictive about the content of magazine articles. In the 1980s the importance of magazines as a form of political communication has grown considerably through the mushrooming of opposition political journals. Since the ROC authorities had banned the publication of new daily newspapers until 1988 and the existing newspapers often provided only scanty or biased coverage of anti-KMT opinions and activities, the opposition had to rely on magazines to air their views and to criticize public officials.

In 1980 there were about 2,000 magazines registered with the Press Bureau in the Executive Yuan; 120 were classified as political journals (Tai-wan sheng-cheng-fu 1985, 119). The total number of magazines may have grown to over 2,600 by 1985, but the number of political journals has remained almost unchanged (Tai-wan sheng-cheng-fu 1985,

122). Most political journals have a short life span, although many suspended ones often transmute into a new form with a new title. Taiwan's magazines nevertheless cover a broad range of political positions from the extreme right, represented by *Lung-ch'i* (Dragon Flag), to the left, with publications like *Hsia-ch'ao* (Summer Tide). Most of the politically influential journals may be described as defenders of the status quo, mild reformists, or advocates of popular democracy. Their views about mainland connections also split between those identifying with greater China and those identifying only with Taiwan.

The chief conservative periodicals are published through the KMT—directly as party organs or by affiliated enterprises and individual KMT leaders—and the Ministry of Defense's General Political Department (Nan 1986a, 17). The most important include *Chung-yang yueh-kan* (Central Monthly), issued by KMT central headquarters; *Shuang-shih-yuan* (Double Ten), the organ of provincial party headquarters; *Huang-ho* (Yellow River), by the KMT Central Committee's Youth Department; and *Ta-chung* (the Public), by the Defense Ministry's General Political Department. These journals defend KMT policies and interests while criticizing the opposition. The most influential conservative journals published by individual KMT leaders are *Lien-ho yueh-kan* (United Monthly), *Chung-hua tsa-chih* (China Magazine), and *Cheng-chih p'ing-lun* (Political Review). Periodicals taking a moderate position but with KMT reformist sympathies are *Shih-pao hsin-wen chou-k'an* (Times News Weekly) and *Chung-kuo lun-t'an* (China Tribune). Both of these publications support the KMT government and are satisfied with the prevailing political and economic arrangements. *Hsin hsin-wen* (the Journalist), which began publication in March 1987, is widely regarded as the best of the centrist political journals.

The last category of political journals is linked with the opposition political movement. These opposition magazines are often suppressed by the authorities, but the publishers bring them back under different titles. Key editors often shift from one journal to another. Consequently it is difficult to classify the opposition journals and their backers, although in general they express the views of the non-KMT democratic movement that has emerged since the Chungli Incident of 1977. They advocate political democratization, increased civil rights on Taiwan, the reform of government institutions, a free press, and the legalization of opposition parties. They even oppose the promulgation of new laws on state security, organized groups, and political activities since the suspension of martial law. In their view all members of the three national representative bodies must be subject to periodic popular election without provisions for a quota of seats reserved for the mainlanders. They favor legalizing contacts that improve Taiwan–mainland relations. But among themselves they differ over the strategy and tactics to achieve these goals. During 1984–1985 several of these publications took up a steady drumbeat of personal criticism of major KMT leaders for their allegedly corrupt life-styles and conspiratorial arrangements used to protect their own interests.

The moderate opposition critics follow the lead of K'ang Ninghsiang, a member of the Legislative Yuan. K'ang, who is also a DPP Central Standing Committee member, and his associates have published a number of political journals, such as *T'ai-wan cheng-lun* (Taiwan Political Review), *Pa-shih nien-tai* (the Eighties), *Ya-chou jen* (the Asian), and *Nuan-liu* (Warm Current). Although all these journals criticize the KMT and demand political reform, they advocate incremental reforms and acknowledge the KMT's dominant role in the political process. The moderate reformers favor electoral politics as the main avenue for achieving parliamentary democracy, and they reject mass movements. In their journals they consciously avoid the flamboyant style favored by radical opposition publications. Overall these non-KMT moderates subscribe to the standard elements of Western liberalism.

The vast majority of opposition publications are more militant than the moderate journals. They are heirs to the journalistic tradition initiated in 1978 by *Mei-li-tao* (Formosa), which stressed sweeping reforms and a strategy based on mass organization to challenge KMT domination. Since then journals such as *Feng-lai-tao* (Formosa Weekly), *Shen keng* (Deep Plough), *Kuan-huai* (Great Sympathy), *Sheng ken* (Striking Roots), *Hsin ch'ao-liu* (New Trends), *Hsin lu-hsien* (New Line), *Hsin kuan-tien* (New Perspective), and *Min-chu shih-tai* (Age of Democracy) have continued at one time or another the less restrained editorial criticism begun by *Mei-li-tao*. While stressing immediate political reform, all these so-called militant journals also promote native Taiwanese consciousness. As such, they have earned an undue reputation of favoring political independence for Taiwan. Most support street protests and mass rallies as important tactics to gain political concessions from the KMT authorities. Key figures who advocate such militant tactics include Ch'iu I-jen, Hung Ch'i-ch'ang, Cheng Nan-jung, Ch'en Shui-pien, and more recently Hsieh Ch'ang-ting. Ch'en, Hung, and Hsieh are members of the DPP Central Standing Committee.

Mei-li-tao and its successor militant journals, as well as moderate magazines published by K'ang Ning-hsiang and his associates, form the mainstream of opposition journalism (Nan 1986a, 27–28). Beyond these are a few journals representing the left wing or marginal left wing of the political spectrum. *Hsiao-ch'ao* (Summer Tide), for instance, clearly favors socialism and an eventual unification with the mainland; *Ch'ien-chin* (Forward), published by Lin Cheng-chieh and Chang Fu-chung, took a more cautious editorial stance but seemed to favor democratic socialist ideas while also being receptive toward rapprochement with the mainland. Altogether the circulation of these militant opposition journals reached a height of about 150,000 copies a month in 1978 and has not changed since (Li Li 1983, 11).

The more militant writers and magazine editors, commonly referred to as "the new generation" (hsin-sheng-tai), have organized the Association of Nonparty Editors and Writers (Tang-wai Pien-lien-hui). In 1985 the association had more than 150 members, mostly young and college educated. The association's credo calls for "political democracy, self-determination for Taiwan inhabitants, and respect for human rights" (*TWMP*, August 24, 1985, 1). Its magazines criticize the moderates and mount vicious verbal attacks on KMT officials. The association's militancy did not abate after the formation of the DPP and the KMT announcement of an end to martial law. From March to June of 1987 the association organized a wave of mass rallies and street demonstrations against the proposed new state security law due to go into effect when martial law ended in July 1987. *Min-chin-pao* (Democratic Progressive News), the DPP's official publication, is under the editorial control of these militants and endorses the tactic of promoting street demonstrations.

THE KUOMINTANG AND THE MASS MEDIA

Taiwan does not have the type of free press that prevails in the western democracies and Japan. In the past the authorities did not tolerate criticism that questioned the legitimacy of the government, the fundamental policy of anticommunism, the reunification of China based on the Three Principles of the People, or the rejection of Taiwan independence. All four topics are gradually finding their way into the newspapers and political journals. Although the government's press policy is liberalizing, blunt criticism still runs the risk of official sanction. The political system provides several instruments for promoting official policies and sanitizing the media. Laws and regulations governing the mass media are enforced by both the ROC's civilian administrative agencies and the military's Garrison Command headquarters. The KMT party apparatus also plays an important role in monitoring media activities. Outright violations of the laws and regulations as well as overt challenges to the regime's fundamental policies will call down a variety of sanctions. Censorship continues in the ROC even though the Taiwan press is generally more independent than is typical in "most developing or communist countries" (Jacobs 1976b, 785). But given the growing popular demand for liberalization and the KMT's policy of sanitizing unwanted views, what is the balance between party control and freedom of the press?

The task of managing the press belongs to the KMT Central Committee's Department of Cultural Affairs (DCA) (Goldstein 1986e, 26). Since 1963 the DCA has held work conferences for the press to convey KMT policies about press work and to transmit party directives on the standards, format, and content of the media. Only KMT members attend these conferences, in which leading KMT functionaries give lectures on the party's expectations. According to a DCA report, 244 persons participated in the Fourth Press Work Conference held in April 1974 (KMT, 1974, 83–88). The participants included (1) 131 KMT publishers, board chairmen, or general managers of major newspapers and electronic media, plus editors and department heads from all major media; (2) 100 KMT party functionaries in charge of propaganda activities in the party or government administrations; and (3) 13 KMT scholars and experts specializing in communications. The conference discussed ways to bring press policy in line with the Three Principles of the People, to mobilize the media to support the nation's development programs, to coordinate the media's anti-PRC coverage through joint efforts with party and government offices, and to improve the content and management of the mass media to serve the interests of the nation. The participants were expected to gain a clearer notion of how to perform their jobs to fulfill the regime's aims.

As one means of monitoring the press, the KMT makes certain that editors, particularly those of daily newspapers and electronic media, are party loyalists. Editors, after all, act as gatekeepers to prevent politically unacceptable materials from reaching their audience (Goldstein 1986e, 26). The DCA is particularly concerned about media coverage of elections and other major political events, domestic or foreign, that may affect the political stability of the island. As Carl Goldstein of the *Far Eastern Economic Review* observed: "Starting several months before island-wide elections were to be held . . . party officials began meeting with the publishers and top editors of major newspapers to discuss the proper orientation of press coverage of the elections" (Goldstein 1986e, 27). It is also not surprising that press coverage of the U.S. derecognition of the ROC in 1978–79 by the four leading daily newspapers—the *Central Daily News,* the *United Daily News,* the *China Times,* and *Taiwan Hsin-sheng News*—had a party-directed uniformity in both editorial interpretation and news reports (Lai 1979, 14–31). From time to time KMT officials may also approach local reporters about "how the party [hopes] to see certain issues covered" (Goldstein 1986e, 27).

The KMT's intrusion into media activities does not in practice guarantee editors' or reporters' compliance. Although ownership of the major media is restricted to "reliable persons," competition for market share and the profit motive have led to frequent deviations from the official position in bids to increase circulation. Since business goals sometimes run counter to party interests, Taiwan's newspapers, including some of the KMT affiliates, can maintain a degree of independence not found in other authoritarian systems.

The conflicts between party discipline and press professionalism are growing among media personnel. Following the principles of their professional training, many journalists are eager to see a reduction in political supervision. They believe that close monitoring by KMT officials is unnecessary and retards their professional performance. According to some surveys these sentiments have become widespread among editors and reporters (Hsu, Pan, and Chao 1978, 35; Wang Liang-fen 1982, 69). But KMT loyalists still hold the party line by controlling the employment of editors and reporters (Jacobs 1976b, 785). There are documented cases in which editors and reporters have lost their jobs because of pressure from the DCA.

LAWS AND REGULATIONS

The ROC's regulation of the mass media is extensive. But laws and regulations governing printed materials often do not uniformly apply to radio and television broadcasting because most of the laws were enacted long before electronic media became popular. Regulation thus weighs more heavily on print journalism, which also has a history of seeking greater freedom of expression than the electronic media.

The Press and Other Printed Materials

Elaborate sets of laws and regulations govern the press and other printed materials. The main regulations applicable to print journalism follow (Hu Yuan-hui 1982, 8; Yang Su-min 1984, 38–42):

1. *The National Mobilization Law.* Two articles in the National Mobilization Law are especially applicable to the press. Article 22 stipulates that the government may restrict or prohibit newspapers, press wire services, and the printing of articles and other materials (such as pamphlets or books) whenever it deems necessary. Article 23 empowers the government to restrict the freedoms of speech,

publication, correspondence, popular assembly, and association if circumstances should require such actions. These articles have been enforced in Taiwan because of what the government considers a threatening political and military situation with regard to the mainland.

2. *Martial Law.* Article 11 stipulated that in areas falling under martial law, the senior commander could prohibit popular assembly, organized associations, mass rallies, and petitions and could impose sanctions against speeches, lectures, presses, magazines, photographs, postcards, and other printed materials deemed harmful to the military. Taiwan Garrison Command headquarters, an arm of the Ministry of Defense, was empowered to carry out these restrictive provisions following an administrative decree issued by the president. The State Security Law that replaced the suspended martial law has not inherited most of the latter's regulatory authority over publications.

Article 4 empowered the Taiwan garrison commander to conduct precirculation censorship. Article 3 defined speech and writing seditious if they were deemed propaganda for the Chinese Communists, slandered the head of state, stirred up animosity between the government and the people, or violated the national policy of anticommunism. Since violations were loosely defined, the regulations granted wide latitude to suppress opposition periodicals (Goldstein 1986e, 26). These martial law provisions have either been removed from the new State Security Law or incorporated into the revised Publication Law since 1987.

3. *The Publication Law.* Enforced by the Press Bureau of the Executive Yuan, this law addresses the registration of newspapers and magazines. It gives the bureau the authority to deny registration or to suspend publication when articles are deemed seditious or likely to incite social disorder.

4. *Detailed regulations for implementing the Publication Law.* The best known of these regulations issued by the Executive Yuan for operating the Press Bureau deals with the authority to restrict the number of pages a newspaper may print. The ROC authorities imposed strict page limits on all newspapers; the maximum in 1988 rose from twelve to twenty pages.

Obviously these laws and regulations overlap. The authority of the Taiwan Garrison Command headquarters and the Press Bureau of the Executive Yuan, the two main enforcement agencies, are intertwined in practice to provide a broad range of discretionary power applicable to any publication considered undesirable. There is little or no recourse for publishers whose publications are placed under sanction, and they have no means to seek judicial redress against the authorities. Thus the press restrictions always seem arbitrary. Since the lifting of martial law in 1987, control over publications has loosened and many laws and regulations have been revised. It is still unclear how much press freedom the government will eventually permit.

Press Censorship

Government censorship of books, periodicals, and newspapers has generated ill feelings in Taiwan and abroad. In recent years, as the *tangwai* movement has intensified, periodicals published by the political opposition have increased their criticism of both fundamental national policies and the KMT leaders' personal lives. The opposition press has also criticized the one-party system, martial law, and press censorship. As the opposition publications have become increasingly belligerent, the KMT authorities have resorted to wholesale censorship of *tangwai* political journals.

Censorship on Taiwan is carried out under the provisions of various laws and regulations concerning published materials. One study disclosed that from 1950 to 1981, 141 books were censored under the Publication Law and 142 under the regulations for the control of published materials under martial law (Hu Yuan-hui 1982, 23). Thus the civilian government and the Garrison Command roughly divided the responsibility for censorship. In the four years from 1979 to 1983 alone, 33 books by *tangwai* authors were censored.

Before the lifting of martial law, the censorship of opposition periodicals was frequent and controversial. Censorship meant the banning or confiscation of a single issue of a magazine or the suspension of publication, usually for one year. According to Table 8.2 confiscations and bannings increased from 9 instances in 1980 to 295 in 1986. Censorship had escalated since 1984, reflecting the growing challenges by editors and writers as well as the authorities' increasing vigilance. The number of magazine suspensions stood at about 7 per year except in 1984 and 1985, when suspensions leapt to 35 and 15 respectively. Censorship during 1980–1986 increased partly because there were more political journals in those years. But harsh censorship actions by the Garrison Command have taken their toll against even the respected moderate opposition journals *Ya-chou jen* (the Asian) and *Pa-shih nien-tai* (the Eighties), both driven from publication in 1986. At the end of 1986, 5 weekly and 4

_____ TABLE 8.2 _____
PRESS CENSORSHIP IN TAIWAN, 1980–1986

	Confiscations and bannings	Suspensions	Total
1980	9	7	16
1981	13	6	19
1982	23	4	27
1983	26	7	33
1984	176	35	211
1985	260	15	275
1986	295	7	302

SOURCE: International Committee for Human Rights in Taiwan (1987), 20.

monthly opposition publications remained. In 1987 several suspended opposition journals registered for publication under new titles.

A spokesman for the Taiwan Garrison Command stated the reasons why the government continues to censor the press:

> In recent years, some political journals have frequently published radical views under the pretext of freedom of the press. They fabricate stories and spread false tales about the present anticommunist policy of the nation and important government actions. They openly advocate the separatist idea of Taiwan independence, agitating bad feelings between the government and the people. They defame the head of state, and they serve the propaganda purposes of the Chinese Communists. All of these actions have greatly damaged the future of the nation and threatened social order. (*CYJP*, May 12, 1985)

To stop the spread of such "radical and harmful" views, the Garrison Command headquarters insists that censorship must continue (*CYJP*, May 12, 1985). But the opposition regards the Garrison Command's position as a convenient excuse for continued restrictions on their civil rights. Press censorship has thus become a partisan political issue.

A closer look reveals that the reasons given for banning articles are not always in line with criteria set forth by the Garrison Command's spokesman in 1985. According to Table 8.3 half the articles banned during January to July of 1984 were suppressed either for "exposing" the KMT leaders' personal "secrets" or for publicizing the sensitive issue of political prisoners. Another 33 articles were banned in connection with

_____ TABLE 8.3 _____

A CONTROL ANALYSIS OF BANNED ARTICLES, JANUARY–JULY 1984

	Number of banned articles	Percent
"Historical secrets" (mainly pertaining to President Chiang and other high KMT officials)	58	26.9
Prison conditions and political prisoners	50	23.1
Domestic issues (such as coal mine disasters)	33	15.3
Future status of Taiwan	26	12.0
Suggesting the establishment of opposition parties	21	9.7
Taiwan's diplomatic isolation	14	6.5
Undemocratic structure of the central government	9	4.2
Succession after President Chiang Ching-kuo	5	2.3
Total	216	100.0

SOURCE: International Committee for Human Rights in Taiwan (1986), 16.

the government's handling of three serious coal mine disasters. Fourteen articles were banned for discussing the ROC's diplomatic isolation. Indeed, all these issues are politically sensitive in Taiwan, and the authorities do not want them to be freely discussed in the mass media. Since the opposition journals need to present events dramatically to capture readers' interest, their writing style contains stronger language and more accurate content than the KMT-dominated press. At issue here is whether the Garrison Command should have the discretion to decide if an article "damages the future of the nation" or "threatens social order."

The ROC's censorship policies place publishers, especially those with a *tangwai* orientation, in a continuing state of watchfulness over the content of their publications. The problem is obviously political rather than legal. Opposition groups rely on publications to express their views; only by criticizing the authorities can they expect to gain the citizens' support. The tendency to defame KMT leaders and to exaggerate government misconduct has become part of the DPP's conscious strategy to belittle the ruling party and thus to diminish its authority. Censorship serves as a weapon for the KMT to counter the opposition's criticisms without answering the charges. Since 1985 the KMT has applied the legal process to these so-called slanderous cases. But the failure of the courts to act independently from the KMT in such cases has damaged the credibility of the judiciary (Tien 1987b, 9–10).

The Electronic Media

Television and radio broadcasting operated without any governing laws until 1976, when the Broadcasting Law was adopted. Before then broadcasting enterprises were subject to constantly changing administrative regulations (Cheng Su-min 1985, 2). Even the responsibility for monitoring broadcasting shifted from one ministry to another, creating much confusion at times. Before the first television stations went on the air in 1962, regulatory activities were needed only for radio broadcasts. At different times from 1950 to 1961 the KMT's Department of Cultural Affairs, the Ministry of Education, and the Ministry of Communications assumed principal regulatory responsibility for radio broadcasting (Li Chan 1973, 258–59). Most of these regulations concerned licenses, program supervision, and the collection of license fees.

In 1961 the Executive Yuan's Press Bureau became responsible for monitoring both radio and television broadcasts. Two years later the bureau issued standards for monitoring radio and television programs to regulate both the content and the scheduling of programs (Li Chan 1973, 259). One consequence was to reduce the number of programs aired in native Taiwanese dialects (Jao et al. 1982, 260). From 1967 to 1973 the Bureau of Cultural Affairs in the Ministry of Education replaced the Press Bureau as the government's regulatory agency. The Broadcasting Law of 1976 created an Office of Broadcasting Enterprises in the Press Bureau as the government agency to implement the new law (Hsu En-p'u 1980, 73).

Efforts to draft a broadcasting law began in 1965. The draft was sent to the Legislative Yuan in 1972, but a long series of revisions followed until the Executive Yuan completed the final draft in 1975. To sanitize the content of broadcasts the bill stipulated that "popular entertainment shows must be educational and must be based on promoting Chinese culture." In addition, Mandarin was declared the official broadcasting dialect, and television programs were prohibited from conflicting with the national policies of anticommunism and the recovery of the mainland (Hsu En-p'u 1980, 65). The Broadcasting Law was officially promulgated in 1976; a year later the Press Bureau announced its detailed regulations concerning broadcasting programs. Both are enforced by the bureau's Office of Broadcasting Enterprises.

Because the views expressed by Taiwan's mainstream electronic media have always been in line with party-government policies, the authorities have not needed to be concerned with deviations from official positions. Instead they have worried about the proliferation of Taiwanese-dialect programming and, more recently, foreign programs, especially those from the United States and Japan, which can be either dubbed and broadcast or imitated in local productions (Cheng Su-min 1985, 2). The government's sanitization policy aims to reduce such programs out of a fear of their long-term influence. Taiwanese-dialect programs may perpetrate an indigenous identity, which runs counter to the regime's claim to represent the whole of China. Japanese programming worries the authorities because of a potential revival of the Taiwanese affinity for things Japanese that stems from the 1895–1945 period of Japanese colonial rule. But commercial pressures and network competition for popular programming have rendered these government regulations extremely difficult to implement.

THE MEDIA AND PUBLIC COMMUNICATION

With the proliferation of electronic networks and the ever growing circulation of newspapers and magazines, the modern mass media have pervaded all levels of society on Taiwan. Still, face-to-face personal communication—a characteristic of traditional society—remains a salient force in opinion formulation. Some argue that in Taiwan, as elsewhere in highly developed societies, the mass media system simply "embeds traditional channels of contact within a new system of intercourse" (Hoselitz and Moore 1970, 8). The effectiveness of the media is still connected with the forms of face-to-face social contact common to the island: nuclear and extended families, economic enterprises, administrative offices, neighborhoods, associations, factional networks, and so on. In each of the various social contexts, opinion leaders transmit messages from the mass media to average citizens through personal contacts. The traditional forms of face-to-face communication continue in Taiwan because social interaction still reflects a strong pattern of social relations based on intricate personal ties.

Education, age, geographic location, and subject matter all influence the form of media most effective for various elements of Taiwan society. One survey conducted in the early 1970s showed a direct correlation between higher education and a reliance on newspapers and magazines for information (Chiang Ping-lun 1974a, 4–11). People with elementary and junior high school educations relied heavily on the broadcasting media for information. The illiterate and some of those with only an elementary school education derived their information almost exclusively from interpersonal verbal communications. In addition, young adults (ages 18–39) tended to read newspapers and magazines more frequently than the middle-aged and elderly. In contrast, those age 51 or over depended heavily on face-to-face communication for information. All age groups within the adult population had substantial contact with the electronic media, but contact frequency was higher among those in the 18–50 age group. Above age 50 contact with the electronic media gradually declined, perhaps because the older age cohort has less education. Thus the greater reliance of the elderly on traditional means of communication may be a function of illiteracy or marginal literacy, not age.

What about media sources on politically sensitive topics? How do people know what sources to rely on? Empirical studies provide some insights into these two aspects of political communication. Taiwan's voters do not necessarily rely on the mass media for information on electoral campaigns. They attend large public rallies so that they can see the candidates in person and hear them firsthand. They also read pamphlets prepared by the candidates' campaign organizations and even meet with the candidates in person during their frequent door-to-door visits. Hence voters get considerable information through personal contacts. Opposition candidates in particular must rely on interpersonal communications to reach the voters to overcome the disadvantages of limited or biased coverage by a majority of Taiwan's mass media.

Among different types of mass media, newspapers and television broadcasts are the two most frequent sources of information, followed by radio broadcasts and magazines. Table 8.4 shows the results of a November 1980 survey conducted in metropolitan Taipei. According to this study, 78 percent of the sample indicated that newspapers were their usual source of campaign information, while an additional 18 percent cited newspapers as an occasional source. Of the same people surveyed, 68 percent were also usual viewers of television as a source of information, while 25 percent were occasional users. Another 12 percent depended on radio broadcasts as a usual source, and 17 percent were occasional listeners. But 71 percent said they either rarely or never used the radio as a source of information about candidates or campaign issues. Magazines were cited as a still less frequent source of campaign information. Over 80 percent of those surveyed either rarely or never used magazines for this purpose—perhaps because magazines, usually published on a weekly or monthly basis, do not provide the timely information most voters seek.

Among the newspapers, the *China Times* and the *United Daily News* were read by 73 percent of those surveyed who regularly or occasionally used newspapers as a source of campaign information (Hsu Hui-ling 1982, 74). The readership of these two major dailies published in Taipei is lower in central and southern Taiwan, where numerous local newspapers offer strong competition. Among the three television networks, TTV

_____ TABLE 8.4 _____

MASS MEDIA SOURCES OF CAMPAIGN INFORMATION, NOVEMBER 1980

	Usual	Occasional	Rare	Never	Total[a]
Newspapers	113 (78%)	26 (18%)	5 (3%)	0 (0%)	144 (100%)
Television	98 (68%)	36 (25%)	9 (6%)	1 (1%)	144 (100%)
Radio	17 (12%)	25 (17%)	39 (27%)	63 (44%)	144 (100%)
Magazines	6 (4%)	21 (15%)	39 (27%)	78 (54%)	144 (100%)

SOURCE: Hsu Hui-ling (1982), 73.
[a]Percentages do not all add to 100 because of rounding.

with its strong Taiwanese connections drew the most viewers on campaign events, followed by CTV and CTS in that order (Cheng Shih-min 1982, 36).

The pattern of media influence differs considerably when it involves news of major political events. Two major events that shocked the population of Taiwan illustrate the point: the death of President Chiang Kai-shek in 1975 and the U.S. derecognition of the ROC in 1978. In their political consequences, these events may be regarded as the two most significant events in Taiwan since 1949. According to a mail survey conducted soon after the death of Chiang Kai-shek, 34 percent of the general public learned the news from face-to-face contacts, 29 percent from radio broadcasts, 20 percent from newspapers, and 17 percent from television (Yang Hsiao-jung 1975, 17–18). About 46 percent of Taipei citizens heard the news of the unexpected U.S. shift of diplomatic relations from face-to-face contacts, 34 percent from television, 16 percent from radio broadcasts, and only slightly more than 2 percent from daily newspapers (Yang Chih-hung 1979, 22–23). (The news arrived in Taipei after the morning newspapers had been published, so they could not serve as a source in this case.)

These two dramatic events illustrate a great diversity of influence for the media in Taiwan. But because the surveys do not help us understand the initial public impressions of these major political events, we cannot fully assess the influence of the media. Nor do we always have reliable information on whether or how the regime intervened in the handling of these or other news events.

We do have evidence on the ROC's handling of the fall of Ferdinand Marcos in the Philippines. The news networks were initially allowed extensive freedom to report and analyze the February 7, 1986, election in the Philippines and the subsequent political upheaval, but the KMT soon became alarmed by the tenor of the reporting. About a week after the election, as Marcos's political situation deteriorated, the KMT Department of Cultural Affairs directed the *China Times* and the *United Daily News* "to reduce the amount of space devoted to the story," but the order was ignored (Goldstein 1986g, 16–17). Apparently KMT authorities thought that the deposing of a long-dominant leader might stir up opposition to the Chiang family on Taiwan.

CONCLUSION

Taiwan's mass media has clearly diversified and plays an important role in the political process. The KMT and government authorities cannot monopolize media enterprises in an increasingly pluralistic society. Censorship continues on Taiwan, particularly for *tangwai* political journals; yet opposition publications have been allowed to reappear under new titles within a short time. The party and the government still monitor the press closely, but party opinions are not reflected either strictly or uniformly. Furthermore, a greater volume of information is now available from sources outside the ROC. In these overseas sources only information on the Chinese mainland and the Soviet bloc are subject to tight scrutiny. Since the 1970s, as the authorities have tolerated more dissent, the mass media have developed a greater diversity of viewpoints. Even influential daily newspapers such as the *China Times,* published by a prominent KMT leader, do not hesitate to depart from official views on many topics.

In the light of these developments we can say that although Taiwan's mass media continue to show the effects of political sanitization and increasing commercialism, they also show clear signs of decreasing ideological control. Whether the liberalization of press censorship will continue depends largely on the success of current KMT political reforms and on the DPP's conduct once it is fully legal.

— 9 —

Foreign Relations and International Status

Challenges and Constraints

To be viable an independent nation-state requires legal recognition from other nation-states; the nation-state must also be able to conduct wide-ranging activities in the international arena. By the same token the legitimacy of a political regime depends on external diplomatic recognition. Although the ROC held formal diplomatic recognition in the world community before 1971, events since 1971, when the China seat in the United Nations was given to the PRC, have cast doubt on the ROC's continuing viability as an independent state. In 1988 the ROC government retained membership in only eight international government organizations.[1] It has diplomatic ties with merely 22 of the 160 states in the world. None of these nations is a major power, and only South Africa, Saudi Arabia, and South Korea may be considered regional powers.

On Taiwan growing diplomatic isolation has undermined the foundations of the national governments's legitimacy. Those who hold key positions in the government and the national legislatures derive their authority from their claim to represent all the provinces on the Chinese mainland. Since the international community no longer accepts that claim, the rationale for maintaining the ROC's present state structure has lost a major source of its authority and has become subject to growing popular criticism at home. Under the circumstances, the KMT regime has found it increasingly difficult to justify its present political structure. Hence the ROC's international status is not merely a foreign relations issue; it also affects the rationale on which the ROC's political institutions and power are maintained on Taiwan.

From the KMT leaders' standpoint, China's civil war is still unfinished. Since 1949, when the KMT regime moved to Taiwan, the ROC authorities have insisted that there is only one China and that the ROC government is its sole representative. Like their counterparts in Peking, the KMT authorities have refused to accept either the "one China, one Taiwan" or the "two Chinas" formula in diplomatic relations. That rigid stance is responsible in part for Taiwan's growing international isolation. Yet there is no easy solution to the ROC's dilemma. Any fundamental change in policy would require the transformation of the ROC political system, severely testing the KMT elite's legitimacy. This requirement explains why the KMT has been unwilling to entertain any significant changes in its foreign policy.

This chapter examines the recent history of the ROC's external relations as well as the dilemma posed by its diplomatic isolation. The discussion focuses on an analysis of the three major issues: (1) the changing status of the ROC in international organizations, both governmental and nongovernmental, and in bilateral diplomacy; (2) relations with the United States; and (3) the challenge of the PRC's unification campaigns. In many ways these three issues intertwine.

INTERNATIONAL INVOLVEMENT AND FOREIGN RELATIONS

Before 1949 the international community recognized the KMT government as the sole legitimate government of China. During World War II China, led by the KMT, was one of the major allies of the United States fighting against Japan. During the KMT-CCP civil war of 1945–1949, the ROC had full diplomatic recognition even by the Soviet Union and occupied a seat in the United Nations Security Council as one of the U.N.'s five permanent members. Military defeat on the mainland and the retreat to Taiwan cast uncertainty over the Nationalist regime's future in 1949–1950. As the communist forces appeared to be gathering across the Taiwan Strait for an invasion, U.S. Secretary of State Dean Acheson decided that the United States should stand clear from Chiang Kai-shek and his regime in anticipation of a final communist victory (Riggs 1952, 6). The outbreak of the Korean War in June 1950 and the subsequent U.S. military involvement in the war dramatically altered the military and diplomatic situation in the Taiwan Strait. The Truman administration began to value the ROC as a noncommunist ally in its fight with communist China. In 1954 the U.S.-ROC Mutual Defense Treaty made the two nations military allies as part of the Eisenhower-Dulles global strategy of containing communism through military alliances.

U.S. hostility toward the PRC during the 1950s and the 1960s guaranteed U.S. support for the ROC's position in the world community. During these two decades of the cold war, the world split into two contending power blocs: U.S. allies and communist nations. The United States' perception of monolithic international communism anchored at Moscow dictated Washington's view of the Peking regime as a puppet of the Soviet Union. As a U.S. ally and with U.S. support, the KMT government sustained most of its pre-1949 acceptance as the sole representative of China even though the KMT had lost the mainland to the Communists.

Participation in International Organizations

As a charter member of the United Nations, the ROC government held seats in virtually all U.N. bodies and affiliated organizations, both governmental and nongovernmental. It was one of the five permanent members of the Security Council. This status in the U.N. not only supported the KMT's claim to China but also provided an important rationale for the form of government it established on Taiwan. The Chinese Communists also understood the importance of U.N. membership. Once the civil war ended on the mainland, the newly established PRC government took immediate action to challenge the ROC's representation. In January 1950 Chou En-lai (Zhou Enlai), then PRC premier and foreign minister, demanded that U.N. Secretary-General Trygve Lie take action to oust the ROC and install the Peking regime in its stead (Clough 1984a, 525). The outbreak of the Korean War, the U.N.-sanctioned military intervention in Korea, and the PRC's entrance into the war on North Korea's behalf—all in the last six months of 1950—ended the PRC's first attempt to enter the U.N.

Throughout the 1950s and the 1960s the United States continued to support the ROC as the holder of the China seat in international organizations. In the 1950s, when U.S. allies in Europe and Latin America constituted a majority in the General Assembly, there was no difficulty in defeating Soviet-bloc resolutions to seat the PRC. As a growing number of newly independent Third World nations became members of the U.N., the United States after 1961 resorted to parliamentary maneuvers to maintain the ROC's position (Clough 1978, 529). Over time these parliamentary tactics became a dubious means of preserving the ROC's international status. There was no sign that the communist regime would collapse on the mainland. The ROC's claim to represent China seemed increasingly a fiction of anticommunist ideology. Even the U.S. government was losing interest in supporting the Taiwan government in the face of popular criticism at home and abroad.

The turning point came in July 1971 when President Nixon announced his plan to visit the Chinese mainland the following year. The announcement was accurately interpreted as a drastic shift of the United States' China policy. The ROC leaders, still adhering to their "one China" policy, rejected proposals that would have given the China seat to the PRC while admitting the ROC government as a separate member of the General Assembly. In October 1971, in yet another U.N. vote on the China seat, the United States dropped its lobbying on the ROC's behalf and the China seat went to Peking. The ROC had been ousted from the United Nations.

What followed were successive ousters of the ROC from all U.N. affiliated organizations (Hsieh 1985, 5). By 1980, when the PRC joined the World Bank and the International Monetary Fund, the ROC had been forced to withdraw from all but ten international governmental organizations. Among these ten only the Asian Development Bank (ADB), the International Union for Publication of Customs Tariffs, and the Permanent Court of Arbitration were considered important. Membership in the ADB is important in part because the ROC joined in 1966 as a charter member under the name "China" (Galang 1985, 101). Many officials and opinion leaders in Taiwan view the ADB as Taiwan's last foothold in governmental organizations.

The ADB was founded in 1966. Of its 45 members—31 Asian-Pacific and 14 European and North American nations—the ROC has been one of the leaders. Between 1966 and 1982 Taipei contributed over U.S. $21 million to the bank. In 1983 the ROC gave an additional U.S. $2 million to the ADB's soft-loan arm, the Asian Development Fund (Galang 1985, 101). Thus the ROC's membership has been an important financial asset to the ADB.

Then in 1983, when the PRC showed interest in joining the ADB, the Reagan administration favored retaining Taiwan's membership. The question became what name the ROC would use to remain in the organization. Peking categorically rejects the continued use of the designation "Republic of China" because it implies there are two Chinas. The KMT authorities appeared willing to adopt the name "China (Taiwan)" and proposed it as a solution that would permit both governments to participate in the ADB. Teng Hsiao-p'ing (Deng Xiaoping) in June 1983 publicly stated that he would not oppose the name "China, Taipei" (Chiu, 1986b, 1). But the PRC leader later changed his mind and insisted in a 1985 agreement that although the ADB could use "China, Taipei" in Chinese texts, the English version should read "Taipei, China," an exact parallel of the "Hong Kong, China" formula used in other contexts (Lin Yi-ling 1987, 15).

In March 1986 the ADB officially announced its acceptance of the PRC as a member while retaining the ROC under the new name "Taipei, China." The announcement touched off a heated debate in Taiwan's mass media and in KMT ruling circles. Subsequently the ROC decided to follow a "three no's" policy—no acceptance, no participation, no withdrawal—pending further negotiations (Kau 1986, 5). The ADB declined to accommodate the ROC and admitted the PRC, delivering a devastating blow to the ROC's leaders. The result of their insistence on a rigid policy of no compromise over the national title demoralized the more pragmatic leaders and a majority of the general public, who favor flexibility and realism in diplomatic conduct (Chiu 1986b, 1; Chen Hao, 1986b, 15; *MCJP,* December 20, 1985, 2). In an effort to salvage a reputation for realism, the ROC's leaders decided to stay in the ADB, though not actively participating in an official capacity in its meetings. After a period of absence, the ROC government decided to attend the April 1988 ADB annual meeting under the label of "Taipei, China." This move came in the wake of growing flexibility toward international affairs under the new leadership of President Lee Teng-hui.

The PRC has sought to expel the ROC from nongovernmental international organizations. The most conspicuous case has been the battle over Taiwan's proper name in the International Olympic Committee (IOC), which determines the name the Taiwan team is allowed to use in the Olympic Games. Until 1976 Taiwan used the title "Republic of China" for its teams, but at the Olympic Games in Montreal in 1976 the Canadian government declared that Taiwan could no longer use that name in Olympic competition. After negotiations involving both the PRC and the ROC, the IOC in November 1979 formally announced its decision to accept Peking's claim to form the sole national committee of China. Two years later the Nationalist government finally accepted a new name, "Chinese Taipei Olympic Committee," and agreed to abandon, as required, the ROC flag and national anthem when participating in future Olympic Games (Weng 1984, 467; Clough 1984a, 531–32). Since then the Taipei authorities have used the IOC formula in a bid to broaden Taiwan's involvement in other nongovernmental organizations. By 1987 Taiwan had joined over 700 such organizations by using some variation of the Olympic formula, which implies that the Nationalists are both Chinese and based in Taiwan but does not imply that there are two Chinas (Chou Hsi 1987, 41).

Diplomatic Relations

The development of the ROC's bilateral relations with individual states parallels its difficulties in international organizations. The issue involves the intense competition between the two rival Chinese regimes to be the legitimate China. In 1971, at the peak of the ROC's diplomatic fortunes, Taipei registered formal diplomatic ties with 68 nations while only 53 recognized the PRC. At that time the PRC's partially self-imposed isolation, which began in 1950, had reached its height after the turbulent Cultural Revolution. Conversely the ROC had derived considerable diplomatic success from its efforts to court Third World nations with a variety of goodwill missions.

Among the major nations in the noncommunist world, the United Kingdom never extended diplomatic recognition to the ROC regime after the retreat to Taiwan in 1949. Nonetheless, the British maintained a consulate in Taiwan until 1972. In 1964 France became the first Western European power since 1949 to break ties with the ROC and recognize the Peking regime. In 1970 Canada and Italy followed suit. Two years later, in February 1972, President Nixon made his historic journey to the mainland in an effort to reconcile the differences between the two powers. Japan promptly shifted diplomatic recognition from Taipei to Peking in September 1972.

Despite these changes in formal diplomatic relations, most of these same nations have not endorsed Peking's territorial claim to Taiwan. Countries that have established diplomatic links with the Peking regime have preferred to use such ambiguous diplomatic terms as "take note," "understand," and "acknowledge" to accommodate Peking's claim to Taiwan (Copper 1984, 5). The U.S. government, for instance, only "acknowledges" in the 1972 Shanghai Communiqué that "all Chinese on either side of the Taiwan Strait maintain there is but one China and that Taiwan is a part of China"—a position the Peking authorities insisted on (Kissinger 1979, 1079).

Although U.S. influence was important, the initial success of the ROC's diplomatic efforts in the Third World during the 1960s depended on other factors as well. Some nations, particularly those in Central America, maintained diplomatic relations with Taipei on the grounds of mutual anticommunism. Also, as more nations gained political independence the ROC began ambitious programs of economic and technical assistance in exchange for diplomatic ties (Hsieh 1985, 186–90). The ROC experimented with aid programs in Liberia; by 1971, 31 nations—including Liberia, Iran, Thailand, South Vietnam, the Dominican Republic, Brazil, Chile, Mexico, Panama, Peru, Ecuador, and Guyana—had assistance from Taiwan (Hsieh 1985, 186; Clough 1978, 151). Taiwan sent agricultural teams and technical specialists to remote rural villages where they worked side by side with local peasants. In addition Taiwan provided training in Taipei for over 7,500 foreign technicians from 50 developing nations during the period 1954–1975 (Clough 1978, 151).

Few nations in the world have offered as much aid to others as the ROC has, but the true intent of the KMT regime was to solidify the ROC's diplomatic foundations, which they understood were shaky at best. They had known long in advance that an all-out challenge to Taiwan's diplomatic status would come from Peking sooner or later. In 1971, when the ROC was expelled from the U.N., its diplomatic status began to crumble. As Table 9.1 shows, 12 nations severed diplomatic ties with Taipei that year. And after President Nixon's trip to the PRC, the situation worsened as another 15 nations switched diplomatic recognition to Peking. Of the states that had formal diplomatic relations with the ROC in 1971, 45 percent switched ties to the PRC from 1971 to 1973.

From then on, additional derecognitions took place nearly every year; by 1988 a total of 55 countries (80 percent) had switched. During these years Taiwan gained diplomatic recognition from 9 countries, but except for South Africa they were all tiny states in the Caribbean and the South Pacific. South Africa had long had consular relations with Taipei and in 1976 upgraded its representation to the ambassadorial level. Other nations that currently recognize the ROC are the Holy See, Malawi, Swaziland, Costa Rica, the Dominican Republic, Dominica, El Salvador, Guatemala, Haiti, Honduras, Nauru, Panama, Paraguay, St. Christopher and Nevis, St. Lucia, St. Vincent and the Grenadines, the Solomon Islands, Saudi Arabia, South Korea, Tonga, and Tuvalu (Hsi 1986, 32). All maintain diplomatic representation of some kind in Taipei except Nauru, which has only a consulate-general's office. Of these nations only 13 have full-fledged diplomatic missions in Taipei. With the exception of Saudi Arabia, South Africa, and South Korea, none is regarded as influential even by its neighbors. In fact trade between the ROC and these 22 nations amounts to less than 10 percent of Taiwan's annual foreign trade. Only 6 of these nations have annual exports to Taiwan worth U.S. $1 million or more; of these only 3—South Korea, Saudi Arabia, and South Africa—have substantial trade and other economic relations with the ROC. Each of the 13 smaller states has an annual trade with Taiwan of less than U.S. $1 million (Chen Ch'i-ti 1985, 72).

Informal Relations

It is uncertain whether the ROC will be able to retain diplomatic ties with these small nations in the years ahead. Rumors persist that Peking has approached Panama, the Vatican, and Saudi Arabia about a possible

TABLE 9.1
A CHRONICLE OF DIPLOMATIC RELATIONS
WITH THE REPUBLIC OF CHINA

	Countries breaking ties with the ROC	Total	Countries establishing ties with the ROC	Total
1971	Austria, Belgium, Cameroon, Chile, Ecuador, Iran, Kuwait, Lebanon, Mexico, Peru, Sierra Leone, Turkey	12		
1972	Argentina, Australia, Chad, Luxembourg, Madagascar, Maldives, Malta, New Zealand, Ruanda, Senegal, Togo	15	Tonga	1
1973	Bahrain, Spain, Upper Volta, Zaire	4		
1974	Botswana, Brazil, Gabon, the Gambia, Malaysia, Niger, Venezuela	7		
1975	Philippines, Portugal, Thailand, Samoa, Vietnam	5		
1976	Central African Republic	1	South Africa	1
1977	Barbados, Jordan, Liberia	3		
1978	Libya	1		
1979	United States of America	1	Tuvalu	1
1980	Colombia	1	Nauru	1
1981			St. Vincent and the Grenadines	1
1983	Ivory Coast, Lesotho	2	Dominica, Solomon Islands, St. Christopher and Nevis	3
1984			St. Lucia	1
1985	Bolivia, Nicaragua	2		
1988	Uruguay	1		
Total		55		9

SOURCES: Hsi (1986), 33; *CYJP* (February 4, 1988), 1.

switch. Even South Korea, the ROC's quasi-ally, has improved relations with the PRC in recent years. South Korea's two-way trade with the PRC, both direct and indirect through Hong Kong and Japan, has increased sixfold from U.S. $250 million in 1983 to U.S. $3 billion in 1987 (*SPCK,* December 22, 1985, 21; McBeth 1988, 15). Furthermore, the South Korean government has carefully avoided taking steps that might antagonize Peking, thus raising doubts in Taiwan about the long-term viability of Taipei-Seoul ties. The South Korean embassy in Taipei has been reduced to only seven diplomats, and Seoul's cabinet-level officials have avoided Taiwan for years for fear of offending Peking (Hoon 1988a, 27). In August 1988 a new commercial shipping route was established between Ch'ing-tao (Qingdao) on the mainland and Pusan in South Korea. Full diplomatic ties could be expected by 1990 (Hoon 1988a, 2).

The ROC's increasing diplomatic isolation comes as no surprise to the KMT leaders. To a large extent, the ROC's diplomatic fortunes have declined not because of a worldwide rejection of the ROC and its policies but because of external factors such as the changing balance of international power, the United States' strategic decision to improve relations with the PRC, and a worldwide realization that the Taipei government plainly can no longer represent the mainland. But internal elements in the ROC have contributed to the situation too. Some blame the KMT leadership for ineptness and lack of innovation as its international position began to shift after 1970 (Copper 1984, 18). As Michael Y. M. Kau has argued:

> By choosing to adhere rigidly to the dogmatic position of absolutely "no coexistence with the Communist bandits," the Nationalist (KMT) leadership has indeed entrapped itself with its own political rhetoric and has been forced to rule out *a priori* any possibility of accepting a "dual membership," side by side with the PRC, in international organizations and/or arranging for a dual recognition when confronted by Beijing's (Peking's) competition for exclusive diplomatic ties with a third country. (Kau 1986, 5)

Other scholars believe that the KMT policy of keeping alive the Chinese civil war and continuously threatening the mainland regime has "played directly into the hands of Chinese Communist foreign policy" (Johnson 1969, 160; Tien 1975, 643–44).

With few nations willing to recognize the ROC as the sole representative of China, the KMT authorities have so far refused to explore seriously either a "two Chinas" or an "independent Taiwan" policy. They fear that such a policy change might undermine the KMT's credibility to govern Taiwan and threaten the mainlanders in power there. Native Taiwanese could claim more power in the government and party in the event of a major political realignment in the ROC (Copper 1984, 16). Consequently, as formal diplomatic ties evaporate, the KMT leadership has sought to maintain Taiwan's political role in the world community by means of substantive foreign relations (*shih-chih wai-chiao*). That approach emphasizes the promotion of bilateral or multilateral nondiplomatic relations in sports, culture, science and technology, investment, trade, and banking.

Taiwan's nongovernmental relations with Japan and the United States have prospered since the cutoff of diplomatic ties in 1972 and 1978 respectively. Formal state-to-state relations between Taiwan and the United States are handled by the quasi-embassies of the Coordination Council for North American Affairs and the American Institute in Taiwan, which was created by the Taiwan Relations Act in 1979. Bilateral ties between Taipei and Tokyo have been handled by the ROC's East Asia Association and Japan's Interchange Association. U.S. and Japanese personnel in these quasi-embassies are actually career diplomats who are technically retired from their official capacities to serve in Taiwan.

U.S. and Japanese investment in Taiwan has remained steady over the years. From 1952 to 1986 U.S. investment totaled U.S. $1.85 billion, compared with U.S. $1.38 billion from Japan. In 1986 alone the United States invested U.S. $138.4 million and Japan U.S. $253.6 million (*FCJ*, May 18, 1987, 2). Trade has also grown steadily since derecognition. In 1986 the United States and Japan combined accounted for over half the ROC's trade volume. Imports from the United States stood at U.S. $5.4 billion, or 22.4 percent of total imports; those from Japan totaled U.S. $8.3 billion, or 34.2 percent. In the same year Taiwan's exports to the United States reached U.S. $19 billion, or 47.7 percent of the total, while exports to Japan were U.S. $4.5 billion, or 11.4 percent (*TSDB*, 1987, 215, 220). Bilateral tourism and cultural contacts have grown as well. But the enormous imbalance in Taiwan-U.S. trade has come to threaten the close relations between the two nations. In 1986 alone Taiwan incurred a surplus of U.S. $14 billion in trade with the United States (*CYJP*, March 25, 1988, 1). ROC officials are trying to avoid protectionist measures by the U.S. administration or the Congress.

The ROC maintains trade and other commercial ties with over 140 other nations. To facilitate bilateral activities at least 21 nations that have severed formal diplomatic ties have trade or cultural offices in Taipei like those of the United States and Japan. To coordinate and promote global economic activities the ROC has established the China External Trade Development Council (CETDC) with at least 48 offices throughout the world that function under a variety of names (Clough 1984a, 550). Trade has become the main element of Taiwan's foreign relations. In 1953 Taiwan's trade volume ranked 61st of all trading nations; by 1987 Taiwan's trade volume of U.S. $880 billion had leapt to 13th place, with an annual surplus of over U.S. $19 billion (*CYJP,* January 8, 1988, 1). By 1985, 32 foreign banks were operating in Taiwan, compared with only 1 in 1961 (Lu Min-jen 1985, 4). Foreign investment in Taiwan has not faltered either; in 1986 it rose to U.S. $770.4 million (*FCJ,* May 16, 1987, 2). For January–November 1987 investment reached a record high of U.S. $1.25 billion (*CYJP,* December 5, 1987, 1). Aside from the obvious economic importance of foreign investment in Taiwan, it has also had a positive psychological impact on domestic investors who otherwise might have lost confidence in their own economy.

The island's banking and industrial circles are also diversifying into overseas ventures. Major corporations such as the International Commercial Bank of China, the First Commercial Bank, Formosa Plastics, Tatung Electric Company, and Sampo Company have set up branch offices and factories in the United States, Europe, and Southeast Asia (Clough 1984a, 542–44). These corporations have expanded overseas because of market factors as well as a need for foreign resources. Above all, these overseas operations help foster Taiwan's informal ties with other nations. Since 1979 the ROC approved trade with Eastern European countries—Yugoslavia, East Germany, Poland, Hungary, Bulgaria, Romania, and Czechoslovakia—to break the tradition of complete economic isolation from the communist world. In recent years Eastern European merchant vessels have been allowed to dock at Kaohsiung, the island's largest port. Taiwan's businessmen and trade missions have visited Eastern Europe to participate in trade fairs and garment shows (Clough 1984a, 541). In 1988 additional measures were taken to promote direct trade with Eastern Europe and the U.S.S.R. Two-way trade between Taiwan and Eastern Europe rose from U.S. $40 million in 1986 to U.S. $240 million in 1987, and the volume is expected to grow rapidly throughout 1988 (Liu and Chin 1988, 33). Taipei is also making a strong effort to promote trade relations with Western Europe. Eleven European nations now have trade offices in Taipei; since 1980 twelve European banks have opened offices there (Martin 1986, 4).

Furthermore, the Nationalist government has pursued noncommercial foreign contacts through various cultural centers and the representatives of the Central News Agency. That body was reorganized in 1973 as a private corporation rather than a KMT organ in the hope that it might play a useful role in Taiwan's changing foreign relations. In some countries cultural centers serve as quasi-embassies. For example, the Sun Yat-sen Cultural Center in Spain serves in that capacity. Many private but government-funded organizations on Taiwan—such as the Institute of International Relations, the Asia and World Institute, and the Pacific Cultural Foundation—also sponsor international conferences in Taipei to drum up people-to-people diplomacy. The Nationalists have established military training programs in Taiwan for Singapore, the Philippines, and certain Central American nations.

All these nondiplomatic activities have flourished as formal diplomatic ties have disappeared. President Chiang Ching-kuo pressed for these "substantive" ventures beginning in 1975 when he instituted the "all-out diplomacy" campaign. Yet in the absence of formal diplomatic ties, Taiwan's officials and businessmen as well as ordinary citizens often encounter difficulties when traveling abroad. Applications for visas may be delayed or denied. Access to officials in nations without diplomatic ties can also be difficult. In commercial dealings there is little recourse when a foreign country or business fails to honor commitments (Specter 1983, 48–49). Problems with the European Economic Community (EEC) exemplify how substantive relations without diplomatic ties can be detrimental to trade (Chen Jui-kuei 1986, 14). On occasion the EEC has subjected Taiwan to unilateral quotas on some imports. Obstacles to negotiations over trade arrangements have evolved simply because of the lack of official involvement. Moreover, without diplomatic missions Taiwan's business community is hard-pressed to acquire needed trade information in many nations.

In the end we can conclude that substantive relations no matter how extensive, cannot make up for the facilities available through formal diplomatic relations. Some of these difficulties have been minimized only because of Taiwan's growing economic leverage, but Taiwan's external relations could worsen if Peking's diplomatic pressure continues to offset Taiwan's status as a government independent of Peking.

U.S.-ROC RELATIONS

U.S.-ROC ties have been the keystone of the ROC's foreign relations. Over the decades different phases in the relationship have been shaped by U.S. ideological currents, changing strategic calculations, and other considerations of U.S. national interest. Sometimes, as with the strong support urged by the China lobby for the ROC during the 1950s, the influence of U.S. domestic political forces has dictated the direction of the relationship. Because the United States is a major power, its policy directions often determine the essence of these bilateral ties. Because of the ROC's overwhelming dependence on the United States for support, the shifts in Washington-Taipei relations have had an inevitable impact on the leadership and the general public in Taiwan, who perceive the ROC's survival to be tied closely to U.S. support.

Over the four decades since 1949, U.S.-ROC relations moved through four phases, each reflecting a shift in the United States' policy. During the initial phase from January 1949, when Washington began to formulate a policy on the ROC government on Taiwan, to June 1950, when the Korean War broke out, the Truman administration clearly dissociated itself from the KMT. But after the outbreak of the Korean War, General Douglas MacArthur's unilateral embrace of Chiang Kai-shek as an ally, and the PRC military intervention in the war in November 1950, the U.S. government shifted to a policy of definite support for the ROC on Taiwan and a pledge to sustain Taiwan's security. In the 22 years of this second phase, from 1950 to 1972 the ROC became a key U.S. ally in the policy of containing communism in East Asia, and Taiwan received massive military and economic aid from Washington.

President Nixon's historic journey to the mainland in February 1972 marked the third shift in U.S.-ROC ties. Relations over the next six years marked the United States' strategic and diplomatic disengagement from Taiwan, culminating in the December 1978 normalization of U.S. diplomatic relations with the PRC by the Carter administration. Since then the United States has essentially followed a "one and one-half China policy," recognizing the Peking regime as the sole legitimate government of China while maintaining nondiplomatic but substantive relations with Taiwan.

Today Taiwan ranks fifth among U.S. trading partners. Continuing arms sales from the United States provide the basic defense requirements of the island, and a strong defense is seen as an important stabilizing factor in Taiwan's future economic development. Without these military and economic links the ROC would find it even more difficult to fend off the PRC's unification campaign. Thus the Chinese Communists portray these substantive relations between Taipei and Washington as a hindrance to improvements in Washington-Peking ties.

Uncertainty and Dissociation

The KMT and Chiang Kai-shek expected a Dewey victory in the 1948 presidential election and before the election had shown their displeasure with the incumbent Democratic administration. Truman's victory thus presented the ROC with a serious problem, for the entire U.S. aid program to the ROC immediately came up for reappraisal. Under the circumstances, Madame Chiang Kai-shek (Soong Mei-ling) flew to Washington on December 1, 1948, "to revise and expand the China Lobby," which had been formed in the summer of 1940 by her brother, T. V. Soong, then the ROC foreign minister, in an effort to garner U.S. support against Japan (Koen 1974, 35). As the civil war loomed in China after World War II, the Truman administration sent George Marshall to forge a KMT-CCP coalition government to avert another military contest in China. Marshall's mission failed, and during the subsequent civil war that began in 1947, the Democratic administration grew increasingly disenchanted with the Chiang Kai-shek government after U.S. mediation efforts failed.

The Communists' victories in the Northeast (Manchuria) and in northern China raised concern in Washington about the viability of the ROC government. General Chen Cheng was sent to fortify Taiwan in late 1948 in preparation for the eventual retreat of President Chiang Kai-shek and his loyalists. By January 1949 the Department of State and Joint Chiefs of Staff had concluded that for U.S. strategic considerations in the Pacific Taiwan should be denied to the Communists. They believed that the communist threat to Taiwan would not be an amphibious invasion but would take the form of infiltration, agitation, and revolt. Although officials in the Department of State recognized that at some stage the United States would have to take military action to deny Taiwan to the Communists, they argued that that "time is not yet upon us" (U.S. Department of State 1974, 266). In line with these judgments, the National Security Council on February 3 and March 3, 1949, adopted resolutions approved by President Truman to lend only diplomatic and economic support to the KMT forces already on Taiwan (U.S. Department of State 1974, 337–41). The deployment of U.S. military forces to defend Taiwan was specifically ruled out. In an internal memorandum issued on May 24, 1949, high-level officials within the Department of State criticized General Chen Cheng, then governor of Taiwan. The memorandum instructed the Office of Far Eastern Affairs to follow "a policy of calculated inaction colored with opportunism" in the absence of U.S. military commitment to defend Taiwan (Riggs 1952, 6).

The policy of the Truman administration coupled with the unfriendly attitude of State Department officials caused high anxiety in the KMT, which viewed the United States as its principal supporter; meanwhile the ROC's friends in the United States expressed outrage over the situation. In July 1949 Mao Tse-tung's (Mao Zedong's) public declaration of the PRC's intention to side with the Soviet Union caused increasing concern in U.S. political and bureaucratic circles. By December the CCP had forced a total retreat of the Nationalists from their mainland footholds. At that point many influential Republican leaders, such as Senators Robert A. Taft and William F. Knowland, as well as General Douglas MacArthur in Tokyo openly urged U.S. military protection for Taiwan. Even the Joint Chiefs of Staff, under the chairmanship of General Omar Bradley, recommended dispatching a military mission to Taiwan; President Truman rejected the recommendation (Chiu Hungdah 1979, 149). Subsequently the Department of State instructed its Far East officers to expect Taiwan to fall to the Chinese Communists. On January 5, 1950, Truman publicly stated: "The United States will not pursue a course which will lead to involvement in the civil conflict in China. Similarly the United States Government will not provide military aid and advice to the Chinese forces on Formosa" (Riggs 1952, 6). In May the communist forces captured the island of Hainan, and a full-scale invasion of Taiwan appeared imminent. One month later, after the outbreak of the Korean War, the reluctant Truman administration ordered the U.S. Seventh Fleet to patrol the Taiwan Strait, thereby interposing U.S. military power between the PRC on the mainland and the ROC on Taiwan.

The U.S.-ROC Alliance

Once the U.S. government had reversed its policy toward the ROC, bilateral relations were quickly renewed. The new Central Intelligence Agency made Taiwan its chief operational base in Asia and became a partner in the airlines run by former General Claire Chenault (Riggs 1952, 443). Meanwhile General MacArthur, in his message to the Veterans of Foreign Wars on August 27, 1950, advocated the inclusion of Taiwan in a chain of U.S. island bases ringing the western Pacific (Riggs 1952, 6). He even called for direct KMT military involvement in the Korean conflict. The Joint Chiefs of Staff also viewed the defense of Taiwan as critical to the U.S. presence in the Far East. The Military Assistance Advisory Group (MAAG) was dispatched to President Chiang's military headquarters. By the middle of 1951 the United States had allocated U.S. $50 million in military equipment and supplies and an additional U.S. $42 million in economic aid to the ROC (Clough 1978, 10). As the war in Korea progressed, some U.S. military leaders intensified their efforts to involve KMT troops in Korea, but to no avail (Cohen et al. 1971, 42). Nonetheless, the United States increased aid to Taiwan to modernize its economy and strengthen the KMT forces. The 1951–1952 foreign aid bill earmarked U.S. $300 million for Taiwan alone, a third of the total allotted to the Far East (Riggs 1952, 8).

Although neither Truman nor Eisenhower ever allowed KMT troops to set foot on the battlefield in Korea, Taiwan benefited from the war there. In 1954 the United States officially forged a military alliance with the ROC by signing the Mutual Defense Treaty. Taiwan became a strategic element in John Foster Dulles's global chain of defensive alliances to contain communism. The overall political climate in the United States, coupled with the strong anticommunist views of the Eisenhower administration, enhanced the importance of the formal ties of the alliance. During a meeting in Geneva in August 1955, U.S. representatives, encouraged by ROC initiatives, proposed that Peking renounce the use of force against Taiwan. The PRC representatives, however, insisted that the "liberation" of Taiwan was a Chinese domestic issue (Clough 1984a, 527). In 1958 Peking resorted to belligerence to settle the Taiwan question by conducting a massive artillery bombardment of Quemoy from August 23 to October 4, 1958 (Chiu Hungdah 1979, 170). During the crisis the United States supplied the ROC with new weapons, including air-to-air Sidewinder missiles, to help defend Taiwan's offshore islands and forestall a PRC invasion.

Despite the U.S. military commitment to Taiwan's defense, Washington never considered assisting Chiang Kai-shek's forces in a military effort to retake the mainland. On the contrary, the United States actually imposed constraints on ROC military action against the PRC. According to A. Doak Barnett, in 1958 and 1962 the United States took concrete steps to leash the ROC forces to preclude any major military action against the mainland (Barnett 1977, 236). The U.S. policy objective was to neutralize the Taiwan Strait, preventing either the PRC or the ROC from resuming armed conflict.

When the ROC arrived on Taiwan, its armed forces were demoralized and underequipped. The island's shaky economy was in no position to sustain the half-a-million-strong ROC military and the over one million civilian refugees from the mainland. The United States thus had to assume a large portion of the financial burden of supporting the exiled regime of Chiang Kai-shek. According to Karl Lott Rankin, U.S. ambassador to Taipei in the 1950s, in the three years after the signing of the 1954 Mutual Defense Treaty, Washington gave Taipei U.S. $2 billion worth of military and economic aid and stationed five thousand U.S. servicemen on the island (Rankin 1964, 288). Estimates of U.S. military aid range from U.S. $2.5 billion to U.S. $3 billion in the two decades from 1950 to 1970 (Whiting 1971, 86; Barnett, 1977, 244). The United States also gave more than $1 billion in economic aid, invigorating Taiwan's civilian economy by improving the island's infrastructure as well as providing direct assistance to the manufacturing industry (Kuo 1983, 14).

According to one writer, when President Johnson escalated U.S. military involvement in Vietnam from late 1964 on, he considered having the ROC send ground forces to Indochina; but high-level bargaining failed, perhaps because of President Chiang Kai-shek's request for nuclear weapons and U.S. support for a Nationalist invasion of the mainland (Seagrave 1985, 455).[2] Even without direct involvement in the Vietnam conflict, Taiwan served as a major source of repair and refitting for U.S. military equipment as well as a source of supply for U.S. forces in Southeast Asia. In 1965 Taichung's Ch'ing Ch'uan Kang airfield was enlarged to provide a convenient base for U.S. "KC-135 jet tankers refueling B-52s enroute from Guam to Indochina, as well as B-52s under emergency weather conditions" (Whiting 1971, 90). At the peak of U.S. involvement in Indochina ten thousand U.S. military personnel were stationed in Taiwan.

Overall U.S.-ROC relations during the late 1950s and the 1960s were about as good as could be expected between any two nations. U.S. involvement in Indochina indirectly strengthened those ties. The Johnson administration saw the U.S. involvement in Vietnam as part of its strategy to stop Chinese communist expansion into Southeast Asia. As the rival Chinese government opposing Peking, Taiwan's KMT regime stood to gain strategic importance if the United States succeeded in Vietnam. Under the circumstances, as A. Doak Barnett has argued, "if the Nationalists in the late 1950s or early 1960s had opted to move toward independence, the United States might have approved and possibly much of the international community would have gone along" (Barnett 1977, 237). But Chiang Kai-shek never entertained any political option other than the "one China" policy, which would both fulfill his vision of the KMT's role and also justify the institutional and governing structure of Taiwan. Once the international political environment changed in the early 1970s, the political option of an independent Taiwan separate from the mainland had already been severely compromised.

Alliance in Transition:
The Rapprochement Between Washington and Peking

ROC relations with the United States first became uncertain in 1969 when the new Nixon-Kissinger team looked to the end of the Indochina conflict. The Republican administration hoped not simply to end the conflict in Indochina but to restructure the world's balance of power by seeking détente with both the Soviet Union and the PRC. Americans also wanted a respite to repair the serious damage to their national strength and sociopolitical cohesion caused by the prolonged and divisive Vietnam War. From a strategic standpoint, the Sino-Soviet border clashes in the late 1960s finally convinced Washington policymakers of a genuine rift between Peking and Moscow. Nixon and Kissinger also realized that the anticipated U.S. withdrawal from Indochina would remove a serious obstacle to U.S.-PRC rapprochement. The turning point came in 1971 when the ROC lost the China seat in the U.N. In July of that year National Security Adviser Henry Kissinger journeyed to Peking for a secret meeting with Premier Chou En-lai to lay the groundwork for the subsequent Nixon visit in February 1972.

One of the main issues in the secret negotiations between Kissinger and his Chinese counterpart—Foreign Minister Ch'iao Kuan-hua (Qiao Guanhua)—was the Taiwan question. The PRC wanted U.S. troops to be withdrawn from Taiwan, but the U.S. negotiating team insisted that Peking promise a peaceful solution of Taiwan as a prior condition (Kissinger 1979, 1075–77). Unable to compromise, both sides agreed to state their different positions about Taiwan in the 1972 Shanghai Communiqué:

> The Chinese side reaffirmed its position: the Taiwan question is the crucial question obstructing the normalization of relations between China and the United States; the government of the People's Republic of China is the sole legal government of China; Taiwan is a province of China which has long been returned to the motherland; the liberation of Taiwan is China's internal affair in which no other country has the right to interfere; and all U.S. forces and military installations must be withdrawn from Taiwan. . .
>
> The U.S. side declared: The United States acknowledges that all Chinese on either side of the Taiwan Strait maintain there is but one China and that Taiwan is a part of China. The United States government does not challenge that position. It reaffirms its interest in a peaceful settlement of the Taiwan question by the Chinese themselves. With this prospect in mind, it reaffirms the ultimate objective of the withdrawal of all U.S. forces and military installations from Taiwan. (Tien 1983, 213).

Since Peking refused to make a firm commitment to settle the Taiwan question peacefully, the United States stopped short of making key concessions regarding its relations with Taiwan. Thus the communiqué merely "acknowledges" and "does not challenge" the Chinese position on Taiwan. The Nixon visit, however, laid a foundation for improving U.S.-PRC relations.

In April 1973 the United States and the PRC exchanged liaison officers and established diplomatic missions. That was followed by a growing number of cultural, athletic, and scientific exchanges. Trade improved after more than two decades of bilateral embargoes. Reciprocal visits by official delegations multiplied, culminating in the November 1975 visit of President Ford to China. But diplomatic relations stalled after 1973, despite progress in other areas, because of Peking's three demands: the severance of Washington's diplomatic ties with Taipei, the abrogation of the U.S.-ROC Mutual Defense Treaty, and U.S. military withdrawal from Taiwan. The U.S. government refused to accept these points as prior conditions for normalizing diplomatic relations. As Vice President George Bush, former CIA director and a previous U.S. representative to the PRC, stated in 1978: "The United States had consistently balked at these terms, insisting that it would not formally recognize Peking until there was a firm, explicit commitment to settle the Taiwan issue peacefully" (Bush 1978, D3). Although the Chinese Communists assert that this is a domestic issue, many Peking leaders since 1972 have expressed the peaceful intentions of their unification campaigns for Taiwan.

After the signing of the Shanghai Communiqué in 1972, U.S. officials and the public softened their hostility toward the PRC. Many Americans who had proclaimed the ROC as a staunch anticommunist friend ceased to regard the Taipei regime as "an ideological symbol of a worldwide struggle against communism" (Barnett 1977, 238). The United States in the 1970s gradually cut back its military presence on Taiwan.

On December 15, 1978, President Carter announced his decision to establish formal diplomatic relations with the PRC effective January 1, 1979. The move entailed the derecognition of the Nationalist regime and an abrogation of the U.S.-ROC Mutual Defense Treaty, which would take effect one year later. All U.S. military personnel thus would be withdrawn from Taiwan before January 1, 1979. The announcement came as a surprise in both Washington and Taipei, particularly because the Carter administration had failed to extract any concessions from Peking after accepting the latter's three publicized conditions for normalization. Later it was disclosed that "the Carter Administration during the formal negotiation period never asked Peking for a pledge not to use force to regain Taiwan" (Chang Jaw-ling 1985, 4). In Taipei the startled ROC reacted without rage, but it did mobilize a number of controlled mass protests.

There was widespread sentiment in Washington in favor of retaining some form of U.S.-Taiwan relations. Some Americans denounced the normalization agreement as a sellout of Taiwan, but a more pragmatic bipartisan effort in Congress quickly drafted a new Taiwan Relations Act that spelled out provisions for continuing U.S.-Taiwan ties. Senator Edward Kennedy clearly expressed the sentiments in favor of continuing U.S. support for Taiwan when he outlined two important arguments for the passage of the act. Kennedy urged that U.S.-Taiwan ties be "unimpaired" and "actually enhanced because we have finally removed Taiwan as a diplomatic issue between China and the United States" (Wolff and Simon 1982, 1).

The powerful Congressman Clement Zablocki, another Democrat and chairman of the House Foreign Affairs Committee, told House members that the Taiwan Relations Act was "absolutely necessary"; it reflects "our [Americans'] strong desire for Taiwan's continued security and for continuing, without interruption, our commercial, cultural, and other nondiplomatic relations with Taiwan" (Wolff and Simon 1982, 8).

The Taiwan Relations Act contains several provisions of particular importance. Section 2 (b) reiterates the policy of the United States

1. to declare that peace and stability in the area (Taiwan) are in the political, security, and economic interests of the United States and are matters of international concern;

2. to make clear that the United States' decision to establish diplomatic relations with the People's Republic of China rests on the expectations that the future of Taiwan will be determined by peaceful means;

3. to consider any effort to determine the future of Taiwan by other than peaceful means, including by boycotts or embargoes, a threat to the peace and security of the western Pacific area and of grave concern to the United States;

4. to provide Taiwan with defensive arms; and

5. to maintain the capacity of the United States to resist any resort to force or other means of coercion that would jeopardize the security and the social or economic system of the people of Taiwan (Wolff and Simon 1982, 8).

The act also states that "whenever the laws of the United States refer or relate to foreign countries, nations, states, governments, or similar entities, such terms shall include and such laws shall apply with respect to Taiwan" (Sc. 4 (b) (1)). This provision makes the treatment of the ROC like that of a sovereign nation. In regard to Taiwan's military security, the Taiwan Relations Act states that "the United States will make available to Taiwan such defense articles and defense services in such quantity as may be necessary to enable Taiwan to maintain a sufficient self-defense capability" (Sec. 3 (1)). This clause seems to offer less protection than the ROC had under the old treaty, but in fact it makes a unilateral defense pledge from the United States to Taiwan that goes further than the previous Mutual Defense Treaty (Barnett 1981, 5). It also treats Taiwan as the functional equivalent of an independent state. The Taiwan Relations Act was widely acclaimed in the United States and allayed the anxiety of Taiwan's residents about their military security, but it drew strong objections from the PRC (Tien 1984, 9–12).

The American Institute in Taiwan (AIT) was subsequently established to administer Washington's unofficial relations with Taiwan. In return Taiwan's Coordination Council for North American Affairs (CCNAA) in Washington, D.C., and its ten branch offices were set up to handle what in formal relations are called diplomatic and consular matters. AIT and CCNAA have conducted business essentially as embassies. Mutual relations have not suffered substantially, except that CCNAA representatives do not have easy access to U.S. officials.

Relations Under the Reagan Administration

The evolution of U.S.-Taiwan relations since 1971 clearly shows that these connections form one side of a U.S.-PRC-ROC triangle. Relations have been further complicated by Washington's overriding concern with the more important U.S.-Soviet-PRC strategic triangle. U.S. efforts to counter Soviet expansionism have been a critical factor in the U.S.-PRC rapprochement. As long as the two superpowers remain adversaries, the PRC carries important strategic weight that would be useful on the U.S. side. In fact during the last two years of the Carter administration efforts had already been made to explore U.S.-PRC bilateral strategic interests. Consequently the PRC became a U.S. strategic partner to curb Soviet expansionism, and that effort limited Washington's commitment to the ROC on Taiwan. During the 1980 presidential campaign, candidate Reagan, a strong supporter of the ROC, publicly declared his intention to restore official relations with Taiwan, thus shifting U.S. support back to the Taipei government. Although Mr. Reagan obviously had great personal sympathy with the ROC and distrusted the Chinese Communists, in the end his personal views and sentiments yielded to U.S. global strategic interests. Once elected President Reagan did not swing the China policy back toward the ROC but maintained the general framework of U.S.-PRC relations laid down by the Carter administration. A number of examples illustrate this point.

One test case was Taiwan's request to buy advanced military fighter aircraft, the so-called FX planes, the F-16/J79 and the F-5G. The question of selling such planes to Taiwan was an issue for Reagan during 1981, his first year in office. Opinions within the administration were divided. The Taiwan Relations Act gives the president discretionary authority to judge if weapons sought by Taiwan are "defensive" and necessary "to maintain a sufficient self-defense capability" (TRA, Sec. 3 (a)). Both of these FX military aircraft are superior to the F-5E, which Taiwan coproduces with the Northrop Corporation as the backbone of the island's air defense. The ROC argued that the more advanced FX aircraft were needed to maintain the balance of forces in the Taiwan Strait.

Some administration officials and members of Congress believed that the offensive capabilities of the FX aircraft would preclude them from the classification of defensive weapons (Barnett 1981, 2, 36–39). The F-16/J79 "can loiter for one hour and then fly some 550 miles to unload its bombs," whereas the F-5G has a smaller range (Friedman 1981, 2). The F-16s would have provided Taipei with offensive air penetration of the mainland in times of military hostility. The PRC interpreted the proposed FX sale as an example of blatant U.S. insensitivity to its views on the Taiwan issue and threatened to retaliate (Barnett 1981, 3). After much debate in Congress and within his administration, President Reagan decided in December 1981 to deny Taiwan's request for the FXs but agreed to extend the cooperative manufacture of F-5Es by Northrop and Taiwan (Seib 1982, 1).

What Peking wants is a total cutoff of U.S. arms sales to Taiwan. On August 17, 1982, the Reagan administration issued a nine-point communiqué on the question that contained concessions to Peking. The communiqué stated that the U.S. government "does not seek to carry out a long-term policy of arms sales to Taiwan" and "will not exceed, either in qualitative or quantitative terms, the level of those supplied in recent years since the establishment of diplomatic relations—and intends gradually to reduce its sale of arms to Taiwan, leading, over a period of time, to a final resolution" (Tien 1982, 7). The U.S. concessions supposedly derive from the PRC's fundamental policy to "strive for a peaceful resolution of the Taiwan question" (Tien 1982, 4). To alleviate anxiety on Taiwan about those concessions, President Reagan announced his approval to sell 60 additional F-5E fighters to Taiwan. John Holdridge, assistant secretary of state for Asian and Pacific affairs, later disclosed that the United States had conveyed six assurances to the ROC (*NYT*, August 18, 1982, A13):

1. The United States will not set a date for ending arms sales to Taiwan.
2. U.S. officials will not agree to prior consultation with Peking on arms sales to Taiwan.
3. The United States will not mediate between Taipei and Peking.
4. The United States will not revise the Taiwan Relations Act.

5. The United States has not changed its position on the sovereignty of Taiwan.

6. Washington will not exert pressure on Taipei to negotiate with Peking.

The August 1982 communiqué defined the upper level of U.S. arms sales to Taiwan but did not mandate a termination schedule. Since 1982 the United States has continued to sell arms to Taiwan worth U.S. $830–750 million annually. From 1983 to 1986 the level of sales declined by U.S. $30 million per year. At that rate U.S. military sales to Taiwan would continue until 2011.

Despite the skirmish over the arms sales issue and a separate issue involving Peking's apparent unwillingness to enter a stronger anti-Soviet strategic partnership with the United States, U.S. relations with the PRC improved under the Reagan administration. After all, China's growing need for foreign assistance for its domestic modernization programs forced Peking to tolerate U.S. arms sales to Taiwan. By late 1983 the Reagan administration had modified its China policy with a new emphasis on encouraging internal economic liberalization and enlarging the United States' role in mainland China's economic transformation.

In the spring of 1984 President Reagan visited the mainland for the first time. While in China he met with the top Chinese leaders, delivered a televised speech, toured several cities, and signed three agreements on corporate investment taxes, nuclear cooperation, and cultural exchanges (*NYT,* April 30, 1984, 7). White House aides declared the trip "highly successful"; Reagan himself was quoted as saying, "My trip to China has been as important and enlightening as any I've taken as President" (*NYT,* May 2, 1984, 1). Thus Reagan not only set aside his earlier personal opinions about the PRC but greatly improved U.S.-China relations. This improvement is evident in the steadily increasing visits of leaders, including top defense officials, from the two countries in recent years.

Perhaps the warming of U.S.-PRC relations has enabled the Reagan administration to help Taiwan with little risk of rupturing its ties with Peking. Under Reagan two additional CCNAA branches (functionally equivalent to a consulate general) have reopened in Boston and Kansas City. In 1987 Taipei was able to purchase up to U.S. $720 million worth of weapons, though the amount represents an annual reduction of U.S. $30 million from the previous year—a rate of decrease followed by the Reagan administration since the August 17, 1982, Washington-Peking communiqué on arms sales to Taiwan. But the apparent gap is more than offset by a significant growth in sales of commercial items with military applications. Those sales rose to U.S. $150 million in fiscal 1987 (Gold-stein 1986e, 26).

Generally speaking, Taiwan officials have found it easier to gain direct access to U.S. government officials under the Reagan administration than during Carter's days, provided that meetings do not take place in government offices. Thus the ROC authorities have been satisfied with the Reagan administration as far as substantive relations are concerned. But issues such as Taiwan's large trade imbalance and the continuing patent piracy by firms on Taiwan could still cause serious conflicts with Washington.

As smooth as substantive relations may seem, Taiwan's domestic political situation has captured growing attention on Capitol Hill, particularly among liberal Democrats. Past congressional resolutions called for more political democratization and the termination of martial law on Taiwan. In March 1986 Senators Edward Kennedy and Claiborne Pell cosponsored a bill to press Taiwan to legalize opposition parties and hold popular elections for the ROC president and national legislators (*CP,* March 28, 1986, 2; *Taiwan kung-lun-pao,* March 31, 1986, 1). Such congressional pressures have eased considerably since martial law was lifted, the DPP was legalized, and Taipei leaders promised parliamentary reform.

THE CHALLENGES FROM
PEKING'S UNIFICATION CAMPAIGNS

The real battles of the KMT-CCP civil war had already ended on the mainland by late 1949, but hostility continues as Peking and Taipei both claim to be the legitimate regime of China, including Taiwan. As long as Taiwan is separate from the mainland, neither side can acknowledge that the civil war is over. Each is waiting for the opportune time to subjugate the other and terminate the war. The Communists clearly have the upper hand given the asymmetry of power, population, and territory. Moves toward unification since the 1950s mark periods of action or inaction by the PRC. Peking's threats to pursue unification by force give rise to a recurring siege mentality in Taiwan. Any tension or hostility in the Taiwan Strait has far-reaching implications for Taiwan's internal political stability. The ROC leaders see themselves wrestling with shifting PRC efforts for unification while trying on Taiwan to maintain a political equilibrium between demands for change and concerns about security. To a large extent politics on Taiwan takes place under the shadow of this still unfinished KMT-CCP feud.

Events Before 1978

The year 1978 marked the turning point in the PRC's approach to the Taiwan question. In December of that year Teng Hsiao-ping and his associates scored a victory in their power struggle against the Maoists during the Third Plenum of the Eleventh Central Committee. One of the many policies of the new leadership was that unification of Taiwan would be pursued by peaceful means.

Until then the PRC had oscillated between approaches. At times large military forces were deployed along the Fukien coast poised to "liberate" Taiwan, as in the 1960s and early 1970s when Peking openly advocated a military solution. Peking propaganda defined the Taiwan issue by the Marxist-Leninist concept of class struggle. It described a Taiwan enduring "systematic oppression of its population by the dictatorship of bureaucrats, landlords, and big bourgeoisie." The People's Liberation Army would be deployed in the class struggle to eliminate the "Chiang Kai-shek reactionary clique" (Hsiao and Sullivan 1980, 784). Even after the 1972 Shanghai Communiqué, the more radical leaders in Peking continued to press for a military assault on Taiwan. On September 6, 1975, Chang Ch'un-chiao (Zhang Chunqiao), one of the Gang of Four, told a visiting overseas delegation that military means should be used to support a peaceful settlement of the Taiwan issue. In July 1976, when Chang met with a U.S. delegation headed by Senator Hugh Scott, he still insisted that peaceful unification was impossible and that Taiwan must be "liberated by force" (King C. Chen 1979, 139). Even after the arrest of the Gang of Four in the fall of 1976, the militant line on Taiwan continued at least among the more radical leaders. In May 1977, for instance, the radical Politburo member, Chi Teng-k'uei (Ji Dengkui) spoke of the "many counter-revolutionary elements in Taiwan" whose existence would justify the use of force to "liberate" Taiwan's populace (Hsiao and Sullivan 1980, 793).

The more pragmatic leaders, however, emphasize a less belligerent approach to the Taiwan question. As early as 1956 Chou En-lai, speaking at a National People's Congress, stated that "the Chinese people would seek to liberate Taiwan by peaceful means so far as it is possible" (Clough 1984a, 533). In the 1970s two factors greatly influenced Peking's perception of the unification issue. One was the rumored contact between the Soviet Union and the KMT (Garver 1978, 755–57; King C. Chen 1979, 139–44). The other was the Shanghai Communiqué, in which the United States reaffirmed "its interest in the peaceful settlement of the Taiwan question." Thus when reports of visits to Taiwan in 1969 by the well-known Soviet journalist Victor Louis were circulating, Chou En-lai urged the PRC to be patient on the Taiwan question by declaring China's willingness to "wait five years, ten years, or one hundred years" (King C. Chen 1979, 139). The PRC's desire to improve relations with the United States may also have influenced China's swing toward the peaceful unification approach. On December 15, 1978, the same day President Carter announced the normalization of U.S.-PRC relations, Teng Hsiao-p'ing declared that Peking would seek a third CCP-KMT united front to achieve unification with Taiwan. He also promised that after unification Taiwan would retain its separate socioeconomic system, life-style, foreign investments, and local armed forces (Yen 1985, 1). Teng's statement represented a clear departure from Peking's earlier declarations of the need for a military solution.

The PRC's Unification Proposals

Since January 1979 the PRC has advanced several proposals for a peaceful unification of Taiwan with the mainland. Four of these are particularly important because they outline steps on the road to Peking's peaceful unification policy.

1. "A Message to Compatriots in Taiwan," issued by the Standing Committee of the PRC National People's Congress in January 1979, proposed the establishment of "three links" (mail, trade, and air and shipping services) and "four exchanges" (relatives and tourists, academic groups, cultural groups, and sports teams).

2. A nine-point proposal made by Yeh Chien-ying (Ye Jianying), the chairman of the National People's Congress, on September 30, 1981, spelled out the principles that would serve as guidelines for CCP-KMT negotiations. The document contained the earlier three links and four exchanges, with added provisions defining Taiwan's status as a local autonomous government that, while part of China, would be permitted to maintain a separate socioeconomic system.

3. A six-point supplement to Marshal Yeh's nine-point proposal was advanced by Teng Hsiao-p'ing on June 26, 1983, during a conversation with a visiting Chinese-American scholar, Winston Yang. In this version Teng broadened the areas in which Taiwan would be autonomous of Peking, specifically excluding the armed forces, security, intelligence, and certain forms of external affairs. Thus Teng's formula stopped short of complete autonomy for Taiwan (*JMJP,* July 30, 1983, 1; Tien 1985c, 40–41).

4. The Sino-British Accords on the Future of Hong Kong, announced on September 26, 1984, contained eight detailed points on Hong Kong's transition to the mainland political system. The Hong Kong accords contain the "one nation, two systems" formula the PRC evidently intends to apply to Taiwan as well. In short, the formula allows Hong Kong to retain separate social, economic, cultural, and judicial systems for 50 years after the PRC formally assumes sovereignty in 1997.

The proposals articulate the PRC's approach to the peaceful resolution of the Taiwan question. The ultimate goal is amalgamating Taiwan with the mainland, but for at least half a century the PRC will allow the KMT and its armed forces to continue on Taiwan along with the island's different social, economic, and political systems. The proposal for "one nation, two systems" incorporates all the elements in previous PRC statements. According to one PRC writer, this formula is specifically safeguarded by the PRC constitution and therefore cannot be modified at the whim of a future set of leaders in Peking. In this interpretation the PRC constitution grants regions with different sociopolitical systems autonomy within a unified nation—China—and thus they cannot exercise sovereign authority in matters of diplomacy and national defense, including the rights to declare war and negotiate peace (Yen 1985, 3). Moreover, since the "one nation, two systems" formula must operate within the current PRC unitary government system, it excludes any possibility of a federal or commonwealth arrangement (*CP,* February 4, 1986, 1). But the tolerance of different systems, including capitalist—would seem to be subject to the *a priori* constraints of socialism, the foundation of the PRC's politico-economic system.

Unification Campaigns

In the 1980s the PRC strategy for unification has been to induce KMT leaders to negotiate. So far these efforts have been unsuccessful; ROC leaders have repeatedly balked at Peking's unification appeals. On October 7, 1981, the late President Chiang Ching-kuo issued a statement alluding to the "bitter lessons" the KMT had learned during two previous collaborations with the Communists (Tien 1983, 241–45). His statement was a rejoinder to Marshal Yeh Chien-ying's nine principles of September 30, 1981. Chiang Ching-kuo emphatically stated that "we shall never negotiate with the Chinese Communists" and called for the unification of China under a completely different formula based on the Three Principles of the People as enunciated by Dr. Sun Yat-sen, the founding father of the ROC. Subsequently, on June 10, 1982, ex-Premier Sun Yun-suan, in another well-publicized rejoinder to Peking, rejected Marshal Yeh's proposals (Tien 1983, 264). Premier Sun emphasized that differences between the political, economic, social, and cultural standards on both sides are a hindrance to unification. Taiwanese politicians and opinion leaders have also rejected Peking's appeal, often on these same grounds (Tien 1985c, 41–43).

The KMT's unwillingness to negotiate is based on six points (Chiu 1983, 1081–84):

1. The party has had bad experiences in the past with the Chinese Communists;
2. The CCP lost credibility in such matters by its handling of Tibetan reunification during the 1950s and the early 1960s;
3. The PRC continues to exert relentless pressure to isolate the ROC in the world community;
4. Taiwan's internal political balance would not permit the KMT to negotiate on Peking's publicized terms;
5. The PRC's guarantee of Taiwan's autonomy after unification lacks credibility; particularly in the light of point 6.
6. The PRC has a history of internal political instability and major shifts in policy.

For the KMT leaders to enter negotiations now or in the foreseeable future would also provoke "a serious risk of undermining its own legitimacy and credibility, and thereby unleashing a process of uncontrollable political protest and instability" on Taiwan (Kau 1986, 7).

Peking's strategy for unification, of course, does not depend exclusively on peaceful appeals and inducements. The peace formula has been contaminated by pressures and threats as the PRC waves both the carrot and the stick (Kau 1986, 9). Since the early 1970s Peking has tried to isolate the ROC from the international community. Its insistence on the "one China" principle has led to the ROC's ouster from most international governmental organizations. Peking has pressured nations to abrogate diplomatic relations and other ties with Taiwan. Even in international nongovernmental organizations, it has forced the ROC to accept the name "China-Taiwan," "Taipei, China," or "China-Taipei"—with their implication that Taiwan is part of China—as a condition for retaining membership. Peking keeps finding new ways to isolate Taiwan diplomatically. For instance, in June 1983 Peking notified all countries having diplomatic relations with the PRC that it was not proper to honor visas issued in Taiwan for the ROC personnel of international nongovernmental organizations (Liu P'ing-lin 1983, 2).

Partly to show that the PRC can threaten Taiwan militarily, the Communists tested their submarine-based missiles in the East China Sea, north of Taiwan, in October 1982 (Chiu 1983, 1091). These tests were followed by the launching of a guided missile at a target only 300 kilometers north of Taiwan in October 1985. More evidence of the military stick that Peking can wield surfaced in Teng Hsiao-p'ing's 1985 conversation with a group of Japanese visitors when he said Peking would not rule out a naval blockade of Taiwan (Tien 1985a, 84). Hu Yao-pang (Hu Yaobang), speaking to an overseas-Chinese journalist, emphasized the same point, adding that once the decision were made to blockade, Peking leaders could have complete confidence in a successful outcome (Lu K'eng 1985, 17–19). And in recent years PRC leaders have repeatedly warned that force would be used against Taiwan if the ROC allied itself with the Soviets, declared Taiwan's independence, or indefinitely postponed negotiations for unification. On Taiwan few people expect the PRC's peaceful approach to endure.

The threats of military coercion are heard clearly in Taipei's ruling circles, but the PRC has mounted a general propaganda campaign to elicit support for its peace efforts. Directed by the Leadership Team on Taiwan Work (Tui T'ai Kung-tso Chih-tao Hsiao-tsu), a network of united-front organizations support the central authorities' efforts.[3] In the Chinese Communist Party's Central Secretariat, the United Front Department coordinates unification-related propaganda activities as one of its main functions. The Work Team for the Unification of the Motherland was set up in the National Political Consultative Council, a symbolic body of representatives from various noncommunist parties and mass organizations. Within the state council, a Taiwan office directs branch offices throughout the provinces and cities. In addition the PRC has created, among others, the Taiwanese Friendship Association and the Association of Taiwan Classmates to win the support of native Taiwanese. These efforts have brought results. In 1985 and 1986 visits to the mainland from Taiwan were made confidentially and indirectly through Hong Kong, Singapore, Manila, the United States, and Japan. Beginning in late 1987 Taiwan openly permitted people not in the military or government service to visit relatives on the mainland. Peking also offers trade and investment incentives and sponsors conferences and lecture tours to attract "Taiwan compatriots" to the mainland for visits. From November 1987, when Taiwan's ban on visits to the mainland was lifted, to early November 1988, 220,000 persons registered for the visits as required by the ROC authorities (CKSP, November 3, 1988, 3).

The most significant form of contact, however, has been the informal trade between Taiwan and the mainland. Since direct trade with the mainland is still illegal in Taiwan, trade is handled indirectly through Japanese trading companies or middlemen in Hong Kong and sometimes by Taiwan's fishing boats, which make unacknowledged but routine visits to Fukien and Kwangtung harbors across the Taiwan Strait. This trade was insignificant before 1980, when it consisted mostly of exports of mainland medicines and delicacies to Taiwan. But beginning in 1980 Taiwan's exports to the mainland multiplied to hundreds of millions of U.S. dollars per year. The trade includes a wide variety of modern consumer goods, such as household appliances, clothing, and entertainment items such as music tapes and videos. In 1981 the PRC authorities, in a move obviously intended to foster economic interdependence between the mainland and Taiwan, announced duty-free treatment for all incoming merchandise bearing Taiwan manufacturers' labels. Although duty-free status was modified a year later to correct abuses by trading agents in Hong Kong, Taiwan products have continued to enjoy customs rates lower than products from other countries. By 1983 Taiwan's indirect exports to the mainland grew to U.S. $300 million (Weng 1984, 471). Two-way trade soared to U.S. $1.5 billion in 1987, of which exports from Taiwan reached U.S. $1.2 billion and imports from the mainland U.S. $300 million (*CKSP,* March 14, 1988, 6). This new foreign trade outlet came at an opportune time, since Taiwan's economy experienced a mild downturn in 1985 and has encountered growing difficulties in exports to the United States—its principal market—because of the appreciation of the New Taiwan dollar and U.S. protectionism. The sudden spurt in exports to the PRC may have saved some labor-intensive manufacturing firms on Taiwan from bankruptcy. This indirect trade is especially valuable as Taiwan faces internal economic difficulties in its transition from a labor-intensive to a more technologically advanced industrial structure. Thus the Taipei authorities, while remaining firmly opposed to direct contacts with the PRC, have given the green light to this lucrative indirect trade (Wen Man-ying 1985, 18).

In addition, a semiclandestine form of direct trade has quietly taken place on the Fukien and, to a lesser extent, Kwangtung coasts. Fishermen from both sides exchange such goods as cigarettes, watches, and tape recorders from Taiwan for medicine, liquor, silver coins, and antiques from the mainland (Weng 1984, 471). Some of this trade is permitted by the PRC while some involves prohibited goods, but still Taiwan smugglers use fishing boats to carry goods across the strait to sell at reception centers in Fukien (Oka 1984, 7). From 1981 to 1986, 7,000 fishing boats and 15,000 people from Taiwan had reportedly called at Pingtan, the first of four reception centers in Fukien opened during 1978–1981 for Taiwan fishermen and visitors (Nan 1987b, 18–19; Wen Li Chung 1986, 98–100). Since then both Fukien and Kwangtung provinces have established additional boat-trading points and reception centers along the southeastern coast (*TS,* June 1984, 32; May 1987, 14–15). Although the Taiwan authorities have tried to stop this illegal trade, their efforts have been ineffective, giving rise to speculation that the official disapproval is only a face-saving measure. The peculiar direct trade continues. No one knows its exact value, but it could easily be worth tens of millions of U.S. dollars each year.

Even though the PRC has had an unwanted overall trade deficit of hundreds of millions of U.S. dollars each year since 1980, the trade with Taiwan serves two important purposes. First, Taiwan's inexpensive semi-finished products and machinery can help the PRC achieve a competitive edge in its drive to develop new export industries. Consumer products from Taiwan are acceptable on the mainland because they satisfy consumer demand, particularly when domestic industries lag behind in output and quality. The PRC authorities and some of the public on the mainland seem more receptive to Chinese goods from Taiwan than to Japanese or other foreign products. Second, continuing the trade creates real economic links between the PRC and Taiwan that may someday make Taiwan's economy dependent on the mainland market. That would give Peking an element in the equation for unification it has lacked so far.

As the PRC steps up its unification campaign, trade can also be used as a propaganda ploy to win greater support from Taiwan's business community. Peking's purpose is to create a system of trade that would help integrate the two economic systems. Peking's leaders also hope that growing trade ties will spill over into investment activity. Efforts are made to attract Taiwan businessmen, usually via overseas channels, to enter joint ventures in Shen Chun (Shenzhen) and other special economic zones along the coast. The modes of economic production in these zones are rapidly becoming "Hong Kongized" or "Taiwanized," according to one writer (Gold 1987a, 314).

The PRC's efforts to promote trade and other economic relations have produced a growing debate on Taiwan over the desirability of legalized direct trade and investment in the mainland. The popular outcry for opening trade with the mainland comes largely from those business and industrial circles likely to benefit from the change in policy. And many mainlanders—older people, especially former ROC military men without families on Taiwan—are eager to visit the mainland. Liberal academic and many DPP activists also favor improved contacts with the mainland on humanitarian grounds, and such a position is popular politically. But

ROC authorities worry that once the door is open, PRC propaganda campaigns would capitalize on the situation. As nongovernmental contacts grow, their impact on political relations between Taiwan and the mainland could be profound. So far Taiwan tends to benefit more in trade. Permitting visits to the mainland could generate pro-PRC sentiments among the island's residents, as the authorities fear. But some evidence suggests that many who have visited their mainland relatives have returned totally disillusioned (*WSJ*, February 17, 1988, 1).

CONCLUSION

Since the early 1970s the ROC has faced external challenges to its survival as an independent nation. These challenges have become more threatening as Taiwan's isolation in the international diplomatic community grows. The ROC has found it more difficult to maintain official ties with other governments; bilateral diplomatic relations with major nations have almost all been cut. Through considerable effort and innovation the ROC has retained a broad range of so-called substantive relations, but they fall short of the convenience and advantages of diplomatic protocol. Besides, without the full sovereignty implied by diplomatic ties, the ROC's survival as a nation-state in the international community cannot be certain in the long run. The great test of Taiwan's viability as an independent state would come with a serious downturn in the island's economy and trade. For now, Taiwan's growing international isolation and deteriorating diplomatic prospects do little to support the ROC regime's legitimacy as the government of both Taiwan and the mainland. Pressures are mounting within Taiwan for a revision of the existing political institutions so that they represent Taiwan's status in the world more realistically; yet the KMT perceives any change in the status quo as a threat to its power without a sure prospect of enhancing its international diplomatic status.

Moreover, the PRC's unification campaigns could undermine the KMT regime's popular support and in the meantime inspire feelings of uncertainty about Taiwan's future. Most people on Taiwan remain unwilling to accept Peking's terms for unification, but they worry that Taiwan might be gobbled up by the much larger and militarily more powerful PRC after Hong Kong's return to China in 1997. A growing segment of the population would like, for a variety of reasons, to see more freedom of contact with the mainland. For some this contact is necessary to reduce tension in the Taiwan Strait, while others are thinking of their own interests—for example, business gains, unrestricted visits to family on the mainland, and even tours of famous historical sites and scenic spots.

Lately some businessmen have been reluctant to make long-term investments in Taiwan precisely because of their concern about Taiwan's future (Gold 1986, xi, 109). The government wants to alleviate this fear by strengthening national defense. Yet, the purchase of sophisticated weapons from abroad, particularly from the United States, is becoming more restricted. In recent years Taiwan's military has begun to manufacture its own advanced weapons. In March 1986, for instance, the ROC announced the successful testing of a surface-to-air Sky Bow missile, presumably capable of knocking down invading PRC aircraft (*FCJ*, March 31, 1986, 1). A month later the first Taiwan-developed air-to-air missile—the Sky Sword—was successfully test fired (*FCJ*, May 26, 1986, 1). The Sky Sword resembles the U.S.-made Sidewinder and is carried by an F-5E jet fighter now manufactured on Taiwan. The Defense Ministry has also entered joint ventures with foreign high-tech industries to research and develop weapons. There are rumors that Taiwan may be able to manufacture nuclear weapons. Yet the PRC military still enjoys about a ten-to-one advantage over the ROC in nearly every major category of conventional military capability (International Institute for Strategic Studies 1987, 114–16, 134–35). Meanwhile the Reagan administration recently approved the sale to the PRC of high-tech items with military applications. Such sales could significantly upgrade Peking's technological capacities to overcome the ROC's advantage in that area in the years ahead (*NYT*, April 9, 1986, 3).

As long as the PRC remains preoccupied with defending its borders with the Soviet Union, India, and Vietnam—three actual or potential adversaries—and with its ambitious domestic modernization program, there is little likelihood of an attack against Taiwan. Such a military venture could severely strain the PRC's relations with the United States and Japan, which see peace and stability in the Taiwan Strait as vital to their own interests. Still, the future military balance in the Taiwan Strait could shift more in favor of the PRC. Consequently the fear of an impending PRC military threat confirms Taiwan's need to remain in a state of emergency and military preparedness. In turn, the threat of military conflict blocks changes in Taiwan's domestic political process that would rapidly democratize and liberalize the government on Taiwan. In short, this sense of emergency constrains a political system facing continuing demands for political change. The emergency also helps justify the power of the military security apparatus and the old-guard political elite who resist change on Taiwan. Such is the dilemma the ROC faces, for it needs both military security and democratic political reform.

_ 10 _

Conclusion

In 1949 the KMT government and armies arrived on Taiwan from the mainland after their defeat in the Chinese civil war. Since then both the Peking and Taipei regimes have claimed sovereignty over the land controlled by the other side. This de facto political division perpetuates the notion that China's civil war remains unfinished. On this premise the ROC authorities have maintained on Taiwan a governmental structure to match their claim of jurisdiction over the PRC-controlled mainland. Consequently the legitimacy of the ROC as a state is closely linked to its claim to be the government of China.

During the 1950s and the 1960s the ROC received widespread diplomatic recognition from the world community, and its legitimacy had no difficulty withstanding external and internal challenges. But this stance had to change with the rapid diplomatic shifts of the 1970s. The states with formal diplomatic ties to Taiwan dwindled to 22 by 1988, and none of these is a global power. In contrast, the PRC regime in Peking is recognized by 133 nations as the sovereign government of China. Moreover, the ROC government, a founding member of the United Nations, has been unseated and replaced by the PRC in practically all international governmental organizations. Diplomatic isolation thus raises profound questions about the ROC's legitimacy as the sovereign government of China, threatening its existence as a nation-state. The ROC's legitimacy further erodes over time as more of the national parliamentarians and other government personnel who came from the mainland pass away each year. The drastic reduction in their numbers undermines the constitutional basis of a regime that claims mainland representation.

Such changes have compelled the KMT authorities to seek a new source of legitimacy in Taiwan's extraordinary economic performance and its more moderate political democratization. To salvage some international standing, the ROC tries relentlessly to expand what it calls substantive relations, that is, unbroken nondiplomatic links with foreign nations through trade, cultural exchanges, athletic competitions, wide-ranging commercial and economic ties, KMT party-to-party connections, and military cooperation. Taiwan's phenomenal development as a major trading state in the world economic system is the principal reason these unofficial relations are possible. Through such links the ROC has managed to survive as a political entity in the community of nations. As long as the ROC government can sustain economic prosperity and a network of substantive ties, it can at least partially offset its diplomatic isolation.

In recent years the PRC has launched well-coordinated campaigns to induce KMT leaders to negotiate the unification of Taiwan with the mainland, but to no avail. Since 1980 Peking has developed a peaceful unification approach according to a "one nation, two systems" (*i-kuo liang-chih*) formula that would allow Taiwan to retain considerable autonomy as a province within a unified state structure defined by the PRC's constitution and controlled by the Chinese Communist Party at the top. Peking leaders continue to threaten coercion as an alternative to negotiation should all peaceful efforts fail or should Taiwan declare independence by severing territorial ties with the mainland. This state of affairs creates serious problems for the ROC in its international conduct, perpetuates feelings of hostility across the Taiwan Strait, and complicates the island's internal politics. Although KMT authorities have begun to Taiwanize the regime in response to the growing Taiwanese demands for power sharing, they have been equally interested in maintaining the façade of a political system with mainland connections. The PRC's inducements and threats thus impose external constraints on change in Taiwan's political process, making progressive reforms all the more difficult.

External factors contribute to an atmosphere of siege, but they are not solely responsible for the essentially authoritarian character of the island's political system. On Taiwan the party-state has retained features of the Leninist model as far as the KMT's relations with the state and society are concerned. As the preceding chapters have demonstrated, the ruling KMT maintains a position of primacy in government as well as in social control. It has penetrated the government apparatus, the legislatures, and the armed forces, and it dominates the mass media and group activities by manipulating rules, appointing personnel, and allocating resources. It has established a network of party organizations that permeate society and may be second to none in the noncommunist world in its horizontal and vertical penetration. Under the circumstances civil liberties are restricted and the sociopolitical life of the citizens is constrained. But the KMT party-state's effective governing has brought four decades of political stability—valued both in their own right and as a necessary precondition for Taiwan's successful economic development.

The success of economic modernization has generated the momentum for recent trends toward liberalization and democratization in political life. Economic prosperity and industrialization have given rise to four conditions conducive to progressive political development. First, a large middle class is emerging. A substantial segment of this economically prosperous and well-educated social stratum is demanding political participation and institutional reforms. The opposition political movements that have emerged since the 1970s have been propelled largely by disenchanted elements from the middle class. Even within the ruling KMT, they press for reductions in the level of authoritarian control. Second, the expansion of the private economic sector has created great private wealth and autonomous sources of funds that can be channeled into activities outside state and party control. Over time the percentage of people dependent on state and KMT patronage for a living has declined. Individuals with sources of income and career patterns independent of the state and the KMT are less likely to be subject to the authorities' political dictates. Third, social pluralism is on the rise in lieu of increasing social stratification, the proliferation of issue-oriented and vocational groups, and the general affluence of the middle class. Social pluralism lays the foundation for political pluralism. The party-state has found it increasingly difficult to manipulate group activities for its own purposes. Finally, there has been an explosive growth of mass media. With rising education and affluence, demands have intensified for access to a variety of mass media and previously prohibited information. As the media enterprises cater to market demands and commercial needs, the authorities' long-established efforts to sanitize the media for political purposes have met with growing resistance.

Since the 1970s Taiwan has witnessed rapid socioeconomic changes clearly favoring democratic political development. Such changes have come about largely because of the KMT regime's tolerance of new nonstate socioeconomic development. Thus Taiwan, although structured on a Leninist model of party-state rule, has adopted political forms of the industrial democracies. Even the ruling KMT has to adapt to socioeconomic changes by modifying its roles and transforming the party structure. Two other factors that favor democratization in the ROC are missing in Marxist-Leninist states. The KMT leadership, personified by the late President Chiang Ching-kuo, has believed that reforms and democratization are both necessary and inevitable. Although Chiang and other reformist leaders have stressed the favorite Chinese goals of stability and harmony, they have perceived a direct correlation between these twin political goals and concessions that increase liberalization and democracy. The KMT's official ideology—Sun Yat-sen's Three Principles of the People—stresses the party's commitment to the goal of political democracy and thus contributes to the KMT's rationale for democratization. The issue therefore has never been whether the ROC should uphold its democratic goal; rather controversy has resolved around the timing and tempo of democratization. Democratic development itself is inherent in KMT ideology.

The substantial liberalization and democratization that have taken place in Taiwan make the ROC political system unusual. The ROC has progressed toward these goals despite the state of siege owing to KMT-CCP hostility, increasing international isolation, an entrenched Leninist party-state structure, and ethnic strife between the mainlanders and the indigenous Taiwanese. Political changes already under way suggest that a once exclusionary authoritarian system is now in transition. The one-party system on Taiwan is giving way to a dominant-party system in which the ruling party must compete with the DPP and several smaller parties in the electoral process. Since the KMT is likely to maintain control over the government administration, the armed forces, the mass media, the legislatures, and group activities, democratic development must occur within a corporatist structure. Conversion to a pluralistic democracy will continue to be constrained by the KMT's links to the state and society.

Yet the authorities' ability to manipulate organized groups is subsiding as newly formed associations acquire more autonomy. Freedom of the press, though still limited, has expanded because of commercialization and a growing appetite for opposition views. Liberalization is also stimulated by the influx of new ideas and information brought home by hundreds of thousands of citizens now permitted to travel abroad each year. Taiwan is no longer the tightly monitored closed society it was in the 1950s and 1960s. With the suspension of martial law social movements and protest activities have already escalated. If the current pace of liberalization continues, an open society on Taiwan is just around the corner.

The Taiwanization of the KMT, broader electoral competition, and the emergence of an organized political opposition are all signs of democratization. Since the 1970s more Taiwanese have been recruited into the KMT; in 1988 over 70 percent of its 2.4 million members are Taiwanese, and they also constitute 52 percent of the KMT's ruling Central Standing Committee. The number of parliamentary seats open for electoral competition is also on the rise. The proposed reform of the parliamentary bodies under study in 1988 will surely create additional seats for popular election. Meanwhile, the opposition has gained real strength in the last decade. With the birth of the Democratic Progressive Party in 1986 and other similar parties since then, the KMT's monopoly over political life has come to an end. As the DPP and other opposition parties become institutionalized, political competition will inevitably heat up.

Taiwan's political life is clearly moving toward a dominant-party system in a society with a growing democratic character. Under the leadership of Lee Teng-hui, a Taiwanese who succeeded Chiang Ching-kuo as president and KMT chairman after Chiang's death in January 1988, political reforms have continued both within the KMT and in the ROC political system. Lee has the political support of key military leaders, including the powerful Chief of General Staff Hau Pei-tsun—a backing that is crucial for Taiwan to sustain democratic development under civilian rule. But more time is needed before we can be sure that military acquiescence to democratic civilian rule will continue on Taiwan. Myron Weiner argues convincingly that when the military is strongly opposed to civilian democratic rule in the contemporary Third World, such countries have no chance to institute a stable democracy under civilian leadership (Weiner 1987, 860–66). Moreover, KMT leaders have yet to reach a consensus on the scope and direction of political liberalization and democratic reforms. The most troublesome issue is the political rift between strong proponents of the unification of Taiwan with the mainland and those who advocate independence for Taiwan. If the ROC embraces a democratic system and the KMT substantially reduces its dominance over the state and society despite the unsettling issues cited above, Taiwan will become one of the few authoritarian countries in the Third World ever to accomplish such a political transition.

Appendix

The Constitution of the Republic of China

*Adopted by the National Assembly on December 25, 1946, promulgated by the national
government on January 1, 1947, and effective from December 25, 1947*

The National Assembly of the Republic of China, by virtue of the mandate
received from the whole body of citizens, in accordance with the teachings be-
queathed by Dr. Sun Yat-sen in founding the Republic of China, and in order to
consolidate the authority of the State, safeguard the rights of the people, ensure
social tranquility, and promote the welfare of the people, do hereby establish this
Constitution, to be promulgated throughout the country for faithful and perpet-
ual observance by all.

CHAPTER 1. GENERAL PROVISIONS

Article 1. The Republic of China, founded on the Three Principles of the People, shall be a democratic republic of the people, to be governed by the people
and for the people.

Article 2. The sovereignty of the Republic of China shall reside in the whole
body of citizens.

Article 3. Persons possessing the nationality of the Republic of China shall be
citizens of the Republic of China.

Article 4. The territory of the Republic of China according to its existing national boundaries shall not be altered except by resolution of the National Assembly.

Article 5. There shall be equality among the various racial groups in the Republic of China.

Article 6. The national flag of the Republic of China shall be of red ground
with a blue sky and a white sun in the upper left corner.

CHAPTER II. RIGHTS AND DUTIES OF PEOPLE

Article 7. All citizens of the Republic of China, irrespective of sex, religion, race, class, or party affiliation, shall be equal before the law.

Article 8. Personal freedom shall be guaranteed to the people. Except in case of *flagrante delicto* as provided by law, no person shall be arrested or detained otherwise than by a judicial or a police organ in accordance with the procedure prescribed by law. No person shall be tried or punished otherwise than by a law court in accordance with the procedure prescribed by law. Any arrest, detention, trial, or punishment which is not in accordance with the procedure prescribed by law may be resisted.

When a person is arrested or detained on suspicion of having committed a crime, the organ making the arrest or detention shall in writing inform the said person, and his designated relative or friend, of the grounds for his arrest or detention, and shall within 24 hours, turn him over to a competent court for trial. The said person, or any other person, may petition the competent court that a writ be served within 24 hours on the organ making the arrest for the surrender of the said person for trial.

The court shall not reject the petition mentioned in the preceding paragraph, nor shall it order the organ concerned to make an investigation and report first. The organ concerned shall not refuse to execute, or delay in executing, the writ of the court for the surrender of the said person for trial.

When a person is unlawfully arrested or detained by any organ, he or any other person may petition the court for an investigation. The court shall not reject such a petition, and shall, within 24 hours, investigate the action of the organ concerned and deal with the matter in accordance with law.

Article 9. Except those in active military service, no person shall be subject to trial by a military tribunal.

Article 10. The people shall have freedom of residence and of change of residence.

Article 11. The people shall have freedom of speech, teaching, writing, and publication.

Article 12. The people shall have freedom of privacy of correspondence.

Article 13. The people shall have freedom of religious belief.

Article 14. The people shall have freedom of assembly and association.

Article 15. The right of existence, the right of work, and the right of property shall be guaranteed to the people.

Article 16. The people shall have the right of presenting petitions, lodging complaints, or instituting legal proceedings.

Article 17. The people shall have the right of election, recall, initiative, and referendum.

Article 18. The people shall have the right of taking public examinations and holding public offices.

Article 19. The people shall have the duty of paying taxes in accordance with law.

Article 20. The people shall have the duty of performing military service in accordance with law.

Article 21. The people shall have the right and the duty of receiving citizens' education.

Article 22. All other freedoms and rights of the people that are not detrimental to social order or public welfare shall be guaranteed under the Constitution.

Article 23. All the freedoms and rights enumerated in the preceding Article shall not be restricted by law except by such as may be necessary to prevent infringement crisis, to maintain social order, or to advance public welfare.

Article 24. Any public functionary who, in violation of law, infringes upon the freedom or right of any person shall, in addition to being subject to disciplinary measures in accordance with law, be held responsible under criminal and civil laws. The injured person may, in accordance with law, claim compensation from the State for damage sustained.

CHAPTER III. THE NATIONAL ASSEMBLY

Article 25. The National Assembly shall, in accordance with the provisions of this Constitution, exercise political powers on behalf of the whole body of citizens.

Article 26. The National Assembly shall be composed of the following delegates:

1. One delegate shall be elected from each hsien, municipality, or area of equivalent status. In case its population exceeds 500,000, one additional delegate shall be elected for each additional 500,000. Areas equivalent to hsien or municipalities shall be prescribed by law;

2. Delegates to represent Mongolia shall be elected on the basis of four for each league and one for each special banner;

3. The number of delegates to be elected from Tibet shall be prescribed by law;

4. The number of delegates to be elected by various racial groups in frontier regions shall be prescribed by law;

5. The number of delegates to be elected by Chinese citizens residing abroad shall be prescribed by law;

6. The number of delegates to be elected by occupational groups shall be prescribed by law.

Article 27. The function of the National Assembly shall be as follows:

1. To elect the President and the Vice President;

2. To recall the President and the Vice President;

3. To amend the Constitution; and

4. To vote on proposed Constitutional amendments submitted by the Legislative Yuan by way of referendum.

With respect to the rights of initiative and referendum, except as is provided in Items 3 and 4 of the preceding paragraph, the National Assembly shall make regulations pertaining thereto and put them into effect, after the abovementioned two political rights shall have been exercised in one-half of the hsien and municipalities of the whole country.

Article 28. Delegates to the National Assembly shall be elected every six years.

The term of office of the delegates to each National Assembly shall terminate on the day on which the next National Assembly convenes.

No incumbent government official shall, in the electoral area where he holds office, be elected delegate to the National Assembly.

Article 29. The National Assembly shall be convoked by the President to meet 90 days prior to the date of expiration of each presidential term.

Article 30. An extraordinary session of the National Assembly shall be convoked in any of the following circumstances:

1. When, in accordance with the provisions of Article 49 of this Constitution, a new President and a new Vice President are to be elected;

2. When, by resolution of the Control Yuan, an impeachment of the President or the Vice President is instituted;

3. When, by resolution of the Legislative Yuan, an amendment to the Constitution is proposed; and

4. When a meeting is requested by not less than two-fifths of the delegates to the National Assembly.

When an extraordinary session is to be convoked in accordance with Item 1 or Item 2 of the preceding paragraph, the President of the Legislative Yuan shall issue the notice of convocation; when it is to be convoked in accordance with Item 3 or Item 4, it shall be convoked by the president of the Republic.

Article 31. The National Assembly shall meet at the seat of the Central Government.

Article 32. No delegate to the National Assembly shall be held responsible outside the Assembly for opinions expressed or votes cast at meetings of the Assembly.

Article 33. While the Assembly is in session, no delegate to the National Assembly shall, except in case of *flagrante delicto,* be arrested or detained without the permission of the National Assembly.

Article 34. The organization of the National Assembly, the election and recall of delegates to the National Assembly, and the procedure whereby the National Assembly is to carry out its functions, shall be prescribed by law.

CHAPTER IV. THE PRESIDENT

Article 35. The President shall be the head of the State and shall represent the Republic of China in foreign relations.

Article 36. The President shall have supreme command of the land, sea, and air forces of the whole country.

Article 37. The President shall, in accordance with law, promulgate laws and issue mandates with the counter-signature of the President of the Executive Yuan or with the counter-signatures of both the President of Executive Yuan and the Ministers or Chairmen of Commissions concerned.

Article 38. The President shall, in accordance with the provisions of this Constitution, exercise the powers of concluding treaties, declaring war, and making peace.

Article 39. The President may, in accordance with law, declare martial law with the approval of, or subject to confirmation by, the Legislative Yuan. When the Legislative Yuan deems it necessary, it may by resolution request the President to terminate martial law.

Article 40. The President shall, in accordance with law, exercise the power of granting amnesties, pardons, remission of sentences, and restitution of civil rights.

Article 41. The President shall, in accordance with law, appoint and remove civil and military officials.

Article 42. The President may, in accordance with law, confer honors and decorations.

Article 43. In case of a natural calamity, an epidemic, or a national financial or economic crisis that calls for emergency measures, the President, during the recess of the Legislative Yuan, may, by resolution of the Executive Yuan Council, and in accordance with the Law on Emergency Orders, issue emergency orders, proclaiming such measures as may be necessary to cope with the situation. Such orders shall, within one month after issuance, be presented to the Legislative Yuan for confirmation; in case the Legislative Yuan withholds confirmation, the said orders shall forthwith cease to be valid.

Article 44. In case of disputes between two or more Yuans other than those concerning which there are relevant provisions in this Constitution, the President may call a meeting of the Presidents of the Yuans concerned for consultation with a view to reaching a solution.

Article 45. Any citizen of the Republic of China who has attained the age of 40 years may be elected President or Vice President.

Article 46. The election of the President and the Vice President shall be prescribed by law.

Article 47. The President and the Vice President shall serve a term of six years. They may be reelected for a second term.

Article 48. The President shall, at the time of assuming office, take the following oath:

"I do solemnly and sincerely swear before the people of the whole country that I will observe the Constitution, faithfully perform my duties, promote the welfare of the people, safeguard the security of the State, and will in no way betray the people's trust. Should I break my oath, I shall be willing to submit myself to severe punishment by the State. This is my solemn oath."

Article 49. In case the office of the President should become vacant, the Vice President shall succeed until the expiration of the original presidential term. In case the office of both the President and the Vice President should become vacant, the President of the Executive Yuan shall act for the President; and, in accordance with the provisions of Article 30 of this Constitution, an extraordinary session of the National Assembly shall be convoked for the election of a new

President and a new Vice President, who shall hold office until the completion of the term left unfinished by the preceding President. In case the President should be unable to attend to office due to any cause, the Vice President shall act for the President. In case both the President and Vice President should be unable to attend to office, the President of the Executive Yuan shall act for the President.

Article 50. The President shall be relieved of his functions on the day on which his term of office expires. If by that time the succeeding President has not yet been elected, or if the President-elect and the Vice-President-elect have not yet assumed office, the President of the Executive Yuan shall act for the President.

Article 51. The period during which the President of the Executive Yuan may act for the President shall not exceed 3 months.

Article 52. The President shall not, without having been recalled, or having been relieved of his functions, be liable to criminal prosecution unless he is charged with having committed an act of rebellion or treason.

CHAPTER V. ADMINISTRATION

Article 53. The Executive Yuan shall be the highest administrative organ of the State.

Article 54. The Executive Yuan shall have a President, a Vice President, a certain number of Ministers and Chairmen of Commissions, and a certain number of Ministers without Portfolio.

Article 55. The President of the Executive Yuan shall be nominated and, with the consent of the Legislative Yuan, appointed by the President of the Republic.

If, during the recess of the Legislative Yuan, the President of the Executive Yuan should resign or if his office should become vacant, his functions shall be exercised by the Vice President of the Yuan, acting on his behalf, but the President of the Republic shall, within 40 days, request a meeting of the Legislative Yuan to confirm his nominee for the vacancy. Pending such confirmation, the Vice President of the Executive Yuan shall temporarily exercise the functions of the President of the said Yuan.

Article 56. The Vice President of the Executive Yuan, Ministers and Chairmen of Commissions, and Ministers without Portfolio shall be appointed by the President of the Republic upon the recommendation of the President of the Executive Yuan.

Article 57. The Executive Yuan shall be responsible to the Legislative Yuan in accordance with the following provisions:

1. The Executive Yuan has the duty to present to the Legislative Yuan a statement of its administrative policies and a report on its administration. While the Legislative Yuan is in session, Members of the Legislative Yuan shall have the right to question the President and the Ministers and Chairmen of Commissions of the Executive Yuan.

2. If the Legislative Yuan does not concur in any important policy of the Executive Yuan, it may, by resolution, request the Executive Yuan to alter such a policy. With respect to such resolution, the Executive Yuan may, with the approval of the President of the Republic, request the Legislative Yuan for recon-

sideration. If, after reconsideration, two-thirds of the Members of the Legislative Yuan present at the meeting uphold the original resolution, the President of the Executive Yuan shall either abide by the same or resign from office.

3. If the Executive Yuan deems a resolution on a statutory, budgetary, or treaty bill passed by the Legislative Yuan difficult of execution, it may, with the approval of the President of the Republic and within 10 days after its transmission to the Executive Yuan, request the Legislative Yuan to reconsider the said resolution. If, after reconsideration, two-thirds of the members of the Legislative Yuan present at the meeting uphold the original resolution, the President of the Executive Yuan shall either abide by the same or resign from office.

Article 58. The Executive Yuan shall have an Executive Yuan Council, to be composed of its President, Vice President, various Ministers and Chairmen of Commissions, and Ministers without Portfolio, with its President as Chairman.

Statutory or budgetary bills or bills concerning martial law, amnesty, declaration of war, conclusion of peace or treaties, and other important affairs, all of which are to be submitted to the Legislative Yuan, as well as matters that are of common concern to the various Ministries and Commissions, shall be presented by the President and various Ministers and Chairmen of Commissions of the Executive Yuan to the Executive Yuan Council for decision.

Article 59. The Executive Yuan shall, three months before the beginning of each fiscal year, present to the Legislative Yuan the budgetary bill for the following fiscal year.

Article 60. The Executive Yuan shall, within four months after the end of each fiscal year, present final accounts of revenues and expenditures to the Control Yuan.

Article 61. The organization of the Executive Yuan shall be prescribed by law.

CHAPTER VI. LEGISLATION

Article 62. The Legislative Yuan shall be the highest legislative organ of the State, to be constituted of members elected by the people. It shall exercise legislative power on behalf of the people.

Article 63. The Legislative Yuan shall have the power to decide by resolution upon statutory or budgetary bills or bills concerning martial law, amnesty, declaration of war, conclusion of peace or treaties, and other important affairs of the State.

Article 64. Members of the Legislative Yuan shall be elected in accordance with the following provisions:

1. Those to be elected from the provinces and by the municipalities under the direct jurisdiction of the Executive Yuan shall be five for each province or municipality with a population of not more than 3,000,000; one additional member shall be elected for each additional 1,000,000, where the population exceeds 3,000,000;

2. Those to be elected from Mongolian Leagues and Banners;

3. Those to be elected from Tibet;

4. Those to be elected by various racial groups in frontier regions;

5. Those to be elected by Chinese citizens residing abroad; and
6. Those to be elected by occupational groups.

The election of members of the Legislative Yuan and the number of those to be elected in accordance with Items 2 to 6 of the preceding paragraph shall be prescribed by law. The number of women to be elected under the various items enumerated in the first paragraph shall be prescribed by law.

Article 65. Members of the Legislative Yuan shall serve a term of three years, and shall be re-eligible. The election of Members of the Legislative Yuan shall be completed within three months prior to the expiration of each term.

Article 66. The Legislative Yuan shall have a President and a Vice President, who shall be elected by and from among its Members.

Article 67. The Legislative Yuan may set up various committees.

Such committees may invite government officials and private persons concerned to be present at their meetings to answer questions.

Article 68. The Legislative Yuan shall hold two sessions each year, and shall convene of its own accord. The first session shall last from February to the end of May, and the second session from September to the end of December. Whenever necessary a session may be prolonged.

Article 69. In any of the following circumstances, the Legislative Yuan may hold an extraordinary session:
1. At the request of the President of the Republic;
2. Upon the request of not less than one-fourth of its members.

Article 70. The Legislative Yuan shall not make proposals for an increase in the expenditures in the budgetary bill presented by the Executive Yuan.

Article 71. At the meetings of the Legislative Yuan, the Presidents of the various Yuan concerned and the various Ministers and Chairmen of Commissions concerned may be present to give their views.

Article 72. Statutory bills passed by the Legislative Yuan shall be transmitted to the President of the Republic and to the Executive Yuan. The President shall, within ten days after receipt thereof, promulgate them; or he may deal with them in accordance with the provisions of Article 57 of this Constitution.

Article 73. No Member of the Legislative Yuan shall be held responsible outside the Yuan for opinions expressed or votes cast in the Yuan.

Article 74. No Member of the Legislative Yuan shall, except in case of *flagrante delicto,* be arrested or detained without the permission of the Legislative Yuan.

Article 75. No Member of the Legislative Yuan shall concurrently hold a government post.

Article 76. The organization of the Legislative Yuan shall be prescribed by law.

CHAPTER VII. JUDICIARY

Article 77. The Judicial Yuan shall be the highest judicial organ of the State and shall have charge of civil, criminal, and administrative cases, and over cases concerning disciplinary measures against public functionaries.

Article 78. The Judicial Yuan shall interpret the Constitution and shall have the power to unify the interpretation of laws and orders.

Article 79. The Judicial Yuan shall have a President and a Vice President, who shall be nominated and, with the consent of the Control Yuan, appointed by the President of the Republic.

The Judicial Yuan shall have a certain number of Grand Justices to take charge of matters specified in Article 78 of this Constitution, who shall be nominated and, with the consent of the Control Yuan, appointed by the President of the Republic.

Article 80. Judges shall be above partisanship and shall, in accordance with law, hold trials independently, free from any interference.

Article 81. Judges shall hold office for life. No judge shall be removed from office unless he has been found guilty of a criminal offense or subjected to disciplinary measures, or declared to be under interdiction. No judge shall, except in accordance with law, be suspended or transferred or have his salary reduced.

Article 82. The organization of the Judicial Yuan and of the law courts of various grades shall be prescribed by law.

CHAPTER VIII. EXAMINATION

Article 83. The Examination Yuan shall be the highest examination organ of the State and shall have charge of matters relating to examination, employment, registration, service rating, scale of salaries, promotion and transfer, security of tenure, commendation, pecuniary aid in case of death, retirement and old age pension.

Article 84. The Examination Yuan shall have a President and a Vice President and a certain number of Members, all of whom shall be nominated and, with the consent of the Control Yuan, appointed by the President of the Republic.

Article 85. In the selection of public functionaries, a system of open competitive examination shall be put into operation, and examinations shall be held in different areas, with prescribed numbers of persons to be selected according to various provinces and areas. No person shall be appointed to a public office unless he is qualified through examination.

Article 86. The following qualifications shall be determined and registered through examination by the Examination Yuan in accordance with law:

1. Qualifications for appointment as public functionaries; and

2. Qualifications for practice in specialized professions or as technicians.

Article 87. The Examination Yuan may, with respect to matters under its charge, present statutory bills to the Legislative Yuan.

Article 88. Members of the Examination Yuan shall be above partisanship and shall independently exercise their functions in accordance with law.

Article 89. The organization of the Examination Yuan shall be prescribed by law.

CHAPTER IX. CONTROL

Article 90. The Control Yuan shall be the highest control organ of the State and shall exercise the powers of consent, impeachment, censure and auditing.

Article 91. The Control Yuan shall be composed of Members who shall be elected by Provincial and Municipal Councils, the local Councils of Mongolia and Tibet, and Chinese citizens residing abroad. Their numbers shall be determined in accordance with the following provisions:

1. Five Members from each province;

2. Two Members from each municipality under the direct jurisdiction of the Executive Yuan;

3. Eight Members from Mongolian Leagues and Banners;

4. Eight Members from Tibet; and

5. Eight Members from Chinese citizens residing abroad.

Article 92. The Control Yuan shall have a President and a Vice President, who shall be elected by and from among its Members.

Article 93. Members of the Control Yuan shall serve a term of six years and shall be re-eligible.

Article 94. When the Control Yuan exercises the power of consent in accordance with this Constitution, it shall do so by resolution of a majority of the Members present at the meeting.

Article 95. The Control Yuan may, in the exercise of its powers of control, request the Executive Yuan and its Ministries and Commissions to submit to it for perusing the original orders issued by them and all other relevant documents.

Article 96. The Control Yuan may, taking into account the work of the Executive Yuan and its various Ministries and Commissions, set up a certain number of committees to investigate their activities with a view to ascertaining whether or not they are guilty of violation of law or neglect of duty.

Article 97. The Control Yuan may, on the basis of the investigations and resolutions of its committees, propose corrective measures and forward them to the Executive Yuan and the Ministries and Commissions concerned, directing their attention to effective improvements.

When the Control Yuan deems a public functionary in the Central Government or in a local government guilty of neglect of duty or violation of law, it may propose corrective measures or institute an impeachment. If it involves a criminal offense, the case shall be turned over to a law court.

Article 98. Impeachment by the Control Yuan of a public functionary in the Central Government or in a local government shall be instituted upon the proposal of one or more than one Member of the Control Yuan and the decision, after due consideration, by a committee composed of not less than nine Members.

Article 99. In case of impeachment by the Control Yuan of the personnel of the Judicial Yuan or of the Examination Yuan for neglect of duty or violation of law, the provisions of Articles 95, 97 and 98 of this Constitution shall be applicable.

Article 100. Impeachment by the Control Yuan of the President or the Vice President of the Republic shall be instituted upon the proposal of not less than one-fourth of the whole body of Members of the Control Yuan, and the resolution, after due consideration, by the majority of the whole body of Members of the Control Yuan, and the same shall be presented to the National Assembly.

Article 101. No Member of the Control Yuan shall be held responsible outside the Yuan for opinions expressed or votes cast in the Yuan.

Article 102. No Member of the Control Yuan shall, except in case of *flagrante delicto,* be arrested or detained without the permission of the Control Yuan.

Article 103. No member of the Control Yuan shall concurrently hold a public office or engage in any profession.

Article 104. In the Control Yuan, there shall be an Auditor General who shall be nominated and, with the consent of the Legislative Yuan, appointed by the President of the Republic.

Article 105. The Auditor General shall, within three months after presentation by the Executive Yuan of the final accounts of revenues and expenditures, complete the auditing thereof in accordance with law, and submit an auditing report to the Legislative Yuan.

Article 106. The organization of the Control Yuan shall be prescribed by law.

CHAPTER X. POWERS OF THE CENTRAL AND LOCAL GOVERNMENTS

Article 107. In the following matters, the Central Government shall have the power of legislation and administration:

1. foreign affairs;
2. national defense and military affairs concerning national defense;
3. nationality law, and criminal, civil, and commercial laws;
4. judicial system;
5. aviation, national highways, state-owned railways, navigation, postal and telegraph service;
6. Central Government finance and national revenues;
7. demarcation of national, provincial, and hsien revenues;
8. state-operated economic enterprises;
9. currency system and state banks;
10. weights and measures;
11. foreign trade policies;
12. financial and economic matters affecting foreigners or foreign countries;
13. other matters relating to the Central Government as provided by this Constitution.

Article 108. In the following matters, the Central Government shall have the power of legislation and administration, but the Central Government may delegate the power of administration to the provincial and hsien governments:

1. general principles of provincial and hsien self-government:
2. division of administrative areas;

3. forestry, industry, mining, and commerce;

4. educational system;

5. banking and exchange system;

6. shipping and deep-sea fishery;

7. public utilities;

8. cooperative enterprises;

9. water and land communication and transportation covering two or more provinces;

10. water conservancy, waterways, agriculture, and pastoral enterprises covering two or more provinces;

11. registration, employment, supervision, and security of tenure of officials in the Central and local governments;

12. land legislation;

13. labor legislation and other social legislation;

14. eminent domain;

15. census-taking and compilation of population statistics for the whole country;

16. immigration and land reclamation;

17. police system;

18. public health;

19. relief, pecuniary aid in case of death, and aid in case of unemployment;

20. preservation of ancient books and articles and sites of cultural value.

With respect to the various items enumerated in the preceding paragraph, the provinces may enact separate rules and regulations, provided these are not in conflict with national laws.

Article 109. In the following matters, the provinces shall have the power of legislation and administration, but the provinces may delegate the power of administration to the hsien;

1. provincial education, public health, industries, and communications;

2. management and disposal of provincial property;

3. administration of municipalities under provincial jurisdiction;

4. province-operated enterprises;

5. provincial cooperative enterprises;

6. provincial agriculture, forestry, water conservancy, fishery, animal husbandry, and public works;

7. provincial finance and revenues;

8. provincial debts;

9. provincial banks;

10. provincial police administration;

11. provincial charitable and public welfare works;

12. other matters delegated to the provinces in accordance with national laws.

Except as otherwise provided by law, any of the matters enumerated in the various items of the preceding paragraph, in so far as it covers two or more provinces, may be undertaken jointly by the provinces concerned.

When any province, in undertaking matters listed in any of the items of the first paragraph, finds its funds insufficient, it may, by resolution of the Legislative Yuan, obtain subsidies from the National Treasury.

Article 110. In the following matters, the hsien shall have the power of legislation and administration;

    1. hsien education, public health, industries, and communications;

    2. management and disposal of hsien property;

    3. hsien-operated enterprises;

    4. hsien cooperative enterprises;

    5. hsien agriculture and forestry, water conservancy, fishery, animal husbandry, and public works;

    6. hsien finance and revenues;

    7. hsien debts;

    8. hsien banks;

    9. administration of hsien police and defense;

    10. hsien charitable and public welfare work;

    11. other matters delegated to the hsien in accordance with national laws and Provincial Self-Government Regulations.

Except as otherwise provided by law, any of the matters enumerated in the various items of the preceding paragraph, in so far as it covers two or more hsien, may be undertaken jointly by the hsien concerned.

Article 111. Any matter not enumerated in Articles 107, 108, 109, and 110 shall fall within the jurisdiction of the Central Government, if it is national in nature; of the province, if it is provincial in nature; and of the hsien, if it concerns the hsien. In case of dispute, it shall be settled by the Legislative Yuan.

CHAPTER XI. SYSTEM OF LOCAL GOVERNMENT

Section 1. The Province

Article 112. A province may convoke a Provincial Assembly to enact, in accordance with the General Principles of Provincial and Hsien Self-government, regulations, provided the said regulations are not in conflict with the Constitution.

The organization of the Provincial Assembly and the election of the delegates shall be prescribed by law.

Article 113. The Provincial Self-Government Regulations shall include the following provisions:

    1. In the province, there shall be a Provincial Council. Members of the Provincial Council shall be elected by the people of the province.

    2. In the province, there shall be a Provincial Government with a Provincial Governor who shall be elected by the people of the province.

    3. Relationship between the province and the hsien.

The legislative power of the province shall be exercised by the Provincial Council.

Article 114. The Provincial Self-Government Regulations shall, after enactment, be forthwith submitted to the Judicial Yuan. The Judicial Yuan, if it deems any part thereof unconstitutional, shall declare null and void the articles repugnant to the Constitution.

Article 115. If, during the enforcement of the Provincial Self-Government Regulations, there should arise any serious obstacle in the application of any of the articles contained therein, the Judicial Yuan shall first summon the various parties concerned to present their views; and thereupon the Presidents of the Executive Yuan, Legislative Yuan, Judicial Yuan, Examination Yuan and Control Yuan shall form a committee, with the President of the Judicial Yuan as Chairman, to propose a formula for solution.

Article 116. Provincial rules and regulations that are in conflict with national laws shall be null and void.

Article 117. When doubt arises as to whether or not there is a conflict between provincial rules or regulations and national laws, interpretation thereon shall be made by the Judicial Yuan.

Article 118. The self-government of municipalities under the direct jurisdiction of the Executive Yuan shall be prescribed by law.

Article 119. The local self-government system of the Mongolian Leagues and Banners shall be prescribed by law.

Article 120. The self-government system of Tibet shall be safeguarded.

Section 2. The Hsien

Article 121. The hsien shall enforce hsien self-government.

Article 122. A hsien may convoke a hsien assembly to enact, in accordance with the General Principles of Provincial and Hsien Self-Government, hsien self-government regulations, provided the said regulations are not in conflict with the Constitution or with provincial self-government regulations.

Article 123. The people of the hsien shall, in accordance with law, exercise the rights of initiative and referendum in matters within the sphere of hsien self-government, and shall, in accordance with law, exercise the rights of election and recall of the magistrate and other hsien self-government officials.

Article 124. In the hsien, there shall be a Hsien Council. Members of the Hsien Council shall be elected by the people of the hsien. The legislative power of the hsien shall be exercised by the Hsien Council.

Article 125. Hsien rules and regulations that are in conflict with national laws, or with provincial rules and regulations, shall be null and void.

Article 126. In the hsien, there shall be a Hsien Government with a hsien magistrate who shall be elected by the people of the hsien.

Article 127. The hsien magistrate shall have charge of hsien self-government and shall administer matters delegated to the hsien by the Central or Provincial Government.

Article 128. The provisions governing the hsien shall apply *mutatis mutandis* to the municipality.

CHAPTER XII. ELECTION, RECALL, INITIATIVE AND REFERENDUM

Article 129. The various kinds of elections prescribed in this Constitution, except as otherwise provided by this Constitution, shall be by universal, equal, and direct suffrage and by secret ballot.

Article 130. Any citizen of the Republic of China who has attained the age of 20 years shall have the right of election in accordance with law. Except as otherwise provided by this Constitution or by law, any citizen who has attained the age of 23 years shall have the right of being elected in accordance with law.

Article 131. All candidates in the various kinds of elections prescribed in this Constitution shall openly campaign for their election.

Article 132. Intimidation or inducement shall be strictly forbidden in elections. Suits arising in connection with elections shall be tried by the courts.

Article 133. A person elected may, in accordance with law, be recalled by his constituency.

Article 134. In the various kinds of elections, the number of women to be elected shall be fixed, and measures pertaining thereto shall be prescribed by law.

Article 135. The number of delegates to the National Assembly and the manner of their election from people in interior areas, who have their own conditions of living and habits, shall be prescribed by law.

Article 136. The exercise of the rights of initiative and referendum shall be prescribed by law.

CHAPTER XIII. FUNDAMENTAL NATIONAL POLICIES

Section 1. National Defense

Article 137. The national defense of the Republic of China shall have as its objective the safeguarding of national security and the preservation of world peace. The organization of national defense shall be prescribed by law.

Article 138. The land, sea, and air forces of the whole country shall be above personal, regional, or party affiliations, shall be loyal to the state and shall protect the people.

Article 139. No political party and no individual shall make use of armed forces as an instrument in a struggle for political power.

Article 140. No military man in active service may concurrently hold a civil office.

Section 2. Foreign Policy

Article 141. The foreign policy of the Republic of China shall, in a spirit of independence and initiative and on the basis of the principles of equality and reciprocity, cultivate good-neighborliness with other nations, and respect treaties and the Charter of the United Nations, in order to protect the rights and interests of Chinese citizens residing abroad, promote international cooperation, advance international justice and ensure world peace.

Section 3. National Economy

Article 142. National economy shall be based on the Principle of the People's Livelihood and shall seek to effect equalization of land ownership and restriction of private capital in order to attain a well-balanced sufficiency in national wealth and people's livelihood.

Article 143. All land within the territory of the Republic of China shall belong to the whole body of citizens. Private ownership of land, acquired by the people in accordance with law, shall be protected and restricted by law. Privately-owned land shall be liable to taxation according to its value, and the Government may buy such land according to its value.

Mineral deposits which are embedded in the land, and natural power which may, for economic purposes, be utilized for the public benefit shall belong to the State, regardless of the fact that private individuals may have acquired ownership over such land.

If the value of a piece of land has increased, not through the exertion of labor or the employment of capital, the State shall levy thereon an increment tax, the proceeds of which shall be enjoyed by the people in common.

In the distribution and readjustment of land, the State shall, in principle, assist self-farming land-owners and persons who make use of the land by themselves, and shall also regulate their appropriate areas of operation.

Article 144. Public utilities and other enterprises of a monopolistic nature shall, in principle, be under public operation. In cases permitted by law, they may be operated by private citizens.

Article 145. With respect to private wealth and privately-operated enterprises, the State shall restrict them by law if they are deemed detrimental to a balanced development of national wealth and people's livelihood.

Cooperative enterprises shall receive encouragement and assistance from the State.

Private citizens' productive enterprises and foreign trade shall receive encouragement, guidance, and protection from the State.

Article 146. The State shall, by the use of scientific techniques, develop water conservancy, increase the productivity of land, improve agricultural conditions, plan for the utilization of land, develop agricultural resources, and hasten the industrialization of agriculture.

Article 147. The Central Government, in order to attain a balanced economic development among the provinces, shall give appropriate aid to poor or unproductive provinces.

The provinces, in order to attain a balanced economic development among the hsien, shall give appropriate aid to poor or unproductive hsien.

Article 148. Within the territory of the Republic of China, all goods shall be permitted to move freely from place to place.

Article 149. Financial institutions shall, in accordance with law, be subject to State control.

Article 150. The State shall extensively establish financial institutions for the common people, with a view to relieving unemployment.

Article 151. With respect to Chinese citizens residing abroad, the State shall foster and protect the development of their economic enterprises.

Section 4. Social Security

Article 152. The State shall provide suitable opportunity for work to people who are able to work.

Article 153. The State, in order to improve the livelihood of laborers and farmers and to improve their productive skill, shall enact laws and carry out policies for their protection.

Women and children engaged in labor shall, according to their age and physical condition, be accorded special protection.

Article 154. Capital and labor shall, in accordance with the principle of harmony and cooperation, promote productive enterprises. Conciliation and arbitration of disputes between capital and labor shall be prescribed by law.

Article 155. The State, in order to promote social welfare, shall establish a social insurance system. To the aged and the infirm who are unable to earn a living, and to victims of unusual calamities, the State shall give appropriate assistance and relief.

Article 156. The State, in order to consolidate the foundation of national existence and development, shall protect motherhood and carry out the policy of promoting the welfare of women and children.

Section 5. Education and Culture

Article 158. Education and culture shall aim at the development among the citizens of the national spirit, the spirit of self-government, national morality, good physique, scientific knowledge, and the ability to earn a living.

Article 159. All citizens shall have equal opportunity to receive an education.

Article 160. All children of school age from six to twelve years shall receive free primary education. Those from poor families shall be supplied with books by the Government.

All citizens above school age who have not received primary education shall receive supplementary education free of charge and shall also be supplied with books by the Government.

Article 161. The national, provincial, and local governments shall extensively establish scholarships to assist students of good scholastic standing and exemplary conduct who lack the means to continue their school education.

Article 162. All public and private educational and cultural institutions in the country shall, in accordance with law, be subject to State supervision.

Article 163. The State shall pay due attention to the balanced development of education in different regions, and shall promote social education in order to raise the cultural standard of the citizens in general. Grants from the National Treasury shall be made to frontier regions and economically poor areas to help them meet their educational and cultural expenses. The Central Government may either itself undertake the more important educational and cultural enterprises in such regions or give them financial assistance.

Article 164. Expenditures of educational programs, scientific studies and cultural services shall not be, in respect of the Central Government, less than 15 percent of the total national budget; in respect of each province, less than 25 percent of the total provincial budgets; and in respect of each municipality or hsien, less than 35 percent of the total municipal or hsien budget. Educational and cultural foundations established in accordance with law shall, together with their property, be protected.

Article 165. The State shall safeguard the livelihood of those who work in the fields of education, sciences and arts, and shall, in accordance with the development of national economy, increase their remuneration from time to time.

Article 166. The State shall encourage scientific discoveries and inventions, and shall protect ancient sites and articles of historical, cultural or artistic value.

Article 167. The State shall give encouragement or subsidies to the following enterprises or individuals:

1. Educational enterprises in the country which have been operated with good record by private individuals;

2. Educational enterprises which have been operated with good record by Chinese citizens residing abroad;

3. Persons who have made discoveries or inventions in the fields of learning and technology; and

4. Persons who have rendered long and meritorious services in the field of education.

Section 6. Frontier Regions

Article 168. The State shall accord to the various racial groups in the frontier regions legal protection of their status and shall give them special assistance in their local self-government undertakings.

Article 169. The State shall, in a positive manner, undertake and foster the development of education, culture, communications, water conservancy, public health, and other economic and social enterprises of the various racial groups in the frontier regions. With respect to the utilization of land, the State shall, after taking into account the climatic conditions, the nature of the soil, and the life and habits of the people, adopt measures to protect the land and to assist in its development.

CHAPTER XIV. ENFORCEMENT AND AMENDMENT OF THE CONSTITUTION

Article 170. The term "law," as used in this Constitution, shall denote any legislative bill that shall have been passed by the Legislative Yuan and promulgated by the President of the Republic.

Article 171. Laws that are in conflict with the Constitution shall be null and void.

When doubt arises as to whether or not a law is in conflict with the Constitution, interpretation thereon shall be made by the Judicial Yuan.

Article 172. Ordinances that are in conflict with the Constitution or with laws shall be null and void.

Article 173. The Constitution shall be interpreted by the Judicial Yuan.

Article 174. Amendments to the Constitution shall be made in accordance with one of the following procedures:

1. Upon the proposal of one-fifth of the total number of the delegates to the National Assembly and by a resolution of three-fourths of the delegates present at a meeting having a quorum of two-thirds of the entire Assembly, the Constitution may be amended.

2. Upon the proposal of one-fourth of the members of the Legislative Yuan and by a resolution of three-fourths of the members present at a meeting having a quorum of three-fourths of the members of the Yuan, an amendment may be drawn up and submitted to the National Assembly by way of referendum. Such a proposed amendment to the Constitution shall be publicly published half a year before the National Assembly convenes.

Article 175. Whenever necessary, enforcement procedures in regard to any matters prescribed in this Constitution shall be separately provided by law.

The preparatory procedures for the enforcement of this Constitution shall be decided upon by the same National Assembly which shall have adopted this Constitution.

TEMPORARY PROVISIONS EFFECTIVE DURING THE PERIOD OF COMMUNIST REBELLION

(Adopted by the National Assembly on April 18, 1948, promulgated by the National Government on May 10, 1948, amended by the National Assembly on March 11, 1960, amended by the extraordinary session of the National Assembly on February 7, 1966, amended by the National Assembly on March 19, 1966, and amended by the fifth session of the National Assembly at its ninth plenary meeting March 17, 1972)

In accordance with the procedure prescribed in Paragraph 1 of Article 174 of the Constitution, the following Temporary Provisions to be effective during the Period of Communist Rebellion are hereby enacted:

1. The President during the Period of Communist Rebellion may, by resolution of the Executive Yuan Council, take emergency measures to avert an imminent danger to the security of the State or of the people or to cope with any serious financial or economic crisis, without being subject to the procedural restrictions prescribed in Article 39 or Article 43 of the Constitution.

2. The emergency measures mentioned in the preceding paragraph may be modified or abrogated by the Legislative Yuan in accordance with Paragraph 2 of Article 57 of the Constitution.

3. During the Period of Communist Rebellion, the President and the Vice President may be reelected without being subject to the two-term restriction prescribed in Article 47 of the Constitution.

4. During the Period of Communist Rebellion, the President is authorized to establish, in accordance with the constitutional system, an organ for making major policy decisions concerned with national mobilization and suppression of the Communist rebellion and for assuming administrative control in war zones.

5. To meet the requirements of national mobilization and suppression of the Communist rebellion, the President may make adjustments in the administrative and personnel organs of the Central Government, as well as their organizations.

6. During the period of national mobilization and the suppression of the Communist rebellion, the President may, in accordance with the following stipulations, initiate and promulgate for enforcement regulations providing for elections to strengthen elective offices at the Central Government level without being subject to the restrictions prescribed in Article 26, Article 64, or Article 91 of the Constitution:

(1) In free areas, additional members of the National Assembly, the Legislative Yuan, and the Control Yuan may be added through regular elections. Members of the Legislative Yuan and Control Yuan that must be elected by Chinese citizens living abroad who are unable to hold elections shall be chosen according to regulations established by the President of the Republic.

(2) Representatives elected to the National Assembly, Legislative Yuan, and Control Yuan in the first elections were chosen through popular vote by the people of the entire nation. These representatives exercise their powers of office in accordance with law; the same principle applies to the representatives elected to fill vacancies or provide additional representation.

Elections for the National Assembly, Legislative Yuan, and Control Yuan shall be held on the Chinese mainland, one by one, as each area is recovered.

(3) Additional members elected to serve in the National Assembly, Legislative Yuan, and Control Yuan, shall exercise the same powers of office in accordance with law as the members elected in the first elections.

Additional members of the National Assembly shall stand for reelection every six years; members of the Legislative Yuan, every three years; and members of the Control Yuan, every six years.

7. During the Period of Communist Rebellion, the National Assembly may enact measures to initiate principles concerning Central Government laws and submit Central Government laws to referendum without being subject to the restriction prescribed in Paragraph 2 of Article 27 of the Constitution.

8. During the Period of Communist Rebellion, the President may, when he deems necessary, convoke an extraordinary session of the National Assembly to discuss initiative or referendum measures.

9. The National Assembly shall establish an organ to study, during its recess, problems relating to constitutional rule.

10. The termination of the Period of Communist Rebellion shall be declared by the President.

11. Amendment or abrogation of the Temporary Provisions shall be resolved by the National Assembly.

INTERPRETATION OF
"TOTAL MEMBERSHIP OF THE NATIONAL ASSEMBLY"

(Adopted by the Council of Grand Justices at its 138th Meeting on February 12, 1960; No. Shih-85)

The total membership of the National Assembly under the Constitution shall be counted on the basis, in the present situation, of the number of delegates who are duly elected according to law, and able to answer summons to attend the meeting of the Assembly.

Reasons for the Interpretation

This case was referred successively by the Executive Yuan and the Secretariat of the National Assembly for interpretation as to the basis of counting the total membership of the National Assembly during its coming third session, when the quorum shall be computed on the total membership, since re-election of delegates to the Assembly cannot be held and vacancies can also in no way be filled.

The total membership of the National Assembly under the Constitution or other laws was counted, during the first and second sessions of the present Assembly, on the basis of the number of the delegates scheduled to be elected. It has been, however, a decade since the fall of the mainland, and the country is undergoing a grave crisis. Many of the delegates thereby being deprived of the liberty of movement, were unable to attend the meetings of the Assembly. And for those members disqualified for various reasons, their position being vacant, few candidates could be found to succeed them or to fill the vacancies. Organs created by the Constitution are presumed to be able to transact their business. If, due to the aforementioned predicament, the Assembly is restrained from exercising the functions conferred by the Constitution, it will be something unanticipated to its framers. In the present situation, which is unlike the past, the doctrine of *rebus sic stantibus* shall apply. Due respect is to be paid to original intentions of the Constitution in setting up the National Assembly. The total membership shall be construed as consisting of the delegates duly elected according to law and able to go at summons to the meeting at the seat of the Central Government, including those who are free to, but do not actually attend.

Notes

CHAPTER 2

1. The dramatic rise in per capita income partially reflected the fall of the U.S. dollar relative to the New Taiwan (N.T.) dollar. The average exchange rate for 1987 was U.S. $1 to N.T. $31.7. Before the current fall of the U.S. dollar began in 1986, the exchange rate was U.S. $1 to N.T. $38.

2. According to Haggard and Cheng (1987, 87), between 1952 and 1962 U.S. aid financed 38 percent of gross domestic capital formation. Domestic savings, merely N.T. $330 million in 1952, went up to N.T. $2.9 billion in 1960 and over N.T. $10 billion in 1964 (*TSDB*, 1987, 57).

3. Figures reflect the current prices of New Taiwan dollars and an exchange rate of U.S. $1 to N.T. $40.

4. Available figures suggest that the total industrial workforce was over 7.7 million out of a national population of almost 20 million in 1987 (*TSDB*, 1987, 15; Hoon 1988, 18).

5. The student population includes those in kindergarten, schools for the handicapped, and college preparatory schools.

CHAPTER 3

1. The JCRR is an official body directing agricultural reform in Taiwan, staffed and funded jointly by the Republic of China and the United States.

2. Recently organized independent unions such as the Brotherhood Association are the only exceptions.

CHAPTER 4

1. These six functional groups deal with political issues, party affairs, finance and economics, social problems, education, and legal institutions. Each member volunteers to serve in one or more groups. Such functional divisions prepare the Central Standing Committee to exercise a form of collective leadership in the post–Chiang Ching-kuo era.

2. Lee Huan is the KMT secretary-general; Sung Shih-hsun was chairman of the Party Provincial Committee and head of the party's Organization Department from 1979 to 1987.

3. In early 1964 Peng Ming-min, Hsieh Ts'ung-min, and Wei T'ing-ch'ao prepared 10,000 copies of an eight-point manifesto entitled *A Declaration of Formosan Self-salvation*. The manifesto questioned the government's policy of returning to the mainland and called for replacing "Chiang Kai-shek's regime" with a "government freely elected." Peng and Wei were sentenced to eight years in prison and Hsieh to ten years.

4. The DPP issued a statement reaffirming Taiwan's independent sovereignty and rejecting the PRC's claim of jurisdiction over Taiwan at the special session of the party congress in April 1988 (see *Tzu-li chao-pao*, April 18, 1988, 2).

5. President Lee publicly issued this statement on February 22, 1988, in his first press conference as president (see *CKSP*, February 23, 1988, 2).

6. The Labour Party had a serious split in May 1988. Vice Chairman Liu Mei-wen and some leaders connected with the Summer Tide Association left the party. They tried to form a separate Workers' Party (*Lao-tung tang*) in the following month.

CHAPTER 5

1. For instance, Article 38 of the constitution states that "the president shall, in accordance with the provisions of this constitution, exercise the powers of concluding treaties, declaring war, and making peace."

2. Taiwan's older KMT mainlander leaders still insist that the Chinese Communists are "rebels" and that their "rebellion" will someday be suppressed. This view is not shared by the majority of Taiwan's residents.

3. The Executive Yuan will add Ministries of Labor, Agriculture, Culture, and Health and Social Welfare and the Ministry of Economic Affairs will be renamed the Ministry of Industry and Commerce, according to an official reorganization proposal. The proposal is expected to complete the legislative process by the end of 1988 (*CKSP*, February 27, 1988, 1).

CHAPTER 6

1. Based on the February 1988 exchange rate of U.S. $1 to about N.T. $28.

2. *Chao-chi-jen* means literally "convener of committee meetings." His status

and power are equivalent to a committee chairman in European parliaments. In Taiwan's Legislative Yuan, each standing committee has two conveners.

3. "One-Four" refers to Monday and Thursday, the days this group used to hold regular caucuses.

CHAPTER 7

1. Based on a 1983 exchange rate of U.S. $1 to N.T. $40.

CHAPTER 9

1. The Republic of China is able to use its official title in the following international bodies: the International Union for Publication of Customs Tariffs, the Permanent Court of Arbitration, the International Committee of Military Medicine and Pharmacy, the International Office of Epizootics, the International Cotton Advisory Committee, the Asian Productivity Organization, the Afro-Asian Rural Reconstruction Organization, and the Asian and Pacific Council.

2. Seagrave's speculation is farfetched; the United States must have worried about possible PRC military involvement in Vietnam if Taiwan troops had engaged in the war.

3. The leadership team is the highest directing agency of the PRC united-front activities related to Taiwan. In recent years it has been headed by Yang Shang-kun, a CCP politburo member and Teng Hsiao-p'ing's confidant on military affairs.

Abbreviations

AS *Asian Survey*, Berkeley.

CEPD Council for Economic Planning and Development, Executive Yuan.

CHNC *Chung-hua Min-kuo nien-chien* (China yearbook). Taipei: Hilit. Various years.

CKLT *Chung-kuo lun-t'an* (China Tribune), Taipei.

CKSP *Chung-kuo shih-pao* (China Times), Taipei.

CP *Chung pao* (China News), New York.

CPTC *Chin-pu tsa-chih* (Progressive Magazine), Taipei.

CQ *China Quarterly*, London.

CSNT *Chin-shih nien-tai* (the Nineties), Hong Kong.

CYACL Chinese Youth Anti-Communist League (Chung-kuo Ching-nien Fan Kung Chiu-kuo-t'uan).

CYJP *Chung-yang jih-pao* (Central Daily News), Taipei.

ES *Educational Statistics of the Republic of China*, Taipei: Ministry of Education. Various years.

FCJ *Free China Journal*, Taipei.

FEER *Far Eastern Economic Review*, Hong Kong.

FLT *Feng-lai-tao* (Formosa Weekly), Taipei.

HHW *Hsin hsin-wen* (the Journalist), Taipei.

JMJP *Jen-min jih-pao* (*Remin ribao*, People's Daily), Peking

KCJP Kuo-chi jih-pao (International Daily News), Los Angeles.

KHJC Kuang-hua tsa-chih (Sinorama), Taipei.

KMT Kuomintang (Nationalist Party).

LHP Lien-ho pao (United Daily News), Taipei.

LHYK Lien-ho yueh-k'an (United Monthly), Taipei.

MCJ Min-chu-jen (Democrat), Taipei.

MCJP Min-chung jih-pao (People's Daily), Kaohsiung.

MLT Mei-li-tao (Formosa), Taipei.

NYT New York Times, New York.

PRC People's Republic of China.

PSNT Pa-shih nien-tai (the Eighties), Taipei.

QNET Quarterly National Economic Trends, Taipei.

ROC Republic of China.

RDEC Research, Development, and Evaluation Committee, Executive Yuan.

SAI Statistical Abstract of the Interior, Taipei: Ministry of the Interior. Various years.

SCJP Shih-chieh jih-pao (Chinese Daily News), Los Angeles.

SGK Sheng ken (Striking Roots), Taipei.

SI Social Indicators of the Republic of China. Taipei: Directorate-General of Budget, Accounting, and Statistics. Various years.

SK Shen keng (Deep Plough), Taipei.

SPCK Shih-pao chou-k'an (China Times Weekly), New York.

SPHWCK Shih-pao hsin-wen chou-k'an (Times News Weekly), Taipei.

SPTC Shih-pao tsa-chih (China Times Magazine), Taipei.

SY Statistical Yearbook of the Republic of China. Taipei: Directorate-General of Budget, Accounting, and Statistics. Various years.

TCNC T'ung-chi nien-chien (Statistical yearbook), Taipei: Directorate-General of Budget, Accounting, and Statistics. Various years.

THTC Tien-hsia tsa-chih (Commonwealth), Taipei.

TLWP Tzu-li wan-pao (Independence Evening Post), Taipei.

TS Tai sheng (Taiwanese Voice), Peking.

TSDB. Taiwan Statistical Data Book. Taipei: Executive Yuan. Various years.

TWCL Tai-wan cheng-lun (Taiwan Political Review), Taipei.

TWKC Tai-wan kuang-ch'ang (Taiwan Square), Taipei.

TWMP Tai-wan min-pao (Taiwan People's Journal), Los Angeles.

TWTW Tai-wan tang-wu (Taiwan Party Affairs), Taipei.

WSJ Wall Street Journal, New York.

Bibliography

A Pu-cheng [pseud.]. 1983a. "Kuo-min-tang te ti-fang tzu-chih shen-hua" (Local self-government under the Kuomintang: A fairy tale). *SGK*, no. 15 (August 15): 22–25.

———. 1983b. "Leng-yen hui-ku 'pan-shan' yu T'ai-wan cheng-t'an" (Taiwanese returned from the mainland and their political careers in Taiwan). *SGK*, no. 19 (September 10): 42–45.

Almond, Gabriel A. 1970. *Political Development*. Boston: Little, Brown.

Almond, Gabriel A., and Powell, G. Bindham, Jr., eds. 1984. *Comparative Politics Today: A World View*. Boston: Little, Brown.

Almond, Gabriel A., and Verba, Sidney. 1963. *The Civic Culture, Political Attitudes and Democray in Five Nations*. Princeton: Princeton University Press.

Appleton, Sheldon. 1976. "The Social and Political Impact of Education in Taiwan." *AS* 16, no. 8 (August): 705–710.

Apter, Davis. 1964. *Ideology and Discontent*. New York: Free Press.

———, ed. 1965. *The Politics of Modernization*. Chicago: University of Chicago Press.

Armstrong, John A. 1978. *Ideology, Politics, and Government in the Soviet Union*. 4th ed. New York: Praeger.

Barnett, A. Doak. 1977. *China and the Major Powers in East Asia*. Washington, D.C.: Brookings Institution.

———. 1981. *The FX Decision: Another Crucial Movement in U.S.-China-Taiwan Relations*. Washington, D.C.: Brookings Institution.

Belloni, Frank P., and Beller, Dennis C., eds. 1978. *Faction Politics: Political Parties and Factionalism in Comparative Perspective*. Santa Barbara: ABC Clio.

Bennet, Dirk. 1984 "Chiang's Changes." *FEER*, March 31, 11.

Berger, Peter; Hsiao Hsin-huang; Wen Ch'ung-i; Li I-yuan; and Huang Kuang-kuo. 1984. "T'sung Taiwan ching-yen k'an shih-su-hua ju-chia yu tzu-pen chu-i fa-chan" (The Taiwan experience: A perspective on the development of secular Confucianism and capitalism). *CKLT*, no. 222 (December 25):13–34.

Berry, Jeffrey M. 1984. *The Interest Group Society.* Boston: Little, Brown.

Black, C. E. 1967. *The Dynamics of Modernization.* New York: Harper & Row.

Braibanti, Ralph. 1969. *Political and Administrative Development.* Durham, N.C.: Duke University Press.

Brelis, Dean. 1985. "India: A Landslide for Gandhi." *Time*, January 7, 68–69.

Burns, John F. 1985 "Vessey in China: Two-Edged Symbolism." *NYT*, January 20, 3.

Bush, George. 1974 "Our Deal with Peking: All Cost, No Benefit." *Washington Post*, December 24, D3–4.

Chai, Trong R. 1986. "The Future of Taiwan." *AS*, 26, no. 12 (December 12): 1309–23.

Chai Sung-lin. 1983a. "I tz'u ch'eng-kung te hsuan-chu" (A successful election). *SPCK*, no. 212 (December 25): 15.

_____. 1983b. "Mien tui shih-mo-yang te chu-jen" (Taiwan's sovereign populace). *SPTC*, no. 201 (October 5): 9–18.

_____. 1985. "1945, 1985, 1995 she-hui pien-ch'ien ho kuo-min sheng-huo yi-hsiang te tiao-ch'a yen-chiu" (A study of social change and citizens' life-styles in 1945, 1985, and 1995). *LHP*, November 25–26, 2.

Chang Ch'i-yun. 1952. "Tang-wu pao-kao yao-lueh" (A summary of the report on party affairs). Taipei: KMT Headquarters.

Chang Ch'un-hua. 1984. "Ts'ung lao-chi-fa te chih-ting k'an kung-hui te li-hsiang yu hsien-shih" (The Labor Standard Law and the prospect for trade unions). *SPTC*, no. 251 (September 19): 27–29.

_____1986. "Min ch'ing liang tang ch'iang ta cheng-chih pa-shih?" (Will the China Youth Party and Democratic Socialist Patry join the political bandwagon?). *SPTC*, no. 91 (November 22): 16–18.

Chang Ch'un-hua and Chi Hui-jung. 1987. "Pei ch'i shih-tzu-chia, tso tsai shih-tzu-lu" (March on the crossroads with the cross on their backs). *SPHWCK*, no. 46 (April 14): 64–68.

Chang Hsiao-ts'un. 1988. "Lao-kung yao cheng ch'uan-li kung-hui yao ch'iu tzu-chu" (Workers strike for rights while unions seek autonomy). *MCJP*, January 30, 3.

Chang Hsi-che. 1975. "Chung-kuo Kuo-min-tang yu cheng-tang cheng-chih" (The KMT and party politics). *Fu-hsing-kang hsueh-pao* (Fu-hsing-kang Journal) 13 (January): 15–37.

_____. 1977. "Chung-kuo Kuo-min-tang yu cheng-chih" (The KMT and politics). *Chung-hua hsueh-pao* (China Journal) 4:2.

Chang Hua-jen. 1983. "Chih-yeh t'uan-ti hsuan-ch'ing li-ts'e" (A preview of electoral contests in vocational groups). *SPTC*, no. 209 (November 30): 33–34.

Chang Hung. 1983. "Li-fa-yuan te chuan-li tou-cheng" (Power struggle in the Legislative Yuan). *Chung-ku-lou* 1 , no. 4 (April): 4–8.

Chang I-lun. 1985. "Chien-t'ao chih-cheng-tang te t'i-ming wen-t'i" (Examine the issue of the ruling KMT's nomination practice). *LHYK*, no. 46 (May): 6.

Chang, Jaw-ling Joanne. 1985. *Peking's Negotiating Type: A Case Study of U.S.-PRC Normalization*, Occasional Papers/Reprints Series in Contemporary Asian Studies, no. 5. Baltimore: University of Maryland, School of Law.

Chang Mao-kuei and Hsiao Hsin-huang. 1987. "Ta-hsueh-sheng te 'chung-kuo chiech' yu 'Tai-wan chieh'" (College Students' ties to "China" and to "Taiwan"). *CKLT* 25, no. 1 (October 10): 34–53.

Chang, Parris H. 1983a. "Supplemental Elections of the Legislative Yuan: A Field Study Report." Paper prepared for the North American Taiwanese Professors Association.

———. 1983b. "Taiwan in 1982: Diplomatic Setback Abroad and Demands for Reforms at Home." *AS* 23, no. 1 (January): 39–44.

———. 1984. "Taiwan in 1983: Setting the Stage for Power Transition," *AS* 24, no. 1 (January): 122–24.

Chang Shu-ming. 1986. "Chuan-li he-hsin cha-hsien hsin-cho" (Sudden shifts in the center of power). *SPCK*, no. 69 (June 22): 6–9.

Chang Shu-ming, and Lin Yi. 1986. "Tang-wai kung-cheng-hui hung yun t'u ch'i" (Tangwai public policy association gaining new life). *SPCK*, no. 61 (April 26): 59–63.

Chang Wang. 1984. "Shui shih ying chia? Kung min ying chi-kou jen ts'ai chiao li chan" (Which is the winner? Competition for qualified personnel between public and private sectors). *SPTC*, no. 222 (February 22): 5.

Chao, Yung-mao. 1978. *Taiwan ti-fang p'ai-hsi yu ti-fang chien-she chih kuang-hsi* (Local factions and local reconstruction in Taiwan). Kaohsiung: Tung-yi.

Chen Ch'ao-p'ing. 1982. "Chin-ch'ien, cheng-ke, shih" (Money, politicians, and corruption). *LHYK*, no. 10 (May): 16–21.

Chen Che-ming. 1987. "Tang-ch'ien wu ta she-hui yun-tung ti tung-li, tsu-li, ya-li" (Five major social movements: The dynamics, obstacles, and pressures). *SPHWCK*, no. 46 (April 14): 37–51.

Chen Cheng-nung. 1987a. "Ch'u fan k'e-i k'ua-tang, wen cheng pu-neng lien-shou: (The party line may be crossed at the dinner table, but not on the legislative floor). *HHW*, no. 6 (April 20): 48–50.

———1987b. "Szu shih nien lai i ch'ang en-yuan" (Four decades of friction). *HHW*, no. 8 (May 4): 34–39.

Chen Chih-hao. 1981. "Chung-kuo Kuo-min-tang pa shih yu nien lai tui li-shih chih kung-hsien" (Historical contribution of the KMT over eight decades). *Chung-kuo ti-fang tzu-chih* (Local self-government in China) 33, no. 9 (January): 31–35.

Chen Ch'ing-hsi. 1986. "T'i-sheng li-fa p'in-chih, ch'iang-fa i-su kung-neng" (Improve legislative quality, strengthen policy interpellation). *SCJP*, February 12, 5.

Chen Ch'i-ti. 1985. "Wo-kuo te wai-chiao ch'u-ching yu ch'u-lu" (ROC diplomatic status and prospects for breakthrough). *SPTC*, no. 317 (December 25): 72.

Chen Ch'un-hsiang. 1984. "Tang-pien, tang-kun hsien-hsing-chi't'ou-shih pei-shih i-hui tang-t'uan yin-tso" (Party discipline in action: The case of the Taipei city council). *PSNT*, no. 40 (July 15): 38–41.

Chen En-tse. 1984. "Kuo-min-tang chan-k'ai tang-nei chieh-pang" (Succession of power in the KMT). *SPTC*, no. 239 (June 27): 62–63.

————. 1986. "P'ai-hsi te tung-yuan yu shih-li te cheng-ho" (Mobilization and integration of factional forces). *SPCK*, no. 50 (February 9): 71.

Chen Fu-hsing. 1983. "Tang-wai chung-yang hou-yuan-hui ch'eng-li chi-shih" (Report on founding of the *tangwai* central compaign committee). *SK*, no. 17 (September 25): 15–20.

Chen Hao. 1984. "Kuo-min-tang p'ai-hsi feng-p'o liu-shih-nien" (Six decades of KMT factional strife). *SPTC*, no. 228 (April 11): 27–30.

————. 1986a. "Cheng-chih kai-ke te ching-kao" (Warning for political reform). *SPCK*, no. 60 (April 20): 15–16.

————. 1986b. "Ch'ien Fu tsai T'ai-pei" (Ch'ien Fu in Taipei). *SPCK*, no. 47 (January 19): 15.

Chen I-shen. 1981. "Chung-san hsien-shen i tang chih kuo te kuan-nien shen-hsi" (An analysis of Sun Yat-sen's concept of party-state). *CKLT* 12, no. 3 (May 10): 40–42.

Chen I-t'ien. 1984. "Sheng tang-pu yu ti-fang tzu-chih" (Provincial party headquarters and local autonomy). *SPTC*, no. 250 (September 12): 31.

Chen Jui-Kuei. 1986. "Ch'iao k'ai tui Ou te mao-i ta men" (Exploring the European market for exports). *SPTC*, no. 320 (January 25): 13–14.

Chen, King C. 1979. "Taiwan in Peking's Strategy." In Hungdah Chiu, ed., *China and the Taiwan Issue*, 127–44. New York: Praeger.

Chen Kou-hsiang and Hu Sun. 1982. "Cheng-chih ch'uan-li shih sheng-ts'ai kung-chu" (Wealth is acquired through political power). *LHYK*, no. 8 (March): 9–14.

Chen Li-ch'ing. 1980. "Wo kuo pao-chih pao-tao sheng i-hui hsin-wen hsing-t'ai chih yen-chiu" (A study of news coverage on the provincial assembly in the Taiwan press). *Hsin-wen-hsueh yen-chiu* (Studies of Journalism) 26 (December 25): 69–135.

Chen Lin-sheng. 1984. "Kung-hui ch'u-chin ho-hsieh" (Trade unions promote harmony). *SPTC*, no. 239 (June 27): 11–12.

Chen Li-shen. 1979. "Cheng-tang cheng-chih, cheng-tang fa" (Party politics and party law). *Min-chu ch'ao* (Democratic Tide) 29, no. 11 (November): 8–11.

Chen Min-feng. 1987. "Tsou shang chieh t'ou" (March on the streets). *HHW*, no. 30 (October 26): 19–23.

Chen Ming-k'uan. 1984. "Yu Kuo-hwa nei-ke te ho-hsin jen-wu" (The nucleus of Yu Kuo-hwa's cabinet). In *T'o shih ch'uan-li pien-chu* (The power structure in transition), vol. 6. Taipei: Feng-yun Lun-t'an-she.

Chen Shih-min. 1982. "Ching ch'ueh hsin-wen pao-tao te ti-i pu" (First step toward accurate press reports). *SPTC*, no. 134 (June 29): 34–37.

Chen Shun-chih. 1984. "Li-fa-yuan Kuo-min-tang hua" (The Legislative Yuan monopolized by the KMT). *PSNT*, no. 40 (July 15): 34–37.

Chen Ti-chuan. 1983. "Kuo-min-tang fa-t'ung ching-ying sheng to-shao?" (How many of the legislative old guards are still alive?). *PSNT*, no. 1 (April 3): 19–22.

Chen Wen-tse. 1986. "Pai-hsi te tung-yuan yu shih-li te cheng-ho" (Factional mobilization and aggregate strength). *SPCK*, no. 50 (February 9): 71.

Chen Yang-hao. 1983a. "Li-fa-yuan hsuan-pa-fa pien-lun shih-lu chi p'ing-hsi" (Report and commentary on the debate of the election and recall law in the Legislative Yuan). *MCJ*, no. 6 (April 16): 35–48.

————1983b. "Li-fa-yuan pao chin ta pien-lun p'ing-yi" (The great debate on newspaper bans in the Legislative Yuan: A commentary). *MCJ*, no. 5 (April 1): 13–15.

Chen Yang-te. 1978. *T'ai-wan ti-fang min-hsuan ling-tao jen-wu chih pien-tung* (Change in popularly elected local officials in Taiwan). Taipei: Ssu-chi.

Cheng Chi-en. 1984a. "T'ai-wan chung-ch'an chieh-chi te ching-chi" (The economy of Taiwan's middle class). *SPTC*, no. 244 (August 1): 53–56.

————. 1984b. "T'ai-wan pa ta ch'i yeh ling-hsiu" (Taiwan's eight great entrepreneurs). *SPTC*, no. 249 (September 5): 32–43.

Cheng Ching. 1986. "Tui wai tzu-t'ai ti, tui nei ch'i-yan kao, Kuo-min-tang chung-liang-chi yuan-lao wei-hsieh tang-wai" (Outwardly low profile and inwardly inflammatory: The KMT heavyweight old guard threaten the *tangwai*). *Hsien-feng shih-tai chou-k'an* (Herald's Time Weekly), January 13, 28–39.

Cheng Chu-yuan. 1986. "T'ai-wan te ching-chi ch'eng-chang" (Taiwan's economic growth). *SCJP*, March 2, 9.

Cheng Mu-hsin. 1985. *T'ai-wan sheng-i-hui chih pien-chu* (Change in the Taiwan Provincial Assembly). Taipei: Pa-shih Nien-tai.

Cheng Nan-jung. 1983. "Kuan Chung t'iao-chan Tai-pei tang-wai, Tai-pei tang-wai ju-ho fan-chi" (Taipei *tangwai* face Kuan Chung's challenge: How to react?). *MCJ*, no. 13 (August 1): 15.

Cheng Shu-chieh. 1984. "Kuo-min-tang kao-ts'eng jen-shih t'iao-cheng te ching-wei" (Reshuffles of high-level personnel in the KMT). *LHYK*, no. 36 (July): 15–17.

Cheng Su-min. 1985. "Mass Media in the Information Age." *FCJ*, September 22, 2.

Ch'eng Ch'uan-sheng. 1975. Tang-ch'ien cheng-tang cheng-chih te ch'u-shih" (Current status of party politics). *Tzu-yu ch'ing-nien* (Free Youth) 53, no. 5 (May): 54–59.

Ch'i Chih. 1982. "Wo-men tui tang-nei tsu-chih hsing-t'ai te chien-she" (Our efforts on intraparty organization). *Kuo-hui* (Parliament) 12, no. 1 (January): 9–17.

Ch'i Hsi-sheng. 1982. *Nationalist China at War: Military Defeat and Political Collapse, 1937–1945*. Ann Arbor: University of Michigan Press.

Chiang Chia. 1984. "Ti-fang ts'ai-cheng te p'ing-ching" (The bottleneck of local finance). *SPTC*, no. 250 (September 12): 29.

Chiang Ching-kuo. 1979. "Chung-kuo Kuo-min-tang wei kuo-chia yu min-chung tso liao hsieh shih-mo?" (What has the KMT done for the country and the people?). *CYJP*, November 12, 1.

Chiang Hsueh-ch'ing. 1987. "Ko-ch'i t'ung t'ung chin hsien-chai k'ai yi tien chiang-lai teng cho ch'iao" (Censorship in the past, freer now, and the future is yet to be decided.) *HHW*, no. 18 (July 13): 20–23.

Chiang Liang-jen. 1987. "T'ai-wan-jen ti erh ke shang-chiang" (Second Taiwanese general). *HHW*, no. 39 (December 7): 8–11.

Chiang Ping-lun. 1974a. "She-hui tung-yuan yu cheng-chih tung-yuan, T'ai-wan ke-li yen-chiu" (Social mobilization and political mobilization: The case study of Taiwan). *Hsien-cheng su-ch'ao* (Constitutional Ideas) 27 (July): 4–11.

————. 1974b. "T'ai-wan ti-ch'u chih-yeh pien-tung te fu-tu chi ch'i ch'u-hsiang" (The level and trend of occupational changes in Taiwan). *Tang-fang tsa-chih* (Eastern Magazine) 8, no. 3 (September): 5–9.

————. 1985. "Wo-kuo cheng-tang cheng-chih te hsien-k'uang yu wei-lai" (The future of party politics in the Republic of China). Paper presented at Nan-yuan Conference, Taipei, December 27–29.

Ch'ien Tuan-sheng. 1950. *The Government and Politics of China*. Cambridge: Harvard University Press.

Ch'in Huai-pi. [pseud.]. 1984. "Li-fa wei-yuan te chiao-she ch'ung-t'u" (Conflicting roles of Legislative Yuan members). *LHYK*, no. 14 (September): 57–58.

————. 1986. "T'ai-wan tang-wai lien-hsien chan-ho chih to-shao?" (How much did the Taiwan opposition gain in running a coordinated electoral campaign?). *CP*, February 6, 2.

China Yearbook. 1984. Taipei: China Publishing. Various years.

Ch'ing Yen. 1985. "Leng yen k'an hsuan-chu, p'ing-hsin lun te shih" (An objective analysis of the election results). *LHYK*, no. 53 (October): 7.

Chiu Hungdah, ed. 1979. *China and the Taiwan Issue*. New York: Praeger.

————. 1983. "Prospect for the Unification of China: An Analysis of the Views of the Republic of China on Taiwan." *AS* 22, no. 10 (October): 1081–94.

————. 1986a. "Ch'ung-shih chung-yung min-yi chi-kuang wen-t'i fen-hsi" (An analysis of the issue of change in the national representative institutions). *SPCK*, no. 60 (April 20): 8–12.

————. 1986b. "Lun Ya-chou K'ai-fa Yin-hang te Chung-kuo hui-chi wen-t'i" (China membership question in the Asian Development Bank). *Fa-yu k'uai-pao* (Sino Express), March 24, 1.

Chiu Hungdah and Leng Shao-ch'uan, eds. 1984. *China: Seventy Years After the 1911 Hsin-hai Revolution*. Charlottesville: University Press of Virginia.

Ch'iu Jung-chu. 1984a. "Chih-cheng tang jen-shih i-tung te i-yeh li-shih" (The ruling party's personnel reshuffles: A historical perspective). *SPTC*, no. 237 (June 13): 17–23.

————. 1984b. "Kuai-shou shen-chin li-fa-yuan" (The invisible hand in the Legislative Yuan). *SPTC*, no. 238 (June 20): 14–18.

———. 1984c. "T'ai-wan ti-ch'u nung-hui chi chiang kai-hsuan" (Taiwan's farmers' associations to hold elections soon). *SPTC*, no. 264 (December 19): 31–32.

———. 1984d. "Tang-wai fen-fen ho-ho san-shih-nien" (The nonpartisans: Three decades of unity and feud). *SPTC*, no. 241 (July 11): 31–35.

Ch'iu Jung-chu and Li Pi-ju. 1984. "San shih wu nien nei-ke ta-kuan" (Cabinets in the past 35 years: An overview). *SPTC*, no. 227 (April 4): 19–25.

Chou Hsi, 1987. "Wo-kuo wai-chiao ch'u-ching hui-sheng chung" (Improving the diplomatic status of our country). *Yuan chien* (Global Views Monthly), no. 8 (February 1): 38–42.

Chou Yangsun and Nathan, Andrew J. 1987. "Democratizing Transition in Taiwan." *AS* 27, no. 3 (March): 277–99.

Chu Hai-yuen. 1982. "Cheng chiao kuan-hsi te su-k'ao: T'ai-wan chi-tu chang-lao-hui" (On state and church relations: The Taiwan Presbyterian Church). *LHYK*, no. 6 (January): 38–49.

Chu Yun-han. 1988. "Liang an ching mao kuan-hsi chu-tung ch'u chu" (Take positive action to deal with Taiwan-Mainland trade relations). *CKSP*, December 18, 2.

Ch'ü Chao-hsiang. 1984. "Cheng-tang yu cheng-chih ch'an-yu, Min-Kuo ch'i-shih-erh nien t'ai-pei-shih li-fa-wei-yuan hsuan-chi chung-kuo kuo-min-tang te cheng-chih chiao-she te yen-chiu" (Party and political participation: A study of the KMT role in the 1983 supplementary election in Taipei). Master's thesis, National Taiwan University, Taipei.

Chuang Feng-ho, 1985. "Kuo-min-tang te she-hui k'ung-chih shu" (Social control of the KMT). *PSNT*, no. 87 (October 19): 49–51.

Chung Wong. 1985. "Industries Gain Momentum." *FCJ*, March 24, 2.

Chung-hua Min-kuo hsin-wen nien-chien (ROC news media yearbook). 1981. Taipei: Hsin-wen Chi-che Kung-hui.

"Chung-kuo min-chu-tang yu tzu-yu chung-kuo" (China Democratic Party and free China). 1983. *LHYK*, no. 25 (August): 16.

Clough, Ralph. 1978. *Island China.* Cambridge, Mass.: Harvard University Press:

———. 1984a. "The Republic of China and the World, 1949–1981." In Hungdah Chiu and Shao-ch'uan Leng, eds. *China: Seventy Years After the 1911 Hsin-hai Revolution.* Charlottesville: University Press of Virginia.

———. 1984b. "Taiwan's Expanding World Connections." *American Asian Review* 1, no. 4 (Winter): 3–6.

Cohen, Jerome Alan; Friedman, Edward; Hinton, C. Harold; and Whiting Allen S. 1971. *Taiwan and American Policy.* New York: Praeger.

Copper, John Franklin. 1982. "Taiwan in 1981: In a Holding Pattern." *AS* 22, no. 1 (January): 41, 48–49, 51.

———. 1984. "Taiwan's Foreign Policy: Diplomacy to Prevent Isolation." Paper presented at the Annual Meeting of the Mid-Atlantic Association for Asian Studies, Princeton, N.J., November 10–11.

Copper, John Franklin, with Chen, George P. 1984. "Taiwan's Elections: Political Development and Democratization in the Republic of China." Occasional

Papers/Reprints Series in Contemporary Asian Studies, no. 5. Baltimore: University of Maryland School of Law.

Cornelius, Wayne A., and Craig, Ann L. 1988. "Mexico." In Gabriel A. Almond and G. Bindham Powell, Jr., eds., *Comparative Politics Today.* Boston: Little, Brown.

Crissman, Lawrence W. 1975. "Government and Political Oppositions." In Fred Greenstein and Nelson W. Polsby, eds., *Macropolitical Theory.* Reading, Mass.: Addison-Wesley.

———. 1981. "The Structure of Local and Regional Systems." In Emily Martin Ahern and Hill Gates, eds., *The Anthropology of Taiwanese Society.* Stanford: Stanford University Press.

Cutright, Phillips. 1963. "National Political Development: Measurement and Analysis." *American Sociological Review,* no. 28: 253–64.

CYACL. 1982. "Lu ch'i p'iao-yang san shih nien" (The green flag: Thirty years' swaggering in the sky). Taipei: CYACL Headquarters.

Dahl, Robert A. 1966. "Patterns of Opposition." In Robert Dahl, ed,. *Political Oppositions in Western Democracy.* New Haven: Yale University Press.

———. 1971. *Polyarchy, Participation, and Opposition.* New Haven: Yale University Press.

———. ed. 1974. *Regimes and Opposition.* New Haven: Yale University Press.

———. 1975. "Government and Political Opposition." In Fred I. Greenstein and Nelson W. Polsby, eds. *Macropolitical Theory.* Reading, Mass.: Addison-Wesley.

Deutsch, Karl W. 1961. "Social Mobilization and Political Development." *American Political Science Review* 55, no. 3 (September): 507.

———. 1966. *Nationalism and Social Communication.* 2d ed. Cambridge, Mass.: MIT Press.

Dix, Robert H. 1974. "Latin America: Oppositions and Development." In Robert Dahl, ed. *Regimes and Opposition.* New Haven: Yale University Press.

Domes, Jurgen. 1981. "Political Differentiation in Taiwan." *AS* 21, no. 10 (October): 1011–29.

Duverger, Maurice. 1963. *Political Parties.* New York: Wiley.

Eastman, Lloyd E. 1974. *The Abortive Revolution: China Under Nationalist Rule, 1927–1937.* Cambridge, Mass.: Harvard University Press.

Eckstein, Harry. 1961. *The Theory of Stable Democracy.* Princeton: Princeton University Press.

———. 1966. *Division and Cohesion in Democracy: A Study of Norway.* Princeton: Princeton University Press.

———. 1982. "The Idea of Political Development: From Dignity to Efficiency." *World Politics* 34, no. 4 (July): 451–86.

Emerson, Rupert. 1978. *Political Modernization: The Single-Party System.* Denver: University of Denver.

Engstrom, Richard L., and Chu Chi-hung. 1984. "The Impact of the 1980 Supplementary Election on Nationalist China's Legislative Yuan." *AS* 24, no. 4 (April): 454–57.

Enloe, Cynthia H. 1973. *Ethnic Conflict and Political Development*. Boston: Little, Brown.

Fan Hsiang-lin. 1984. "Fang Chen Chin-jang t'an pei shih tang-wu"(An interview with Chen Chin-jang on Taipei party affairs). *SPTC*, no. 252 (September 26): 20–21.

Fang Yen. 1982. "Ts'ung hsuan-chu k'an ti-fang tang-wu ho ch'u ho ts'ung" (Elections and the prospect of future local party affairs). *Ta-hsueh tsa-chih (College Journal)*, no. 155 (June): 16–17.

Fang Yi-jen. 1985. "Hsien chieh-tuan shih-hsing lao-chi-fa te wen-t'i" (Problems of implementing the labor law now). *LHYK*, no. 48 (July): 10–14, 77–88.

"Fang-wen pien-lien-hui chung-kan-shih Liu Shou-ch'eng" (Interview with Liu Shou-cheng, general director of the Tangwai Editors' Association). 1985. *TWMP*, August 24, 2.

Fei, C. H.; Gustav, Ranis; and Kuo, Shirley W. Y. 1979. *Growth with Equality: The Taiwan Case*. New York: Oxford University Press.

Feldman, Harvey J. "The Development of United States–Taiwan Relations, 1948–1987." Paper presented at the Third International Congress of Professors, World Peace Academy, Manila, August 24–29, 1987.

"Five Years of U.S.–Chinese Relations." 1984. *Christian Science Monitor,* April 23, 14–15.

Foltz, William J. 1974. "Political Opposition in Tropical Africa." In Robert A. Dahl, ed., *Regimes and Opposition*. New Haven: Yale University Press.

Friedman, Edward. 1981. "Military Security on Taiwan and the Sale of Advanced Military Aircraft." U.S. House of Representatives. Committee on Foreign Affairs. Memo, March 18.

Friedrich, Carl J., and Brzezinski, Zbigniew K. 1975. *Totalitarian Dictatorship and Autocracy*. 2d ed. Cambridge, Mass.: Harvard University Press.

Fromm, Joseph, and Hildreth, James. 1984. "What Reagan Wants from Peking." *U.S. News and World Report,* April 20, 31–33.

Fukui, Haruhiro. 1978. "Japan: Factionalism in a Dominant-Party System." In Frank P. Belloni and Dennis C. Beller, eds., *Faction Politics: Political Parties and Factionalism in Comparative Perspective*, 43–72. Santa Barbara: ABC Clio.

Galang, Jose. 1985. "A Lot's in a Name: China Appears on the Point of Joining ADB." *FEER*, December 5, 101.

Galenson, Walter, ed. 1979. *Economic Growth and Structural Change in Taiwan*. Ithaca: Cornell University Press.

Gallin, Bernard. 1963. "Land Reform in Taiwan: Its Effect on Rural Social Organization and Leadership." *Human Organization* 22, no. 2 (Summer): 109–12.

_____. 1964. "Rural Development in Taiwan: The Rule of the Government." *Rural Society* 29: 317–18.

_____. 1968. "Political Factionalism and Its Impact on Chinese Village Social Organization in Taiwan." In Marc J. Swartz, ed., *Local-Level Politics*. Chicago: Aldine.

Gallin, Bernard, and Gallin, Rita S. 1977. "Sociopolitical Power and Sworn Brother Groups in Chinese Society: A Taiwanese Case." In *Anthropology of Power.* New York: Academic Press.

Gamarnikow, Michael. 1967. "Poland's Political Pluralism in a One-Party State." *Problems of Communism* 16, no. 4 (July–August): 1–13.

Garver, John W. 1978. "Taiwan's Russian Option: Image and Reality." *AS* 18, no. 7 (July): 755–57.

Gastil, Raymond D. 1987. *Freedom in the World: Political Rights and Civil Liberties, 1985–1986.* New York: Greenwood Press.

Gates, Hill. 1981. "Ethnicity and Social Class." In Emily Martin Ahern and Hill Gates, eds., *The Anthropology of Taiwanese Society.* Stanford: Stanford University Press.

Gerth, H. H., and Mills, C. Wright. 1958. *From Max Weber: Essays in Sociology.* New York: Oxford University Press.

Gold, Thomas B. 1986. *State and Society in the Taiwan Miracle.* New York and London: M. E. Sharpe.

_____. 1987a. "Popular Culture and Society in Taiwan." Paper presented at the China Council Conference on Taiwan Entering the 21st Century, The Asia Society, New York, April 23–25.

_____. 1987b. "The Status Quo Is Not Static: Mainland-Taiwan Relations." *AS* 27, no. 3 (March): 300–315.

Goldstein, Carl. 1985a. "Eye in the Tang Wai." *FEER,* February 14, 21–22.

_____. 1985b. "The New Ending Story." *FEER,* September 12, 93–94.

_____. 1986a. "Dominance of Taipei's Big Two." *FEER,* December 26, 27–29.

_____. 1986b. "Growing Economic Ties but No Political Trust." *FEER,* July 24, 24–25.

_____. 1986c. "KMT Power Grows out of a Holstered Gun." *FEER,* May 8, 24–25.

_____. 1986d. "Power of the Old Guard." *FEER,* April 10, 16.

_____. 1986e. "The Straight and Narrow." *FEER,* December 26, 26–28.

_____. 1986f. "Taiwan Seeks Outlets for Burgeoning Reserves." *FEER,* January 23, 46.

_____. 1986g. "A View from the Wings." *FEER,* March 20, 16–17.

_____. 1987a. "A Gift in Power." *FEER,* February 26, 12–13.

_____. 1987b. "Political Muscle-Flexing." *FEER,* March 5, 40–41.

_____. 1987c. "Rally for Democracy." *FEER,* December 3, 40–41.

_____. 1987d. "Students Seek Freedoms." *FEER,* February 12, 21–22.

Grant, Wyn, ed. 1985.*The Political Economy of Corporatism.* London: Macmillan.

Greenhalgh, S. 1984. "Networks and Their Nodes: Urban Society on Taiwan."*CQ* 2 (September): 531–40.

Greenstein, Fred I., and Huntington, Samuel P. 1975. "Political Development." In Fred I. Greenstein and Nelson W. Polsby, eds., *Macropolitical Theory.* Reading, Mass.: Addison-Wesley.

Gregor, A. James, and Chang, Maria Hsia. 1983. *The Republic of China and U.S. Policy: A Study in Human Rights.* Washington, D.C.: Ethics and Public Policy Center.

_____. 1983. *Essays on Sun Yat-sen and the Economic Development of Taiwan.* Occasional Papers/Reprints Series in Contemporary Asian Studies, no. 1. Baltimore: University of Maryland, School of Law.

Gurr, Ted Robert. 1973. "The Revolution–Social Changes Nexus."*Comparative Politics* 5 (April): 363–78.

Gurtuv, Melvin. 1967. "Recent Development in Formosa." *CQ* 31: 59–95.

Haberman, Clyde. 1985. "An Opposition Party Gets Strong Support in South Korea Vote." *NYT* February 13, 1.

Haggard, Stephan, and Cheng Tun-jen. 1987. "State and Foreign Capital in the East Asian NICs." In Frederic C. Deyo, ed., *The Political Economy of the New Asian Industrialism,* 4–129. Ithaca: Cornell University Press.

Han I. 1984. "Kou yao tzu-chi te wei-pa, Li-fa-yuan te p'ai-hsi tou-cheng" (Dogs bite their own tails: Factional struggle in the Legislative Yuan). *Chien-chin shih-chieh* (Progressive World) 4 (April 7): 9–13.

Hardgrave, Robert L., Jr. 1980. *India: Government and Politics in a Developing Nation.* 3d ed. New York: Harcourt Brace Jovanovich.

Harrison, Reginald J. 1980. *Pluralism and Corporatism: The Political Evolution of Modern Democracies.* London: Allen & Unwin.

Hau Ming-yi and Yang Shao-huan. 1988. "Chu-hsi ti ku-shih" (The story of the KMT Chairman). *SPCK,* no. 154 (February 6) : 6–9.

Hau Yu-mei. 1981. *Chung-kuo Kuo-min-tang t'i-ming chih-tu chih yen-chiu* (A study of the KMT's nomination system). Taipei: Cheng-chung.

Himmelstrand, Ulf. 1964 "Depoliticization and Political Involvement." In Erik Allardt and Yijo Littunen, eds., *Cleavages, Ideologies and Party System.* Turku: Westermarck Society.

Hinton, Harold C. 1985. "Taiwan's Future Responses to International and Regional Challenges: A North American Perspective." Paper prepared for the Alantic Council of the United States, George Washington University, March.

Ho Chen-fen. 1985a. "Hsien shih chang hsuan-ch'ing fen-hsi" (An analysis of electoral campaigns for mayors and county magistrates) *LHYK,* no.45 (April): 14–18.

_____. 1985b. "Sheng yi-yuan hsuan-ch'ing fen-hsi" (An analysis of electoral campaigns for the provincial assemblymen). *LHYK,* no. 45 (April): 23–26.

Ho, Samuel P. S. 1987. *Economic Development of Taiwan, 1860–1970.* New Haven: Yale University Press.

Hofheinz, Roy, Jr. 1969. "The Ecology of Chinese Communist Success: Rural Influence Patterns, 1923-1945." In A. Doak Barnett, ed. *Chinese Communist Politics in Action,* 3–77. Seattle: University of Washington Press.

Hoon, Shim Joe. 1988a. "Parting of the Ways." *FEER,* August 18, 27.

_____. 1988b. "Sweet Sorrow for Those Long Parted." *FEER,* January 14, 40–41.

_____. 1988c. "Taiwan: Clairon Call to Workers." *FEER,* January 21, 18–19.

Hoselitz, Bert, and Moore, Wilbert, eds. 1970. *Industrialization and Society.* Paris: UNESCO, Mouton.

Hsi Hsien-te. 1985. "Yu Tai-fei cheng-tun shih-chi k'an kuo-ying shih-yeh ch'ien-t'u" (Putting Taiwan fertilizer company in order: The future of national enterprises). *LHYK,* no. 47 (June): 77–79.

_____. 1986. "Tang ch'ien wai-chiao kung-tso te ping yu you" (The ailing state of current diplomacy). *LHYK,* no. 47 (June): 7–39.

Hsiang Ch'ang-ch'uan. 1969. *T'ai-wan ti-fang hsuan-chu chih fen-hsi yu chien-t'ao* (An analysis of Taiwan's local elections). Taipei: Shang-wu.

_____. 1972. *T'ai-wan ti-fang i-hui yu ti-fang cheng-fu chih ch'uan-tse yu ch'i hsiang-hu kuang-hsi chih chien-t'ao* (Local legislatures and local governments on Taiwan: An overview of their powers and mutual relations). Taipei: Shang-wu.

Hsiao, Frank S. T., and Sullivan, Lawrence R. 1980. "The Politics of Reunification: Beijing's Initiative on Taiwan." *AS* 20, no. 8 (August): 784–93.

Hsiao Hsin-huang. 1984. "Shui tsai Li-fa-yuan wei lung-yeh ch'ing-ming?" (Who works for the agricultural interests in the Legislative Yuan?). *SPTC,* no. 184 (June 12): 8–11.

_____. 1985. "Tai-wan she hui chieh-ko chuan-hsing te tsai t'an-so" (An inquiry into the transition of Taiwan's social structure). Paper presented at Nan-yuan Conference, Taipei, December 27–29.

Hsiao Li-ch'eng. 1986. "Lien-ho tso-t'an-hui p'ai ch'ou-mu chu chin tang kuo yuan-lao ta chang p'ai-hsi ch'i-ku" (*Lien-ho tso-t'an-hui* factions raises huge funds signaling revival of factional strife among party old guards). *PSNT,* no. 104 (March 27): 26.

Hsieh Chiao Chiao. 1985. *Strategy For Survival.* London: Sherwood Press.

Hsieh Ch'un-sheng. 1984. "Ti-fang i-hui chung te Kuo-min-tang ying-tzu" (KMT shadow over local legislatures). *PSNT,* no. 40 (July 15): 31–33.

Hsieh Fu-sheng. 1983. "Hsuan-chü, cheng-tang yu min-chu"(Elections, political party, and democracy). *LHYK,* no. 27 (December): 5–8.

Hsieh Tzu-i. 1979. "Hsin-sheng-tai te hui-hsiang, chen-chih to yuan hua" (Repercussions from the younger opposition activists—political pluralism). *Kuo-chia lun-t'an* (National Review) 12, no. 10 (October): 5–6.

Hsu Chia-shih, Pan Chia-ch'ing, and Chao Ying. 1978. "Kai-chin T'ai-wan ti-ch'u ta-chung ch'uan-po kuo-chia chih fa-chan kung-neng ti yen-chiu" (Nation-building functions of the mass media in Taiwan). *Hsin-wen-hsueh yen-chiu* (Studies of Journalism), no. 21 (May 20): 1–14.

Hsu En-p'w. 1980. *Wo-kuo kuang-po tien-shih fa chih-ting kuo-ch'eng te yen-chiu* (Legislative process of the ROC's Broadcasting Law). Master's thesis, Cheng-chih University, Mucha, Taiwan.

Hsu Fu-ming. 1984. *Chung-kuo Kuo-min-tang te kai-chao 1950–1952* (Reorganization of the KMT, 1950–1952). Master's thesis, National Taiwan University, Taipei.

Hsu Hui-ling. 1982. "Wo-kuo pao-chih yi-t'i she-ting kung-neng chih yen-chiu" (A study of topical selection in Taiwan's newspaper columns). Master's thesis, Cheng-chih University, Mucha, Taiwan.

Hsu Ya-yüan. 1983. "Lao-kung li-fa pu-jung hu-shih" (Do not ignore labor law legislation). *SPTC,* no. 12 (July 10): 45–47.

Hu Fo. 1983. "Tzu-chu, tzu-chih, to-yuan ch'uan" (Autonomy, self-governance, and pluralistic power). *CKLT* 17, no. 5 (December 10):18–19.

_____. 1985. "Hsien-cheng chieh-kuo te liu-pien yu ch'ung-cheng" (Change and consolidation in constitutional order). Paper presented at Nan-yuan Conference, Taipei, December 27–29.

Hu Fo and Yu Ying-lung. 1983. "Hsuan-min te tang-p'ai hsuan-tse: T'ai-tu ch'u-hsiang chi ko-jen pei-ching te fen-hsi" (Partisan choice of the Voters: An analysis of their attitudes and background). *Cheng-chih hsueh-pao* (Journal of Politics), no. 21 (December 16): 31–53.

Hu Hung-jen and Lin Ho-ling. 1981. "T'ai-wan ti-fang p'ai-hsi ta-kuan" (An overview of Taiwan's local factionalism). *LHYK,* no. 3 (October): 12–23.

Hu Kuang-ch'i. 1986. "I wei t'ui-hsiu chung-chiang te kao-pai"(Revelation of a retired general). *PSNT,* no. 100 (January 25): 4–10.

Hu Yüan-hui. 1982. "San shih nien lai wo-kuo hsien-fa pao-chang hsia ch'u-pan tzu-yu chih yen-chiu" (A study of three decades of freedom of the press in Taiwan under constitutional protection). *Chen-chih ta-hsueh cheng-chih yen-chiu-so nien-k'an*(Annual Bulletin of Political Science, Cheng-chih University) 16 (June 15): 6–13.

Huang Chen-hui. 1987. "Pen-t'u-hua, shih tzu-jan yeh shih pi-jan" (Taiwanization: Both natural and inevitable). *SPHWCK,* no. 51 (May 19): 12–16.

Huang Hui-chen. 1983. "Ts'ung chieh-kou yu kung-neng k'an Kuo-min-tang ch'i jen t'i-ming hsiao-tsu" (Structural and functional significance of the KMT seven-man nomination committee). *SPTC,* no. 193 (August 14): 10–13.

_____. 1985. "Liu wei li jen chung-yang tang-pu pi-shu-chang te ching-li" (Profile of six KMT Central Committee secretary generals). *SPCK,* no. 351 (February 16): 60–61.

Huang Kuang-kuo. 1984. "Ts'ung T'ai-wan ching-yen k'an shih-su fa ju-chia yu tzu-pen chu-i fa-chan" (Confucianism and capitalist development: The Taiwan experience). *CKLT,* no. 222 (December 25): 3–8.

_____. 1987. "Chung-kuo chieh yu T'ai-wan chieh: Tui-k'ang yu ch'u-lu" (China ties and Taiwan ties: Confrontation and reconciliation). *CKLT,* no. 289 (October 10): 1–18.

Huang Su-chi. 1983. "Li-fa-yuan te chin-jih ch'un-ch'iu" (The Legislative Yuan in action). *LHYK,* no. 12 (July): 9–21.

Huang Su-chuan. 1986a. "Chui-chiu shih-hsin che-jen" (Hold the tenth credit case accountable). *LHYK,* no. 19 (August): 21–26.

_____. 1986b. "Shih-hsin feng-pao tai-chia ch'an-chung"(High cost of the stormy tenth credit scandal). *LHYK,* no.54 (January): 24–25.

Huang, Wei-hsiang. 1986. "Jang Kuo-min-tang t'ou t'ung i t'ou, chiao t'ung i chiao pa!" (Let the KMT solve its problems when they surface!). *SK,* no. 17 (September 10): 30–31.

Huang Yen-tung. 1984. *Liu shih nien lai Chung-kuo Kuo-min-tang tang cheng kuang-hsi chih yen-chiu* (Six decades of KMT party-state relations). Taipei: San-min-chu-i Institute, National Taiwan University.

Hung Chin-chu. 1984. "Ch'eng-chang chung te lao-tzu chiu-fen" (The growth of labor disputes). *SPTC*, no. 239 (June 27): 7–10.

Huntington, Samuel P. 1968. *Political Order in Changing Societies*. New Haven: Yale University Press.

Huntington, Samuel P. 1984. "Will More Countries Become Democratic?" *Political Science Quarterly* 99, no. 2 (Summer), 193–218.

Huntington, Samuel P., and Dominiquez, Jorge I. 1978. "Political Development." In Fred I. Greenstein and Nelson W. Polsby, eds., *Macro-political Theory*. Reading, Mass.: Addison-Wesley.

Huntington, Samuel P., and Moore, Clement H. 1970. *Authoritarian Politics in Modern Society*. New York: Basic Books.

Ike, Nobutaka. 1957. *Japanese Politics: Patron-Client Democracy*. 2d ed. New York: Knopf.

International Committee for Human Rights in Taiwan. 1985. *Taiwan Communiqué*, no. 18 (February 8): 16–18.

––––––. 1986. *Taiwan Communiqué*, no. 24 (February 8): 16.

––––––. 1987. *Taiwan Communiqué*, no. 29 (March 28): 19–20.

International Institute for Strategic Studies. 1987. *The Military Balance*. London: International Institute for Strategic Studies.

Jacobs, J. Bruce. 1973. "Taiwan 1972: Political Season." *AS* 13, no. 1 (January): 101–12.

––––––. 1974. "Taiwan 1973: Consolidation of the Succession." *AS* 14, no. 1 (January): 22–29.

––––––. 1976a. "The Cultural Bases of Factional Alignment and Division in a Rural Taiwanese Township." *Journal of Asian Studies* 36, no. 1 (November): 81–82.

––––––. 1976b. "Taiwan's Press: Political Communications Link and Research Resource." *CQ* 68 (December): 778–85.

––––––. 1978. "Paradoxes in the Politics of Taiwan: Lessons for Comparative Politics." *Politics* 13, no. 2 (November): 240, 243–46.

––––––. 1979. "Taiwan 1978: Economic Success, International Uncertainties." *AS* 19, no. 1 (January): 20–28.

––––––. 1980. *Local politics in Rural Chinese Cultural Settings*. Canberra: Australian National University, Contemporary China Centre.

––––––. 1981. "Political Opposition and Taiwan's Political Future." *Australian Journal of Chinese Affairs*, no. 6 (July): 21–40.

Jacoby, Neil. 1966. *U.S. Aid to Taiwan*. New York: Praeger.

Jao Hsiao-ming. 1982. *Chung-hua Min-kuo tien-shih shih-yeh te hui-ku yu ch'ien-chan* (The development of Taiwan's TV enterprises and their future prospect). Taipei: China Television Corporation.

Johnson, Chalmers A. 1962. *Peasant Nationalism and Communist Power: The Emergence of Revolutionary China, 1937–1945*. Stanford: Stanford University Press.

———. 1969. "A China Policy for the Seventies." In Paul Seabury and Aaron Wildavsky, eds., *U.S. Foreign Policy: Perspectives and Proposals for the 1970s.* New York: McGraw-Hill.

———, ed. 1984. *Change in Communist System.* Stanford: Stanford University Press.

———. 1987. "Political Institutions and Economic Performance: The Government-Business Relationship in Japan, South Korea, and Taiwan." In Frederic C. Deyo, ed., *The Political Economy of the New Asian Industrialism*, 136–64. Ithaca: Cornell University Press.

Johnstone, Bob. 1988. "Diverting the Brain Drain." *FEER*, January 28, 70–71.

Jung Wu-t'ien. 1985. "Huang Chun-ch'iu ch'an-yu t'i-ming chueh-ts'e" (Huang Chun-ch'iu participates in the party's nomination exercise). *LHYK*, no. 49 (August): 16.

Kang Ning-hsiang. 1985. "T'ai-wan cheng-chih ho wai-chiao te ch'u-lu" (Taiwan's political and diplomatic prospects). *PSNT*, no. 17 (November): 53.

Kao Ch'eng-shu. 1985. "T'ai-wan szu shih nien lai she-hui chieh-ko pien-ch'ien ch'u t'an" (A study of Taiwan's social change in four decades). In Taiwan Provincial Government, *T'ai-wan kuang-fu szu shih nien chuan-chi* (A commemorative volume on Taiwan after four decades' return to China). Taichung: Taiwan Provincial Government.

Kao Hui-yu. 1981. "Kuo-min-tang chung-yang ch'uan-li chi-ko te ch'iang-hua" (Strengthen the KMT's central power organs). *LHP*, April 4, 2.

Kao Yung. 1986. "Min-chu-chin-pu-tang p'ai-hsi pen-cheng fen-hsi" (An analysis of factional conflicts in the Democratic Progressive Party). *CP*, November 22, 2.

Kaplan, John. 1981. *The Court-Martial of the Kaohsiung Defendants.* Berkeley: University of California, Institute of East Asian Studies.

Kataoka, Tetsuya. 1974. *Resistance and Revolution in China.* Berkeley and Los Angeles: University of California Press.

Kau Michael Y. M. 1986. "Challenges to Taiwan's International Position." Paper presented at the annual meeting of the Association for Asian Studies, Chicago, March 21–23.

Kaufman, Robert R. 1974. "The Patron-Client Concept and Macropolitics: Prospects and Problems." *Comparative Studies in Society and History* 16, no. 3 (June): 284–308.

Kaufman, Susan, and Purcell, John F. H. 1980. "State and Society in Mexico." *World Politics* 32, no. 2 (January): 199–208.

Kerr, George H. 1965. *Formosa Betrayed.* Boston: Houghton Mifflin.

Key, V. O. 1964. *Politics, Parties and Pressure Groups.* New York: Thomas Y. Crowell.

Kim, Chong Lim; Green, Justin; and Patterson, Samuel C. 1976. "Partisanship in the Recruitment and Performance of American State Legislators." In Heinz Eulau and Moshe M. Czudnowski, eds., *Elite Recruitment in Democratic Politics: Comparative Studies Across Nations.* New York: Sage.

Kissinger, Henry. 1979. *White House Years.* Boston: Little, Brown.

KMT. 1951. *Taiwan tang-wu* (Taiwan party affairs), February 16, 24.

————. 1953. *Taiwan tang-wu* (Taiwan party affairs), July 16, 43–49.

————. Department of Cultural Affairs. 1974. *Ti ssu tz'u hsin-wen kung-tso hui-t'an shih-lu* (A documentary on the fourth work conference of the press). Taipei: Kuo-min-tang Wen-kung-hui.

————. Party History Commission. 1981. *Chung-kuo Kuo-min-tang liu shih chiu nien kung-tso chi-shih* (KMT party work in 1980). Taipei: Chin-tai Chung-kuo.

Ko Yung-kuang. 1980. *Chung Jih Han cheng-tang pi-chiao yen-chiu: Cheng-chi hsi-tung te kung-neng fen-hsi* (A comparative study of political parties in the Republic of China, Japan, and South Korea: A functional analysis of political systems). Master's thesis, National Taiwan University, Taipei.

Koen, Rose Y. 1974. *The China Lobby in American Politics*. New York: Harper & Row.

Kornhauser, William. 1969. *The Politics of Mass Society*. New York: Free Press.

K'ou Ssu-lei. 1982. "T'ou-shih li-fa ch'eng-hsu shang te tang-cheng hsueh-t'iao" (A close look at party-state relations in the legislative process). *LHYK*, no. 17 (December): 18–21.

K'ou Wei-yung. 1983. "Ts'ung tsai-yeh tsa-chih shih-chien k'an Ch'ing-nien-tang" (The China Youth Party and the Tsai-yeh Magazine Incident). *LHYK*, no. 19 (February): 24–33.

Kraar, Louis. 1986. "Taiwan: Trading with the Enemy." *Fortune*, February 17, 89.

Kuan Fan-chieh. 1985. "I ke kuo-chia, liang chung chih-tu yu k'ou-ta ai-kuo t'ung-i chan-hsien wen-t'i" ("One nation, two systems" and the question of a broader patriotic united front). *Cheng-chih-hsueh yen-chiu* (Studies of Political Science), no. 2 (Spring): 8–11.

Kuan Ta-kung. 1987. "Min-chin-tang ling-tao pan-tzu ta huan hsueh" (A great turnover in the Democratic Progressive Party leadership). *HHW*, no. 36 (November 16): 15–19.

————. 1988. "'Chi-szu-hui' k'ai-ch'iu Kuo-min-tang luan le" ("The breakfast club for common views" kicks off, and the KMT becomes divided). *HHW*, no. 59 (April 25): 18–22.

Kung T'ung-wen. 1981. "T'sung ch'ung-t'u tao t'iao-shih chih lu: T'ou-pien chung te li-ya-yuan tang-cheng kuan-hsi" (From conflict to conciliation: The changing party-state relations in the Legislative Yuan). *SPTC*, no. 88 (August 9): 6–7.

Kuo Ch'ung-lun. 1987. "Hsin p'ai-hsi ho-tsung, lao p'ai-hsi lien-heng" (New allies, old factions). *SPHWCK*, no. 47 (April 21): 50–54.

Kuo Hung-chi. 1987. "Chin shu chin shu wo ai ni" (Censored books, I love you). *HHW*, no. 18 (July 13): 16–20.

Kuo, Shirley W. Y. 1983. *The Taiwan Economy in Transition*. Boulder: Westview Press.

Kuo, Shirley W. Y.; Ranis, Gustav; and Fei, John C. H. 1981. *The Taiwan Success Story: Rapid Growth with Improved Distribution in the Republic of China, 1952–1979*. Boulder: Westview Press.

Kurian, George T. 1984. *The New Book of World Rankings*. New York: Facts on File.

Kuznets, Simon. 1979. "Growth and Structural Shifts." In Walter Galenson, ed., *Economic Growth and Structural Change in Taiwan*. Ithaca: Cornell University Press.

Lai Kuang-lin. 1983. *Ch'i shih nien Chung-kuo pao-yeh shih* (Seven decades of press history in China). Taipei: Chung-yang jih-pao.

Lai Kuo-chou. 1979. "Chung mei tuan-chiao ch'ien hou ssu pao yao-wen she-lun ch'u-li chih yen-chiu" (A study of four major newspapers: News coverage and editorial treatments of U.S. diplomatic derecognition of the ROC). *Pao hsueh* (Journalism) 6, no. 3 (December): 14–31.

Lai Tsu-i. 1987. "Szu-i-chiu fen-lieh; wu-i-ch'iu t'uan-chieh" (Is the April 19 Incident cause for friction and the May 19 Incident for unity?). *HHW*, no. 7 (April 27): 20–21.

Landé, Carl H. 1977. "Introduction: The Dyadic Basis of Clientelism." In Steffen W. Schmidt, James C. Scott, Carl Landé, and Laura Guasti, eds., *Friends, Followers, and Factions*, xiii–xxxvii. Berkeley and Los Angeles: University of California Press.

LaPalombara, Joseph, and Weiner, Myron, eds. 1966. *Political Parties and Political Development*. Princeton: Princeton University Press.

Lee Teng-hui. 1983. *Agriculture and Economic Development in Taiwan*. Vols. 1, 2, and 3. Taichung, Taiwan: Ta-hung.

Lei Chen. 1952. "Kung-hsien kei Li-fa-yuan chi tien yi-chien" (A few suggestions for members of the Legislative Yuan). *Chih-yu Chung-kuo* (Free China), 7, no. 7 (April 1), 209–11.

———. 1978. *Lei Chen hui-i-lu* (Lei Chen's memoirs). Hong Kong: Ch'i Shih Nien-tai.

Lemarchand, René, and Legg, Keith. 1972. "Political Clientelism and Development: A Preliminary Analysis." *Comparative Politics*, 4, no. 2 (January): 151–52, 158.

Lerman, Arthur J. 1977. "National Elite and Local Politicians in Taiwan." *American Political Science Review* 71, no. 4 (December): 1420–21.

———. 1978. *Taiwan's Politics: The Provincial Assemblyman's World*. Washington, D.C.: University Press of America.

Lerner, Daniel. 1958. *The Passing of Traditional Society*. Glencoe, Ill.: Free Press.

Li Ao. 1983. "Kuo-min-tang ta sheng? hai-shih tang-wai ta sheng?" (A great victory for the KMT or the Tangwai?). *MCJ*, no. 23 (December 16): 4–8.

Li Chan. 1973. *Pi-chiao tien-shih chih-tu chien-lun wo-kuo tien-shih fa-chan chih fang-hsiang* (Comparing TV broadcasting systems, and a study of Taiwan's television development). Mucha, Taiwan: Graduate Department of Journalism, Cheng-chih University.

———. 1974. *Wo-kuo tien-shih hsi-t'ung yu cheng-ts'e chih t'an-t'ao* (A study of Taiwan's TV broadcasting system and its policy). Taipei: RDEC.

Li Chan-t'ai. 1982. *T'ai-wan ti-ch'u nung-hui chih yen-chiu* (A study of Taiwan farmers' associations). Master's thesis, National Taiwan University, Taipei.

Li Chieh. 1984. "Chien-ch'a chih-tu tsou-tao le chin-t'ou?" (Have the Control Yuan functions reached a dead end?). *SPTC*, no. 217 (January 15): 12–15.

Li Chien-hsing. 1984. "Chiu-kuo-t'uan yu-suan chih to-shao?" (What is the budget of the Chinese Youth Anti-Communist League?). *TWKC*, no. 3 (June 29): 13–15.

Li Heng-li. 1984. "Hsiao-yuan chung te tang cheng chin t'uan t'e" (Party and state agencies on campuses). *TWKC*, no. 6 (July 20): 6–11.

Li Hung-hsi. 1983. "Hsien-fa chi-pen kai-nien chih ch'eng-ch'ing" (Clarifying basic concepts in the constitution). *CKLT* 16, no. 185 (June 10): 14–16.

———. 1985. "Chan-hou T'ai-wan fa-chih t'i-chih fa-chan chih cheng-chieh" (Dilemma of post–World War II development of legal institution in Taiwan). In *T'ai-wan ti-ch'u she-hui pien-ch'ien yu wen-hua fa-chan* (Social change and cultural development in Taiwan), 179–209. Taipei: Chung-kuo Lun-t'an.

Li I-kuang. 1984. "Shengi-hui Kuo-min-tang tang-pien fu-ch'en-lu" (The ups and downs of KMT party discipline in the Provincial Assembly). *SPTC*, no. 253 (October 31): 41–47.

Li Kung-ch'uan. 1984. "T'ai-wan Li-fa-yuan te kuei-fan" (Norm of conduct in Taiwan's Legislative Yuan). *Hsien-tai kuo-chia* (Modern Nation) 108, no. 9 (January).

Li Kuo-ting. 1978. *T'ai-wan ching-chi k'uai-shih ch'eng-chang te ching-yen* (The Taiwan experience in rapid economic growth). Taipei: Cheng-chung.

Li Li. 1983. "Tang-wai te wen-tzu yu wen-jen" (Tangwai literatures and writers). *SGK*, no. 8 (May 10): 10–12.

Li Shouqui and He Fang. 1986. "The Relation Between Taiwan and the Mainland in Perspective." Paper presented at the anuual meeting of the Association for Asian Studies, Chicago, March 21–23.

Li Tien-meng. 1985. "Chung-chiao t'uan-t'i jo-hsin hung-yi ching-shen k'e-p'ei" (Praiseworthy public spirit of religious groups). *CYJP*, May 25, 2.

Li Wang-ch'eng. 1983. "Tang-wai te san ke ch'iang-pang" (*Tangwai*'s three tough figures). *MCJ*, April 1, 8–12.

Li Wang-t'ai. 1983. "T'ai-wan ti-fang p'ai-hsi hsin tung-hsiang" (New trend in Taiwan's local factionalism). *LHYK*, no. 22 (May): 21–25.

Li Wen-lang. 1987. "T'ai-wan te she-hui pien-ch'ien yu sheng chi wen-t'i chieh-chieh chih tao" (Social change in Taiwan and the solution to ethnic problems). *KCJP*, May 19, 2.

Li Wen-shih. 1983. "Lun kao-p'u k'ao sheng-chi yu-tai ts'un fei wen-t'i" (Quota by provincial origins in the civil service examinations: Should it continue?). *LHYK*, no. 23 (June): 46–50.

Li Ya-ch'ing. 1985. "Ch'iang-tiao ch'iang-jen che-hsueh te Kuan Chung" (Kuang Chung and his strongman philosophy). *SPTC*, no. 297 (August 7): 61.

Liang Shang-yung. 1985. "T'ai-wan kuang-fu szu shih nien lai chiao-yu wen-hua te fa-chan yu chan-wang" (Four decades of educational and cultural developments in Taiwan). In Taiwan Provincial Government, *T'ai-wan kuang-fu szu shih nien chuan-chi* (A commemorative volume on Taiwan after four decades' return to China). Taichung: Taiwan Provincial Government.

Liang Shuang-lien. 1984. "Chung-yang hsing-chen chi-kuan kung-wu jen-yen chih-tsu jen-t'ung te yen-chiu" (Party identity of civil servants in the national administration). Ph.D. diss., National Taiwan University, Taipei.

Liao Cheng-hung. 1985. "T'ai-wan ti-ch'u wei-lai shih nien chih jen-k'o yu jen-li tzu-yuan" (Taiwan's population and human resources in the next decade). Paper presented at Nan-yuan Conference, Taipei, December 27–29.

Liao Chi-ch'ing and T'ang Ming-yueh. 1984. *Hui-kuo hsueh-jen chi liu-hsueh-sheng fu-wu chuang-k'uang chih yen-chiu fen-hsi* (An analysis of overseas returned students and their employment situations). Taipei: Commission on Youth Assistance and Guidance, Executive Yuan.

Liao Chin-Kuei. 1988. "Shui lai wan-chiu chung-yang jih-pao?" (Who can rescue the *Central Daily News* from sinking circulation?). *HHW*, no. 75 (August 15): 76–78.

Ligphart, Arendt. 1975. *The Politics of Accommodation*. 2d. ed. Berkeley and Los Angeles: University of California Press.

Lin Cheng-chieh and Chang Fu-chung. 1978. *Hsuan-chu wan-shui* (Long life election). Washington, D.C.: Taiwan Monitor Reprint.

Lin Chia-ch'eng. 1983. "Chiang ya-li t'uan-t'i ho-tung na-ju cheng-kuei" (Accept the roles of pressure groups in the process of governing). *CKLT*, 16, no. 2 (April 25): 18–20.

Lin Chien-hsing. 1985. "Hsi-shou shih-san hsiung-ti" (A close view of the Thirteen Brothers). *SPTC*, no. 300 (August 28): 14–18.

Lin Ch'ing-ching. 1978. "Tui Kuo-min-tang hsien shih wei-yuan-hui te chi-tien kai-chin i-chien" (A proposal for improving the KMT county and city party committees). *Cheng-chih p'ing-lun* (Political Review) 36, no. 6 (July): 12.

Lin Ching-yuan. 1973. *Industrialization in Taiwan*. New York: Praeger.

Lin Chin-k'un. 1986a. "Fei-shui chih chan: An ch'ao hsiung-yung te shui-li-hui hsuan-chu" (Wealth in water: Turbulent election for members of the water irrigation association). *SPCK*, no. 60 (April 20): 69–73.

_____. 1986b. "Tang-wai tsu tang tien-shan lei-pen" (*Tangwai* forming political party at thundering speed). *SPCK*, no. 84 (October 4): 3–9.

_____. 1986c. "Ts'ung shou-tu k'ai-shih" (Begin with the capital). *SPCK*, no. 9 (May 25): 24–25.

Lin Ch'ung-hsuan. 1984. "Lung-chao T'ai-wan ch'ing-nien te chiu-kuo-t'uan" (Chinese Anti-Communist Youth League overshadows the life of Taiwan youth). *TWKC*, no. 3 (June 29): 18.

Lin Feng-sung. 1986. "Chi-ch'eng hsuan-chu te yi-han" (A regrettable local election). *SPCK*, no. 50 (February 9): 69–71.

Lin Hen. 1986. "San chung ch'uan-hui te jen-shih tiao-tung" (Personnel reshuffles at the KMT Third Plenum). *CSNT*, May, 46–48.

Lin I-Shu. 1985. "Tang-wai ch'an-hsuan hou-yen ts'e-lei" (*Tangwai* electoral campaign strategy). *SPTC*, no. 303 (September 18): 10.

Lin K'ai-hsiang. 1987. "Chiang Ching-kuo an p'ai hsieh-jen hou cheng-chu" (Chiang Ching-kuo shaped up the ruling circle for the future). *Lei sheng*, (Thunder) no. 176 (August 10): 4–11.

Lin Kuei-p'u. 1970. "Chung-kuo tang cheng kuan-hsi te p'o-shih" (Anatomy of ROC's party state relations). *Chung-shan hsueh-shu wen-hua chi-k'an* (Chung-shan Academic and Cultural Bulletin), no. 5 (March 12): 85–86.

Lin Po-sheng. 1985. "T'ai-wan wei-lai shih-nien tui-wai mao-i fa-chan chih fang-hsiang yu chan-wang" (Direction of and prospects for Taiwan's trade development in the next decade). Paper presented at Nan-yuan Conference, Taipei, December 27–29.

Lin Sheng fen, Chao Yung-mao, Tang Kuang-hua, and Wei Min. 1983. "Shui lai ch'iao tseng-erh li-fa wei-yuan chih men?" (Who lobbies the supplementary legislators?) *CKSP*, June 30, July 1.

Lin Yi-ling. 1987. "Ch'ueh-hsi te hui-yuan, chi-mo te wai-chiao-pu" (An absent member, the lonely foreign ministry), *LHYK*, no. 70 (May 1987): 14–15.

Lin Yo-yu. 1981. "T'ai-pei shih tang nei wai ching-hsuan ts'e-lei fen-hsi" (An analysis of KMT and opposition campaign strategies in Taipei). *LHYK*, no. 4 (November): 34–35.

Lindblom, Charles E. 1977. *Politics and Markets: The World's Political Economic Systems*. New York: Basic Books.

Linz, Juan J. 1970. "An Authoritarian Regime: Spain." In Erik Alardt, ed. *Mass Politics: Studies in Political Society*. New York: Free Press.

———. 1974. "Opposition in and Under an Authoritarian Regime: The Case of Spain." In Robert Dahl, ed., *Regimes and Opposition*. New Haven: Yale University Press.

———. 1975. "Totalitarian and Authoritarian Regimes." In Fred I. Greenstein and Nelson W. Polsby, eds., *Macropolitical Theory*. Reading, Mass.: Addison-Wesley.

Lipset, Seymour Martin. 1959. "Some Social Requisites of Democracy: Economic Development and Political Legitimacy." *American Political Science Review* 53 (March): 69–105.

Liu, Alan P. L. 1982. *Social Change on Mainland and Taiwan, 1949–1980*. Occasional Papers/Reprints Series in Contemporary Asian Studies, no. 3. Baltimore: University of Maryland, School of Law.

———. 1985. *The Political Basis of the Economic and Social Development in the Republic of China, 1940–1980*, Occasional Papers/Reprints Series in Contemporary Asian Studies, no. 1. Baltimore: University of Maryland, School of Law.

Liu Ch'ang-shu. 1980. *Hsien tsung-t'ung Chiang kung ta-chung ch'uan-po ssu-hsiang chih yen-chiu* (A study of the late President Chiang Kai-shek's views on mass communication). Taipei: Cheng-chung.

Liu Feng-sung. 1986. "Chi ch'eng hsuan-chi te i-han" (Regrettable local elections). *SPCK*, no. 50 (February 9): 69–71.

Liu Jen-yüan. 1983. "Chien-ch'a-yuan tang-nien hsiung-feng ho-tsai?" (Where is the Control Yuan's past activism?). *SPTC*, no. 182 (May 29): 8–10.

Liu P'ei-yuan and Chin Shih-hsiu. 1988. "Hsiung-ya-li kung shang fang-went'uan" (The trade mission from Hungary). *SPHWCK*, February 9, 32–33.

Liu P'ing-lin. 1983. "T'an chung-kung ho-p'ing tung-i lun-tiao te k'o-hsin-hsing" (Credibility of the PRC's peaceful unification strategy). *CKSP*, October 19, 2.

Liu Shang-jen. 1974. "Kuo-min-tang te tung-chih chia-chu lung-tuan Tai-wan cheng-ch'uan" (The KMT ruling families monopolize Taiwan's political power). *FLT*, no. 3 (July 23): 18–21.

Liu Tung-sheng. 1984. "Shih san hsiung-ti tien chiang lu" (Who's who on the Thirteen Brothers). *FLT*, no. 3 (June 26): 10–15.

Lo Kuo-chun. 1984. "Li-fa-yuan ch'i-shih-wu hui-ch'i ch'eng-chi-tan" (A record of the 75th Legislative Yuan session). *LHYK*, no. 49 (August).

Lowi, Theodore J. 1969. *The End of Liberalism*. New York: Norton.

Lu K'eng. 1985. *Hu Yao-pang fang-wen chi* (A visit with Hu Yao-pang). Hong Kong: Pai-hsing.

Lu Min-jen. 1985. "Wei-lai shih nien wo-kuo chin-jung fa-chan te chan-wang" (Prospects for Taiwan's banking development in the next decade). Paper presented at Nan-yuan Conference, Taipei, December 27–29.

Lu Ya-li. 1984. "T'ai-wan ti-ch'u chung-ch'an chieh-chi te cheng-chih chiao-she" (Political roles of Taiwan's middle class). *SPTC*, no. 244 (August 1): 44–46.

———. 1985. "T'ai-wan ti-ch'u cheng-chih fa-chan te ching-yen yu chan-wang" (The Taiwan experience in political development). In *T'ai-wan ti-ch'u she-hui pien-ch'ien yu wen-hua fa-chan* (Social change and cultural development in Taiwan). Taipei: Chung-kuo Lun-t'an.

McBeth, John. 1988. "South Korea: A Bridge to China." *FEER*, January 7, 15–16.

McGregor, James. 1988. "Taiwan Ruling Party's Many Businesses Are Beginning to Be an Embarrassment." *WSL*, July 22, 17.

Mancall, Mark, ed. 1964. *Formosa Today*. New York: Praeger.

Mancur, Olson. 1967. *The Logic of Collective Action*. Cambridge, Mass: Harvard University Press.

Martin, Charmian. 1986. "Trade with Europe Improving: Taiwan Products Are Competitive." *FJC*, February 3, 4.

Masumi, Junnosuke. 1964. "A Profile of the Japanese Conservative Party." In Eril Allardt and Yujo Littunen, eds., *Cleavages, Ideologies and Party System*. Turku: Westermarck Society.

Meisner, Maurice. 1977. *Mao's China: A History of the People's Republic*. New York: Free Press.

Mendel, Douglas. 1970. *The Politics of Formosan Nationalism*. Berkeley and Los Angeles: University of California Press.

Montgomery, John, and Siffin, William, eds. 1966. *Approaches to Development Politics, Administration and Change*. New York: McGraw-Hill.

Mooney, Paul. "Braving the KMT Ban." *FEER*, October 9, 1986, 19–20.

Moore, Barrington, Jr. 1966. *Social Origins of Dictatorship and Democracy*. Boston: Beacon Press.

Mu Hsin. 1979. "Pu pu sheng-kao te sheng-i-hui cheng-ch'uan yun-tung" (Power struggles in the Provincial Assembly intensify). *MLT*, no. 4 (November 25): 7–11.

Myers, Ramon H. 1983. "The Contest Between Two Chinese States." *AS* 23, no. 4 (April): 536–52.

———. 1984. "The Economic Transformation of the Republic of China in Taiwan." *CQ* 2 (September): 508–28.

———. 1987a. "Grievances, Social Tensions and Social Violence: October 15, 1946–May 15, 1947." Paper presented at the annual meeting of the Association for Asian Studies, Boston, April 10–12.

———. 1987b. "Political Theory and Recent Political Development in the Republic of China." *AS* 27, no. 9 (September): 1003–22.

Nan Min [pseud.]. 1986a. "Tai-wan te chen chia tang-wai tsa-chih" (Real and falsified opposition periodicals in Taiwan). *CSNT*, August, 12–15.

———. 1986b. "Tui Kuo-min-tang shan chung ch'uan-hui ti kuan-ch'a" (An observer's views on the third Plenum). *CSNT*, May, 1–2.

———. 1987a. "T'ai-wan hui yu chi ke cheng-tang?" (How many parties will Taiwan have?). *HHW*, no. 20 (July 27): 22–26.

———. 1987b. "Ta-lu tui-tai cheng-t'se feiling-jen ts'ai-i," (PRC's Taiwan policy puzzling). *HHW*, no. 24 (August 31): 18–21.

———. 1988. "San ke ta chia-tsu ts'ai-fu ta kung-k'ai" (The Chiang, Kung, and Soong families: Disclosures of their wealth). *HHW*, no. 48 (February 8): 22–25.

Nathan, Andrew J. 1978. "An Analysis of Factionalism of Chinese Communist Party Politics." In Frank Belloni and Dennis Beller, eds., *Faction Politics: Political Parties and Factionalism in Comparative Perspective*. Santa Barbara: ABC Clio.

Nathan, Andrew J., and Chou Yangsun. 1987. "Democratizing Transition in Taiwan." *AS* 27, no. 3 (March): 277–99.

Nations, Richard. 1982. "A New Dogfight over Taiwan." *FEER*, January 15, 8.

———. 1984. "They're Going Steady." *FEER*, January 26, 24.

Neubauer, Deane E. 1967. "Some Conditions of Democracy." *American Political Science Review* 61, no. 4 (December): 1005.

Nordlinger, Eric A. 1968. "Political Development: Time Sequences and Rates of Changes." *World Politics* 20, no. 3 (April): 500–509.

O'Donnell, Guillermo A. 1973. *Modernization and Bureaucratic-Authoritarianism: Studies in South American Politics*. Berkeley: University of California, Institute of International Studies.

O'Donnell, Guillermo A.; Schmitter, Phillip C.; and Whitehead, Laurence, eds. 1986. *Transitions from Authoritarian Rule: Prospects for Democracy*. Baltimore: Johns Hopkins University Press.

Oka, Takashi. 1982a. "China on Taiwan Arms Sales." *Christian Science Monitor*, January 13, 2.

———. 1982b. "Reagan: No Advanced Jets to Taiwan." *Christian Science Monitor*, January 12, 1, 6.

———. 1984. "Secret Trips Across Formosa Strait Defy Barriers Between Taiwan and China." *Christian Science Monitor*, March 7, 7–8.

Oke, Claude. 1967. "Political Integration and Political Stability: A Hypothesis." *World Politics* 19 (April): 486–499.

Olson, Mancur, Jr. *The Logic of Collective Action: Public Goods and the Theory of Groups.* Cambridge, Mass.: Harvard University Press.

Packenham, Robert A. 1970. "Legislatures and Political Development." In Allan Kornberg and I. Musolf, eds., *Legislatures in Developmental Perspective.* Durham, N.C.: Duke University Press.

Padgett, L. Vincent. 1976. *The Mexican Political System.* 2d. ed. Boston: Houghton Mifflin.

P'an chia-ch'ing. 1983. "Tai-wan ti-ch'u te yueh-t'ing-jen yu mei-chieh nei-jung" (Mass media recipients and media content in Taiwan). *Hsin-wen-hsueh yen-chiu* (Studies of Journalism), no. 31 (May 2): 35–63.

P'an Fu-chien. 1987. "Liang tang tsu-chih chan ti-fang ch'iang ti-p'an" (KMT-DPP competition for local support). *SPCK*, no. 146 (December 12): 44–48.

———. 1988. "Li-fa-yuan shen-ch'a yu-hsuan pan-fa ting an" (Legislative process on national budget finalized). *SPHWCK*, no. 88 (February 2): 27–28.

P'an Hung-chin. 1982. "T'ai-wan ti-ch'u ch'uan-kuo-hsing chi k'ua-yueh sheng shih chiao-t'ung kung-kung shih-yeh kung-hui tsu-chih chih hsien-k'uang yu kai-chin" (Union organization in Taiwan's public communication enterprises: Present situation and prospects for improvement). Master's thesis, Wen-hua University, Taipei.

P'an K'e-k'uan. 1983. "Ts'ung T'ai-wan hsuan-chu k'an min hsuan ching-ying te chuan-hsing" (Taiwan election and the changing orientation of elected officials). *LHYK*, no. 29 (December): 24–27.

Peng Ming-min. 1972. *A Taste of Freedom.* New York: Holt, Reinhart & Winston.

P'eng Huai-en. 1979. "Ssu ko tien-ting T'ai-wan san shih nien an-ting te kuan-chien cheng-ts'e" (Four critical policies laying the foundation of stability in Taiwan over the past three decades). *Hai-wai hsueh-jen* (Overseas Scholars), no. 89 (December): 19–21.

———. 1981. *Chung-hua min-kuo cheng-chih t'i-hsi te fen-hsi* (An analysis of the Republic of China's political system). Taipei: Shih-pao Wen-hua.

———. 1983. "Kung-ch'uan-li te wei-chi yu chuan-chi" (Crisis and opportunity of public authority). *SPTC*, no. 166 (February 6): 7–11.

P'eng Li-mei. 1986. "Yi chung ch'iu t'ung kung mo ho-hsieh" (Let's seek common ground from diversity to achieve political harmony). *CYJP*, May 14, 1.

Pepper, Suzanne. 1978. *Civil War in China: The Political Struggle, 1945–1949.* Berkeley and Los Angeles: University of California Press.

Pien Yu-yuan. 1978. *T'ai-wan ching-chi fa-chan yu so-te fen-p'ei* (Economic development and income distribution in Taiwan). Ph.D. diss., National Taiwan University, Taipei.

Pienkos, Donald. 1976. "Poland's United Peasants Party: A Minor Party's Place in a Socialist State." *Poland and Germany* 18, no. 1: 17–28, 24–26, 31–33.

Plummer, Mark. 1970. "Taiwan: Toward a Second Generation of Mainland Rule." *AS* 10, no. 1 (January): 18.

Pollack, Jonathan D. 1986. "The Military Balance in the Taiwan Strait and The Implications of China's Military Modernization." *AEI Foreign Policy and Defense Review* 6, no. 3: 35–42.

Purcell, Susan Kaufman, and Kaufman, John F. H. 1980. "State and Society in Mexico: Must a Stable Polity Be Institutionalized?" *World Politics* 32, no. 2: 204.

Putnam, Robert D. 1971. "Studying Elite Political Culture: The Case of Ideology." *American Political Science Review* 65, no. 3 (September): 657–65.

Pye, Lucian W. 1966. "Party System and National Development in Asia." In Joseph LaPalombara and Myron Weiner, eds., *Political Parties and Political Development*. Princeton: Princeton University Press.

———. 1968. *The Spirit of Chinese Politics: A Psychocultural Study of the Authority Crisis in Political Development*. Cambridge, Mass.: MIT Press.

———. 1986. *Aspects of Political Development*. Boston: Little, Brown.

Pye, Lucian W., and Verba, Sidney, eds. 1965. *Political Culture and Political Development*. Princeton: Princeton University Press.

Rankin, Karl Lott. 1964. *China Assignment*. Seattle: University of Washington Press.

Ranney, Austin. 1975. *The Governing of Men*. 4th ed. Hinsdale, Ill.: Dryden Press.

RDEC. 1977. *Ch'iang-fa chih-yeh t'uan-t'i tsu-chih kung-neng yen-chiu pao-kao* (A study of how to strengthen organizational functions of vocational groups). Taipei: Executive Yuan.

———. 1983. *Annual Review of Government Administration, Republic of China, 1981–1982*. Taipei: Executive Yuan.

———. 1987. *Chung-hua Min-kuo hsing-cheng kai-k'uang* (Annual review of government administration). Taipei: Executive Yuan.

Riggs, Fred W. 1952. *Formosa Under Chinese Nationalist Rule*. New York: Macmillan.

ROC Economy Yearbook. 1985. Taipei: Economic Daily News.

Rustow, Dankwart A. 1967. *A World of Nations: Problems of Political Modernization*. Washington, D.C.: Brookings Institution.

———. 1970. "Transition to Democracy: Toward a Dynamic Model." *Comparative Politics* 2 (April): 156–344.

Salisburg, Robert A. 1969. "An Exchange Theory of Interest Groups." *Midwest Journal of Political Science* 13, no. 1 (February): 3–20.

Salisbury, Robert H. 1975. "Interest Groups." In Fred Greenstein and Nelson Polsby, eds., *Non-Governmental Politics*. Reading, Mass.: Addison-Wesley.

Sartori, Giovanni. 1964. "The Typology of Party Systems: Proposals for Improvement." In Erik Allardt and Yujo Littunen, eds., *Cleavages, Ideologies and Party System*. Turku: Westermarck Society.

Scalapino, Robert, and Masumi, Junnoskui. 1967. *Parties and Politics in Contemporary Japan*. Berkeley and Los Angeles: University of California Press.

Schattschneider, E. E. 1966. *The Semisovereign People*. New York: Macmillan.

Schmidt, Steffen W.; Scott, James C.; Landé, Carl; and Guasti, Laura, eds. 1977. *Friends, Followers, and Factions*. Berkeley and Los Angeles: University of California Press.

Schmitter, Philippe. 1979. "Still the Century of Corporatism?" In Philippe Schmitter and Gerhard Lehmbruck, eds., *Trends Toward Corporatist Intermediation*. Beverly Hills and London: Sage.

———. 1982. "Reflections on Where the Theory of Neo-Corporation Has Gone and Where the Proof of Neo-Corporation May Be Going." In Gerhard Lehmbruck and Philippe C. Schmitter, eds., *Patterns of Corporatist Policy-Making*. London: Sage.

———. 1986. "An Introduction to Southern European Transitions from Authoritarian Rule: Italy, Greece, Portugal, Spain, and Turkey." In Guillermo O'Donnell, Philippe C. Schmitter, and Laurence Whitehead, eds., *Transition from Authoritarian Rule: Prospects for Democracy*. Baltimore: Johns Hopkins University Press.

Schurmann, Franz. 1968. *Ideology and Organization in Communist China*. 2d ed. Berkeley and Los Angeles: University of California Press.

Scott, James C. 1972. *Comparative Political Corruption*. Englewood Cliffs, N.J.: Prentice-Hall.

Seagrave, Sterling. 1985. *The Soong Dynasty*. New York: Harper & Row.

Seib, Gerald F. 1982. "U.S. Won't Sell Advanced Jets Taiwan Sought." *WSJ*, January 12, 1.

Seldon, Mark. 1971. *The Yenan Way in Revolutionary China*. Cambridge, Mass.: Harvard University Press.

Sheng Ken. 1983. "Kuo-min-tang ching-hsuan shih-wu liu-ch'eng chin-tu piao" (The KMT's schedule for managing electoral campaigns). *SGK*, no. 10 (June 10): 1–3

Shih Wei-chien. 1981. *Chin* (Censorship). Taipei: Su-chi.

———. 1983. "Mei-li-tao shih-chien i-lai te cheng-chih chih-shu" (Banned books on politics since the Kaohsiung Incident). *SGK*, no. 10 (June 10): 5–7.

Shih Yi-jen. 1987. "T'o an-ch'uan tan-sheng le!" (It is safely born!). *HHW*, no.16 (June 29): 10–17.

Shils, Edward. 1966. *Political Development in the New States*. The Hague and Paris: Mouton.

Silm, Robert H. 1976. *Leadership and Values: The Organization of Large-Scale Taiwanese Enterprises*. Cambridge, Mass.: Harvard University Press.

Simon, Denis Fred. 1986. "Taiwan's Political Economy and the Evolving Links Between the PRC, Hong Kong, and Taiwan." *AEI Foreign Policy and Defense Review* 6, no. 3: 42–51.

Skillings, H. Gordon. 1970. "Group Conflict and Political Change." In Chalmers Johnson, ed., *Change in Communist Systems*. Stanford: Stanford University Press.

Smith, Hedrick. 1982. "Fruits of the Trip." *NYT*, May 1, 1, 6.

———. 1984. "The Streets Can Be Eerily Deserted Even in a Nation of a Billion People." *NYT*, April 20, 7.

Snyder, Edwin K., and Gregor, A. James. 1981. "The Military Balance in the Taiwan Strait." *Journal of Strategic Studies* 4, no. 3 (September): 307.

Spector, Michael. 1983. "Success at a Price." *FEER*, December 8, 48–49.

Stavis, Benedict. 1974. *Rural Local Government and Agricultural Development in Taiwan*. Ithaca: Cornell University, Rural Development Committee.

Stinchombe, Arthur L. 1975. "Social Structure and Politics." In Fred I. Greenstein and W. Polsby, eds., *Macropolitical Theory*. Reading, Mass.: Addison-Wesley.

Su Hsien-ya. 1982. "Leng yen p'ang-kuan pan nien lai te Li-fa-yuan" (The Legislative Yuan in the last six months). *LHYK*, no. 13 (August): 23.

———. 1987. "Shih kai t'ui-hsiu tan pu-shih wo" (They should be retired, but not me). *SPCK*, no. 146 (December 12): 50–51.

Su Ming-ta. 1985. "Li-fa-yuan ch'eng-hsien ta-fu-tu fa-lo hsien-hsiang" (Substantial decay of the Legislative Yuan as a law-making institution). *MCJP*, January 16, January 17.

Su-ma Wen-wu (Chiang Ts'un-nan). 1986. "Chieh-chia pu chieh-tien te chiang-chun" (The retired generals who refuse to stay out of sight). *PSNT*, January 11, 3–4.

———. 1988. "Hau Po-ts'un pu chai cho ch'iang-jen?" (Is General Hau Pei-ts'un no longer a strongman?). *HHW*, no. 49/50 (February 15): 42–46.

Sun Ch'ing-shan. 1985. "T'ai-wan ti-ch'u cheng-chang te mo-shih yu ch'u-shih" (Pattern of urban growth in Taiwan). In Taiwan Provincial Government, *T'ai-wan kuang-fu szu shih nien chuan-chi* (A commemorative volume on Taiwan after four decades' return to China). Taichung: Taiwan Provincial Government.

Sun Man-p'ing. 1987. "Shui shih ming-jih pao-yueh ti-san shih-li?" (Which newspaper enterprise will be the third force in the future?). *THTC*, no. 78 (November 1): 26–27.

Sun Meng-ch'eng. 1984. "San shih nien nei-ke ch'uan-li chieh-kou pien-ch'ien ta-shih" (Change in the cabinet power structure during the past three decades). In *T'ou-shih ch'uan-li pien-chu* (The power structure in transition), vol. 6. Taipei: Feng-yun Lun-t'an She.

Sung Chiang-ts'un. 1984. "Li-fa-yuan p'ai-hsi ta tui-chieh" (A great showdown of the Legislative Yuan factions). *SPTC*, no. 253 (October 3): 30.

Sung, Dixson D. S., and Ho, Lawrence. 1988. *Republic of China: A Reference Book*. Taipei: Hilit.

Sung Hsi. 1976. *Chung-kuo Kuo-min-tang cheng-kang cheng-ts'e te yen-shuo* (Policy speeches regarding the Kuomintang party platform). Taipei: Cheng-chung.

Ta Yen [Pseud.]. 1981. "Tang-wai jen-shih t'an chih-cheng-tang ho tsu-tang wen-t'i" (Conversation with the *tangwai* opposition regarding the KMT and organization of a new party). *Cheng-chih p'ing-lun* (Political Review) 39, no. 1 (February): 32–33.

Tai Hung-ch'ao. 1970. "The Kuomintang and Modernization in Taiwan." In Samuel P. Huntington and Clement H. Moore, eds., *Authoritarian Politics in Modern Society*. New York: Basic Books.

Tai-wan sheng-cheng-fu. 1985. *T'ai-wan ching-chi fa-chan te ching-yen yu mo-shih* (Taiwan economic development: Experience and model). Taichung: Taiwan Prov.ncial Government.

Tanzer, Andrews. 1983a. "Divide and Rule?" *FEER*, November 24, 27–28.

_____. 1983b. "Exporters' Dream is Bankers' Nightmare." *FEER*, December 22, 43–46.

Thompson, Stuart. 1984. "Taiwan: Rural Society." *CQ* 2 (September): 554–58.

Tien Hung-mao. 1972. *Government and Politics in Kuomintang China, 1927–1937.* Stanford: Stanford University Press.

_____. 1975. "Taiwan in Transition: Prospects for Socio-political Change." *CQ* 64 (December): 622–25, 643–44.

_____. 1980. "Uncertain Futures: Politics in Taiwan." In *Taiwan Yesterday and Today*, 59–77. New York: China Council of the Asia Society.

_____. 1981. "Lei Ken cheng-fu te chung-kuo cheng-ts'e" (The Reagan administration's China policy). *Yuan-tung shih-pao* (Far Eastern Times), June 29, 2.

_____. 1982. "Lun erh-hao Shang-hai kung-pao yu T'ai-wan ch'ien-t'u" (The second Shanghai Communiqué and the future of Taiwan). *CKSP*, September 2, 4.

_____, ed. 1983. *Mainland China, Taiwan and U.S. Policy.* Cambridge, Mass.: Oelgeschlager, Gunn & Hain.

_____. 1984. *Political Development in Taiwan.* Hearing before the Subcommittee on Asian and Pacific Affairs of the Committee on Foreign Affairs. U.S. House of Representatives. Washington, D.C.: U.S. Government Printing Office.

_____. 1985a. "Chung-kung ning-tao te tui t'ai cheng-ts'e yu chien-chieh" (PRC leaders' policy and views concerning Taiwan). In Lu K'eng, ed., *Hu Yao-pang fang-wen-chi* (An interview with Hu Yaobang). Hong Kong: Pai Shing Semi-monthly, 79–87.

_____. 1985b. "Hsien chieh-tuan yu t'ai-wan wei-lai te nei-wai cheng-chu" (The present and the future of Taiwan's internal and external political situation). *CKLT* 21, no. 7 (January 10): 13–28.

_____. 1985c. "In Pursuit of Political Amalgamation: The PRC and the Future of Hong Kong and Taiwan." In Jack F. Williams, ed., *The Future of Hong Kong and Taiwan.* Occasional paper no. 9. East Lansing: Michigan State University, Center for East Asian Studies.

_____. 1987a. "Social Change and Political Development." Paper presented at the Third International Congress of Professors, World Peace Academy, Manila, August 24–29.

_____. 1987b. "Taiwan in 1986: Reforms Under Adversity." In John S. Major and Anthony J. Kane, eds., *China Briefing, 1987*, 131–54. Boulder: Westview Press.

Tien Yu-shih. 1982. "Chiang Ching-kuo tsung-t'ung te chih-kuo li-ch'eng" (The political career of President Chiang Ching-kuo). *Ch'ing-nien chan-shih pao* (Young Soldiers' Press), July 31.

Ting Wei-jen. 1985. "San shih nien lai li-wei kuo-hui lun-cheng te ta so-ho" (Contributions of the opposition legislators in the Legislative Yuan over the past three decades). *MCJ*, no. 5 (April 1): 4–7.

Ts'ai Shih-p'ing. 1983. "Min-chu cheng-chih ho ya-li cheng-chih" (Democracy and pressure politics). *LHYK*, no. 26 (September): 20–28.

Tseng Chi-ch'un. 1976. *Li-fa-yuan ch'ang she wei-yuan-hui chih yen-chiu* (A study of the Legislative Yuan's standing committees). Taipei: Cheng-chung.

——. 1985. *Chung-hua Min-kuo Li-fa-yuan chih chih-tsu yu chih-ch'uan fen-hsi* (An analysis of the Legislative Yuan's structure and functions in the Republic of China). Taipei: Shang-wu.

Tung Hsiang-fei. 1974. "Tang ch'ien hsiang-chen chih-ch'eng hsing-cheng te ping-hsiang" (The pathology of present local government administration). *Tung-fang tsa-chih* (Far East Magazine) 8, no. 3 (September): 31–35.

Tung Shu-fan. 1971. "Cheng-tang cheng-chih yu kung-kung cheng-ts'e chih chih-hsing" (Party politics and implementation of public policies). *Cheng-chih p'ing-lun* (Political Review) 26, no. 11 (March): 26–27.

U.S. Department of State. 1974. *Foreign Relations of the United States, 1949*. Volume 9, *The Far East and China*. 1974. Washington, D.C.: U.S. Government Printing Office.

Von der Mehden, Fred R. 1969. *Politics of the Developing Nations*. 2d ed. Englewood Cliffs, N.J. Prentice-Hall.

Wang Liang-fen. 1982. *Wo-kuo hsin-wen chi-tse fa chih yen-chiu* (A study of laws governing news reporters in Taiwan). Master's thesis, Cheng-chih University, Mucha, Taiwan.

Wang Li-hsia and Chang Hsiao-ch'un. 1987. "Kung-hui yu kung-yun, T'ai-wan lao-kung yun-tung te hsien-tsai yu wei-lai" (Trade unions and labors: Prospects for Taiwan's labor movement). *LHYK*, no. 70 (May): 84–88.

Wang Pai-mei. 1983. "T'ai-wan te yang-pan kung-hui" (The model trade union in Taiwan). *SGK*, no. 7 (April 25): 7–9.

Wang Po-jen. 1987. "Tsai-yeh tang t'uan hua ling wei cheng" (Opposition party being organized in the Provincial Assembly). *SPHWCK*, no. 53 (June 2): 77–79.

Wang, Tom. 1985. "Free China's Trade Winds Expand to 140 Countries." *FCJ*, December 30.

Wang Tuan-cheng. 1972. "Tai-wan ti-fang hsuen-chi cheng-tang pu-hsuan huan-chuan chih fang-shi yu ch'i hsiao-kuo" (Methods and effects of party campaign propaganda in Taiwan's local elections). *Hsin-wen-hsueh yen-chiu*, no. 9 (May 20): 153.

Wang Yi-shang. 1984. "Shih san hsiung-ti p'an-shang tso-t'an-hui-p'ai" (The Thirteen Brothers joined the Tso-t'an-hui faction). *FLT* 3 (June 26): 8–9.

Ward, Robert E. 1978. *Japan's Political System*. Englewood Cliffs, N.J.: Prentice-Hall.

Ward, Robert E., and Rustow, Dankwart A., eds. 1964. *Political Modernization in Japan and Turkey*. Princeton: Princeton University Press.

Wei Cheng-t'ung. 1985. "San shih tuo nien lai chih-shih-fen-tzu chui-ch'iu tzu-yu min-tsu ti li-ch'eng" (In pursuit of freedom and democracy by the intelligentsia—A record of over three decades' endeavors). In *Tai-wan ti-ch'u she-hui pien-ch'ien yu wen-hua fa-chan* (Social change and cultural development in Taiwan). Taipei: Chung-kuo Lun-t'an-she.

Wei Yung. 1976. "Modernization Process in Taiwan: An Allocative Analysis." *AS* 16, no. 3 (March): 262–66.

———. 1983. "T'u-p'o yuen-lan hai-wai jen-ts'ai te p'ing-ching" (Breaking through bottlenecks in recruiting overseas talents). *THTC*, no. 25 (June): 29–30.

"Wei ch'uan-sheng chi-ch'eng hsing-cheng t'i-hsi pa-mai" (Diagnosis of Taiwan's local government administration). 1984. *LHYK*, no. 36 (July): 70–77.

Weiner, Myron. 1987. "Empirical Democratic Theory and the Transition from Authoritarianism to Democracy." *PS* (American Political Science Assocation newsletter), Fall 1987, 861–66.

Weisman, Steven R. 1985. "Hundreds of Pakistanis Arrested as Elections Near." *NYT*, February 22, 1.

Wen Chang. 1984. "Ts'ung jen-ts'ai wai-liu tao jen-ts'ai hui-lin" (From the exit of qualified scientists and technicians to their return). *LHYK* no. 32 (March): 60–66.

Wen Ch'ung-i. 1985. "T'ai-wan ti kung-yueh-hua yu she-hui pien-ch'ien" (Industrialization and social change in Taiwan). In *T'ai-wan ti-ch'u she-hui pien-ch'ien yu wen-hua fa-chan* (Social change and culture development in Taiwan). Taipei: Chung-kuo Lun-t'an-she.

Wen Hsien-shen. 1984. "Ching-chien-hui te kuo-ch'i hsien-tsai yu wei-lai" (The Economic Planning and Development Council: Past, present, and future). *THTC*, no. 41 (November): 20–24.

———. 1988. "Chieh chang-lao-hui cheng chiao kuan-hsi chih mi" (Solve the riddle of the Presbyterian Church's political ties). *Yuan Chien* (Global Views Monthly), no. 19 (January 1): 96–105.

Wen Man-ying. 1985. "Pu pu ching-hsien te t'ao-chin lu, chuan k'o mao-yi" (The transit trade: A risky route to gold mine). *THTC*, no. 50 (August): 12–18.

Wen Li-chung. 1986. "K'an t'ai-hai liang an yu-min chiao-i" (Taiwan-mainland fishermen's trade). *LHYK*, no. 62 (September): 98–101.

———. 1987. "K'an ch'un-chung hsi yun-tung" (A close look at the mass movements). *Yuan chien* (Global Views Monthly), no. 9 (March): 28–36.

———. 1988. "Ts'ung-cheng Kuo-min-tang ku-fen yu-hsien kung-szu" (Reorient KMT, Inc.). *Yuan chien* (Global Views Monthly), no. 21 (March): 15–18.

Weng, Byron S. J. 1984. "Taiwan's International Status Today." *CQ* 3 (September): 464–81.

Wesson, Robert. 1985. *Modern Government, Democracy and Authoritarianism*, 2d ed. Englewood Cliffs, N. J.: Prentice-Hall.

Whiting, Allen S. 1971. "Morality, Taiwan, and U.S. Policy." In Jerome Alan Cohen, Edward Friedman, C. Harold Hinton, and Allen S. Whiting, eds., *Taiwan and American Policy*, 79–105. New York: Praeger.

Who's Who in Taiwan Industry and Business (Kung shang jen-ming-lu). Various years. Taipei: Chunghua Tseng-hsin-so.

Who's Who in Taiwan Business (Chung-hua Min-kuo shih-yeh ming-jen-lu). 1980. Taipei: Chung-hua Cheng-hsin-so.

Wiatr, Jerzy J. 1964. "One Party Systems: The Concept and Issues for Comparative Studies." In Erik Allardt and Yujo Littunen, eds., *Cleavages, Ideologies and Party System*. Turku: Westermarck Society.

Wilbur, C. Martin. 1984. "Nationalist China, 1928–1950: An Interpretation." In Hungdah Chiu and Shao-ch'uan Leng, eds., *China: Seventy Years After the 1911 Hsin-hai Revolution*. Charlottesville: University Press of Virginia.

Wilson, Frank L. 1983. "Interest Groups and Politics in Western Europe: The New Corporatist Approach." *Comparative Politics* 16, no. 3 (October): 105–23.

Winckler, Edwin A. 1981. "National, Regional, and Local Politics." In Emily Martin Ahern and Hill Gates, eds., *The Anthropology of Taiwanese Society*. Stanford: Stanford University Press.

———. 1984. "Institutionalization and Participation on Taiwan: From Hard to Soft Authoritarianism?" *CQ* 3 (September): 482–99.

Wolff, Lester L., and Simon, David L., eds. 1982. *Legislative History of the Taiwan Relations Act*. New York: American Association for Chinese Studies.

Wu An-shih. 1985. "Chih-cheng-tang tsai Tai-pei shih yin ho sho ts'o?" (Why did the KMT suffer a setback in Taipei?). *LHYK*, no. 53 (December): 198.

Wu Ching-feng. 1988. "Lee Teng-hui nao-tzu-li shih che-yang hsiang te" (This is what Lee Tang-hui has in mind). *HHW*, no. 72 (July 25): 22–24.

Wu Ch'ueh-yuan. 1981. "Hsien chieh-tuan nung-hui ching-chi kung-neng yu she-hui kung-neng fen-hsi chi ch'i yin-ying chih-tao yen-chiu" (An analysis of the farmers' associations' economic and social functions). *Tai-wan tu-ti chin-jung chi-k'an* (Taiwan Land Finance Quarterly) 18, no. 1 (March).

Wu Ch'ueh-yuan and Yeh Hsin-ming. 1984. "Chia-ch'iang nung-hui kung-neng fa-chan yeh-wu chih yen-chiu ti-yi tzu-t'i: Nung-hui hsin-yung yeh-wu chih chien-t'ao yu chia-ch'iang t'u-ching" (The study of strenghtening the farmers' associations' functions: Review of credit operations and their improvement). *Chung-kuo nung-min yin-hang nung-yeh chin-jung lun-t'sung* (Agricultural Finance of the Chinese Farmers' Bank), series no. 2 (January): 422–23.

Wu Feng-shan. 1972. "T'ai-pei shih kung-ying pao-chih yu min-ying pao-chih yen-lun pi-chiao" (Comparing the editorial stands of Taipei's public and private newspapers). *Hsin-wen-hsueh yen-chiu* (Studies of Journalism), no. 9 (May): 232–34.

Wu Hsiang-hui. 1986. "Ming-t'ien te hsing-hsing hui keng-liang" (Tomorrow's stars will be brighter). *PSNT*, January 25, 3–5.

Wu Ke-ch'ing. 1983a. "K'an chih-cheng-tang wan-p'iao" (The KMT's allocation of votes). *SPTC*, no. 209 (November 30): 21.

———. 1983b. "Pai-fen-pi te yu-hsi" (The percentage game). *SPTC*, no. 210 (December 7): 16.

———. 1985. "Ch'uan-yen chung te shih-san-hsiung-ti' men-lin chieh-t'i" (The Thirteen Brotherhood nears break-up). *SPTC*, no. 39 (September 25): 59.

———. 1987. "Liang an ch'in-ch'ing t'an pu chin" (Strong family ties on both sides of the Taiwan Strait). *SPHWCK*, no. 42 (March 17): 14–17.

Wu Keng. 1985. *Ching-chi-pu chi so shu hsing-cheng chi-kan wei-t'o min-chien t'uan-t'i pan-li yeh-wu k'e-hsing-hsing chih yen-chiu* (A study of delegating authority to civic organizations by the Ministry of Economic Affairs and its subordinate agencies). Taipei: Ministry of Economic Affairs.

Wu Nai-te. 1982. "Tai-wan ti-fang p'ai-hsi te wei-chi" (Crisis of Taiwan's local factionalism). *SK*, no. 8 (April 20): 13–16; no. 9 (May 10): 21–26.

———. 1988. "Cheng-tang ying ju-ho mien-tui lau-kung yun-tung" (How should political parties deal with the labor movement?) *CKSP*, February 6, 3.

Wu Ying-ts'un. 1987. "Ch'uan-wei yu shui-yueh pa-ho" (A tug-of-war between power and generational change). *THTC*, no. 70 (March 1): 68–78.

Wu Yuan-li. 1985. *Becoming an Industrialized Nation: The ROC's Development on Taiwan*. New York: Praeger.

Yang Ch'ao-huan and Kuo Ch'ung-lun. 1987. "Tai-wan hsiang chieh-yen hui pei" (Taiwan bids adieu to martial law). *SPCK*, no. 123 (July 4): 7–10.

Yang Chih-hung. 1979. "Ts'ung na-li t'ing-tao mei-kuo yu chung kung chien-chiao te hsiao-hsi?" (How did people hear of the normalization of U.S.-PRC diplomatic relations?). *Ch'ang-ch'iao tsa-chih* (Long Bridge Magazine), no. 13 (June): 22–25.

Yang Hao. 1986. "Tai-wan yu sheng-chi p'ing-heng ma?" (Is there a balance of provincial origins in Taiwan's officialdom?). *CP*, March 20, 6.

Yang Hsiao-jung. 1975. "Tai-wan ch'uan-po t'i-hsi yu-hsiao-hsing fen-hsi" (Efficiency analysis of Taiwan's mass media). *Pao Hsueh* (Journalism) 5, no. 4 (June): 16–22.

Yang Hsiao-p'ing. 1984. "Tung-ho, ning-chu, tsai-ch'u-fa: Lun Chung-kuo Kuo-min-tang ti shih-erh-chieh san-chung chuan-hui" (On the Second Plenum of the KMT's Twelfth Central Committee). *KHJC* 8, no. 3 (March): 71.

Yang Hsien-ts'un. 1987. "Hsin tang hsin chen-jung lan chieh chiu hsi-t'i" (New leaders for the new party, but old problems are hard to resolve). *SPHWCK*, no. 77 (November 17): 12–23.

Yang Hsi-sheng. 1983. "Tai-wan tang-wai yun-tung te san ta feng-p'o" (Three phases of opposition movements in Taiwan). In *T'ou-shih tang-wai shih-li* (An analysis of the opposition forces). Taipei: Feng-yun Lun-tang-she.

Yang Kuo-shu. 1985. "Tai-wan she-hui te to-yuan-hua, hui-ku yu ch'ien-chan" (Pluralization of Taiwan's society and future prospects). In *T'ai-wan ti ch'u she-hui pien-ch'ien yu wen-hua fa-chan* (Social change and cultural development in Taiwan). Taipei: Chung-kuo Lun-t'an.

Yang, Martin M. C. 1970. *Socio-economic Results of the Land Reform in Taiwan*. Honolulu: University of Hawaii, East-West Center.

Yang Shang-hsin. 1988. "I-chen-chen te cho-feng o-yu ts'ui ta po-t'ai: (Interest groups permeate the Control Yuan). *HHW*, no. 49/50 (February 15): 61–65.

Yang Su-min. 1984. "Hsien-cheng cheng-ts'e hsia wo-kuo pao-yeh wen-t'i yen-chiu" (Problems in Taiwan's publishing enterprises under restrictive policies). Master's thesis, Cheng-chih University, Mucha, Taiwan.

Yang Tu. 1987. "San tang ta pa-ho lao-kung cheng-to-chan" (Competition of three political parties for labor support). *SPCK*, no. 146 (December 12): 75–78.

Yen Chia-ch'i. 1985. "I kuo liang chih ho Chung-kuo t'ung-i te t'u-ching" ("One nation, two systems" and the path toward China's unification). *Cheng-chih-hsueh yen-chiu* (Studies of Political Science), no. 2 (April): 1–7.

Yu Ho-ch'ing and Chuang Mei-hua. 1984. *T'ai-wan ti-ch'u nung-hui chih tsu-chih yu chih-chang* (The organization and management of Taiwan's agriculture). Taipei: RDEC.

Yu Hsing-chien. 1977. *Chung-kuo Kuo-min-tang Yu Cheung-kuo kung-hui tsu-chih* (The KMT and China's trade union organizations). Master's thesis, Wen-hua University, Taipei.

Yu Shui-han [pseud.]. 1985. "Yu te p'iao shu k'an T'ai-wan hsuan-chu te kuai-chuang" (Vote distribution and Taiwan's strange elections). *CP*, November 20, 2.

——. 1986. "Kuo-min-tang ch'uan-li ho-hsin ch'u-hsien wei-miao pien-fa" (Subtle change appears at the KMT power center). *CP* (April 29): 2.

"Yu nei-ke pu-hui shou-chang chi ch'i-t'a hsin jen chung-yao shou-chang i-lan-piao" (Who's who in the Yu Kuo-hwa cabinet and other newly appointed ranking officials). 1984. *LHYK*, no. 35 (March): 6–8.

Yuan Sung-hsi. 1981. "Tui Chung-kuo Kuo-min-tang cheng-kang te fen-hsi yu t'i-jen" (The KMT's political platform: An analysis and acknowledgment). *Chung-yang yueh-kan* (Central Monthly Journal) 13, no. 9 (May): 19–27.

Index